ALSO BY BILL CLINTON

The President's Daughter
(with James Patterson)

The President Is Missing
(with James Patterson)

Back to Work: Why We Need a Smart Government for a Strong Economy

Giving: How Each of Us Can Change the World

My Life

Between Hope and History: Meeting America's Challenges for the 21st Century

CITIZEN

Bill Clinton

CITIZEN

My Life After the White House

ALFRED A. KNOPF
NEW YORK
2024

THIS IS A BORZOI BOOK
PUBLISHED BY ALFRED A. KNOPF

www.aaknopf.com

Knopf, Borzoi Books, and the colophon are registered trademarks of Penguin Random House LLC.

Photograph insert designed by Casey Hampton. Editing and research by Colin Bridgham. Every effort has been made to identify copyright holders of photographs; in case of oversight, and upon notification to the publisher, corrections will be made in subsequent printings. Unless otherwise noted, all photographs are from the collection of the Clinton Foundation. The Associated Press: page 1, all; page 4, top right (U.N.) and center left (N. Korea). Author's personal collection: page 2, center right. Barbara Kinney/Hillary for President 2008: page 4, top left. Adam Schultz/Hillary for America: page 7, top left. Angel Ureña: page 7, bottom left.

Library of Congress Control Number: 2024931127
ISBN: 978-0-525-52144-0 (hardcover)
ISBN: 978-0-525-52145-7 (eBook)

Jacket photograph by Russell James
Jacket design by John Gall

Manufactured in the United States of America

FIRST EDITION

Contents

CITIZEN

INTRODUCTION

On January 21, 2001, after twenty-five years in politics and elected office, eight as president, I was a private citizen again. I often joked that for a few weeks, I was lost whenever I walked into a room because no one played a song to mark my arrival. "Hail to the Chief" was now my successor's anthem. I had loved being president, but I supported the two-term limit and was determined not to spend a day wishing I still had the job. I wanted to live in the present and for the future. Except on rare occasions, I have kept that promise to myself, though it got a lot harder after the 2016 election, harder still after the coronavirus struck, George Floyd's killing, the January 6, 2021, attack on our Capitol, and the inventive efforts of the right-wing culture warriors to find new ways to stoke grievances without sensible plans to make things better for themselves and for all the rest of us.

The years after the White House are different for every former president. In 2001, I was only fifty-four, with a lot of energy, useful experience, and contacts from my years in politics that could and should be used to serve the public as a private citizen.

So how should a former president do that? Several of my predecessors had made a real difference in their time, disproving John Quincy Adams's famous maxim that "there is nothing more pathetic in life than a former President." Adams himself served sixteen years in Congress, two of them with Abraham Lincoln, where he led the fight against slavery on the floor of the House. He also represented the captive African Mende people aboard the *Amistad* in the Supreme Court, winning their release before they could be sold into slavery. Theodore Roosevelt started a new party and ran for president, finishing second in 1912, the only third-party candidate to do so. William Howard Taft became chief justice of the Supreme Court. Herbert Hoover led an effort to modernize and reorganize the federal civil service under President Harry Truman. And Jimmy Carter built a remarkable record with his foundation, eliminating the scourge of guinea worm in Africa, overseeing elections in tough places, and becoming, along with Rosalynn, the face of Habitat for Humanity.

Although Hillary was now serving in the Senate, I had always been impressed by the impact she had by working with nongovernmental organizations, beginning with the Children's Defense Fund. And I had learned a lot in our White House years watching her work with civil society groups in Africa, Northern Ireland, India, and elsewhere.

So I decided to set up a foundation with a flexible but clear mission: to maximize the benefits and minimize the burdens of our new century in the United States and across the world. I was excited about the possibilities and hoped I could do it.

Meanwhile, I had a more immediate agenda. I wanted to support Hillary, just starting her service as a senator from New York, and Chelsea, only a few months from graduating from Stanford, so they could stay in public life if they wanted to do so and be financially secure if I didn't live long, which, given my family history, seemed likely. To do that and pay my substantial legal bills run up during the Whitewater investigations and the impeachment process, I had to start making money, something that had never interested me before. As governor of Arkansas, I had made $35,000 until the voters raised it to $60,000 a couple of months before I left office. As president I made $200,000, and paid for most of our family's expenses out of it, in large part because the job provided excellent public housing!

By the time I left office, I had given a lot of thought to how to increase the opportunities and decrease the problems of our interdependence. We had to create more fairly shared prosperity, shoulder more shared responsibilities, and build more communities in which our differences are respected, but our common humanity matters more.

But the America that I found myself working in had changed in many ways since I had started in politics in the 1970s, and even in the short time since I'd left the White House. Two Americas were emerging with very different stories. One believes that our diversity makes us stronger, and better able to achieve shared prosperity through shared opportunities and responsibilities and equal treatment in our local, state, and national communities. The other believes they are in a battle for all that has been lost by our increasing diversity and economic stagnation, mostly in more rural areas. They feel they've lost control over our economy, our social order, and our culture. They're determined not to lose control over our politics, and to use politics to regain control over the other three.

I still believe we all do better when we work together. In such a polarized environment, that means you have to be willing to work with people who don't think like you along with those who do. Almost always, cooperation beats conflict, and when you do have to stand your ground, it's wise to leave the door open for reconciliation. The ability to do that distinguishes great leaders. Think of Nelson Mandela putting the leaders of parties who had imprisoned him for twenty-seven years in his cabinet, or Yitzhak Rabin keeping the peace process alive while acts of terror claimed the lives of innocent citizens and eventually claimed his.

Following this path is challenging even in less violent times. My family has had a lot of experience with highly personal attacks which were not just hurtful to us, but hurt the country by distracting attention from the real debate: how best to meet our common challenges. When the going got rough, I tried to imagine that I was one of those big inflatable toys of the cartoon figures Baby Huey or Casper the Friendly Ghost—they were big favorites of kids when I was in elementary school. You could knock them down and they always bounced right back up. To survive in politics, that's what you have to do, over and over. Maybe we should start producing those bouncing figures again, as representative of happy warriors reaching across our great divide. People could keep them at home and at work, starting and finishing every workday by knocking them down and smiling when they bounce back. It might clear our heads and help us to get back in the building and cooperating business.

A life in public service can be deeply rewarding if you accept that in the constant ebb and flow of history there are no permanent victories or defeats, and never forget that every life is a story that, regardless of time and circumstance, deserves to be seen and heard.

As I entered this new chapter of my life, I knew that I'd keep score the way I always have: Are people better off when you quit than when you started? Do our children have a brighter future? Are we coming together instead of falling apart?

This book is the story of my twenty-three-plus years since leaving the White House, told largely through the stories of other people who changed my life as I tried to help change theirs, of those who supported me, including those I loved and lost, and of the mistakes I made along the way.

I'm very grateful that, with the help of my family, friends new and old, a great staff, and the endurance of my curiosity, energy, and ability to work, I have been able to have a life full of new experiences and new ways to help and empower people as a private citizen while finding real joy in our small but growing family. I've loved cheering Hillary on as a senator, secretary of state, presidential candidate both in 2008 and in 2016, and watching with wonder the life Chelsea has built with her work in the private sector, in academia, the Clinton Foundation and the Clinton Health Access Initiative, with the books she's authored, and her family life with Marc, whom I love and admire. Chelsea says she and Marc are teaching their kids to "be brave and be kind."

It shows. I love being their grandfather, and am so glad Chelsea and Marc welcome Hillary and me to be involved in their lives.

When this book comes out, I'll be seventy-eight—the oldest person in my family since my maternal great-grandparents, straight out of *American Gothic*, made it into their late seventies. But I still think and dream about how people can live better lives together, and still want to help them do it. I can't sit still and can't go back. So, as many people do every day, I aim to get caught trying. It's the real American way.

PART I

What Does a Former President Do?

ONE

The Man with No Face

Someone in Silicon Valley once described software development as "building the plane while you fly it." Those early postpresidential years were like that for me—starting over without really stopping.

My first year out of office was full: the first Clinton Foundation projects and my first missions as an ex-president; paid and unpaid speeches; commemorations and celebrations which often took me to other countries; fundraising and planning for my presidential library; moving from the transition office in Washington to a new permanent one in Harlem; and spending weekends with Hillary when her Senate schedule and work with her constituents allowed.

Just six days after I left office, my first opportunity for postpresidential service came when a massive earthquake struck the Indian state of Gujarat, killing 20,000 people and destroying thousands of homes, schools, hospitals, health clinics, and other buildings in cities, towns, and small villages.

Because I had dealt with many natural disasters as governor and president, I called Prime Minister Atal Bihari Vajpayee and volunteered to help. I had a high regard for Vajpayee, formed when we worked together to restore strong ties badly frayed by decades of Cold War strain. He was a selfless, ascetic, lifelong bachelor who had kept in check the most destructive impulses of his Hindu nationalist party and supported the booming growth of India's high-tech centers. Vajpayee had a clear grasp of the challenges ahead. He said he had the capability to repair the largest cities but lacked the money and organization to restore the towns and villages, many of which were wiped out. He asked me to help organize the Indian American community to do that.

At the time, Indian Americans had the highest education levels and per capita incomes of all of America's many immigrant groups. They had done well in all the professions, especially medicine, high-tech, and finance. There were also a large number of self-made business owners large and small: for example, Indian Americans owned one third of all the hotel rooms in the United States.

Many were already involved in worthy activities in their home communities, but there was no national group able to do what the prime minister had asked. To create one, we reached out to people across the country. Soon the American India Foundation (AIF) was born, with a board composed of prominent members of the Indian diaspora. Lata Krishnan, an IT entrepreneur from Northern California, agreed to become the first president. The group quickly raised $4 million, with fundraisers in New York, California, and Chicago, and gifts from individuals and organizations from coast to coast; established partnerships with effective Indian nongovernmental organizations; and set to work. In April, I visited India with other AIF board members to see some of the hardest-hit areas, where we had worked with the NGOs to provide immediate food, water, shelter, and wheelchairs for the disabled, and to determine what to do next.

In Bhuj, then a city of more than a hundred thousand people, virtually all the stone buildings had crumbled; the rubble was everywhere. Schoolchildren had been marching in a parade in a narrow street with buildings tightly packed together on both sides when the quake hit. The falling stone had killed two hundred of them. People were still living in the debris, without clean water, much less the ability to resume their livelihoods. To help them, we clearly had to raise a lot of money.

With the support of some pharmaceutical companies, AIF had already assisted a group of doctors and nurses from the Stanford Medical Group who had come to India to perform emergency surgeries. We went to visit with them and the people they were helping in a large still-standing open building the Red Cross had turned into a hospital. After getting a report from the medical staff on their work, we thanked them and visited with the patients and families who wanted to say hello and tell us what had happened to them.

As I made my way through the group, I noticed a man at the far end of the room, in a section not well lighted. He was sitting on his bed talking to a woman I assumed was his wife. I glanced at him a few times, wondering why he hadn't come forward. When the man turned to see the goings-on, I understood why.

He had no face. A falling stone had sheared it away. His brows, nose, and lips were gone. I tried to imagine what he must feel, losing parts of himself essential to his health, to his ability to relate to others, to his very identity. Still his gaze was steady and riveting. Whether he stayed in his bed because of embarrassment, pain, or both, I couldn't know. But I knew there was still a person inside. I bowed to him slightly and returned to the people nearby. When I got to the door to leave, I looked at him again. This time he slowly raised his hand in greeting. I waved back, moved by the dignity and courage of a man still hanging on.

His image stayed with me as I traveled to Ahmedabad to visit Mohandas Gandhi's ashram and talk with young Indian leaders about whether Gandhi's vision for India as a peaceful haven for all its people, regardless of their ethnic or religious heritage, could still become a reality. Today, India is enjoying brisk growth and has become the world's most populous country, but the persistence of internal divisions, especially between Hindus and Muslims, leaves open the question of whether Gandhi's vision will ever be fully realized.

After a stop in Mumbai to see political and business leaders, I went to Calcutta, or Kolkata as it's now known, to keep a promise I had made to Mother Teresa before her death in 1997 to visit her Shishu Bhavan, or Homes for the Children. As her successor toured me around, I saw many children with disabilities and others who appeared mixed-race, all either without parents or whose parents were too poor to take care of them. They had found a loving home.

My last stop was in a village ninety minutes north of New Delhi where my friend Vin Gupta grew up and his father was still the village doctor. Vin had built a successful targeted mass mailing business in America and was determined to bring more economic and educational opportunity to people in and near his home village. We dedicated a new nursing school he named for Hillary and Vin announced he would replace the local high school's ill-equipped fifty-seven-year-old chemistry lab with a modern science and technology facility. He did that, too. The high school's performance in STEM—science, technology, engineering, and mathematics—courses went way up and the nursing school graduates all find jobs that pay well.

There were so many Indian Americans and other friends of the nation already working on their own similar projects in India that I flew home confident that we could do what Prime Minister Vajpayee requested. The AIF quickly raised another $30 million and over the next couple of years built more than 1,350 houses, dozens of schools, three hospitals, a primary health center, and held workshops for thousands of artisans skilled in metal sculpting, woodworking, and making clothes. The group also increased the availability of microcredit loans, training for women entrepreneurs, and support for workers on farms, in salt mines, and in poor urban areas. Then, working with sixty Indian NGOs, AIF made information technology available to more than 200,000 students, increased the artisans' ability to produce and market their products, and began to send young Americans, mostly of Indian heritage, to serve as fellows to work with their NGO partners.

AIF is still going strong. Lata Krishnan is still there and has been board cochair for several years. It has been highly rated by Charity Navigator, and continues to attract strong support. Lata's own children were eight and eleven when she started with

AIF. They grew up watching their mother, and supportive father, AJ, prove you can do well and make a difference to others. I had no idea what would happen when I started. But I'm grateful I had the chance to help them get organized, to support their critical decision to work with dedicated local NGOs, and to encounter the man with no face and feel the grace of his greeting. In many ways AIF was a precursor to the work I would do in the future, not only in other natural disasters, but in other Clinton Foundation programs and through the Clinton Global Initiative.

When you leave the White House, even though no one plays a song when you walk in the room anymore, the government does provide support for your transition—six months for a temporary office in Washington, rent, staff salaries, and health insurance for your permanent office staff. My transition office was located in a small building on Jackson Place just across from the White House, and staffed with former White House aides, led by Karen Tramontano, the last of my deputy chiefs of staff in the White House. The first couple of weeks were marred by negative stories that set off a feeding frenzy in the press. The first to hit were stories that, as we moved out of the White House, I had taken two large bedside tables from the master bedroom in the White House; that the "W" key had been removed from the computers and typewriters in the West Wing; and that on my flight to New York on the former Air Force One after President George W. Bush's inauguration, our passengers destroyed government plates and other utensils. The White House staff asked me to take the tables, saying they didn't want to keep or store them, and no one on Air Force One destroyed government merchandise. I didn't know about the alleged removal of the "W" keys, but the whole thing bothered me because I had made it clear that I wanted a smooth, cooperative transition and we had done exactly that. Within a few days some people finally went on the record to say that either no damage had occurred or that the allegations of "W" mischief were greatly exaggerated.

The most serious attack on me was for my pardons of Marc Rich and his partner Pincus Green. Rich was a wealthy Republican oil broker who had strong ties to Israel and elsewhere in the Middle East. He was accused of misstating the income from his business to lessen the taxes he owed to the U.S. by nearly $50 million. Here's why I decided to do it. First, Rich was charged under a racketeering statute, which had been barred by the Justice Department from being used in such cases not long after he was charged. Second, he and the government had agreed that his wholly owned business would pay $200 million in taxes and penalties (four times what the government had said he owed) in a full settlement of the case that allowed him to continue doing business. Third, Israeli leaders from both major parties, Labor and Likud, asked me to do it because of his help with the Palestinians.

So why was the pardon controversial? For starters, because the wealthy Rich stayed in his house in Switzerland or confined his travel to nations that wouldn't extradite him to the United States. And because his ex-wife, Denise, a friend and supporter of mine who, more than a year earlier, had contributed $450,000 to my presidential library fund, wrote to me recommending the pardon. I wish Denise hadn't written to me, for her sake and mine. I knew she had made plenty of money on her own, did not get along with her ex-husband, and didn't know he would apply for a pardon when she gave money to the library fund. I suspected and later confirmed that she sympathized with him because when their much loved daughter died of cancer, the U.S. attorney wouldn't let Rich come home to her funeral without the threat of arrest to prevent his leaving the country. He wanted to visit her grave before he died.

Then Israel got into the act, with leaders of both their dominant parties, including the prime minister, urging Rich's pardon because of his work to support Israel in defusing security threats and solving problems with the Palestinians. Eric Holder, the deputy attorney general and later attorney general in President Obama's administration, said that the foreign policy considerations made him "neutral, leaning yes" toward approving the pardon, in spite of the U.S. attorney's continuing opposition based largely on Rich's refusal to come home.

I decided to grant the pardon because I thought it was the right thing to do: he'd paid four times what the government said he owed, the Justice Department had barred the law he was charged under from ever being used in such cases again, and Israeli officials from left to right said he helped them save lives and preserve the peace process. The press reaction was predictably negative. There was a congressional hearing and I was interviewed by the U.S. Attorney's Office. I welcomed the chance to answer all their questions and I did. The investigation died a quiet death, and the press began to cover the new president. As a condition of the pardon, I required Rich to agree to be charged civilly as others had been. Despite the lower burden of proof in a civil case, he was never charged. I never met him, and he died of a stroke in 2013, without ever seeing his daughter's grave.

The third controversy involved my office space. After reviewing a number of options, my team had recommended the Tower at Carnegie Hall. I was concerned about the cost and the ritzy-sounding address, but the owner had offered us a good price by Manhattan standards. Still, Representative Ernest Istook (R-OK) criticized the rent and Representative Darrell Issa (R-CA) was urging a full-scale investigation if the lease wasn't abandoned. After the dustup began, New York Democrat Charlie Rangel suggested I come to Harlem.

I thought about it for a couple of days and I decided I'd rather be in Harlem than anywhere else, anyway. More than thirty years earlier, when I was a student at Oxford and flew to New York on my way home to Arkansas, I'd stopped in Harlem and walked through the streets, imagining what it was like in the golden age of the Harlem Renaissance. Harlem was included in one of the first Empowerment Zones created as part of my economic plan in 1993, and during my presidency the unemployment rate there fell from more than 20 to 8 percent. I called Charlie and asked, "Can you find me an office in Harlem?" He replied, "Not before tomorrow morning."

We got out of the Carnegie Hall lease. I'm sure the owner was glad to be out of the story, especially since he'd given us a good deal and could make more from someone else. Soon we had a lease on bare space at the top of 55 West 125th Street, also called Dr. Martin Luther King Jr. Boulevard, near the intersection with Malcolm X Boulevard. Karen found a local architect, Navid Maqami, and a gifted young designer, Sheila Bridges, who crafted my personal office as it is today. The Studio Museum, just down the street, agreed to rotate the work of their artists, which would make the office more attractive and expose their art to people from all over the world.

On July 30, 2001, we finally opened the office, with a big Welcome to Harlem ceremony organized by Congressman Rangel and emceed by the wonderful Cicely Tyson. I had long been a fan—entranced by her performance in *Sounder* and impressed that she spent nearly a decade married to the brilliant but difficult Miles Davis. There were a few thousand people in the streets, lots of music and welcoming speeches, even a nice proclamation of William J. Clinton Day in Harlem from the Republican governor, George Pataki. I made brief remarks about walking down 125th Street as a young man, how I always wanted to play the Apollo Theater, just down the street, and how I'd try to be a good neighbor. The joyous event ended with all of us joining a jazz group in singing "Stand by Me." I felt like I was home. And I stayed.

I loved the buildout of my office—lots of wood, shelves that I filled with books about other presidents and pivotal moments in U.S. history, with a section on civil rights history, heroes, and the persistence of racism amidst our growing diversity, and in the conference room, books about Harlem, biographies of leaders I'd served with and admired, and books about Ireland and Northern Ireland, where I'd worked hard for peace. I've loved working there, having guests and feeding them good meals from local restaurants.

In 2005, the Clinton Foundation took over the thirteenth floor, added more space on the eleventh floor in 2008, and stayed until 2011. The Clinton Global Initiative was growing so fast it needed its own space, which was donated by the French property management company Calyon, from 2005 to 2013. The foundation and CGI both moved several times over the next few years as needs grew and space became available. In late 2023, both moved to their current home in the NoMad neighborhood, right on Madison Square Park.

Through it all, I've kept my former president's office in Harlem, hosting visitors from all over, from Make-A-Wish kids and student groups to political, business, and NGO leaders, foreign and domestic. I enjoy sharing my view of Harlem's main drag, including Marcus Garvey Park just across the street, where great youth league baseball is played; the still unfinished Cathedral of St. John the Divine, the world's largest Gothic church; the north end of Central Park, and all Manhattan beyond. I still love Harlem more than fifty years after I first walked down 125th Street.

Back in November of 1999, at the beginning of Hillary's Senate campaign, we'd bought our home in Chappaqua, New York, an old farmhouse built in the late 1890s, and expanded in the 1980s. I really liked the place, but it needed some work. The rooms in the old part of the house were small and there wasn't enough closet space, so we took out the decorative doors and windows between the living room and the glassed-in porch to make a bigger, lighter space and expanded the upstairs closet. We also glassed in a screened-in porch just off the kitchen to make it a usable breakfast room year-round. The third floor had a sauna, which we took out to make a nice office for Hillary, a good-sized den for TV and book space, and two little side rooms, one of which became a music room. It's packed with my saxophones, including two made by Adolphe Sax in the 1860s, with enough space for me to play music, lots of pictures of my favorite musicians, and other memorabilia, including an autographed scarf Elvis Presley wore at a California concert, a drumhead signed by Mick Fleetwood, and an autographed John Coltrane album. The expansion space is mostly two large rooms—a big den on the ground floor with crowded bookshelves, including many old editions I've collected over the decades, and a big bedroom on the second floor with large windows dominating three sides of the room and French doors opening to the back porch.

There was also an old red barn close to the house, which had been converted into an apartment for the previous owner's parent, with outside steps leading up to a converted loft. The Secret Service liked the loft as a site for their office, and I turned the downstairs into an office for me and a gym.

I knew the age of the house, the septic tank system, and other issues would present problems, but I wanted to buy the house from the minute I saw the bedroom. It was bathed in light. I told Hillary that this house would help her win the Senate election, because she'd wake up in a good mood even on cloudy days with all the light streaming in the bedroom windows. Also, I thought we'd have a good time working to make it ours. For more than twenty years now, we have done just that, restoring, remodeling, and reinforcing the house, improving the grounds, planting trees, shrubs, flowers, and a vegetable garden, putting up outdoor sculptures, fixing the plumbing, you name it. We've now lived there longer than any other place. Our home is obviously not a designer creation. It's filled with photographs, art and crafts from our travels, and our old books, all evoking memories of our public and private lives, our families and friends.

Hillary and I both love living in Chappaqua and feel blessed to live in a county where every town of any size has its own public library with free WiFi, the schools are really good, and the parks and wilderness preserves offer nature's bounty to people who can't afford to go far or spend much to find it. All these public spaces, plus our local bookshop, good new and well-established retail stores and restaurants, the Chappaqua Village Market, and Lange's Delicatessen, have given me countless opportunities to meet my neighbors, their kids, and lots of other people, listen to them and answer their questions. Now these neighbors often show me photos they took of me with their kids fifteen or twenty years ago, then tell me what they're doing these days.

I enjoy doing events that matter to people in Chappaqua, from marching with Hillary in our annual Memorial Day parade, to supporting Edward and Maya Manley's Making Headway Foundation, which supports families dealing with brain and spinal cord tumors and other brain-related traumas, to meeting with New York City kids who come up during the summer to visit our county, which has the largest amount of greenspace of any suburban county in the United States.

In the first half of 2001, while the office was being prepared and the office work was still being handled out of our transition headquarters in D.C., I kept busy making our home more livable, giving my first paid speeches, negotiating a book contract with the late Sonny Mehta of Knopf to write my autobiography with the late, legendary Bob Gottlieb as my editor, and signing on with the Harry Walker Agency in New York to handle my paid speeches.

Because Knopf had offered me a big advance on my memoir and the speech offers were coming in, I was feeling better about being able to pay my bills. I wanted to pay off millions of dollars in legal fees as soon as possible. It had embarrassed me to have a legal defense fund in the White House, and to ask my friend Terry McAuliffe to cosign my first mortgage on the Chappaqua house. Thankfully, now we could even afford a second home in D.C.

Hillary had found a wonderful place to live in Washington when the Senate was in session. It's at the end of Whitehaven, a street just off Massachusetts Avenue that runs uphill for just over a block and dead-ends at Dumbarton Oaks Park. You can walk right out the door and into the park, which we've happily done for more than twenty years.

The three-story red-brick structure, built around 1950, sits right on the street but has a beautiful backyard, with a nice swimming pool on the right and on the left a yard with a fish pond and trees in the back. The backyard borders the grounds of the British and New Zealand embassies. The across-the-street neighbors are the Danish embassy, the Hellenic Institute, and the Italian embassy, and down the street on our side are Polish, Brazilian, and Sri Lankan properties. The house was a godsend for Hillary in her Senate and secretary of state years, and for her mother, Dorothy, in the last years of her life.

Normally, when the Senate was in session, Hillary would spend Monday through Thursday in Washington, take the shuttle or Amtrak home Thursday night, and stay in Chappaqua or travel the state through the weekend, then go back to D.C. Monday morning. Of course, there were times when one or both of us traveled outside New York or the U.S., so we had to rely on phone calls as we grew into our new roles. For years I had watched her making positive changes as a citizen activist while I tried to do the same in politics. It struck me one morning when I was shaving that, in essence, we had switched places. I looked into the mirror and blurted out, "My God, I've become an NGO! Now what?"

When I was sure I was going to be able to pay my debts and the costs of maintaining our homes in Chappaqua and in Washington, I began to devote about 10 percent of my speechmaking income to the Clinton Foundation every year, as well as 10 percent of our total earnings to our family foundation to support the foundation and our other charitable interests.

Thanks to Don Walker and the Harry Walker Agency and other requests, I began making speeches in the United States and all over the world. Among the most welcome early ones came from Jewish groups across the country, and eventually from Latin America and Europe. They appreciated my support for Israel and for peace in the Middle East. Over the ensuing years, the largest number of non-U.S. speech offers by far have come from Canada, where I have a lot of friends and supporters, and there is a culture of inviting speakers in communities spanning the country. I've also given speeches across Europe, Asia, Latin America, Australia, and in Nigeria and South Africa.

I've really enjoyed the speeches and have learned a lot from the people I've met, who often have unusually perceptive comments and questions. I almost never tell war stories about the White House years unless asked about them in the question period that follows, or in interviews when sponsors prefer that format. Instead, whether the audience was a hundred or fewer or thousands at big conventions, I always started with an overview of how I view the world.

I'd tell them we had entered a new era of global interdependence being shaped by positive and negative forces. Among the positive ones were advances in science, led by the sequencing of the human genome, which would extend the length and improve the quality of life; the explosion of information technology, which would lower the cost and increase access to information and create unlimited new opportunities to use it; the increase of travel, trade, and immigration, which could build diversity, fuel economic expansion, and reduce racial, religious, and ethnic turmoil; new educational and economic opportunities for women and girls; and a sharp reduction in extreme poverty.

The problem with this new world in which borders look more like nets than walls is that we're all also exposed to the negative forces of interdependence: the world is too unequal in income and in access to education, health, housing, and the capital necessary to create wealth; it's too unstable because of vast differences in nations' governmental capacity, levels of corruption, and willingness to help those hurt by the changing economy, and internal racial, ethnic, and religious conflicts; and it's unsustainable because of our shared vulnerability to climate change, terror, weapons of mass destruction, disease, the opioid epidemic and other health problems, destabilizing cyberattacks, divisive, often dishonest social media sites, and the downsides of artificial intelligence.

The United States is in an excellent position to lead the world to a new era of shared peace and prosperity because of our relative youth, diversity, universities, community colleges and other training opportunities; achievements in science and technology; a powerful network of businesses large and small; a highly productive, trainable workforce; and our massive potential to produce clean energy and increase efficiency. But to make the most of our advantages, it's imperative to address our own problems with inequality, instability, unsustainability, internal conflicts, a sharp decline in our birth rate and in life expectancy for people under sixty-five, and a resistance to increasing our capacity to properly evaluate, accept, or reject the new immigrants, especially those who show up at the southern border. We have to deal with these challenges, help others to do the same, and keep building networks of cooperation.

That in a nutshell has been my speech. I've also told audiences that I filter the questions I'm asked, or ask myself, through a simple screen: Will this or that action increase the positive and decrease the negative forces of our interdependence, or do the reverse? Once I could answer that, I could determine what I was for and what I was against. I ask the people in my audiences to develop their own framework, so that the blizzard of often evolving and conflicting headlines doesn't become for them the political equivalent of chaos theory in physics, and so that they can compare the headlines with longer-term trendlines, which are often better.

After 9/11, I also told my audiences at home and abroad that since we are living in an interdependent world where we can't kill, jail, occupy, or wall ourselves off from all our adversaries, we need to keep building a world with more friends and fewer enemies. We have to fight terror, but do it in a way that doesn't compromise the character of our nation or the future of our children.

Easier said than done, as we have seen with U.S. treatment of captives in places like Abu Ghraib, Putin's war on Ukraine, the Hamas slaughter on October 7, 2023, and the Israeli attacks on Gaza that followed. And that's just a highly abbreviated list of the violence embroiling our world over the last twenty-five years.

Many of these abuses have driven people from their homelands, creating by far the largest migration across national borders since World War II. Wars, economic collapse, racial, ethnic, and religious repression, climate-change-driven drought, floods, wildfires, and storms, and deep cultural conflicts reduce our chances of building a world of shared peace and prosperity. All this was evident even before the global rise of divisive, populist nationalism. The United States, despite repeated threats from the far right after Reconstruction ended in the 1870s and in every decade since, was in the best position of all large countries to resist the poison, but for reasons embedded in our divided political culture, our uneven economic geography, our twisted information ecosystem, and the Electoral College's built-in advantage for divisive tribalism in the less populous states, we fell victim to it in 2016.

I've always tried in my appearances to incorporate the latest developments in science, or persuasive arguments made in new books, and to explain why cooperation works better than conflict for economic, social, and security reasons, hoping I could help people embrace a more inclusive way of looking at things. For example, after the sequencing of the human genome proved that all humans are genetically about 99.5 percent the same, I began asking audiences, especially the more diverse ones, to look at each other and let it sink in that every non-age-related difference they could see was rooted in one half of one percent of our biological makeup. Then I'd ask them why we spend 99.5 percent of our time focused on that half a percent? Shouldn't we all think more about the 99.5 percent that we share with our fellow humans? It always seems to have some effect.

I began to recommend books I found interesting and valuable, beginning with Robert Wright's *Nonzero* and Matt Ridley's *The Origins of Virtue*, then *The Social Conquest of Earth*, by the late, great naturalist and insect biologist E. O. Wilson, and more recently, Steve Brusatte's *The Rise and Fall of the Dinosaurs*. Wilson argues that since the fall of the dinosaurs 66 million years ago, our planet's most durable species are ants, termites, bees, and people, because they have proved to be the best at adapting to changed circumstances that threatened their existence. They have done so, Wilson maintains, by developing life-saving and -enhancing habits of cooperation. Humans have done best because we have both consciousness and a conscience.

Our problem is that we tend to take our intelligence and progress for granted, become arrogant, and push things to the edge of destruction. So far our conscience has kicked in to save the day. But we can't take it for granted, Wilson cautions, so we have to keep widening the circle of "us" and shrinking the circle of those we brand "them." Wilson offered these observations before America began to go off the rails in 2014, although there was lots of evidence, going back to the 1990s, and certainly since the midterm elections in 2010, that we were heading toward the cliff again.

I got interested in particle physics and the discovery of the

Higgs boson, the so-called God particle, which holds atoms together that otherwise would fly apart. I also worked to understand astrophysics and the latest theories of how the universe began, why it continues to expand, how life on our planet began, and the evidence that our planet, solar system, Milky Way galaxy, and eventually our entire universe would come to an end, though no one knows when. I was fascinated by the first photos of a massive black hole 55 million light-years away, identifiable because it was bordered by a fiery rim. The accompanying article said it was so large and its gravitational pull so powerful that if our entire solar system passed by close enough, it would be sucked in and instantly crushed into a tiny pile of dust that would fit in a thimble.

When I describe this to my audiences, I also tell them a story I mentioned in *My Life* about a rock Neil Armstrong picked up during his first moonwalk in 1969. It had been carbon-dated as 3.6 billion years old and had been sealed in a clear, vacuum-packed case. When Armstrong brought it to a White House event in 1994 marking the twenty-fifth anniversary of the moon landing, I asked to borrow the rock for the rest of my term. I put it right in the middle of the table that sits between the facing couches in the Oval Office. Whenever people sitting there arguing got so angry they were shedding more heat than light, I would interrupt the flow of words with something like, "Wait a minute. See that moon rock? It's 3.6 billion years old. We're all just passing through. Let's settle down and try to get something done." It often worked, even during the bitter partisan fights with the Gingrich Congress.

I told those stories and others like them to try to pierce the barriers we all put up when confronting the "other," hoping my audiences would listen to each other, actually hear what was being said, and become more open and inclusive. Sometimes it helped, sometimes it didn't, but I kept working at it, trying to reach people with "I never thought about it that way" moments that made them see themselves in a bigger picture, one that opens them to move outside their "caste" as the journalist and author Isabel Wilkerson calls it, to discover and embrace what they have in common with people beyond it. I had spent a lifetime trying to bridge the divide between "us" and "them." Now, with no political office and red alerts still flashing all around, my speeches seemed a good way to keep doing it.

It's hard to say which speeches I enjoy the most, but the college and other school appearances, large and small, in states red and blue, always leave me optimistic about the future. I could write a whole book about the students and teachers I've met, their unique cultures, achievements, and challenges. Most of them don't fit the stereotypes which have drawn them into the culture wars. In their own ways, almost all of them hope to help build and succeed in a nation and a world we can all share, widening the circle of opportunity, expanding the meaning of freedom, and strengthening the bonds of community.

And I've also had many great chance encounters. On my first postpresidential shuttle out of LaGuardia, the flight attendant, a young Black woman, told me her husband was a music teacher and jazz musician in D.C. who always supported me. But she said what really mattered to her was the Family and Medical Leave Act. She said her parents had both gotten sick and there was no one to take care of them but her and her sister. If it hadn't been for family leave, she wouldn't have been able to do it and keep her job. The bill had been vetoed twice during the previous administration and in 1992 I had promised to sign it if elected. In February 1993, I did. It was my very first bill and perhaps the most popular because of its impact on so many people. I'll never forget the last thing the flight attendant said to me that day: "You know, a lot of politicians talk about family values, but I think how your parents die is an important family value."

In 2023, I was invited back to the White House by President Biden for the thirtieth anniversary of the Family and Medical Leave Act. It's now been used more than 460 million times and enjoys near universal support. It's a good starting point in freeing America from the crazy—but sadly often effective—culture wars and returning to our founding mission, to form a more perfect union.

TWO

The Egyptian American at the Wall

On September 6, 2001, I flew to Australia for three speeches. I really like Australia, which Hillary and I had visited right after my reelection in 1996. After speeches in Sydney and Melbourne, I flew to Port Douglas, a great little town on the beach near both the Great Barrier Reef and the Daintree Rainforest.

On the evening of the eleventh, as we were finishing a late dinner fourteen hours ahead of the East Coast of the U.S., we learned about the first plane hitting the World Trade Center. I rushed back to my hotel room and turned on the TV. Hillary was in Washington, frantically trying to call Chelsea, who had been visiting a friend in lower Manhattan and had joined the thousands of other people in walking north, away from the carnage. Eventually they got in touch and Hillary, and I, could breathe.

When we saw the second plane hit the second tower, I was on the phone with Bruce Lindsey, my longtime friend and counselor who was president of our foundation, and Cheryl Mills, a former White House lawyer who represented me brilliantly during the impeachment proceedings. They were in Cheryl's office in lower Manhattan and saw the whole thing up close. When the second plane struck, I said, "Bin Laden did this." They asked how I knew and I replied that the attack was clearly the result of months of careful planning that required mastery of complex logistics and training, and that only the Iranians and al-Qaeda had the capacity to pull it off. I thought the Iranians wouldn't do it, because our retaliation would wipe them out, but bin Laden was living in a cave in Taliban-controlled territory in Afghanistan; he and his network were more elusive targets.

It was an awful day for America and the world, but especially for New Yorkers, who were proud of their rich racial, ethnic, and religious diversity and their open welcome to the world. They knew when the smoke cleared from the worst attack on U.S. soil since Pearl Harbor, people they knew and loved would be gone.

I wanted to go home. Thankfully, President Bush wanted all the former presidents and vice presidents in the United States, both for security reasons and to show national unity. So the next morning our small group flew on a C-130 transport plane from Australia to Guam, then took another plane to New York's Stewart Air National Guard Base, about an hour's drive from our house. On the way to the airport in Australia, the road was filled with signs supporting the U.S., part of a global outpouring of sympathy for and solidarity with the United States that lasted until the start of the Iraq War. The feeling was embodied by a simple declaration at the top of the French newspaper *Le Monde:* "We are all Americans."

Back in Chappaqua, I got word that Al Gore had tried to fly back to the U.S. from overseas but was stopped in Canada, as all private aircraft were. So he was driving back to Washington from there, and I invited him to spend the night with me. He got to my house after 2 a.m. When Al came up the driveway, I was waiting on the front porch of our old wooden farmhouse, standing next to my refrigerator. We'd had to move it there while renovating the kitchen. As we shook hands, Al looked at the fridge, and cracked, "I know you wanted to bring your Ozarks culture to New York, but this is going too far." After the last forty-eight hours, it was good to have a brief laugh. I missed Al's wry sense of humor as our lives diverged after the White House years. He's built a large clean energy investment fund and continues to speak out for the changes we need to make to avert climate catastrophe. I'm grateful that he has attended a few of our Clinton Global Initiative meetings, where he's always been very effective and well received.

Meanwhile, Hillary was still in Washington, working with the White House and other members of the New York congressional delegation to develop a package of support for the city's work to clean up and rebuild, and for the victims' families. Four hundred twelve members of the police, fire, and emergency departments of New York and New Jersey had been killed, and many others were bound to have long-term physical and mental health problems.

Chelsea and I wanted to show our support, so we went down to the missing persons center at the 69th Regiment Armory in Manhattan, where people had posted hundreds of pictures of missing loved ones in the hope that they might still be alive and that someone had seen them. They were praying for miracles. We all were.

The impact of the photo wall, with the still smoking ruins just blocks away, was gut-wrenching. I found myself staring at the faces next to a very tall man with an olive complexion and hair going gray. Tears were streaming down his cheeks. When I asked him if he'd lost somebody, he answered in a breaking voice: "No, but I am an Egyptian Muslim American. I hate what these people did. And I'm so afraid my fellow Americans will never trust me again."

The man's anger, tears, and fears reflected the new reality we were facing: we had to take care of the families of the killed or disabled, rebuild New York, and do more to prevent and punish terror. And we had to do it in a way that didn't compromise the inclusive character of our country or the future of our children by making a world of more enemies and fewer friends.

President Bush got us off to a good start with a stirring speech to those still sifting through the rubble to find anything that might identify the people who had perished there. He also went to the Islamic Center of Washington six days after the attacks, and in his remarks there reminded us that our enemy was terror, not Islam. Yes, the terrorists were Muslim, but so were several dozen of the victims. Senator Schumer and Hillary met with the president and she asked him directly for $20 billion to help New York recover. President Bush pledged his support. And he kept his word.

Since 9/11, I've tried to take every opportunity to thank the police and firefighters I've encountered and to never forget what they did on that fateful day. Not long after the attacks, I was given the opportunity to do something more. The late tech entrepreneur Andy McKelvey asked me to support his efforts to help pay for the college costs of children and spouses of all those killed or disabled. There were a lot of them—the families of the Trade Center workers and visitors and those in the Pentagon; the crew and passengers of the planes that crashed in New York, Washington, and Pennsylvania; and those who would die prematurely or become disabled because of their exposure to toxic substances during the recovery operations.

McKelvey wanted the effort to be bipartisan and someone, I don't recall who, suggested that I cochair the fund with my 1996 opponent, Bob Dole. I thought that was a good idea. I had my differences with Dole, but I respected him and marveled at the guts he showed in a political career that, because of the severe injury to his arm in World War II, required him to spend fifty minutes every morning just getting dressed. I thought Dole would be a highly credible, strong partner in a worthy endeavor. On September 29, he and I announced the Families of Freedom Scholarship Fund and asked Americans to contribute.

The fund quickly raised $100 million from more than 20,000 individuals, corporations, universities, and philanthropic organizations. Over the next seventeen years, that money, plus investment income and additional donations, has enabled the fund to distribute $152 million to 3,500 students. The fund began by covering 65 percent of college costs, but was forced to reduce the percentage, mostly because the premature death or disability of a large number of the recovery workers increased the number of people eligible for help by about 3,000. The Families of Freedom Fund would like to raise a few million dollars more to cover all the eligible people and cover a higher percentage of the costs. Hopefully they'll be able to do it. I'll always be grateful to the dedicated people who've served on the board of the fund, many of them in honor of lost loved ones, and to Scholarship America, which has administered the fund all these years without charging any fees and will do so until the fund sunsets in 2030.

While I was doing what I could, Hillary was going back and forth between New York and Washington, meeting with survivors, families who'd lost loved ones and businesses, and leaders of police and fire departments that had suffered a heavy toll. We both attended memorial services and fundraising events, and visited with first responders to thank them. Hillary was physically exhausted and emotionally drained for weeks as she encountered more and more people who were hurting and needed help. She was by turns heartbroken and angry, and determined to do all she could to help them recover and begin again. She saw immediately that those involved in the cleanup would have health problems arising from their efforts and introduced legislation to help them. After all our years together, I was still in awe of watching what she called her "extra responsibility gene" in overdrive. Still, I was worried about her, and tried to get her to rest on the weekends so that the energy powering that responsibility gene didn't burn out.

There were a lot of people in tough shape. Two financial firms, Cantor Fitzgerald and Sandler O'Neill incurred staggering losses. Cantor Fitzgerald, a large global investment firm, lost 658 of its 960 New York employees. Its chairman, Howard Lutnick, made sure the families got the assistance they needed, and in 2002 he started an annual Charity Day that raises millions of dollars a year by donating the firm's entire trading revenues from that day's transactions. I try to go every year. In 2011, President George W. Bush and I both went up and down the aisle talking to the traders and thanking them. They raised over $11 million. Howard Lutnick is still doing the Charity Day, having expanded it in recent years to include charitable causes around the world.

Sandler O'Neill was a smaller investment firm, with eighty-three employees in the office atop World Trade Center's South Tower. Sixty-six of them were killed, including two of the firm's three leaders, one the mentor and the other the best friend of the third principal, Jimmy Dunne, who survived because he was out of the office that day. Dunne, who also lost his personal assistant, absorbed his grief and did his duty. He spoke at twenty of his colleagues' funerals, made sure all the affected families got their loved ones' pay, bonuses, and healthcare coverage, and set up a college fund for the children. Then he went to work rebuilding the company.

In 2019, Sandler O'Neill was acquired by Piper Jaffray and renamed Piper Sandler Companies. And Jimmy Dunne, now living in Florida, is still working. Before his passionate efforts to care for his people and rebuild his company, Jimmy was perhaps best known as one of America's finest amateur golfers. I had the honor of playing a couple of rounds with him and he's terrific (I should have been his caddie instead of slowing him down). I also paid a visit to Sandler O'Neill a few years later and saw it reborn.

Of course, those two firms were far from the only ones who lost people that day. I was just fortunate enough to get to know them.

In 2009, George W. Bush and I were asked to help raise the funds to finish a memorial to the people killed when Flight 93 crashed in a field in rural Pennsylvania, near Shanksville. It was the fourth plane in the terrorists' plan. The first three hit the Twin Towers and the Pentagon; the fourth aimed to hit the Capitol. It failed, thanks to the courage and sacrifice of the passengers who attacked the hijackers, fought for control of the plane, and brought it to the ground, upside down, in that Pennsylvania field. I'm glad we were able to help finish the memorial.

The park was dedicated on September 10, 2011, one day shy of the tenth anniversary of 9/11, with Vice President Biden, President Bush, Speaker John Boehner, and me participating. In my remarks, I compared the heroism of the citizens of Flight 93 to that of the soldiers at the Alamo and the three hundred Spartans who fought a massive Persian army at Thermopylae almost 2,500 years before. At the Alamo, the defenders knew they were going to die, but the time they bought paved the way for Sam Houston's victory. The Greek soldiers also knew they were going to die, but the time they bought saved the people and the city-state they served. The people on Flight 93 were civilians, taking what they assumed was a normal trip. They had to make a snap decision, one that prevented the plane from attacking the Capitol, saving many lives and denying the terrorists the symbolic victory of smashing into the center of American government. They, and those who put their lives on the line to save people in the burning towers, also gave us a chance to save the idea of America: to be able to fight terror and maintain liberty, while still welcoming people from all over the world, regardless of race, religion, and culture, as long as they shared our commitment to freedom and the rule of law.

On April 8, 2004, I met with the 9/11 Commission, a bipartisan group established in 2002 to answer important questions: How did it happen? Did my administration do all it could to strengthen our defenses against terrorist attacks? Did the Bush administration take the threat of an attack on the homeland seriously enough leading up to 9/11? Why did the administration believe Iraq was involved in the 9/11 attacks, even though all the intelligence agencies said there was no evidence of it?

By the time I testified, the commission had heard from both of my national security advisors, Tony Lake and Sandy Berger, Secretary of State Madeleine Albright, Secretary of Defense Bill Cohen, CIA director George Tenet, Attorney General Janet Reno, Richard Clarke, the coordinator for counterterrorism in the National Security Council, and several other members of my administration.

The commission itself was an impressive group, with five Democrats and five Republicans, chaired by former GOP governor Tom Kean of New Jersey. The vice chair was former Democratic congressman Lee Hamilton of Indiana, who had retired in 1999 after thirty-four years in the House. I knew and admired them both. The staff was impressive, too, and they'd worked hard to answer the big questions. But I was concerned that with bin Laden still at large and the future of U.S. efforts in Afghanistan and Iraq in doubt, the report might be too dense and too full of carefully qualifying language.

When I walked into the hearing room with no notes, accompanied only by Sandy Berger, I asked to give a brief opening statement. I told them we had done our best to prevent terrorist attacks and bring terrorists to justice, but in the security arena you don't get credit for saves. "I'm not interested in covering my backside, so if you can find anything I did or didn't do that contributed to 9/11, please say so."

They seemed surprised, but it cleared the air and led to several hours of real conversation. At least they were listening carefully when I said I thought my biggest error of omission was in not ensuring the implementation of my 1995 order to have the CIA and FBI place one of their counterterrorism experts in each other's offices so they could share intelligence and work together to prevent terrorist actions, both in the United States and in other countries. They did the staff transfers, but didn't do much sharing, underestimating the value of doing so, especially when they knew there were threats to attack the homeland.

Since Watergate, when the Nixon administration sought to use the Justice Department, the IRS, and other federal agencies for political purposes, presidents and senior White House advisors of both parties had adopted a largely hands-off approach to the FBI and the Justice Department, even giving the FBI director a ten-year term, which could be shortened only for good cause. I followed past policy because I believed the White House shouldn't interfere with the Justice Department on legal matters, though Kenneth Starr's office had used FBI agents to keep pursuing the Whitewater matter, even after Hillary and I were cleared of any wrongdoing by the Resolution Trust Corporation investigation in 1995.

I made the same mistake with the CIA for the opposite reason. We were in constant contact with the CIA director, George Tenet, and he knew I wanted to know everything about our counterterrorism efforts. But before 9/11, I didn't know there was still too little sharing and too much hoarding of information, or about all the management shortcomings in the main FBI headquarters. I didn't know that the CIA didn't tell the FBI or the attorney general about the presence of suspected terrorists in the United States before 9/11, or that the FBI had no system in place to investigate the terrorism warnings of its own agents.

That came back to bite us in 2001, when the CIA included in the Presidential Daily Brief in August that it had picked up chatter that there would be terrorist attacks in the United States using airplanes, a warning made real when FBI agents from Arizona and Minnesota reported to FBI headquarters in Washington that there were men from the Middle East who took flight training at local airports, but didn't practice takeoffs and landings. Those reports not only weren't shared with the CIA, they never even made it up the FBI chain of command, apparently because they were just written down and put in a file.

There were about 2,200 flight schools in the United States. Quick calls or emails to them could have revealed men in other flight training programs doing the same thing. Although that happened after I left office, there were enough red flags about FBI management issues when I was there, including the loss of lab tests and of substantial cash recovered in criminal operations. If we had pushed the attorney general to exert greater oversight and order more intelligence cooperation, it's possible that would have at least brought the local FBI agents' warnings to light and led the FBI and the Federal Aviation Administration to order defensive measures on flights into New York and Washington and a nationwide search for those who had used the flight schools.

Another mistake I flagged at the hearing was our decision not to retaliate against al-Qaeda after the attack on the USS *Cole* on October 12, 2000. I thought it was an al-Qaeda operation from the beginning, but couldn't get agreement from the FBI and other intelligence agencies before I left office. It wasn't until April of 2001 that they all agreed that it was an al-Qaeda attack. For whatever reason, no retaliation occurred.

Then I said I'd welcome the commission's questions. All the members asked good ones, but the first exchange was the most memorable. John Lehman, President Reagan's navy secretary and a strong pro-defense conservative, thanked me for being candid and open to criticism. Then he said something hard to imagine in today's polarized political climate: "Since you've been so open,

I want to start by saying I owe you an apology. I'm a Republican and I believed everything my party's critics said about you. I have now reviewed about a thousand pages of terrorism-related security documents you received. Your handwritten comments and questions are all over them. You cared a lot about this, learned a lot, and wanted to make the right decisions. You also wanted to do more against al-Qaeda. But you were poorly served by an unintended consequence of the Goldwater-Nichols Act."

He said the act, a bipartisan effort passed in 1986, was designed to improve efficient decision-making in the military and reduce interservice rivalries, and had succeeded in doing both by developing a more organized, inclusive decision-making process in the Pentagon, which enabled the chairman of the Joint Chiefs to brief the president on military leaders' consensus recommendations. He said I had followed those recommendations in launching cruise missiles against al-Qaeda targets after the 1998 African embassy bombings, which had killed several Americans and more than two hundred Kenyan and Tanzanian citizens. "But you didn't send ground troops into Afghanistan because you were told the probability of getting bin Laden and destroying al-Qaeda's core leadership was low and the likelihood of significant civilian casualties, and the loss of a lot of our forces, was high." I agreed.

He then explained the Goldwater-Nichols angle: he had learned that the Special Forces commander strongly disagreed with the consensus and felt his troops had a reasonable chance to achieve the mission of severely weakening al-Qaeda and capturing or killing bin Laden and other leaders without large civilian casualties, but I wasn't told that. He asked if I had specifically asked the chairman of the Joint Chiefs whether the Special Forces commander agreed with the recommendations. I said I hadn't. Lehman said I shouldn't have had to, but over time, the Pentagon had grown so comfortable with the new system, they'd stopped considering its potential downside: depriving the president of informed dissenting opinions that deserved to be heard. Lehman said if I'd been told, I might have made the same decision, but at least it would have been a better-informed one.

I'm telling you this to make a larger point. No matter how

smart and on the level you are, if you make enough decisions, some of them will look wrong in light of subsequent events, and these errors will happen more often when you base decisions on unwarranted assumptions or fail to follow up on troubling leads. That's a big reason why, if they share a common goal, diverse groups with different backgrounds and knowledge make better decisions than homogenous ones or lone geniuses. On that day, John Lehman was a patriot in recognizing we shared a common goal—no more 9/11s—and making his contribution to it.

Both the 9/11 report and a supplemental book containing excerpts from the House-Senate joint inquiry and testimony from fourteen witnesses make interesting reading twenty years later, especially the testimony of Richard Clarke, who worked for our government on national security issues from 1973 until 2003. During my terms, he was our point man on terrorism, and in 1998 I made him the National Security Council's coordinator for security, infrastructure protection, and counterterrorism, with "cabinet-level" access. He was smart, tough, and appropriately impatient when he thought our government was too slow in dealing with agile, creative terrorist groups. Dick stayed on for three years under President Bush, assuming leadership of U.S. cybersecurity affairs. He's still doing work in cybersecurity today, identifying vulnerabilities, developing defenses, and sounding alerts. He's a walking alarm bell, always on guard. I wouldn't want to be in a fight without him. There are more people like Dick out there trying to keep us safe than you know—a "deep state" committed to preserving our freedom, not taking it away.

Before meeting with the 9/11 Commission in 2004, I had spoken at the U.S.-Islamic World Forum in Qatar, home of Al Jazeera, Education City, an impressive group of colleges run by American universities, and an important U.S. military base. There were representatives from across the Islamic world, eager to grasp the benefits of modernity and peace without losing their faith or their cultures, and wondering how to proceed in the aftermath of 9/11.

In my remarks I told them that what they wanted was possible only if we were willing to listen to and learn from one another without preconceptions; to improve our capacity for self-criticism; to identify common interests; and to accept that no one can possess the whole truth, even if they believe their faith embodies it. That's what Saint Paul was saying when he compared our short lives on earth with the promise of eternal life in Paradise: "For now we see through a glass darkly, but then face-to-face; now we know in part, but then we shall know even as we are known." Paul's insight led him to the conclusion that of the abiding virtues—faith, hope, and love—"the greatest of these is love." Not romantic love, but *agape*, love of your fellow human beings. The problem with my argument was that in times full of fear and insecurity, rage and resentment, we crave the clarity and certainty of blaming the other and belonging to a group in possession of the whole truth. That creates a lot of opportunities for "true believers" to exploit.

The speech was well received, perhaps because I admitted that no absolutist, faith-based ideology is free of error. After all, the first thing the Christian soldiers did in laying siege to Jerusalem in the First Crusade in 1096 was not to kill the Muslim defenders, but to burn a synagogue full of Jewish families. The important point was that no one has the whole truth. To my surprise, an Islamist member of the Pakistani parliament joined in the standing ovation.

I had no idea whether my remarks would have any impact, but since 9/11, I'd made an effort to get the message out in the United States and across the world, especially to Muslim groups. I kept trying, delivering the message the next week at the Jeddah Economic Forum in Saudi Arabia, the next month at the University of Judaism in Los Angeles (now the American Jewish University), and in April at Tel Aviv University, at a dinner sponsored by my longtime friend and passionate peace activist Danny Abraham.

On every September 11, as many New Yorkers do, I relive that terrible day. I think of those who still grieve the lost, those who ran toward danger to care for others, and those who have labored to keep our city and our nation safe since then. I think of my daughter, walking away from the towers, not knowing what would happen next. I think of Hillary, knowing her job as a senator from New York would be dominated by a duty and a passion no one had even considered when she campaigned.

And I think of the Egyptian American at the wall. If he's still in New York, it's a good bet that he is still welcomed in a city more vibrant and diverse than ever. But out in the country, where the pot of resentment boils, fueled by economic dislocation, cultural anxiety, and fear of political disempowerment in the face of so much demographic and social change, we're still a work in progress. Remembering how we came together in response to 9/11 is a good place to start.

THREE

Work That Follows You Out of Office

When I left the White House, some of the work followed me out, from ceremonies to missions tied to things I'd done and relationships I'd formed when I was president. Some of them were official, like commemorations of historic agreements, or state funerals, while others just came up.

In the summer of 2001, I flew to Buenos Aires to see Argentina's president, Fernando de la Rúa, and then to Brazil to meet with President Fernando Henrique Cardoso, who had a direct interest in seeing his neighbor succeed. Both wanted my help in convincing the Bush administration to support their plan to resolve Argentina's sudden and severe financial crisis. In recession since 1998, Argentina feared the International Monetary Fund's threat to withdraw pledged loan funds unless it sharply curtailed public spending and started paying down its debt immediately. De la Rúa knew the abrupt changes the IMF demanded would make life more difficult for ordinary citizens and destabilize the country's politics. He wanted to turn things around, but he and Cardoso both thought the IMF demands were so tough they would be self-defeating.

Essentially, they wanted the United States to give Argentina a short-term loan that would enable them to make a substantial payment on the debt, and persuade the IMF to spread the repayment schedule over a longer period of time to reduce the severe impact on Argentine citizens. When I was in office, Brazil had similar troubles and we helped with much more money than Argentina needed. Cardoso was a respected economist, widely admired and corruption-free. He vouched for de la Rúa. I considered Cardoso a good and trusted friend. And Argentina had been America's most loyal ally in South America, regardless of the party in the White House. It was the first to answer the call for troops to support the restoration of democracy in Haiti, always supported the United States on tough votes in the U.N., and pegged its currency to the dollar. I said I'd try to help.

When I got home I called President Bush's secretary of the treasury, Paul O'Neill, whom I'd known since I was governor and he was chairman and CEO of Alcoa, which had a large plant in Arkansas. When I made my case for the loan, he responded, "Well, they're in this mess because they screwed up!" I replied, "Of course they did, Paul. That's often when people need help—when they screw up. Argentina has been a friend and ally of our country and they'll be forever grateful if we do help them."

I failed to sway him. The IMF soon put the hammer down. By December there were riots in the streets and President de la Rúa had to resign. Eventually, Argentina defaulted on some of its debts, leading to years of legal, political, and economic turmoil. Argentina is rich in human talent, with one of the most productive agricultural sectors in the world. But since their 2001 credit crisis, the country's politics have held the country back, swinging back and forth from right to center to left, from more corruption to less of it. Regardless, I'm glad I met with Cardoso and de la Rúa and sorry I couldn't persuade our government to help with my old "ounce of prevention is worth a pound of cure" plea. It's one of those "get caught trying" moments I've learned to live with.

Sometimes my efforts were more successful. Earlier in 2001, I had been invited to Hong Kong to speak to a Fortune Global

Forum on the economy. It was an interesting and lucrative offer, but I wasn't sure I could do it. The United States and China were engaged in a word war over the crash of an American spy plane on an island close to mainland China. So far, the Chinese hadn't released the plane and President Bush hadn't spoken to President Jiang Zemin. I called the national security advisor, Condoleezza Rice, told her about the upcoming speech and the fact that the Chinese president would be there. I said, "I know him well. We spent a lot of time together, and if I go, I'll have to meet with him."

I had a lot of respect for Condi's ability and dedication, which was reinforced by efforts she'd made in her previous job as chancellor at Stanford to protect Chelsea's privacy and make her college years as normal as possible, so I was frank. I said, "You know your side bankrupted me when I was in office and I need this speech, but I'm an American first. If you don't want me to go, just say so and I'll cancel. The other choice is to have me deliver a message from the White House to President Jiang. I know we have just one president at a time. Just tell me what you want me to say and I'll do it."

Condi chuckled at the bankruptcy line because she knew it was true and I was clearly ready to can the speech. She said she'd talk to the president and get back to me. Soon she called back and said they wanted me to go and simply tell Jiang that if China would promptly release the plane, he and Bush could make a fresh start.

I scheduled a meeting with President Jiang before my speech. I wanted to get into the plane issue right away and I started to explain the U.S. position. He quickly cut me off, saying, "This is not nearly as serious as your bombing my embassy in Belgrade." That had happened in 1999 during the seventy-seven-day bombing campaign to stop Slobodan Milošević from turning Kosovo into another Bosnia. We had done our best to hit strategic targets and the CIA maps had identified the embassy building as belonging to the Serbian intelligence service, although Serbia had sold it to China two years earlier.

Jiang continued. "But what did you do then? You immediately apologized and tried to call me. When I didn't take the call, you knew I had a political problem to deal with, so you kept trying. I took the third call, the demonstrations against the U.S. stopped, and we went back to normal. President Bush didn't call me and made a tough public statement instead. So I made one in response. This is simple. You spy on us, we spy on you. We didn't shoot your plane down and you can't blame us for taking a look at it. This isn't a big deal. So tell me what you want."

I said, "President Bush wants the plane back, and if you give it to him, I think you'll have a good conversation with him and get back to normal business." I called Condi and told her about the conversation. Soon the plane was returned, the two leaders talked, and that was that. I've learned that most leaders are more likely to respond to blunt talk when it is delivered in private. It makes the message more credible, while saving enough face to avoid a cycle of public bad-mouthing. Of course, that approach doesn't garner as much press coverage, but it is more likely to be effective, and when you do have to take the gloves off in public, people are more apt to listen.

Anyway, it was the beginning of a fascinating relationship with George W. Bush, a man with sharp political instincts who's determined to keep learning and growing, as his love of painting, continued involvement with men and women wounded in military service, and outspoken support for immigration reform demonstrate. He's a good example of what I've often seen in political leaders and other famous people over the years—the public persona rarely captures the whole person.

The next day I met with Hong Kong chief executive Tung Chee-hwa, who was close to President Jiang yet seemed proud of Hong Kong's more democratic open culture. I liked Tung and hoped his positive approach to dealing with the U.S. and with Hong Kong's vibrant, often contentious democracy would prevail. I briefed him on my meeting with Jiang and asked him to support the resolution of the plane issue.

Unfortunately, our relationship with China has deteriorated, with President Xi Jinping's embrace of divisive nationalism and his decision to stay in office indefinitely. Strains have also been increased by China's abandonment of its commitment to maintain Hong Kong's distinctive role in "One China, Two Systems"; by the internment of a million Uighur Chinese citizens; by aggressive efforts to militarize more of the South China Sea islands and intimidate China's neighbors in Southeast Asia and the Philippines; by Xi's public declaration of his desire to "solve the Taiwan problem" on his watch; by China's less than candid sharing of information on COVID-19; and by Xi's 2021 warning that foreign powers will "get their heads bashed" if they attempt to bully or influence the country.

We still need to work with the Chinese on climate change, our economic relationship, North Korea, and a host of other issues. Divorce is not an option. Today it looks like our relationship is stabilizing, but, as always, we need to prepare for the worst while we work for the best. President Biden's 2022 CHIPS and Science Act, already bringing chip manufacturing back to the U.S., is a big step in the right direction.

Over the years, there have been more opportunities to encourage the continuation of hard-won peace agreements, and urge still estranged former adversaries to find common ground. I always cleared the foreign speeches with the current administration and asked for talking points for meetings that were approved.

In May of 2001, I flew to Ireland to deliver a lecture at Trinity College Dublin and be the honoree at a star-studded dinner at Dublin Castle to raise funds for the Northern Ireland Reconciliation Fund. It was the beginning of a twenty-plus-year labor of love to do whatever I could to keep the letter and spirit of the Good Friday Agreement alive. It was vital, and still is, to the future of all the Irish people, and to the dream of a Europe united in peace, prosperity, democracy, and security. I also thought the pillars of the agreement could be applied to other trouble spots in the world: majority rule, minority rights, individual rights, the rule of law, and shared decision-making in government. But first, we had to keep the peace process on track. As always, the devil was in the details of sensitive matters, including policing and accountability for the bloody past, and in the shifting ground that was an inevitable consequence of the changes in political leadership in Northern Ireland and the U.K., the global financial crash, which hit Ireland especially hard, and later, the narrow victory of Brexit in the U.K., which threatened both Northern Ireland's economic future and the Good Friday Agreement itself.

The Dublin dinner raised a lot of money to facilitate the positive changes Northern Ireland needed in the years before Brexit reared its head. It was a memorable night. Both Prime Minister Bertie Ahern, who worked with Tony Blair to finish the agreement, and George Mitchell, who chaired the successful peace talks with a brilliant balance of patience, persistence, and problem-solving, were there. The great actor Richard Harris read a poem, the Three Irish Tenors and The Corrs sang, and many others prominent in all walks of Irish life attended. So did former senator Gary Hart, for whom I'd worked in the McGovern campaign in 1972. Bob Geldof, famed Irish singer-songwriter and AIDS activist, was master of ceremonies. It was all wonderful, a "home game," with the climax a tribute delivered by my friend Bono, the lead singer of U2, who showed up with his wife, Ali, less than twenty-four hours after she gave birth to their fourth child!

All told, I've been to Ireland and Northern Ireland fourteen times since 2001. The latest trip, in May 2023, was a five-day visit to Belfast to celebrate the twenty-fifth anniversary of the Good Friday Agreement, which, despite political and power-sharing setbacks, has kept the peace.

In June 2002, I was invited by Colombian president Andrés Pastrana and his newly elected successor, Álvaro Uribe, to come to their nation during the transition period to speak at a corporate responsibility conference. The real purpose of the conference was to convince the foreign companies operating in Colombia not to give up in the face of violent conflicts between Colombian law enforcement and military forces on one side and the drug cartels and powerful militia groups that supported them on the other.

They wanted me to come and make the case because I had strongly supported and signed the bill to fund Plan Colombia, an ambitious billion-dollar effort to defeat the guerrillas, dismantle the cartels, and support alternatives to coca production. The initiative had strong bipartisan support in Congress and President Bush had pledged to continue it, but we were in the early stages, and Pastrana and Uribe knew that after 9/11 Bush had to concentrate on Afghanistan and terrorism. The Colombian presidents felt that if the international companies believed the United States had lost interest in Colombia, they might conclude the country was a risk no longer worth taking and begin closing their operations there.

The White House quickly approved the trip for the same reason the two presidents had made the request: Colombia is important to America. It is the oldest democracy in South America, an ally and important trading partner, but also the center of the continent's cocaine trade in a region already unsettled by the rhetoric and actions of then-President Hugo Chávez in next-door Venezuela.

At the time President Pastrana proposed Plan Colombia in 1999, about a third of the population was under the effective control of guerrilla groups and the narcotraffickers who paid them a lot of money for protection. Honest police, prosecutors, and judges were targets for assassination and politicians were ripe for corruption by the rich cartels. When the military was unable to defeat the guerrillas protecting the cartels, several wealthy landowners had formed their own militia groups in response, which increased violence and didn't solve the problem. At the bottom of the food chain were the coca farmers, who raised the crop that the cartels turned into cocaine. They felt they had no choice but to keep growing the coca, since they couldn't raise anything else that would make them nearly as much money.

The strategy of Plan Colombia was to defeat the militias, take down the already weakened cartels, and drastically reduce coca production by giving the coca farmers other ways to make a decent living. We also worked hard to cut the demand in the U.S. and reduce access to the American market. In the summer of 2000, I had gone to Colombia with a congressional delegation that included Speaker Dennis Hastert and then-Senator Joe Biden. We met with people who were implementing the plan, then went to a dinner with Colombian officials. Chelsea was with me, and after the dinner President Pastrana took us on a stroll through the beautiful old section of Cartagena.

Soon we came to a square where a crowd had gathered around a group of young musicians in their traditional native dress, singing and dancing for peace. Los Niños del Vallenato were from the northeastern state of Cesar, a place of beautiful valleys running through deeply forested mountains. They were already famous. Their first CD, full of songs urging an end to violence, quickly rose to the top of the charts in Colombia. Soon, President Pastrana, Chelsea, and I were dancing with them. I was so moved by their music and their message of peace and resilience that I invited them to the White House for our last Christmas party and four years later to perform at the dedication of my presidential library.

They were accompanied by their sponsor, Colombian culture minister Consuelo Araújo, who was from the same area as the children and was a big promoter of the annual Vallenato music festival and competition held in the soccer stadium in Valledupar. It drew 30,000 musicians and fans a year. It was also the home of the most revered teacher of Vallenato music, Andrés Gil. Children came from miles away to learn from him, often walking through dangerous areas when bullets were flying. Consuelo was so well known she was referred to only by her first name. Not many cabinet ministers anywhere can say that.

The guerrillas hated these kids and their music, but they knew better than to go after them. They did, however, manage to kidnap Consuelo in September 2001. She was a "two-fer" for them—the woman whose children had galvanized popular opinion against the violence and the wife of the lawyer who had just become attorney general of Colombia.

About two weeks after 9/11, Los Niños del Vallenato were on a long-scheduled trip to the United States to sing at the Kennedy Center. They performed a song pleading for Consuelo's release. It was not to be. A couple of days later, her body was found. She had been shot in the back of the head. Consuelo's funeral was held in the soccer stadium at Valledupar, site of her beloved festival. I was unable to attend, but President Pastrana and her family asked that I deliver a message over the jumbotron. A hundred thousand people came to say goodbye to a brave woman who wanted Colombia's children to grow up in a peaceful, lawful country, where children are free to sing their songs and find their way.

When I called Pastrana to accept his invitation to the conference in 2002, I made just one request: please bring the children to greet me. On the night of June 28, I landed at the Cartagena airport. When the flight crew opened the door, I walked out on the top step to see the children singing a song of welcome. By their side were two adults: one was the new culture minister, the other a representative of Indigenous people. The culture minister was María Consuelo Araújo, Consuelo's twenty-nine-year-old niece. The Indigenous Colombian was there to give me a traditional welcome bracelet woven from red, blue, and yellow strands, the colors of their flag. Although almost no one does it anymore, tradition holds that it should be worn until it falls off. I followed tradition—to honor Consuelo and her brave family, and to remind myself that compared to what so many others face, I never have a bad day. In the spring of 2022, the bracelet finally fell off my right wrist after almost twenty years. It was badly frayed and the colors were no longer bright, but the memories it held never faded.

I've been back to Colombia often over the years, to speak at a conference on Spanish heritage, to support the work of my foundation there, and to see my friend Gabriel García Márquez not long before his passing. He's the only person I know who bragged that he counted both me and Fidel Castro as friends.

In June 2017, I attended the first World Coffee Producers Forum in Medellín and took the opportunity to visit one of the first infrastructure projects to come out of Plan Colombia, an amazing cascade of escalators going all the way up and down the mountain that dominates the Comuna 13 neighborhood, once the home of cartel kingpin Pablo Escobar. Before the escalators, poor women had to walk down the equivalent of a thirty-story building to fill their water jugs, then put them on their heads for the long trek back up. Now the escalators carry them down and up, along with tourists from all over. They stop along the way to view the famous graffiti art on the walls and roofs of tightly packed buildings, or have a meal or a cup of coffee in a cozy café. The coffee conference brought together people from more than forty countries as part of Colombian president Juan Manuel Santos's plan to reduce coca production by shifting more land to coffee growing and increasing the growers' incomes.

Colombia has made progress through Plan Colombia, but the road has not been an easy one. The main guerrilla group officially disbanded, and overall violence went down, but the peace agreement Santos signed was controversial, with former president Uribe heading the opposition from his Senate seat to a deal he thought was too easy on the rebel groups. After Santos ended his term, he was succeeded by Uribe's favored candidate, Iván Duque, a dedicated young leader who promised not to cancel the peace agreement but to make it tougher. Instead, he had to deal with two new problems: the tremendous influx of economic and political refugees fleeing the turmoil in neighboring Venezuela, nearly two million of them, and the ravages of COVID-19. Soon crime, violence, and general discontent were on the rise.

Duque granted the vast majority of the Venezuelan refugees legal status for ten years, provided they register with the government. About two decades earlier, when Venezuela was more stable and Colombia was struggling, more than a million Colombians fleeing the violence at home had found refuge in Venezuela. At first, most Colombians supported the chance to return the favor, but the international community has given them nowhere near the support they need and proved unwilling or unable to resolve the Venezuelan crisis in the face of President Nicolás Maduro's unwillingness to cede or share power.

In the 2022 election, Colombians voted for their first leftist government. They elected President Gustavo Petro, once a guerrilla fighter who had renounced violence long ago, and who, as mayor of Bogotá in 2013, proudly showed me one of his city's electric taxis; and Vice President Francia Márquez, a social activist who is the nation's first Afro-Colombian to hold such a high office. There was a peaceful transfer of power. Around the same time, a citizens' group issued a report sharply critical of Plan Colombia, essentially saying it placed too much emphasis on defeating the cartels and their supporters and too little on finding better ways for the coca farmers to make a living.

That's an understandable but not entirely accurate criticism. Investors have become more wary as the government, with little outside assistance, has been forced to divert funds needed for development, including alternatives to coca production, to deal with the economic burdens of Covid and the massive influx of refugees, creating new opportunities for the cartels and the violence they bring. I'm still glad we helped them get their country back and hope they can build on that.

In mid-2001, Nelson Mandela called and asked me to come speak at a civil society conference he was hosting with Roelf Meyer, the dedicated public servant who had handled President F. W. de Klerk's side of the transfer of power to Mandela after his landslide victory in the first postapartheid election. Mandela said they were trying to build up the nongovernmental sector to help meet pressing needs and strengthen the legitimacy of their new democracy, and asked me to help make the case.

I loved being with Mandela and thought he was onto something. He knew that after he left office, it would be harder to maintain national unity, and a strong network of NGOs supported by diverse groups could help a lot. I asked him if I could bring an example of what they might want to do to his meeting. When he laughed and said, "Please do," I called Eli Segal. A longtime friend of Hillary's and mine, Eli was chief of staff of my '92 campaign, a successful entrepreneur, and the first leader of AmeriCorps, which I sponsored and Congress enacted in 1993. The program provides a modest stipend for mostly young men and women to live and work in rural and urban communities across America for a year or two on locally chosen projects. They also earn the equivalent of G.I. Bill benefits for college aid for each year they work. Every volunteer takes a simple pledge to "get things done." By 2001, more people had served in

AmeriCorps than in the forty-year history of the Peace Corps. In 2024, that number has grown to almost 1.3 million and every year 200,000 AmeriCorps and AmeriCorps Seniors volunteer in more than 40,000 locations.

Eli agreed to come with me and bring a group of alums from City Year, the widely praised Boston-based group that was AmeriCorps' largest affiliate. At the conference, Eli and the young people from City Year enthusiastically described what they had accomplished by doing what local people wanted in a way that gained their support and generated more volunteers to help. I said we would help start a City Year South Africa if they wanted it. They did and it became a rousing success. After that, on all my trips to South Africa I've tried to meet with the City Year volunteers, often where they're working. I've enjoyed our talks and sharing a couple of hours of cleanup duty, fence painting, and answering their students' questions on school playgrounds. Over the years they've given me a bound book of letters and a beautiful basket full of notes. I reread them every now and then when I need to get my hopes back up.

In late September of 2002, I returned to Africa, stopping first in Ghana to refuel, rest for a day, and see President John Kufuor and former president Jerry Rawlings and his wife, Nana. I liked Jerry and Nana a lot and was impressed that he'd left office on schedule, giving a boost for democracy, something that couldn't be taken for granted in many aspiring democracies across the world, then and certainly not now.

On the way to the airport, we stopped so our group could buy kente cloth in a big barn where the stalls had been turned into a market. When we got there, there were about fifty people. Within a few minutes there were hundreds more. We could barely move for all the well-wishers and the Secret Service was on edge. I told the head of my detail to relax, that I was probably safer here than I was back home in Chappaqua. Ghanaians love to gather. When I went there as president, President Rawlings hosted a rally in the vast open square in the heart of Accra, then placed speakers for several blocks down the streets leading to it. The square holds 700,000 and was full and there were a few hundred thousand more in the arteries leading to it, the largest crowd I've ever addressed.

The crowd in the barn calmed down a bit; we made our purchases and went to the airport. As I was walking across the tarmac to our plane, a woman came running to catch me, waving a package and yelling at me to stop. She smiled and said, "Because of you and the African Growth and Opportunity Act [a bill I signed in 2000 to help sub-Saharan countries expand their exports to the U.S.] I am one of three hundred women who have good jobs making shirts. Now we can support our families and all our kids go to school. We are very grateful. So here's your shirt."

I took the shirt and thanked her. When I got home, I placed that shirt on a shelf in my small walk-in closet where I'd see it every day. We were barely a year beyond 9/11 and it reminded me that that woman and her coworkers weren't mad at America. They were pulling for us because we were pulling for them. The shirt is still there. When I wake up doubting our ability to pull back from the "us vs. them" world, I look at it and smile. It's proved to be a more valuable gift than that working mother could have imagined.

In the fall of 2003, I flew to Tel Aviv for the celebration of Shimon Peres's eightieth birthday. The main event was a theater production highlighting the major events in Peres's life, from being a top aide to the first prime minister, David Ben-Gurion, while in his early twenties, to helping create and organize the Israel Defense Forces, to his work to assure the integration of Jewish immigrants, especially those from Ethiopia, to his championing of the Oslo Peace Accords as foreign minister, then becoming prime minister after Yitzhak Rabin was assassinated.

Peres was defeated by Bibi Netanyahu in 1996 by less than a one percent margin after Netanyahu aired the first negative TV ads ever run in an Israeli campaign and Shimon failed to respond quickly or vigorously enough. Three years later, Ehud Barak, Israel's most decorated soldier, ousted Netanyahu in a campaign calling for a return to the peace process with security. In 2001, after he and his cabinet accepted my proposal for a Palestinian state on the West Bank and Gaza with a capital in East Jerusalem, but failing, as I had, to get Yasser Arafat to agree, Barak was defeated by Ariel Sharon. The voters thought if Arafat wouldn't take the deal I offered and Barak accepted, he wouldn't take anything they could accept, so they voted for the candidate they thought would be toughest on security.

So on this night, Peres sat in the front row of the theater with Prime Minister Sharon on his left and me on his right. We three were a picture of Israel's predicament. Peres had often been at odds with Sharon over the decades, but they preserved their personal relationship. And Shimon, who never gave up on anyone, kept trying to convert him.

Amazingly, two years later, Sharon did change his mind, ordering a withdrawal from Gaza, which included the relocation of about 8,000 settlers back within Israel's original borders, a highly controversial move. He formed a new political party, Kadima, and built a coalition for peace. Then, in 2006, he suffered a stroke from which he never recovered. His deputy, Ehud Olmert, succeeded him and pledged to continue the withdrawal until a full peace agreement could be completed. His plans were also derailed by the victory of Hamas in elections in Gaza, effectively splitting Palestinian politics in two, with Fatah, the former Palestinian Liberation Organization, in charge of the West Bank. Then Olmert was forced to resign under corruption charges in 2008. Netanyahu was again elected prime minister in 2009, with a coalition that included many hard-core opponents of any compromise that gave the Palestinians a state in the West Bank and Gaza.

The last performance of the evening was the best, as a choral group of young Jewish and Palestinian Israelis sang the perfect metaphor for Shimon Peres's life, John Lennon's "Imagine." When the audience started singing along, the kids coaxed Shimon and me into joining them on the stage. In spite of everything, we all wanted to imagine a peaceful tomorrow, no one more than the brilliant, vigorous octogenarian we had come to cheer.

In the years ahead, I went back to Israel several more times, speaking at large rallies to honor Yitzhak Rabin on the anniversary of his assassination, supporting the forum my friend Haim Saban held every year to keep people who wanted both peace and security updated on the latest developments, attending Shimon Peres's ninetieth birthday celebration, and speaking at his funeral two years later. But over those years Israel drifted away from peace and grew more divided, with its governments headed by Bibi Netanyahu more determined to hang on to the West Bank, and Arab governments more interested in the economic benefits of cooperation with Israel and less concerned about Palestinian statehood after they took a pass on the peace deal I offered and the Israeli government accepted in 1998.

In 2024, peace looks more distant than ever, after the vicious assault on Israel by Hamas the previous October claimed 1,200 lives, the largest one-day loss of Jewish lives since the Holocaust, and Netanyahu's counterattack, which has claimed many more Palestinian lives. I'll say more on all this later. It's complicated, heartbreaking, and dangerous.

In 2015, I had the privilege of leading the U.S. delegation to Bosnia and Herzegovina to commemorate the twentieth anniversary of the genocide in Srebrenica. That group included Senators Roger Wicker of Mississippi and Jeanne Shaheen of New Hampshire, New York congressman Peter King, and Secretary Madeleine Albright, who had been my U.N. ambassador during the war. Madeleine was a strong voice for our intervention to stop the Bosnian war and later, as secretary of state, for our early aggressive intervention in Kosovo. It was good to have her with us and to see the bipartisan congressional support for peace in the Balkans.

The Dayton Accords, which ended the Bosnian war, set up a power-sharing coalition government in Bosnia that has always been challenging. The nation contains the Federation of Bosnia and Herzegovina and Republika Srpska, which have their own constitutions, as well as the Brčko District, which is jointly administered. A three-member presidency includes a Serb, a Croat, and a Bosniak, with the chairmanship rotating among the three. There is also a prime minister and a bicameral parliamentary assembly. The power-sharing politics, difficult under the best of circumstances, are heavily influenced by neighbors, especially Serbia. Bosnian Serbs in the government have too often used their veto power to block all change, hoping to win their release to become part of neighboring Serbia, and costing all Bosnians, including their own people, precious economic and reconciliation opportunities.

In 2015, a young Serbian prime minister, Aleksandar Vučić, accepted an invitation to the commemoration of the genocide by the Muslim mayor of Srebrenica, Ćamil Duraković, the only member of his school class to have survived the slaughter. The first part of the ceremony took place inside the factory where many of the Bosnian Muslims had been killed. There were a few hundred local citizens and foreign dignitaries who gave him a respectful reception, impressed by his decision to turn the page on the past and by their own mayor's plea for them to do the same. In my remarks, I did my part to support him and the other Bosnian citizens I had worked to save through NATO's brief bombing campaign and the peacekeeping efforts which followed. I hoped the two young leaders could spark a change.

After the program, we all walked out to the adjoining Potočari Cemetery for the formal interment of the recently found remains of about 100 victims, adding to the 6,000 who were already buried there. After twenty years, many victims were still unaccounted for.

The crowd outside was different. The older Bosnians gave me a good reception, still grateful we stopped the killing, but the younger Bosnians were not so welcoming, many clearly angry because so little economic and political progress had been made. Unfortunately, they also hadn't heard the speeches in the factory. When the crowd recognized the Serbian prime minister, there was muted murmuring that quickly grew to angry shouts. Soon the crowd was throwing stones at Prime Minister Vučić as he was chased up a hill with his bodyguards. Too many in the crowd were unwilling to share the painful ceremony with someone they saw as representing those responsible for the genocide.

Mayor Duraković was in many ways a symbol of the progress his city, and the new nation, had made since the war. He was only sixteen in July 1995 when he fled into the mountains as Bosnian Serb troops poured into the city after holding it in a crippling siege for three years. He eventually made his way to the United States, where he spent ten years getting an education. His election as mayor in 2012 was quite a feat for a Bosniak Muslim, because Srebrenica had become mostly Serbian after the massacre and remains so, even though many Bosniaks returned after the Dayton Accords.

Though Duraković was a popular mayor, he lost reelection in 2016 to a Bosnian Serb but was later elected vice president of Republika Srpska. As of the writing of this book, there is peace and some progress. All Srebrenica's mosques have been rebuilt and children of once warring parties go to school and play soccer together. Like many such places in the world, they are looking for outside investment to boost the economy and hoping for the best while making the most of the fragile peace.

Nobody involved in the Dayton peace talks, including our negotiating team brilliantly led by the late Richard Holbrooke, thought the agreement that ended the war would be easy to maintain. They all took an imperfect deal to stop the killing. Yet the peace, while often under great strain, is still alive, in spite of the fact that neither the European Union nor the international community has done enough to bring the kind of prosperity to Bosnia that keeps Northern Ireland moving forward. Of course, history and geography make Bosnian success harder, but ignoring it makes things worse. I still believe we did the right thing to end the war and make the imperfect peace. But as we see in the United States and in post-Brexit Northern Ireland, polarized politics can make any union less perfect.

Possibly my most memorable mission took place several years earlier, in August 2009, a few months after President Obama took office. North Korean soldiers had seized two American journalists, Laura Ling and Euna Lee, along the Chinese–North

Korea border. They were filming a story about desperate North Koreans fleeing their homeland to escape extreme poverty and oppression by going into China, which considered them undocumented immigrants, not refugees, and often sent them back or kept them in various forms of indentured servitude, from forced marriages to prostitution to the growing internet sex trade.

Originally the journalists had intended only to film on the Chinese side of the still frozen Tumen River, which North Koreans used to cross into China. Then their guide urged them and their colleague, Mitchell Koss, to cross the river and take a few steps inside North Korea, where he said they might be able to talk with North Korean officials who sometimes allowed their citizens to cross the river unhindered. Instead they were confronted by two soldiers who chased them back across the river and caught both Euna and Laura. Mitch Koss escaped into China and told their families and their employer, Current TV, a cable company then owned by former vice president Al Gore, what happened.

The story of their arrest broke in the South Korean press two days later. Meanwhile Al and Lisa Ling, Laura's sister and herself a well-known journalist, had swung into action. At the State Department, Hillary had assigned two people to stay in daily touch with the families and Al worked with his friends in the Obama administration and contacts in the Chinese government, hoping to get Chinese help in persuading the North Koreans, with whom the United States had no formal diplomatic relations, to release our citizens. Lisa also contacted Bill Richardson, who served as U.N. ambassador when I was president and had traveled to North Korea a few years earlier to secure the release of an American. He told her that in the end, North Korea would want to deal directly with the United States and would resist Chinese intervention.

At that point, I was unaware of the back-and-forth, but if I had been, I would have agreed with Richardson. This was going to be a big story and North Korea was not about to pass up the political gift of direct contact with the United States on such a highly publicized matter. I also thought that, in the end, the North Korean leader, Kim Jong-il, would be reluctant to send two young American women to prison and squander the chance to leverage the situation to his benefit.

For the next few months, events unfolded in ways that left open the possibility of either freedom or prison for them. Laura and Euna were brought to Pyongyang, the North Korean capital, confined separately, and subjected to almost daily interrogations about what they did, why, and whether they were genuinely remorseful for their efforts to damage the Hermit Kingdom.

In May, Hillary hosted a meeting at the State Department for the families, Al Gore, and the people she had assigned to work on the case. The White House was also involved through the National Security Council, then headed by General Jim Jones. Hillary reported that while so far there had been no response to their diplomatic efforts, there had been some positive signs. The Swedish ambassador to North Korea had been allowed to see Laura and Euna, and they were allowed to send and receive letters from their families and even to make a couple of phone calls. On the other hand, North Korea had just violated a U.N. resolution by conducting a belowground nuclear test following a missile test the month before, and the U.N. Security Council had voted for, but had not yet imposed, additional sanctions. On June 4, North Korea proceeded to try the two journalists, the first trial of American citizens in a North Korean court. They were quickly convicted and sentenced to twelve years in prison.

The best possible outcome was through a humanitarian mission by someone not in the government to provide positive coverage to North Korea, while avoiding the impression of legitimizing the trial or accepting the missile and bomb tests. Al Gore volunteered to go. Hillary thought it was a good idea and I did, too. He was well respected around the world, had won the Nobel Peace Prize, and had been part of our administration's successful efforts to prevent North Korea from producing plutonium before it could be weaponized and to secure a moratorium on the testing of long-range missiles. He was clearly qualified to execute the mission and avoid all the political and diplomatic land mines it would entail.

After the trial and sentencing, the families were understandably worried but were getting signals that the North Korean government wanted the matter resolved if our government responded in what they considered a suitable way. Soon Al called me and said they didn't want him to come because Laura and Euna worked for him and they didn't want to legitimize Current TV. He said the signals were that they would release them to me. Apparently Lisa Ling had gotten the same message from her sister and relayed it to the White House.

I told him I would do it, but only if President Obama approved. He was already dealing with the largest economic crisis since the Depression. I didn't want to add to his burdens.

To anyone who'd followed the back-and-forth between our nations since 1993, the North Korean behavior made sense. The nation was highly secretive, tightly controlled, and so antagonistic to dissent that it kept tens of thousands of its citizens locked up in prison camps in conditions so bad that many of them died every year. They couldn't grow enough food in their mountainous country to feed themselves, but they had an enormous army and a remarkable capacity to build bombs and missiles. The Chinese helped them, but they were still often short of food and fuel. Most people in the world paid attention to them only when they caused trouble.

In pursuit of greater recognition, North Korea always wanted direct contact with the United States, and in 1993 and 1994, my administration, in close cooperation with South Korea, had given it to them on security matters, in tough negotiations to stop their production of plutonium and long-range missiles. Our negotiators made it clear that if North Korea forced me, I was prepared to attack their nuclear facilities, but I wanted a peaceful resolution and more normal relations between North Korea and their neighbors, especially South Korea. I also went out of my way to avoid embarrassing them in public.

The agreement we reached required North Korea to permanently stop producing plutonium and put the spent fuel rods under the control of the International Atomic Energy Agency. In return, the United States, South Korea, and Japan would fund two light-water nuclear reactors whose fuel couldn't be used to make bombs. By the time I left office, it was estimated that the agreement had prevented the production of up to a hundred bombs.

By 2009, with President Obama in office, the North Koreans wanted to get back to direct official contacts with the U.S., while the administration, preoccupied with pressing domestic issues, had decided to stick with the multilateral six-party format established during President George W. Bush's administration. It was probably the only available option after President Bush, following 9/11, included North Korea, along with Iraq and Iran, in the "Axis of Evil." The North Koreans had also started producing enriched uranium, and in 2005 resumed missile testing, violating the spirit if not the letter of the agreement my administration had made with them.

Giving the American journalists to me probably seemed as close as they could get to direct contact, because of my record and the fact that I was married to the secretary of state. That contact was exactly what the White House was concerned about. Still, this was an easy call. The trip would make the problem go away and give Laura Ling and Euna Lee their lives back.

President Obama approved the mission and invited me to the White House to discuss it and get a briefing. The president asked John Podesta to go with me, which was a good idea. John had been my White House chief of staff and was helping the Obama White House formulate climate policy, but was still head of the Center for American Progress, an NGO he founded, so the delegation would be "unofficial." The White House beefed up my staff with two welcome additions: David Straub, a professor of Korean Studies at Stanford, who made sure we were up-to-date on events and the people we'd be meeting, and Minji Kwon, an interpreter with our embassy in South Korea. They joined my regular traveling staff, one of whom had been in touch with Lisa Ling, and the doctor who often accompanied me on international trips. Before I left, I also talked with Leon Panetta, who had been my second chief of staff and was now CIA director.

Because the mission was classified humanitarian and not official, we couldn't fly on a military aircraft. The chairman of Dow Chemical Company, Andrew Liveris, a foundation supporter, furnished a plane to fly to California. There we picked up Straub and flew to Korea on a plane provided by Steve Bing, a longtime friend and foundation supporter who, among his other good deeds, had built the world's first hangar, at John Wayne Airport in Orange County, that produced no greenhouse gas emissions and provided enough extra solar power to electrify about twenty nearby homes.

Originally, the White House wanted me to be on the ground for only a few hours, just enough time for a quiet meeting and picking up Laura and Euna. I was not surprised that the North Koreans insisted I spend the night. It was their show now, and we had to follow their carefully orchestrated plan, which, with one exception, I was willing to do.

When we landed, I was taken directly to the official guesthouse, a handsome building with a large, well-designed garden. Meanwhile John and others in the delegation had to endure Act One of the drama, an intense rehash of the women's violations of North Korean law by the chief prosecutor. Then the group joined me at the guesthouse for Act Two. We were driven to the North Korean parliament building, where I sat with the president of the body, who wanted to talk about reviving the six-party talks, which had been on hold since the North Korean nuclear test and the passage of U.N. sanctions. With the preliminaries over, we were driven to the Koryo Hotel and put in a conference room.

I stood at the closed doors waiting for about fifteen minutes, until they opened to the beautiful sight of Laura and Euna rushing in. I embraced them as they cried with relief and Laura said, "I knew you'd come for us." It was the first time Euna and Laura had seen each other since their imprisonment began. I knew we were still on North Korea's schedule, so I told them that our doctor had to check them to make sure they were well enough to travel. I said I hoped we'd be taking them home the next morning but we all had to be careful.

Soon they were taken back to their confinement and I returned to the guesthouse for my bilateral meeting with Chairman Kim. He was rumored to be gravely ill, and he looked frail, but he seemed full of energy and determined to have a productive meeting devoid of the usual stilted talking points, which he brushed aside every time his subordinates tried to interject them.

Right off the bat, he said that as soon as the United States had confirmed that I would come, the National Defense Commission decided to grant special amnesty to the journalists. Now, he added, we needed to improve relations and eliminate mistrust so that something like this wouldn't happen again.

I asked why he wanted me to come. He replied that he was impressed when I was the first world leader to send my condolences after his father died in July of 1994, and that his father had complimented our negotiations leading to the joint Agreed Framework, which halted plutonium production and put the spent fuel rods, which could produce material for bombs, under international supervision to make sure no bombs were built. He said his father told him I was tough in private but not disrespectful in public. Kim then mentioned our communications while I was in office, and that late in my second term, I had received his special envoy, Vice Marshal Jo Myong-rok, in the White House, then sent Secretary of State Madeleine Albright to North Korea, who invited him to the U.S. and said I'd like to come to North Korea if we could agree to end North Korea's long-range missile program.

Kim said he clearly recalled that I had written him a letter saying I couldn't come to North Korea because of the recount in the close presidential election of 2000 and that I hoped such an exchange could occur even after I left office. He said he was surprised by the negative attitude of the Bush administration toward North Korea, especially after 9/11, which he had nothing to do with, and said that the nuclear issue worsened only after they were included with Iraq and Iran in the "Axis of Evil." He said he believed if the Democrats had won in 2000, the nuclear and missile agreements would have been implemented, North Korea would have had light-water reactors, which produced electricity without producing fuel for nuclear weapons, and the U.S. would have had a new friend in Northeast Asia. I wasn't so sure, but as Hemingway wrote at the end of *The Sun Also Rises*, "Isn't it pretty to think so?"

Turning to the Obama administration, Kim said he was pleased that the president had said while campaigning that he would talk even with hostile countries, but upset that he was still blocking North Korea's right to send satellites into orbit. He reminded me that he and I had agreed to a missile launch moratorium and that he had unilaterally observed it for seven years after I left office (though he did resume nuclear tests), in spite of the fact that the Bush administration ended bilateral talks in favor of the six-party framework. He said if the Obama administration took a more constructive attitude we could reach similar agreements again.

Kim continued, saying it was a mistake to see North Korea's military-first policy as one of permanent hostility to the West. It wasn't a strategy to attack others but one to prevent others from attacking North Korea. Japanese occupation had left a lasting impact, he said, and as a small country surrounded by giants, North Korea's policy was necessary for survival. He reiterated that he did not see the United States as a sworn eternal enemy, and that in a rapidly changing world, the U.S. should see better relations with North Korea as in our strategic interest. Beyond my coming on this trip, he hoped I would pay attention to Korean issues again. Kim closed by saying, "These are personal views that I had on my mind."

I was impressed that Kim had been so open and undogmatic. It was clear to me that he was pushing for a new start with the U.S., but when the conversation moved from the past and our mission to future relations, I knew that I had to be careful. This was the red line the White House didn't want me to cross. I was a private citizen, not authorized to conduct diplomacy. Even before dinner, Chairman Kim had set an inviting table to do just that. Tempting though it was, I couldn't take him up on it.

Instead, I thanked him for granting amnesty to the journalists, for his comments on our time in office, and for the seven years of genuine progress toward peace and security for both North and South Korea and the region. I reminded him that former South

Korean president Kim Dae-jung had played a large role with his Sunshine Policy, including the first cross-border family visits since the Korean War and the then-open Kaesong Industrial Complex, near the border, in which South Korean companies employed tens of thousands of North Korean workers, an indication of the opportunities reconciliation could bring.

I also thanked him for his seven-year missile moratorium and his understanding of my inability to visit North Korea and close the deal during the uncertain recount period after the election. And I told him of another, more important reason that had prevented my coming back in 2000 that involved Yasser Arafat. I'll talk more about Arafat's role later, but for now I'll just say that the consequences of agreeing to Arafat's request and canceling my North Korea trip may have fatally damaged two different peace plans.

Kim was interested in the part of the story he didn't know. Now I wanted to use it to convince him to give the Obama administration a chance to develop an approach he could support. I explained that I was not there to speak for the United States but to offer some personal observations. First, President Obama had inherited the six-party talks and needed the support of South Korea, China, Japan, and Russia to improve relations with North Korea. Second, Secretary of State Clinton, with the president's support, had appointed Ambassador Stephen Bosworth as a special envoy and asked him to visit North Korea. North Korea hadn't yet said yes or no. I urged Kim to say yes, assuring him that Bosworth was respected, trustworthy, and able to help rebuild the relationship with the U.S.

Finally, I said I had been asked to raise the possibility of the release of detained South Koreans and the resumption of the investigation of Japanese abductees (Kim had already released five of them during the recent visit of the Japanese prime minister). I told him he would see the positive response in the U.S. to the journalists' release and the same thing would happen in the neighboring countries if he released their citizens. I painted the best picture I could without crossing the line into direct negotiations.

Finally I said if North Korea denuclearized, it could insist that its security worries be put to rest, but it was important not to ask President Obama to abandon the six-party talks and instead to work with the United States to have both strong bilateral and regional relationships. Kim said he would think about how to do both and implied he would follow up either with Ambassador Bosworth or with Senator John Kerry, then chairman of the Foreign Relations Committee, who was thinking about coming to North Korea in the spring.

After the meeting we went to a dinner with Chairman Kim and members of the cabinet. We had all the business out of the way so Kim and I talked about goings-on in the rest of the world. I had been told he watched CNN International for several hours every day and it showed in his knowledge of wide-ranging topics.

The meal was extravagant, with lots of fish, beef, vegetables, and dessert, all well prepared. I tried a little of everything, torn between showing respect for my host's hospitality and knowing that millions of North Koreans were hungry and malnourished.

During the dinner, Chairman Kim said he wanted us to accompany him to a nearby stadium to watch either a gymnastics competition or an exhibition of traditional Korean dancing. He said the stadium was full of North Korean citizens who wanted to greet us properly. That was the one thing on his agenda the White House had stipulated, rightly, that I could not do. We had already told them we couldn't do public events so my team deflected and pushed back until Kim told his staff to stop pushing.

The only thing we agreed to do for public consumption was pose for an official photo of both delegations. The White House had specifically asked us not to smile, or to frown, just to be as expressionless as possible. It's not as easy as you think. We actually practiced doing it and I think we did pretty well.

We went to bed and got a decent night's sleep. The next morning after a quick breakfast and walk around the garden, we picked up Laura and Euna, and were soon on our way.

We didn't see many people on the street coming into or leaving Pyongyang, but outside the city we saw some beautiful scenery, mostly forest land and well-tended farms. They could be even more productive with better seed and fertilizer, but the country is so mountainous there may not be enough arable land to meet all North Korea's food needs.

As we were taking off, I thought about the missile-ending deal we left on the table as I left office, my offer to finish it after President Bush took office, which was not accepted, and the turmoil since. (After years in failing health, Chairman Kim would die in 2011 and be succeeded by his son, Kim Jong-un, who seems determined to make his father look like a softheaded liberal, authorizing almost ten times as many short-, medium-, and long-range missile tests as his father conducted. But that was in the future.)

The flight home was wonderful. Once we left North Korean airspace, Euna and Laura called their families and were excited about seeing them when we landed. We got them talking about how they coped with their confinement and what life would be like now. They were bright young women, with their idealism, and in Euna's case, strong religious convictions, still intact. And they were eager to get on with their lives. We stopped at Elmendorf Air Force Base in Anchorage to refuel and give our charges the first good American breakfast they'd had in months.

On the last leg home, I told our group that I had decided not to say anything when we arrived in order to keep the focus on Laura and Euna and to reinforce the humanitarian nature of the mission. I thought it was better just to get off the plane and smile while Al Gore made brief remarks and Laura and Euna said whatever they wanted. The homecoming was perfect. Al did a good job, Laura and Euna spoke beautifully, and their families were radiant.

After briefing the president, the secretary of state, and the National Security Council about my talks with Chairman Kim, I headed home, exhausted but grateful for the chance to be helpful.

Over the years I've had several more of these kinds of opportunities. I went to Vietnam in 2010 and 2015 to celebrate the fifteenth and twentieth anniversaries of normalization with the nation that has become a strong ally in Southeast Asia; represented the United States, at the request of the Obama administration, at the state funeral for the founder of Singapore, Lee Kuan Yew, its revered leader who'd built an astonishingly successful Asian Tiger in a tough neighborhood and whose wise counsel had been a great benefit to me; and attended the inauguration of the first new nation of the twenty-first century, Timor-Leste, whose independence I'd supported.

I was pulling for the Timorese. The U.N. effort, led by the Australians and supported by the United States and Thailand, demonstrated how much a coalition of nations sharing a manageable burden could do. The country had real potential in tourism, offshore energy, and agriculture, which Thailand had promised to help them revitalize. I liked and admired the political leaders: José Ramos-Horta, who had been the voice of the Timorese to the outside world, and Xanana Gusmão, the leader of the resistance, whose imprisonment intensified support for independence. Gusmão became the first president, followed a few years later by Ramos-Horta. It's still tough for Timor-Leste, but they've survived. I left more grateful the U.S. had helped them gain the freedom to chart their own course.

Other visits were briefer but nonetheless significant. In 2002, I spoke at the unveiling of Berlin's renovated Brandenburg Gate, under which I had been the first American president to walk after the wall fell. In 2013 in Dar es Salaam, Tanzania, I was honored to take part in a small private ceremony at the American embassy there to commemorate the lives lost in the terrorist bombing in 1998, where I thanked the embassy staff, and reminded them their sacrifice would not be forgotten.

I've been out of the White House so long now there will be fewer opportunities to help in countries where I was active as president, but if they come up, I'll show up if I can.

FOUR

President Bush 41 and the Children's Drawings

The work I had done after the Indian earthquake and 9/11 set the stage for helping out in the wake of more disasters, both natural and man-made. I found it emotionally rewarding, intellectually challenging, and much needed.

On December 26, 2004, a devastating tsunami struck South Asia, triggered by a strong undersea earthquake off the coast of Sumatra in western Indonesia. It sent mountainous waves into Aceh, on the northwest coast of Indonesia, then moved on to Thailand, inundating the gorgeous tourist mecca of Phuket, then on to Sri Lanka and the southeast coast of India. By the end of the day the small island nation of the Maldives had been devastated, and several other countries had also been hit hard enough to cost lives and cause substantial damage. Soon the high waves reached all the way to the Pacific coast of Mexico, raising water levels and destroying drinking water supplies.

The ferocity of the tsunami and the depth of destruction it left as the waves receded were almost impossible to grasp for those of us far away. All told, nearly 230,000 people were killed in fourteen countries.

My staff called the White House to say I wanted to help, and Chief of Staff Andy Card asked if I'd consider a request from the president to join his father in a national appeal. I was glad to accept, knowing this would put the effort beyond politics. On January 3, President Bush invited me to the White House for the announcement, then he, the first lady, his father, and I visited the embassies of Indonesia, India, Sri Lanka, and Thailand to sign condolence books and help raise awareness of the magnitude of the tragedy. We also cut ads for the Advertising Council, and the TV and radio networks donated more than $100 million to run them.

In the beginning we urged people to donate to well-known charities engaged in immediate relief, like the Red Cross, the Red Crescent, UNICEF, Save the Children, and others. Eventually we also put together a small fund of $15 million to finance specific projects, aided by a golfing fundraiser Greg Norman held at his home course in Florida. We started playing in stormy weather but had to stop after only nine holes because of the hard rain.

We knew the Bush-Clinton Houston Tsunami Fund was a drop in the bucket but hoped it would provide examples of effective projects that could be expanded across the region as more money came in. In Indonesia, just to give one example, we helped local fishermen or their survivors resume their work with new boats, but left the choice of boat, more durable aluminum or traditional wood, to them. And we gave them cell phones they could use to monitor fish prices up and down the coast. Knowing what their catch was worth enabled them to increase their income by an average of 30 percent, far more than the cell service cost.

Americans donated more than $300 million in the first week, thanks in no small measure to the excellent in-depth coverage by the news media. When President George H. W. Bush and I were announced, Steven Spielberg pledged $1.5 million, and lots of celebrities followed suit. There was even a celebrity telethon. Eventually Americans would give more than $2.7 billion to the tsunami relief, much of it coming from small donors, many of them giving over the internet for the first time.

It was the first crowdfunding of a disaster. The median contribution was $50. I remember walking through the game booths at the New York State Fair in 2005, which I attended with Hillary almost every year while she was senator, when a woman working there came up to me with a $50 bill. She said, "This is for the tsunami. As you can see I'm busy here and haven't had time to send it over the internet." The IT revolution, though it could also fuel rage, resentment, and paranoia, was empowering ordinary people to do extraordinary things. And President Bush soon pledged $950 million from our government.

Then, U.N. secretary-general Kofi Annan asked me to serve as his special envoy for tsunami relief, hoping I could keep attention focused on rebuilding when the cameras left, and make the massive work ahead as effective, transparent, and corruption-free as possible.

It would be challenging. Hillary and I visited a Buddhist temple in Queens where the monks were collecting clothes and other supplies for people in Sri Lanka. It was touching to see the support they received from Jews, Muslims, Christians, Hindus, Baha'i, and citizens of no religious affiliation. They filled at least one cargo container. Unfortunately, at the airfield in Colombo, Sri Lanka's capital city, cargo containers and other packaging sat out in the open for weeks, because there was no effective supply chain to get the donated goods to the people and places who needed them. Soon most relief organizations were asking for cash only and promising to account for how it was spent. That opened my eyes to a real problem in the relief supply chain, which, thankfully, has improved a lot in the last few years, thanks to groups like Last Mile, a terrific NGO we've worked with over the years that handles deliveries.

On February 18, 2005, President Bush 41 and I flew to Southeast Asia to see the damage and the recovery work underway. We started in Thailand, on the resort island of Phuket, where half the casualties were foreign tourists, including about a dozen Americans. There were still more than 1,500 bodies yet to be identified in a refrigeration center. We also flew north to a fishing village where nearly a third of the population was lost, along with houses, fishing boats, and the mangrove trees that had served as a natural barrier to high winds and rising water. Many people were still overcome by grief, but seemed grateful that we were there and that the U.S. Marines and aid workers had come so quickly and done so much.

The next morning we flew to Indonesia, site of the most destruction. After a brief meeting with President Susilo Bambang Yudhoyono, who pledged a corruption-free recovery effort, we proceeded to Aceh, which bore the brunt of the tsunami, with 163,000 dead. Banda Aceh, the capital, was devastated, with buildings down, debris everywhere, and people still missing. Even where strong structures still stood, the damage was massive. Virtually all official records, including those establishing title to land, had been destroyed.

So many people had lost their lives so quickly. We heard story after story of people who had lost as many as five family members, saw lots of kids who had lost both their parents, listened to women describe watching the waves wash over their fisherman husbands. With their husbands and their livelihoods gone, they didn't know what to do.

As governor I had visited small towns and city blocks laid bare by tornadoes, and had helped our people cope with severe floods on the Arkansas and Red Rivers. As president, I saw wreckage in the wake of hurricanes, the Northridge earthquake, the five-hundred-year Mississippi flood, and the man-made disasters of Oklahoma City and Waco. I had never seen anything like this. Words, especially sympathy-laden adjectives, felt empty in the face of all this death and destruction. Both George and I felt more determined than ever to help.

We left Aceh for Sri Lanka, famous for fine teas and, for decades the site of a hard-fought rebellion by the minority Hindu Tamils against the Buddhist majority, itself torn by two tribal factions. The president, Chandrika Kumaratunga, who had lost her husband and one eye to political violence, was determined to have an inclusive disaster response, hoping it would reduce, perhaps even resolve, the longstanding divisiveness in her country. She hosted a banquet for us in the backyard of her house and sat me next to the parliamentary leader of the Hindu Tamils, with President Bush next to the leader of the main Buddhist opposition.

I enjoyed my conversation with the Tamil leader. He made a comment which stuck with me: "You know, even though you never took us off the terrorist list, I liked you anyway, because I always felt you knew we faced discrimination and you cared about us." That conversation reinforced an important lesson I'd learned as president. Even when you disagree with other leaders, you should make it clear that you understand and care about the people they represent.

President Kumaratunga made much of the fact that President Bush and I had once been bitter rivals who had joined together to help Sri Lankans in "our hour of greatest need." I hoped her far-from-subtle message would have some impact and tried to reinforce it on future visits.

The next morning we went out to a coastal city that had been hard hit, and as we had done in Thailand and Indonesia and would do the next day in the Maldives, sat with children who'd suffered the loss of family and friends. The grief counselors we met were working with kids who were still struggling to express their feelings and often couldn't speak more than a word or two. To bring them back, the counselors in all the affected countries encouraged them to draw pictures of what they were feeling and thinking.

Usually, the pictures were very dark at first, reflecting the impact of death and destruction seen too soon. Then there was a progression to pictures depicting people and objects trapped in the water and attempts to save them, including one showing a U.S. Marine helicopter on a rescue mission. Then the drawings began to reflect more normal, hopeful scenes, usually involving other children. In the final stage, the kids were drawing pictures in bright colors of sunny days, beautiful flowers, and happy, playing children. The art was raw and honest, and it seemed to be working. By the time we got to Sri Lanka, the children were singing and dancing, far from healed but at least able to feel again and live in the moment.

At each stop George and I received the gift of a couple of drawings. They ran the full gamut of emotions and became prized possessions. George held his close to his heart. He felt their losses deeply, perhaps because he and Barbara had lost a young daughter, long ago but never forgotten.

Our final stop was the Maldives, a small nation of 300,000, living on a chain of islands none of which was more than six meters above sea level. Though few fatalities occurred, the equivalent of two thirds of the economy, based on tourism and tuna fishing, was destroyed. Thankfully, the capital city was protected by a large seawall built several years earlier by the Japanese government. They needed fishing boats, quick repair of damaged resorts, and a loud message to the world that the Maldives was still an open, welcoming place. Soon they would be planning for the future, including removing all citizens on sparsely populated islands to thirteen of them closer to the capital and better situated to build defenses against future rising waters. The next morning, after a round of interviews, President Bush flew home to Houston and I went to China, Japan, South Korea, and Taiwan to promote my autobiography and raise money for the foundation.

In the last few days we had begun a friendship that would become one of the great blessings of the rest of my life. According to his biographer, Jon Meacham, the barriers between us began to break when I urged President Bush to sleep in the plane's only bed, in a compartment with its own bathroom and a TV. I thought it was no big deal. He was older, served as president first, and slept more. I used an air mattress and slept on the floor. The friendship was easier for me. I had always liked him and admired his dedication to public service.

As I recounted in *My Life*, I had become a real fan in 1983, when he had hosted the governors at Kennebunkport at the annual conference which was held in Maine. When I introduced him to our then three-year-old daughter, Chelsea's first question to the vice president was "Where's the bathroom?" George took her hand and led her there, stopping only to introduce her to his mother. I never forgot that small act of kindness.

When he was president, I led the Democratic governors in hammering out bipartisan national education goals at a special meeting for all the governors hosted by the University of Virginia. President Bush had asked us to convene and attended the opening press conference, and subsequently invited our chairman, Republican Terry Branstad of Iowa, then a moderate Republican with a good record on education, and me to the 1991 State of the Union address, where he praised our work.

The 1992 campaign was rough, of course. Just four years earlier, the Bush campaign had eviscerated Governor Mike Dukakis of Massachusetts, and I expected no less, although the bloodletting was done largely by surrogates. But politics was still a contact sport, and as long as my rapid-response team could get our side out, I thought we still had a chance.

By late 1993, our relationship was good enough that President Bush joined Presidents Carter and Ford on the White House lawn for the signing of the Oslo Accords by the Israelis and Palestinians on September 13. And the next day, the three of them were at the White House for our efforts to pass the North American Free Trade Agreement. They all did well, but President Bush was in especially good form, and kind and generous to me.

We did lots of other things after I left the White House. For years, I went to Kennebunkport for a day in the summer to visit with him, Barbara, and the family members and friends who were always there. We'd talk some politics and foreign policy, but it was mostly golf, his hair-raising fast boat rides, and friendly meals.

The tsunami recovery work came early on in my postpresidential career. What sealed the bond of affection with me on that trip was watching the way George responded to the kids who had lost so much and how he treasured their drawings, holding them as if they were priceless masterpieces. For him, they were.

The only burden I put on him was talking too long to too many people. But I knew that if I was going to be effective as the U.N. special envoy for two more years, I had to learn a lot more about the people and places most affected and form good working relationships with the local leaders.

Our work together ended with the distribution of the money from the Bush-Clinton Fund, and the completion of pleas for donations. In 2006, a report by Indiana University's Center on Philanthropy concluded that, in addition to the $950 million

President Bush committed and Congress delivered, 25 percent of American households eventually donated $2.78 billion to tsunami relief, often through their religious groups, with $390 million more coming from corporations and foundations. I am still grateful for the generosity of the American people and for the chance President George W. Bush gave his father and me to support the effort.

But my work for the U.N. was just beginning.

The secretary-general gave me an office in the United Nations building just across the street from the main headquarters where the General Assembly and the Security Council meet. I got a small staff of bright, dedicated young people who were eager to be involved in life-changing work on the ground, work different from days dominated by meetings and conferences. This is not meant as a criticism of the U.N. It was established as a forum for allies and adversaries to talk and talk and talk until they reached a resolution that kept them from going to war. (As Churchill famously said, "Jaw, jaw, jaw is better than war, war, war.") Now, in the post–Cold War world, with the sprouting of new countries, the elections of new leaders, and the rise in regional cooperation, there were also real opportunities for the U.N. to directly contribute to relief and recovery work through its operations-oriented affiliates like UNICEF and to coordinate the activities of others who were helping.

Over the next two years, the five original stalwarts on our team were supplemented by others who came on temporarily to do specific things. Because I was also building my own foundation, with its early concentration on doing more on the AIDS crisis and projects in New York, and getting the library and School of Public Service in Arkansas off to a good start, I couldn't run the operation full-time. Thankfully, Erskine Bowles was willing to do the job. Erskine had served as White House chief of staff and my main negotiator with Congress in formulating and passing the first balanced budget in three decades, containing the largest increase in education funding in thirty years, including the largest increase in college student assistance since the G.I.

Bill; health insurance for millions of uninsured children; and large funding increases for science and technology research and development. Erskine is an excellent leader, a wonderful man, and really knows how to make good things happen. For this job, he also had a very able deputy in Eric Schwartz, who was the National Security Council point person on human rights and humanitarian efforts in my administration, later became assistant secretary of state for population, refugees, and migration under President Obama, then served as president of Refugees International. He and Erskine were a solid team.

My main objective was to "build back better," with an effort that maximized good work in all the impacted countries through constant coordination, reporting on results, and quick resolution of policy and other disputes, in a process that was transparent and corruption-free. "Build Back Better" was our mantra, a slogan President Biden later used to capture the essence of his big recovery package in 2021. Even though it didn't all pass, the idea is important. Whenever something is broken, we should all want it replaced with something better.

Over the next few years, I chaired four meetings of the main coordination group, called the Global Consortium for Tsunami Recovery, originally set up just after the disaster by then U.N. undersecretary-general for humanitarian affairs Jan Egeland. The membership included the affected nations, the largest donor nations, the major NGOs, international financial institutions, and the U.N. agencies involved in the recovery effort. Erskine was on board by mid-2005 and cochaired the U.N. Tsunami Task Force, which met twice a month for the rest of 2005 and 2006. We worked with other groups, too, especially the NGOs that were critical to success on the ground.

We had to keep the energy and the enthusiasm going. After the first rush of giving and emergency actions pass, the real work of building back better can be slowed or derailed by the loss of interest from funders, and the reemergence of local political, capacity, and corruption problems. I knew we couldn't avoid all the pitfalls but also knew we'd get a lot more done if we tried.

I visited the region three more times, twice in 2005 and once more in December 2006 when I went back to Banda Aceh. The first trip in May gave me an opportunity to see the recovery efforts in India, which showcased the benefits of cooperation between the state of Tamil Nadu and local and international NGOs. The most impressive economic initiative trained widows of fishermen to make incense candles for Hindu temples and small sculpted pieces from local clay. The women were surprised and proud they could support their families without their husbands' income from fishing. I still have one of their products, a small red-clay elephant, in our home.

The most vexing problem was getting people into livable shelters and permanent housing. The temporary housing in Tamil Nadu was a mixed blessing. To minimize fire risk, the roofs were tin, not straw, but in the stifling heat, the dwellings were almost unbearable in the daytime.

On the other hand, many of the displaced Indians were very poor Dalits, the lowest caste, who had never had access to healthy sanitation facilities before they found themselves in the temporary shelter camp. Later, when I visited a new permanent housing settlement, I was pleased to see that the new houses, in addition to being far more storm-resistant, also had much better sanitation. It was a particular source of dignity to the Dalits, whom it was no longer acceptable to call "untouchable." Thank goodness; it was well past time.

On my trips, I tried to balance complimenting the progress with urging everyone to deal with what still needed to be done. The picture of possibility was different in each nation. In Thailand, where the damage was concentrated and the pre-tsunami economy was healthy, the restoration was largely funded and completed by the Thais themselves. I had seen their skills in action in East Timor in 2002, when the Thai government helped Timor-Leste by improving the lot of small farmers, artisans, and other self-employed people.

In the Maldives, tuna fishing and tourism began to rebound quickly and most of the work involved the relocation of the population outside the capital to fewer islands, building better defenses there, and lobbying for the quick deployment of an Indian Ocean early warning system. But alongside the progress there remained the looming fear that the tsunami was just a harbinger of things to come with global warming and rising sea levels.

I really came to admire the life and culture the small but hardy population had built on this island chain, and I hoped they could make it. In early 2019, the TV show *Madam Secretary* aired an episode in which the secretary of state has to persuade the young president of a Pacific island nation, which had just lost all its more senior leaders in a storm, to evacuate everyone before an even larger water wall covered his entire country for good. He ordered the evacuation just before his nation disappeared. In the last scene, the people are raising their flag on their new homeland, a more elevated island that a friendly neighbor had given them. I couldn't help thinking of the Maldives during the show, hoping it wouldn't happen to them, but that if it did, someone would give them a shot to begin again.

Sri Lanka's big problem before the tsunami was the long and violent civil conflict between the Buddhist majority, which constituted more than 70 percent of the population, and the Hindu minority, at about 18 percent. The Hindus had representation in parliament but felt they would never have their grievances resolved, and many took up arms in a group called the Tamil Tigers. There was also a smaller, long-rooted group of Muslims, about 7 percent of the population, and an even smaller number of Christians.

The eastern shore of Sri Lanka was hardest hit and as the damage moved further north, there were more and more Hindus, bringing ethnic tensions that made the delivery of aid more difficult. As I said, President Kumaratunga hoped the relief effort might lead to an end of the violence. I tried to support that and vividly remember a meeting we held involving fishing families, including Buddhists, Hindus, and Muslims, on the grounds of a Catholic school run by an order of nuns. The biggest problem they all shared was getting back into homes, when the sites of their former houses were in newly declared buffer zones where building was no longer allowed that close to the water. Since most of the rebuilding in rural areas was to be done by the people themselves with cash grants, a lot of people were involved. There were loud squabbles when property ownership wasn't clear, a big problem in many developing countries. Also, the fishing families feared they'd be too far away from the water to protect their boats. My office tried to be helpful on this and I think we were. But the conflict flared up again, continuing until the government appeared to win a decisive military victory over the Tamil Tigers in May of 2009. Sadly, the country's internal struggles are back in the news today. When I ended my U.N. tenure, I was proud of our team's contribution to the restoration of livelihoods, public services, and housing, but regretted that I couldn't do more to end the deep divisions and governance problems that still haunt Sri Lanka.

The best and most enduring results were achieved in Indonesia, in spite of the fact that Aceh and the nearby island of Nias suffered the most damage, cruelly compounded by a severe earthquake in Nias in 2005. The progress was made possible largely by national and local leaders and ordinary people who knew they had to think and act differently to recover and build a better future.

First, President Yudhoyono made the decision to lodge all the authority and the funds in a single body, the Agency for the Rehabilitation and Reconstruction of Aceh and Nias, or BRR, much like our Federal Emergency Management Agency. Then he made an even better decision, appointing a nonpolitical and scrupulously honest businessman, Dr. Kuntoro Mangkusubrototo, better known as Pak Kuntoro, to handle it. The president then told his grumbling cabinet ministers that until Aceh was reborn, Kuntoro, not they, would have authority over all major decisions and expenditures. Pak Kuntoro was one of the ablest public servants I've ever met—intelligent, knowledgeable, good with people, persistent, and tough but good-natured. I pushed strong standards of transparency, and he enthusiastically delivered, with a website posting all contributions and their sources, all expenditures, who got the money and what they used it for, and an after-action performance audit.

Over the next two years a lot of good things happened. Livelihoods were restored and schools, hospitals, and clinics reopened. And a longstanding civil conflict between the national government and the separatist Free Aceh movement was resolved, with an agreement that kept them a part of Indonesia, but with greater local decision-making. The first regional and local elections were held. I met with some of the local leaders to thank them and encouraged them to stay the course. They said they would and asked for more help to develop their economy.

Aceh had a good coffee-producing capacity, which, like everything else, had been damaged. I knew Starbucks chairman Howard Schultz from the fight for healthcare reform when he was a stalwart supporter of Hillary's efforts. Also Schultz's managing director for U.K. and Ireland, Kris Engskov, had worked for me in the White House and I had known him since he was four years old, running around his grandfather's general store in the small Ozark town of Berryville, Arkansas. I was sure they would help if they could.

Starbucks sent people to Aceh to work with the growers to improve the quality of their beans and the sustainability of their operations. At the time, Starbucks featured coffee from a different country every month in its stores, with the beans well marketed in an attractive package. Soon the coffee of the month was from Aceh, in an informative container explaining where it was from and why it tasted the way it did. If my memory is right, the whole month's stock sold out in ten days, giving Aceh coffee more visibility, access to markets, and happier growers.

The one problem we couldn't solve quickly enough was moving the people out of displaced persons camps, where they lived uncomfortably in hot tents waiting to transition to temporary housing. The temporary housing was much better. The houses were made of wood and there was an open public space for children to play, bordered by a mosque and another large building for community activities.

On one of my trips, I knew I had to visit the largest camp, where thousands of people were still stuck in tents six months after I had told them we'd have them out. I was met by the camp's elected leader, his wife, and their ten-year-old son. We communicated through an interpreter, an impressive young woman who'd left her job as a television news announcer to come to work for Pak Kuntoro. She told me she could do more for her people by taking me and others through sweltering camps and ruined villages. When I told her I thought the son of the camp leader and his wife was one of the most beautiful children I'd ever seen, she smiled and agreed that he was very beautiful but that I should know his parents had lost nine relatives in the tsunami. They were grateful for their son's safety but still grieving their loss as they did their best to take care of the people in the camp.

Thousands of people were milling about row after row of large tents, voicing their legitimate complaints about living too long in the tent city. I assured them they would be out soon, but couldn't stop thinking about all the children who should have been there, and how beautiful all of them were to those who loved them.

Our last stop was at the medical tent. It was a clean, well-stocked facility with dedicated and trained staff. After a few minutes, the wife of the camp president joined us with a broad smile on her face, holding the youngest resident of the camp, a two-day-old boy. She explained that she was bringing the baby to me because, in their culture, a new mother is expected to remain in bed for forty days, feeding her baby and regaining her strength. She said that in honor of my visit they wanted me to name the baby. I turned to the interpreter and asked, "Does your language have a name that means 'new beginning'?" She had a few words with the leader's wife, then replied, "Yes, the word is Dawn. Lucky for you, in our language, Dawn is a boy's name. We will call this baby Dawn. He will be the symbol of our new beginning."

In July 2014, I went back to Aceh for the tenth anniversary of the tsunami, to see what had happened. Our first visit was to a park commemorating the event. The main attraction is a sizable ship which still sits where the tsunami took it, more than four miles inland from the coast. We also saw a remarkable before-and-after village which had lost 90 percent of its people, then rode on a highway rebuilt by the U.S. Agency for International

Development (USAID) to a beautiful park where I saw people I'd met during my U.N. service. The couple who had led me through the camp were there. A young man I'd met in 2005 just after he'd lost his dad and brother came with his sisters and uncle. He was twenty and thriving, with his own business and home, and wearing a T-shirt with the phrase, "Faster Than You Know." And Dawn was there with his family. They lived nearby and appeared to be doing fine. Dawn didn't seem to get what the big deal was. Of course, he couldn't remember the circumstances of his birth, and took the rhythms of ordinary life for granted, which felt right to me. I only wish every child could.

FIVE

New Orleans and the Boats of Bayou La Batre

On August 29, 2005, just nine months after the tsunami, hell and high water came to the United States. Hurricane Katrina hit the Gulf Coast with ferocious winds and waves that flooded the coastal areas of Alabama and Mississippi, and breached the levees of Lake Pontchartrain, Louisiana, inundating 80 percent of New Orleans and neighboring parishes. Katrina and Rita, its smaller but still fierce follow-on, killed more than 1,800 people, destroyed or damaged more than 850,000 homes, and spurred countless acts of kindness and courage—fast rescues of people from rooftops and trees, and from cars with windows rolled up and dwindling oxygen inside; doctors and nurses working all night to care for both their patients and the newly injured in facilities with no power; houses of worship open to people without regard to race or creed; volunteers in the Superdome trying their hardest to make an impossible situation bearable for thousands with no other option for shelter.

When President Bush asked me to join his father again to raise money for relief and reconstruction, I was eager to help. More important, so was my staff. They knew we had to do this and were all in, even though I was about to leave for Asia to advance our AIDS work there and it was just three weeks until the first meeting of the Clinton Global Initiative.

For me, Katrina was deeply personal. New Orleans had given me some of my life's most important memories. It is the first big city I ever saw, when my grandmother took me, at three, on the train to see my widowed mother, who had gone back to finish her nursing education at Charity Hospital, which was now badly damaged by Katrina, closed for the first time since 1815, never to reopen in that iconic building. When I was fifteen, my family took its only out-of-state vacation to New Orleans, with brief stops in Gulfport and Biloxi. All three had been hard hit. I was awarded a Rhodes Scholarship in New Orleans just six weeks after my stepfather lost his fight with cancer but not before saying, on his deathbed, that I shouldn't worry—he was sure I'd be selected. Hillary and I went to a law school hiring convention there, staying in the Cornstalk Hotel—a wonderful little place in the French Quarter marked by the yellow corn decorating its wrought-iron fence. I'd been back several times as governor and president, and in the fall of 2004, after a big meal of local cuisine, I was flying home from New Orleans when I had the chest pains that signaled serious heart trouble and led to my bypass surgery. And I was grateful that a big vote from New Orleans helped me carry Louisiana twice. For all these reasons and more I was eager to get to work.

A week after Katrina struck, Hillary and I flew south to see some of the survivors—not to New Orleans, where we would be in the way of urgent relief work still ongoing, but to Houston, which had taken in more than 200,000 evacuees from the Gulf, as did Baton Rouge, nearly doubling its population in the blink of an eye. Quite a few came to Little Rock. And Chicago took more than 6,000, the largest number of any city outside the South.

When we landed, we connected with George and Barbara Bush, and the rest of the star-studded group—Oprah Winfrey, Jesse Jackson, local ministers, and members of Congress, including Senator Barack Obama, who had called to tell us about raising money in Illinois for the victims who had relocated there.

Hillary and I had done an event for his Senate campaign in Illinois, so she invited him to fly down with us. We went to the Reliant Center, an arena next to the Astrodome, where 4,000 evacuees were staying, and began to walk among the rows of cots. My first impression was a humbling reminder that most of Katrina's victims were poor and working-class people who, having lost all they had, were now in a strange city far from home.

The bright spot was the kids, who lifted our spirits and, more important, gave their parents something to force their pain and loss to take a backseat to thinking about their children's tomorrows. I think their energetic running around helped the loneliness of the people there without children, too. In Jesse Jackson's famous words, they were "keeping hope alive." There were a lot of smiling volunteers from the Red Cross and other groups trying to do the same thing. That's about all anyone could do in those early days, with hundreds of thousands of people wiped out, not knowing what to do next or whether they would ever go home again. As it turned out, many didn't.

Talking to the people, getting briefings, and following the thorough print and television reporting convinced me, and President Bush, that we had a lot to do. There was an initial outburst of generosity to support the emergency responses and federal funds would be made available to rebuild homes and restart businesses. But there's no way government programs would cover all the needs in a timely fashion. Insurance would cover a lot of the losses but, as we learned, not all, and sometimes reluctantly. The colleges and schools would be rebuilt, but what would the teachers do for income while waiting for them to reopen, and while the colleges were losing money in tuition refunds when students transferred to other schools? What about the hundreds of houses of worship, mostly small African American and white Christian churches, but also synagogues, mosques, and temples, whose parishioners had limited resources, much of them already being spent on caring for victims? How would they rebuild? And who would fund the new health challenges, especially the need for more mental health services, which were barely adequate even before they were broken by the storm?

We decided to raise more money and distribute it quickly, concentrating on helping the houses of worship and the colleges, and providing discretionary funds to state and local authorities best able to respond to pressing problems. As I said in a press conference outside the arena, we needed a fund to fill in the blanks and help people who would otherwise be totally overlooked.

Over the next two years, George and I raised more than $130 million from more than 100,000 donors in all fifty states and many foreign nations, and distributed it all: $30 million to thirty-eight colleges—including technical and community colleges—and universities, $25 million to 1,151 houses of worship, $40 million to state-designated groups, and $35.6 million to forty-two local community nonprofit efforts. As with the tsunami, this was a relatively small amount of the overall funds from government assistance and private giving, but our funds were raised quickly and invested in areas that needed immediate help to revive essential activities.

All the services from accounting to legal to printing were donated. By the time we stopped accepting donations in July 2007, New Orleans had regained two thirds of its employment, and in the Gulfport-Biloxi area, employment was 93 percent of its pre-Katrina level.

After the trip to Houston, George and I decided that, when possible, we would be together, but we could do more outside New Orleans if we went to different areas. So he'd go west all the way into Southeast Texas, and I'd go east into Mississippi and Alabama.

Many colleges were in big trouble. They didn't have and couldn't raise the money to repair or replace damaged buildings and expensive equipment. They were losing income from loss of enrollment and tuition refunds. And they had to find a way to pay salaries and benefits to retain teachers and staff while the rebuilding was done. We were able to give them $30 million in December, just over three months after the storm.

Tulane had reopened four months after the storm, thanks to its strong financial base and less extensive damage. In the spring of 2005, George and I spoke at the commencement there. We also did an interview with Ellen DeGeneres, a New Orleans native who had been relentless in promoting the revival of her hometown. So had Tulane's president, Scott Cowen, who in 2008 hosted the first Clinton Global Initiative for university students (CGI U). On our service day, students from all over the United States and several other countries helped clean a devastated section of the city in preparation for new affordable and more storm-resistant housing. I'll never forget the energy and pride those students showed in doing their part for the cause.

On October 5, before I set out for Gulfport, Mississippi, and Bayou La Batre, Alabama, I had breakfast in Metairie, Louisiana, just outside New Orleans, with thirty-five relief workers at a Piccadilly restaurant. I wanted to thank them, and our host. Piccadilly had to shut twenty-five restaurants because of the flood but had managed to provide or donate more than 100,000 meals to evacuees and relief workers, and to offer all five hundred of its displaced workers the chance to work at one of its 100-plus still open restaurants, which were also collecting thousands of pounds of food, clothing, and other supplies. Piccadilly's caring and commitment made the breakfast taste even better.

In Gulfport, I met with community leaders and small business owners who were upbeat and pretty far along in their recovery planning. Then I went to a neighborhood that needed more help. Before Katrina, Forest Heights was a nice neighborhood developed twenty-five years earlier by Dr. Dorothy Height and the National Council of Negro Women. Dorothy was a legendary leader and a good friend of Hillary's and mine until she died in 2010, at ninety-eight and still at work. She left a lasting legacy in community building in the United States and in Africa and was especially proud of Forest Heights.

A significant percentage of these hardworking families had finally paid off their mortgages not long before Katrina struck. Now they had to rebuild on 70 percent of the lots and repair the other houses. Meanwhile residents and relief workers were cleaning up.

I had a fascinating conversation with a woman who had been designated to tell me about the challenges they were facing. She was passionate in saying how worried the families who had just paid off their mortgages were because they had been told their insurance might not cover their losses. Apparently, they had hurricane insurance but not flood insurance. Insurance companies were telling them that even though the hurricane's winds had caused so much damage to the area, their homes were inundated by floodwaters, so they didn't have to cover those losses. If insurance companies didn't cover them, then after twenty years or more of never missing a mortgage or premium payment, those people might never be homeowners again.

I knew the aggregate losses would be large, but I thought in the end the insurance companies would have to pay, and I promised to do whatever I could to help. The homeowners eventually sued the insurance companies and won in district court, but in 2007 the decision was overturned by the Fifth Circuit Court of Appeals, who ruled against the homeowners, saying regardless of what caused the flooding, their policies strictly excluded covering it. Other lawsuits against the Army Corps of Engineers were also unsuccessful. Making matters worse, many of the homeowners later got some relief from a federally funded program to elevate homes in flood-prone areas, only to be sued by the government for "misusing" the funds to repair the homes. Happily, in February of 2023, Louisiana dropped the suits, freeing the homeowners from having to repay the grants.

The woman was obviously intelligent and well spoken but there was something else striking about her, something that strengthened my resolve to do more about a problem unrelated to Katrina. She was in a wheelchair with one leg partially amputated, a frequent consequence of diabetes. Type 2 diabetes, given the same dietary and lifestyle habits, is 1.8 times more likely to occur in African Americans as in those of European descent (1.6 times more likely for Hispanics, and two times more likely for Native Americans and Pacific Islanders). Diabetics are also more at risk of heart attacks, strokes, and cancer. With the rate of childhood obesity high and rising, the increased incidence of type 2 diabetes loomed large in America's future. This vibrant woman embodied the consequences for so many others if we didn't change course. That was a cause I soon embraced through the Alliance for a Healthier Generation, a story I'll tell later in the book.

I went back to Forest Heights once more the following March to assess the ongoing recovery effort and to urge survivors to apply for the Earned Income Tax Credit (EITC) if they were eligible for it. The EITC was created in 1975 to provide a refundable tax credit to lower-income workers. It had been praised by Democrats and Republicans alike for being both pro-family and pro-work. The credit was doubled in my 1993 economic plan, and by the time Katrina hit, it provided up to $4,400 a year for people with two or more children if their incomes were $35,000 a year or less. Families with one child and single workers got less. A large number of survivors were eligible for the EITC, but you had to apply and they didn't know anything about it. A couple of years earlier I had set up an effort in New York to address this after I read a news report that more than 100,000 people in New York City alone had earned the refund but hadn't applied for it.

I didn't want that to happen here. These people really needed the money and were legally entitled to it. To help them get it, the Bush-Clinton Katrina Fund approved a $750,000 grant to Operation HOPE's Project Restore HOPE/Gulf Coast Recovery. Operation HOPE was established and run by John Hope Bryant, a remarkable man who started his first business at age fourteen in California, found financial success in his twenties, and walked away from unlimited earning potential to follow his true passion: promoting financial literacy and economic empowerment among low-income people. I had seen him in action in New York and knew he could make a real difference here. John was in Forest Heights, along with H&R Block volunteers, who were doing survivors' tax filings for free while John was helping eligible people apply for the Earned Income Tax Credit and giving his economic literacy and financial counseling course to adults and schoolkids alike. His passionate empowerment message gave renewed hope and confidence to a lot of people after Katrina. I'll always be grateful to John for all he did for them.

After Mississippi, I flew on to Alabama to visit Bayou La Batre, a small town on the Gulf Coast. Its boats brought home shrimp, oysters, and crabs to be processed and sent across the country. I met Mayor Stan Wright, Governor Bob Riley, and a number of families affected by the storm. More than thirty boats were blown out of the water and needed to be removed, then repaired or replaced as soon as possible. Bayou La Batre wasn't your typical small Southern town. It was 53 percent white, 10 percent African American, 15 percent Vietnamese, 10 percent Laotian and Cambodian, 2 percent Latino, and a small number of Native Americans and others. We stood near the boats washed way up on the shore on both sides of the open meeting ground. Their names reflected their owners' roots. The boats on my left had traditional Southern two-word handles, something like *Mary Ann* and *Betty Sue*. On the right were two Vietnamese boats, *Thanh I* and *Thanh II*. Unlike many troubled places I visited at home and around the world with different groups living in close contact, these people weren't at each other's throats. They weren't interested in burning each other's churches or Buddhist temples. They were hardworking, down-to-earth, family-oriented folks who just wanted to go back to work.

And they shared a big problem: they were being screwed over by FEMA, the Federal Emergency Management Agency, which had told them the agency would pay to remove just three boats, because only they posed a health threat to nearby houses. Six weeks after my visit, FEMA said the other twenty-nine stranded vessels would have to be removed by the owners or they could pay FEMA to remove them at $60,000 a boat. The FEMA coordinator even stopped the U.S. Coast Guard, which had done a great job there from day one, from removing the boats without charging the families after it had already signed a contract to do so.

I was dumbfounded. I told President Bush about it and we agreed to give whatever it took to remove the twenty-nine boats and get everybody going again. We got the money to the governor in April 2006 and the job was completed on September 23. The last boat recovered was an eighty-foot trawler fittingly named *Riptide*, flying an American flag near the mast.

New Orleans was so badly hit that it received a large percentage of the grants. Xavier University, with damages in excess of $30 million, reopened just four months after the storm, with 75 percent of their students. They applied for and won a Bush-Clinton Katrina Fund grant of about $1.9 million to restore their buildings. So many public schools were destroyed that the city decided it was best to quickly approve a large number of charter schools, so we gave money to New Schools for New Orleans to help recruit and place teachers, recruit school board members, and provide free legal services. In September 2006, forty public schools opened, enrolling 40,000 students.

The Children's Health Fund, led by Dr. Irwin Redlener, was providing mental health and primary health services to people in New Orleans and throughout the region through mobile health clinics. The fund made a grant to them, too. I saw one of the mobile units helping people who thought no one had noticed their children's injuries.

Henry Juszkiewicz and the Gibson Guitar company launched Music Rising, led by Bob Ezrin and my friend, U2's brilliant guitarist The Edge, to get instruments back into the hands of the city's musicians. They made and sold 300 guitars out of wood collected after the storm. All told, they raised $7 million, including $500,000 from our fund. The money enabled them to replace the instruments lost by professional musicians, 2,700 in New Orleans alone, and to help schools and community centers throughout the Gulf. Among those receiving instruments were the veterans of the French Quarter's famous Preservation Hall, who had played to natives and tourists for decades without making much money, just to keep Dixieland jazz alive. I first heard them when I was fifteen and was so glad we helped them get going again.

We stopped accepting funds in July 2007 and closed the fund on December 31. To support the grantees until their work was completed and continue to inspire future investment, two of our last grants went to Living Cities and the Foundation for the Mid South, two strong philanthropies we trusted to carry on the work.

Afterward, I kept up with the long-term recovery efforts through our partners in the Clinton Global Initiative who made their own commitments, including the previously mentioned AmeriCorps affiliate, City Year, which started a program for Louisiana based in New Orleans that's still going strong.

The annual CGI meeting in 2009 featured two Katrina guests, a single working mother and one of her two children. Having lost their home in the storm, they had recently settled into a new one in New Orleans's Lower Ninth Ward. It was built to better resist floods and hurricanes and was much more energy-efficient. The crowd gasped when the mother reported that she'd just received her electric bill for July, at the time the hottest July on record: $27! Americans still haven't done enough to increase energy efficiency in buildings new and old. There are some really good models in New Orleans.

The federal government also invested a lot of money after some rigorous debate in Congress over "how much and what for." One of the most ardent supporters of more funding and greater flexibility was the junior senator from New York. Working with Senator Mary Landrieu from Louisiana, Hillary reminded her colleagues that the Gulf Coast senators had been there for New York after the death and destruction of 9/11, and they had to be there for the Gulf Coast now. The Republican Majority Leader, Trent Lott, who had once warned that Hillary would come to the Senate unless "maybe lightning will strike and she won't," said that no senator outside the affected states had done more for the people of the Gulf Coast than Hillary had. She had even cast the deciding vote in the Senate on funding a rail line in Mississippi that had to be rebuilt.

Soon, we would need to recapture that spirit, to finish the recovery and strengthen the resilience of Puerto Rico and the U.S. Virgin Islands, and fight severe drought and wildfire problems in the West.

In 2015, New Orleans mayor Mitch Landrieu, who later served ably as coordinator for implementing President Biden's big infrastructure bill, hosted a week-long conference, Katrina 10: Resilient New Orleans, to discuss how far the city had come in the decade after Katrina and what still needed to be done. The mayor also released a Resilience Strategy to keep the progress going. There was a lot of optimism tempered by understanding that the city wasn't all the way back, that uncertainty remained about its vulnerability to future storms, and that not enough housing, especially for African Americans and other low-income residents, had been built to meet the resilience and energy efficiency standards enjoyed by the single working mother's family I had welcomed to the CGI meeting several years earlier.

About the same time, the Kaiser Family Foundation did a survey asking the citizens of New Orleans what they thought about the progress made in the ten years since the storm. There was general agreement that the recovery had come a long way in restoring the economy, schools, public services, and unique culture of the city. They gave high marks to local government, said the federal government had been of real help after getting off to a shaky start, and felt the state hadn't done enough. A big majority of people were still concerned about the crime rate, but thought the city was moving in the right direction. Most of them were also optimistic about the future, although African Americans and low-income residents were less positive about how far they had come and their future prospects, reflecting the persistence of racial disparities in opportunities that long predated Katrina. The conference, in a series of panels filled with knowledgeable people, made a serious effort to address those issues. President Obama, President George W. and Laura Bush, and I all visited locations during the week to see what had been achieved and to cheer them on. On the last day, I gave a talk in which I tried to sum up what most of us were thinking and feeling:

> There's a difference between being happy and being satisfied. . . . What your very best efforts did should make you burst with pride . . . but it should not stop you from trying to erase the last manifestations of the color line, of the economic differences, of the education differences, of the health-care differences. . . . You've got a lot to celebrate tonight, but the celebration must be leavened by rededication. The people who died left behind memories and loved ones and legacies that deserve to be fully redeemed by erasing the lines

that divide us. My take on this is: Have a good time, New Orleans—you earned it. Give yourself a pat on the back—you earned it. Laugh tonight and dance to the music—you earned it. Tomorrow wake up and say, "Look at what we did, I bet we can do the rest, too."

SIX

Haiti and the People Who Keep Going

I've always been drawn to Haiti and its fascinating and unique history, full of promise and tragedy, with far too much of the latter. Both as president and as a private citizen, I've tried to do what I can to help the Haitian people improve their lives, particularly in the wake of the devastation wrought by the 2010 earthquake and as they've wrestled with debilitating political instability before and since.

Haiti was born of struggle, the only republic to be established through a slave revolt, led by Toussaint Louverture in 1791 and culminating in independence from France in 1804. It was at the time the richest island in the Caribbean, full of spices, coffee, rice, and more. The cost and trouble to France of trying to hold on to it was probably a factor in Napoleon's decision to sell the Louisiana territory to the United States in 1803. The freed slaves were largely from the French West African colony Dahomey, called Benin after independence. They shared the island of Hispaniola with native Caribbean people, the Spanish, and people of mixed races. The tensions between them led to conflicts throughout the 1800s that split the island in two, Haiti on the west, and the Dominican Republic on the east.

Before this happened, Haiti suffered a blow from which it never fully recovered. In 1802, Toussaint, a charismatic unifying force, agreed to a meeting with the French to try to work out a peaceful resolution of their differences and a path forward. Toussaint went to the meeting and was never seen or heard from again, with some reports saying he was captured and sent to France to die shortly thereafter in prison. There was a brief power struggle to succeed him between Toussaint's chief diplomat, Jean-Jacques Dessalines, and his top general, Henri Christophe. The general, unsurprisingly, prevailed.

To protect the people against future attacks, Christophe built a string of forts in the mountainous area of the country to which the people could flee in the event of an invasion. The only one still standing is La Citadelle, a massive structure built atop and into a large cliff overlooking the Caribbean. The construction required thousands of laborers who carried the heavy stones up a sheer cliff. A large number of Haitians died doing the dangerous work to erect what is today still the most commanding structure in the Caribbean—built without a trained architect, without anyone with a college degree, by people whose native intelligence, imagination, hard-won skills, and bloodstained sweat revealed their enduring, yet never realized, potential.

For the nearly two hundred years between the opening of La Citadelle in 1820 and the earthquake in 2010, Haiti alternated between periods of violence and calm, of building and breaking vital institutions, of democracy and devastation, with a nineteen-year interlude of occupation by the U.S. Marines, from 1915 to 1934. Through it all, the Haitians preserved their vibrant culture and the determination to make the best of a bad hand. The gaping chasm between what life is in Haiti and what it could be is a large part of why so many people are both drawn to and repelled by it—I am one of them. That's why I've tried to help the Haitians whenever I could, often against the advice of friends and staff who saw my commitment as a fool's errand, with high risks of blame and little chance of success.

It all began for me in December 1975, when Hillary and I first went to Port-au-Prince on a trip that was a wedding gift from our friend David Edwards. We stayed in a small hotel near the city center, where we saw then-President Jean-Claude Duvalier lay a wreath at the symbol of Haiti's independence, a powerful statue of a freed slave breaking his chains and blowing defiantly on a conch shell. The young Haitian in charge of the local Citibank operation introduced us to Haitian art, which we have loved and collected ever since, and took us to meet a voodoo priest named Max Beauvoir and his family. Beauvoir had degrees from the City College of New York and the Sorbonne in Paris and had thrived in various jobs in New Jersey and Massachusetts, then came home to take over his ailing grandfather's voodoo encampment near the capital city. He took us through his village, explained the basic tenets of his faith and how it had been brought to Haiti by the Fon people of what is now Benin, and how it was his job not only to embody the faith and keep bad spirits away, but to provide social services and a system of justice, since the government had little presence outside the larger cities. The day Hillary and I spent with Max Beauvoir was unforgettable. If you're interested, there's a longer account of voodoo, including a ceremony we attended and the punishments employed that gave rise to the zombie legend, in *My Life*.

I didn't go back to Haiti until I was president. Father Jean-Bertrand Aristide, a leftist priest and candidate for president, had won a big victory in late 1990, but was deposed in a military takeover the following year, led by General Raoul Cédras. Cédras kept a grip on popular unrest with iron-fisted tactics, including "necklacing," putting tires around the necks of Aristide supporters and setting them afire. The U.N. called for him to step down, sanctions were imposed, and a deadline for his departure was set, which Cédras ignored. The Haitian community in the United States was outraged, and they and several of Haiti's neighbors in the Caribbean wanted the general to go. He was offered asylum in Panama, but sat tight. Meanwhile the Haitian economy suffered and tensions rose. Aristide's liberal supporters in the U.S. were agitating for Cédras's removal while several Republicans in Congress, led by Senator Jesse Helms, wanted him to stay.

I wanted him to go. Haiti had its first shot at democracy in decades, and without the support of the United States and the lifting of U.N. sanctions, there was little chance that social peace and even moderate economic growth could be restored. In a last-ditch effort to avoid military action, I asked President Jimmy Carter, Senator Sam Nunn, and General Colin Powell to go to Haiti to negotiate a quick exit for Cédras. In case that failed, I also instructed the Pentagon to develop a plan to replace him with a strategy that kept Haitian casualties as low as possible. Carter, Nunn, and Powell all disagreed with my decision to intervene. Carter was against even a U.N.-sanctioned forced return for Aristide, and seemed sympathetic to Cédras, who must have made a good impression when they had met years earlier when the general trained at a military base in Georgia. Nunn thought Haiti's middle class was too small to support a functioning democracy. Powell thought the chaos would get even worse without the military to rein it in. I thought they should tell the Haitian officials (Nunn worked the parliament, Powell the military brass, and Carter the eighty-one-year-old head of state, President Émile Jonassaint) that they disagreed with my policy, but that I was determined to restore Aristide and they needed to be a part of making it as quick, peaceful, and orderly as possible.

When the September 15, 1994, deadline passed, I authorized the well-planned military operation to begin, and got the delegation out of Haiti. By the time the commander of our forces, General Hugh Shelton, stepped off the landing boat, the opposition had thrown in the towel. Aristide took office, and our military kept the peace for a few months until the task was transferred to an international force with soldiers from more than twenty countries.

In 1995, I traveled to Haiti to visit with President Aristide and thank the troops for their work. Unfortunately, Aristide's opponents in Congress, led by Senator Helms, kept the U.S. from providing any meaningful humanitarian or economic development aid. All I could do was to leave the Army Corps of Engineers in the country for a while to rebuild roads and do other infrastructure work.

My next visit was in 2003, when I went to support the Clinton Foundation's efforts to get low-cost lifesaving medicine to people with the highest HIV/AIDS infection rates in the Caribbean. Aristide was back in office, after sitting out a term as required by the Haitian constitution. We had a cordial reunion but my main mission was to assist the people treating and caring for people with AIDS, including Dr. Bill Pape, whose GHESKIO clinic in Port-au-Prince, founded in 1985, was the world's longest-running AIDS hospital; the late Dr. Paul Farmer, the leader of Partners in Health, who had started his clinic and rural care network called Zanmi Lasante in the central highlands in 1988; and the staff at the large public hospital in Port-au-Prince. We had an event at the hospital to highlight what the Clinton Foundation was doing to help them combat AIDS.

Chelsea, who had started emailing with Farmer when she was at Stanford, said that he was "my generation's Albert Schweitzer." Over our many years of working together, he proved to be that and more, a unique blend of passion and professionalism, barely controlled anger at the unaddressed problems of the poor, and an uncanny ability to live with good humor and gratitude. He also spoke Creole fluently and when the U.S. embassy representative was having trouble translating for me at the hospital event, he gamely stepped in to serve as my interpreter.

In 2008, after Haiti had been badly damaged by three severe storms, I asked Clinton Global Initiative members to help. They responded by making thirty-one commitments, valued at more than $100 million. Then, in 2009, U.N. secretary-general Ban Ki-moon asked me to be his U.N. special envoy, helping to secure more financial assistance from governments and multinational donors, more investment from the private sector, and more coordinated help from NGOs to improve health, education, agriculture, and the small business economy. A donors' conference at the U.N. in 2009 resulted in $391.5 million in pledges. Our first job was to keep track of them. When we did, actual receipts more than doubled, from 12 to 30 percent of the pledges.

Since my 2003 trip, Aristide had been forced to leave again, but René Préval, who had succeeded him in the 1990s, had won the most recent election and in the interim had become a much more able political leader, with the support of a large majority in both houses of parliament. We got off to a strong start with an investor conference attended by several hundred people. They were excited by a Haitian government that appeared stronger, more competent, and more focused on doing something to help their people, as evidenced by their recent adoption of an impressive economic strategy, crafted by Dr. Paul Collier, a highly regarded British economist. Haiti secured a billion dollars in aid commitments from donor governments. School enrollment was up and reformers dared hope rising incomes could bring an end to the dreaded *restavek* system, in which poor parents would sell a child into bonded labor to earn enough to feed their families and put their remaining children in school. Though their per capita incomes remained under $800 a year, things were looking up for the long-suffering Haitians.

Then came a disaster greater than all those which had dashed Haiti's hopes in the past. On January 12, 2010, a huge earthquake hit Haiti near the capital of Port-au-Prince, killing more than 200,000 people, injuring countless others, collapsing thousands of buildings and leaving Port-au-Prince and other cities covered in rubble, without water, sanitation, or light. Instead of new factories we were worried about water and food to keep people alive, safe places for them to sleep, and lights to permit emergency night surgeries on the grounds of the badly damaged hospital, often with vodka the only anesthetic.

The next afternoon I went to the U.N. for a meeting with Secretary-General Ban Ki-moon and an emergency session on the disaster with the Security Council. By then we knew our U.N. mission in Haiti, MINUSTAH, had lost several people, including its leader, Hédi Annabi, an able, dedicated Tunisian diplomat. Their bodies were among thousands, dead and alive, still beneath the ruins.

The next day President Obama asked President George W.

Bush and me to help raise funds from Americans for Haiti. I had already established an emergency fund and promised donors that 100 percent of their gifts would be sent quickly to address the most urgent needs. President Bush and I set up another fund designed to help in rebuilding the economy. After a week of meetings, and lots of media interviews urging people to give money, Chelsea and I took a planeload of supplies down to Port-au-Prince to see what remained of the government, console and provide encouragement to those committed to the U.N. mission, and figure out what to do next. We offloaded the supplies and got into our car to go meet with President René Préval and the U.N. mission.

On the way into the city, we passed the straight stretch where, before the quake, dozens of artists had hung their paintings on a long sturdy fence separating the sidewalk from a large open space filled with tents in which craftspeople sold their wares, made of metal, wood, and stone. It was the perfect place to catch tourists coming and going. Amazingly, seven or eight of the painters had already come back to work. I stopped our small motorcade and told everyone to get out and buy something. And to do it without the usual practice of haggling over prices. I chose a couple of pieces I liked and was headed back to the car when a man whose work was a good distance away shouted, "You have to buy something from me. You did when you were here in 2003."

I walked back to the caller, shook his hand, and saw the photo he had kept of our previous encounter. I said, "I can't believe you're back here so soon." He replied, "I have to be here. I have nowhere else to go. My wife and children were killed in the quake. The only way I can honor them is to begin again. We artists are all one big family. They all know my story. If I can be here, they know they should be, too. We have to go on." I bought two more paintings and left knowing why I was there.

President Préval, his top staff, and cabinet had set up temporary offices in a small building adjoining the Presidential Palace, which, along with several nearby government buildings, had been badly damaged or completely destroyed. Préval had survived the collapse of his house and office because when the quake struck he was outside playing with his grandchildren on the large front lawn. He was clearly badly shaken by all the death, crippling injuries, and massive destruction. Nevertheless, he and his team were intensely focused on urgent tasks: to give people a place to stay, food, clean water, and lighting, while searching for survivors and clearing rubble. They needed money to keep the government open and the military on the job. Most of the donations were going to the Red Cross and other established groups like Partners in Health. But governments were reluctant to give—or legally prohibited from giving—money to the Haitian government with its long history of corruption and incapacity. I wish they had been with us that day.

The finance minister, Ronald Baudin, left an indelible impression on me. Tall, well-built, and soft-spoken, Baudin had lost his ten-year-old son in the quake. But he came to work the next day and had been there every day since. His eyes betrayed his pain and heartbreak but he spoke with immense dignity and intensity about what needed to be done now, what the U.N. could do to help, and how somebody had to give the government enough money to function.

I also made a brief stop at the U.N. mission to see people dealing with the shock of losing our leader and other coworkers. Official grieving would have to wait. There was too much to do, so I did my best to encourage them to keep working on the tasks at hand. Later, I would attend memorials to those who lost their lives far from home doing work they believed in.

Soon I was back in Port-au-Prince for an early-morning meeting at the local U.N. headquarters with the elected leaders of the tent camps that housed tens of thousands of Haitians who had no place else to go. They were in effect the mayors of cities who depended on outside support for survival. They told me they needed lights to improve safety conditions at night. So we found companies that donated solar streetlights with battery storage and others who gave smaller lamps that would light tents. They had lots of good ideas like that and, after the meeting, our U.N. staff kept in regular contact with all of them.

The camp "mayors" were all Haitian except one: Sean Penn, the Academy Award–winning actor who was one of several celebrities who came shortly after the quake to help. The only difference was he stayed, living full-time for three months in the muddy ground of the camp at Pétion-Ville, just up the hill from downtown Port-au-Prince. When he had to return to the U.S. to work, he kept coming back often, making sure everything possible was being done for people in his camp and pushing for faster relocation to more permanent, more livable quarters. Sean was quite a sight at that first meeting in his signature white T-shirt and jeans. I could tell he was already deeply committed. After the emergency passed, with the help of philanthropist Diana Jenkins, Sean set up the J/P Haitian Relief Organization, or J/P HRO, to build a small museum to commemorate the earthquake and fund several initiatives to rebuild the country. They're still at it, though with a new name, CORE.

For the next few months, it seemed the whole world was pulling for Haiti and wanted to help. The U.S. sent a medical ship, the USNS *Comfort*, a sort of floating hospital, to help alleviate the crushing load of injured and sick, made much heavier by the damage to local health facilities. China and Cuba sent a large number of doctors and health workers. Other medical personnel from all over showed up to volunteer, including a boyhood friend of mine from Arkansas. Dr. Jim French is a noncosmetic plastic surgeon in Northern Virginia who knew how badly his skills were needed. I was grateful that he made his way to Haiti just a couple of days after the quake. A lot of good people did that.

Money was coming into the emergency fund I set up at the foundation, in amounts large and small. One of the larger gifts was $500,000 from Algeria, which was promptly deployed to the relief effort. Some critics said I shouldn't have taken the money because it violated my pledge to the Obama White House and the Congress not to take money for the Clinton Foundation from countries that had not already given to us before Hillary became secretary of state. I never considered returning it. The money was sent to my foundation because I was the U.N. envoy. Algeria clearly intended it to benefit the Haitian people, so I immediately sent it to NGOs who would spend it quickly and effectively. Had you seen the utter desolation and the massive loss of life, I think you would agree with what I said at the time, that in the first few days after the quake, the needs were so great I would have taken money from the devil himself.

Although celebrities held fundraising events and organizations involved with Haiti gave or raised large amounts, the vast majority of the contributors were small donors, many of them making use of a new process that allowed Americans to donate $10 ($5 in Canada) by texting a number for their designated charity. If the tsunami was the first disaster response crowd-funded by email, Haiti was the first done by text.

In the first few weeks, so many supplies were coming into the Port-au-Prince airport it created a real logistical problem, and President Préval asked the U.S. to help out. Hillary, then secretary of state, negotiated the opening of the airport with him. For about a month the American military took over airport operations as part of Operation Unified Response, and sent a substantial force to help distribute the supplies and take on other tasks, including keeping the peace until replaced by the U.N.-sanctioned multinational force. I was very proud of the job done by our troops, under the command of General Ken Keen. I spent a night in their encampment by the harbor. The troops were dedicated, effective, and sensitive to the feelings of the people, their pain, despair, and the memory of the nineteen-year-long occupation of their country by the U.S. Marines in the early twentieth century. This deployment wasn't an occupation, but an essential lifeline from our country. This time the United States was a good neighbor and then some.

As the emergency relief phased into reconstruction, it was time to start spending the money George W. and I had raised, and to organize a process through which the billions of dollars pledged through the U.N. drive could be collected and deployed with maximum impact, transparency, and accountability. We designed our fund to operate a lot like the Bush-Clinton Fund his father and I had set up after Katrina. In March, we spent an interesting day together getting ideas from Haitians and visiting a large tent camp near the Presidential Palace. After the visit, we put together a board and staff, started looking for projects, and began taking requests for funding.

Meanwhile I spent most of my time doing my U.N. job to raise funds rapidly and invest them effectively. A second donor conference pledged more than $5.6 billion, with individuals and private companies adding another $3.1 billion. We had already delivered tents and clothing for displaced people, telecommunications and radio equipment for the Haitian government, and thousands of tons of medical supplies, along with solar flashlights and whistles to increase protection for vulnerable women in the temporary camps.

We needed the support and input from important sectors of Haitian society—legislators, businesses, trade unions, local officials, leaders of religious groups, civil society, and the diaspora, especially in the United States and Canada. I met with representatives of all those groups, asked for their help, and promised them input in the rebuilding process. I also pledged to involve the major donors and NGOs. There were about 10,000 NGOs operating in Haiti, but the vast majority of financial aid came from a small number of them. We had to try to get the big ones to coordinate their efforts with the government donors and the Haitian government's development plan.

One of my most interesting meetings was with the leaders of the main faiths, Catholic, Episcopal, evangelical Christian, and voodoo. Over a long period of time, the Catholic and Episcopalian clergy had developed an accommodation with the priests and followers of voodoo, many of whom also attended their services. But there was a tension between them and the evangelicals, who considered voodoo ungodly, though its adherents do believe in a creator God. I knew we needed them all on the same page to recover from the quake as quickly as possible.

Shortly before the meeting I saw President Préval, who had urged me to talk to them. He smiled and said, "Oh, you're in for a treat. Your old friend Max Beauvoir is now the Pope of Voodoo." His actual title was chief priest. When I walked into the small meeting room, I took a moment to greet Max and thank him for his kindness to Hillary and me when we met on our first trip as newlyweds thirty-four years before. He allowed himself a smile and brief exchange, but quickly returned to business. His people needed help and there was no time for reminiscing or for the squabbles he had had with the evangelical leaders. Beauvoir still projected a powerful presence, though a lonelier one for having lost his wife and one of his daughters in the years since we first met. Thankfully, his surviving daughter was close by, a professor at the national university. Max Beauvoir passed away in 2015 at age seventy-nine, to the end a devoted servant of his people and his faith.

The Haitian government was a big help in the beginning. First, they asked Paul Collier to update their economic strategy to take into account the earthquake's impact. Then the legislature, in which President Préval's party held two thirds of the seats, gave him the authority for an extended period to take any action not prohibited by the constitution. Préval needed it, with less than a year to act before the inauguration of a new president.

He designated his prime minister, Jean-Max Bellerive, to lead the government's efforts. Bellerive was smart, politically savvy, and well supported by a team that included Gabriel Verret, an economic policy consultant whose sense of humor kept us laughing when we wanted to scream instead. I asked Dr. Paul Farmer to be my deputy. Farmer's work in Haiti (and later in Rwanda) as well as his many books calling for equal opportunities for poor people had brought worldwide respect and support. He was perfect for the job, with his long dedication to better healthcare for poor Haitians, his wonderful Haitian wife, Didi, and daughter, Catherine, and complete fluency in the language, politics, and culture.

On March 31, we announced the creation of the Interim Haiti Recovery Commission (IHRC) at a donor conference which produced pledges with the total now amounting to almost $9.9 billion. The IHRC was formally approved by Haiti's government in April, with an eighteen-month mandate to approve and evaluate major projects and publicly report on their results. On June 1, we held a meeting at a large conference center in the Dominican Republic with representatives of dozens of countries and organizations, including present and potential donors from as far away as East Asia and the Middle East. The Haitians laid out their strategy and made their pitch.

The first meeting of the IHRC, which I cochaired with Prime

Minister Bellerive, was held in Port-au-Prince on June 17. The commission included Haitians from all sectors—local government, business and the professions, labor, religious groups, and NGOs—sitting across from the donors which had pledged $100 million or more, plus legislators, a representative of the international NGO community, and Venezuela and Cuba, who were donating outside the U.N. system, as observers.

Even though the large body was cumbersome and the process of reviewing proposals, receiving progress reports, and giving all the members the chance to ask their questions and speak their minds was time-consuming, the overall impact was very positive. Both the Haitians and the donors were empowered, and in working together, both sides grew more respectful of and responsive to each other.

To maintain the confidence of the donors, aid money was deposited in a special trust account of the World Bank, to be disbursed as the IHRC approved projects and recipients. This decision led to two problems in the beginning that threatened the IHRC's ability to fulfill its mandate. First, I felt strongly that the bank's proposed fee structure was too expensive, and would take too much money away from recovery operations. Second, the World Bank said that since they were holding the money in trust, they should be the final arbiter of what it was spent on and how to evaluate the outcome. That was a huge problem. If the bank got the last call, it would have killed the credibility of the IHRC and undermined the roles of both the Haitians and the major donors in shaping the recovery. Because these donors had bought into the IHRC and it was, after all, their money, we worked things out rather quickly, getting some relief on the costs and an agreement by the World Bank to work with and through the IHRC, which would approve disbursements and was never intended to access the money.

The next eighteen months proved both rewarding and frustrating. We spent a lot of nights with Haitians, donors, and NGO leaders at local restaurants and hotels working out what we had to accomplish to boost the economy and increase the capacity of the government, without sacrificing our efforts to fight corruption and Haiti's long-dominant elites' deeply ingrained resistance to change.

Meanwhile, during the day we toured the country outside of Port-au-Prince, trying to make sure the other damaged areas, mostly in the west, got their fair share of aid, and looking for opportunities to promote sustainable growth throughout the country, all the way to the border with the Dominican Republic.

President Préval had fully embraced Paul Collier's development plan, which urged the creation of economic opportunity centers that would draw people away from Port-au-Prince into other areas of the country. The capital city's population of three million is mostly concentrated in a bowl-shaped area coming from nearby hills down to the coastline. Nature built it to hold 200,000 to 300,000 people. The overload had destroyed topsoil, compromised solid waste disposal, and led to the runoff of unsanitary water into the bay, making the seawater too polluted for fishing for quite a distance. Except for nationally protected forest lands, practically the entire country had been deforested, leading to the loss of topsoil which had once hosted a prosperous agricultural economy, rich in coffee, mango and mahogany trees, sugar, rice, and many other crops. Dispersal of economic activity was very important even before the quake. But Haiti had less than 1,000 miles of paved roads, only 10 percent of the country was connected to the power grid, and the only port that could load and offload cargo containers was in Port-au-Prince.

In terms of home building, one of the biggest problems was establishing good legal title to land. The absence of a land-titling system led to endless ownership disputes, made mortgages impossible, and resulted in a landscape full of houses built piece by piece in a process that often took more than a decade and kept Haitians from using the land as collateral for home mortgages or for small-business and agricultural loans. We would have to fix it or work around it.

The other big obstacle to growth was an electricity system that was ridiculously expensive, often unreliable, and vulnerable to theft by people siphoning off power from the powerlines. We could help at the margins by restoring the damaged and antiquated hydropower system, but to really make a difference Haiti needed to shift production of power away from environmentally damaging and expensive imported oil and diesel fuel toward wind and solar. The sun shines three hundred days a year or more and the wind blows strongly in parts of the country, so the potential for green power is massive. Despite the resistance of the electric company to change its business model, we made some progress with solar power for schools and health facilities.

We already had a fine example of what could be done. Caribbean Harvest was established in 2005 by Valentin Abe, an Ivory Coast native who used his Fulbright scholarship to earn a PhD in Aquaculture at Auburn University and went to Haiti to help people raise and sell fish to increase their incomes and protein consumption. Abe raises fish until they weigh a pound in tanks with aeration and filtration powered by solar energy, then delivers them fresh in solar-powered ice chests to farmers who grow them to full size in lakes. Unlike many fish farms in other parts of the world, they feed the fish high-quality organic food, something Abe insists on. In 2009, the fish that didn't reach full size were sold by women in open markets, enabling them to earn as much in a morning's work as they could working a full day in a factory.

Abe has helped hundreds of farmers with continued expansion of his operation, thanks in part to support from several of our CGI partners. He gave me a tour of his operation early in the U.N. work, and I later met a fisherman with eight children who said that after joining Caribbean Harvest he had tripled his income and was finally able to send all eight of his children to school for the first time. All of Caribbean Harvest's net income goes to the farmers or to development projects in their communities and it now runs the largest fish hatchery in the Caribbean, powered by the sun. In 2010, Valentin Abe was named one of *Time* magazine's 100 Most Influential People in the World. He deserved it, but it would make him happier if more people's lives were powered by opportunity and clean energy.

On both these issues, power and land titling, we came up against the entrenched oligopolies that had controlled the Haitian economy for too long, and sadly, a political leadership reluctant to take them on, even after the parliament had given them the power to do so. So, the IHRC decided to invest the donors' money where it would do the most good, and use the Clinton Bush Haiti Fund and the CGI Haiti Action Network, whose original commitment of $100 million had grown to more than $400 million after the earthquake, to create as much economic, health, education, social, and environmental progress as possible.

Throughout the rest of 2010 and 2011, I urged the donor community to work through the IHRC to fund needed projects, to support the investments of the Clinton Bush Haiti Fund, and to keep expanding the activities of the CGI Haiti Action Network. After a hotly disputed presidential election in November 2010, there were riots over alleged vote rigging, and an investigation by the Organization of American States (OAS) resulted in a runoff election won by Michel "Sweet Micky" Martelly, a popular singer and political novice who won two thirds of the vote.

I went to Martelly's inauguration in May of 2011, hoping he would quicken the pace of recovery with new faces and new energy. I believe one of the reasons President Préval's preferred candidate, Jude Célestin, lost is that Préval, fearful of losing support from the oligarchs that dominated Haiti's economy and financed its politics, including lots of paid demonstrators for and against candidates, never had fully used the power the parliament had given him to make sweeping reforms.

Martelly had trouble with the parliament from the beginning and couldn't get a prime minister confirmed until the fall, when Haitian doctor Garry Conille took leave from our U.N. mission to serve, a move which boosted the IHRC, of which he was now cochairman, and encouraged the donors. Sadly, after a few months Conille resigned and returned to the U.N., a good man ill-suited to the often brutal politics of his homeland and the ever-present threat of corruption, which he resisted but could not defeat, given his lack of support from the president and in the parliament.

In May, Martelly finally got a prime minister confirmed, when parliament approved his foreign minister, Laurent Lamothe. Lamothe was young, energetic, and seemed determined to modernize Haiti, but he and his team didn't have much support in the parliament, which wouldn't even agree to extend the mandate of the IHRC when it expired in October 2011.

The IHRC was time-consuming, but it was also highly resistant to inside deals and corruption, and the results were subject to audits. I worried that without the IHRC, some of the donors wouldn't follow through on their commitments. When the Haitian government announced its own Aid Effectiveness Committee to replace the IHRC and the World Bank agreed to support the new entity, we turned all the IHRC files, records, and donor tracking over to the Haitian government.

When my U.N. mandate ended in December 2012, we issued a report chronicling the status of approved projects, completed the performance audits, and put out a final document urging that more of the aid to Haiti and other developing countries be channeled through local governments, businesses, and NGOs, but maintaining transparency and accountability requirements. On the last day of the year, the Clinton Bush Haiti Fund closed, with about $4 million still in the bank. That money was used to continue funding active small business development projects and to support the Inter-American Development Bank, putting the loan repayments into a revolving fund that would provide financing for future small business proposals. One hundred percent of the fund went to Haiti projects, not a penny to me or anyone in my family.

President Martelly also asked me to stay on to serve as cochair with Prime Minister Lamothe of a committee to attract more private investors to Haiti. I agreed to do so, on the condition that no one I brought to Haiti would ever be asked to pay a bribe. To my knowledge, the commitment was honored, with only one exception: a large investor in wind and solar energy refused to pay and withdrew, costing Haiti a lot of much cheaper, cleaner electricity. The Clinton Foundation Haiti program stayed active through 2016, when we transferred twenty projects to Sean Penn's CORE. But the CGI Haiti Action Network is still going.

So what did it all amount to? Quite a lot, actually. The $30 million given to the Haiti Fund I established went overwhelmingly to reliable groups to provide food, water, shelter, sanitation, medicine, medical care, and surgeries. We got in-kind donations of solar lights and clothing for the camps, and trucks to help remove the massive amounts of rubble. We sent funds to an NGO to buy seed and fertilizer, to strengthen child protection and restore education, to provide job-training programs for women in the camps and poor communities, and to speed disbursements to recovery programs.

The Clinton Bush Fund eventually raised $54.4 million from more than 200,000 individuals, businesses, and organizations. As we wrote in our report to President Obama, we disbursed the money to support "job promotion and smart, sustainable economic development," and "any successes they have achieved have been their successes, not ours." Josh Bolten and Laura Graham, the board's cochairs, and the fund's CEO, Gary Edson, did a thorough job in funding and monitoring projects. As the recipients met certain benchmarks, they got more funds.

All told, the Clinton Bush Fund invested 36 percent of the money in small and growing businesses, 31 percent in job training and workforce development, 10 percent in microfinance, and 23 percent in meeting critical needs from housing repair to addressing a cholera outbreak caused by the introduction of cholera bacteria into the water by U.N. soldiers from South Asia. We gave $100,000 to a new cholera care facility with an aboveground water purification system that eliminated more than 99 percent of all impurities. I hoped it would serve as a model for further construction.

The fund also invested in building systems people in wealthier countries take for granted: affordable insurance for small business people; a mortgage system for lower-income homeowners when title was not in dispute; money to get people out of temporary camps and unsafe housing into rehabilitated neighborhoods; support to help 1,000 entrepreneurs succeed and to reopen the Haiti Hospitality Board and two hotels; funds to help artists in Jacmel, Port-au-Prince, and Croix-des-Bouquets fill production orders from U.S. retailers; and more than $4 million to strengthen the country's healthcare infrastructure.

By the time we closed the fund, there were 7,350 new jobs,

20,000 people trained for available jobs, from at-risk young people to medical professionals, and more than 311,000 people had benefited in some way from the projects. Because so many of the business projects involved repayable loans which could then be loaned again, a lot of that money is still working.

The IHRC approved the investment of $3.2 billion in more than 810 projects, and donors forgave about a billion dollars more in debt. Among the biggest projects were 186 miles of newly paved roads, 46 new health centers, 7 new hospitals, airport repairs and improvements, especially in Port-au-Prince, and many new schools, homes, and rehabilitated buildings.

The largest economic project was the new Caracol Industrial Park built on six hundred acres in northern Haiti near Cap-Haïtien. Its main funder was the United States, at $250 million, represented on the IHRC by Hillary's chief of staff at the State Department, Cheryl Mills. The anchor tenant of the park was a large Korean operation, Sae-A Trading Company, that made and exported textiles, and provided 10,000 jobs there.

Among the donor nations, besides the U.S., the standouts were Brazil, Canada, and Japan. Led by Foreign Minister Celso Amorim, Brazil gave almost $400 million in aid and $1.85 billion to the U.N. peacekeeping operation, including reconstruction after the quake. Canada, a country whose people include a lot of Haitians, gave a staggering $1.1 billion in humanitarian and development aid, and Japan donated $190 million. All of them were active, constructive members of the IHRC.

After the IHRC shut down, I worked with Prime Minister Lamothe to bring in eighty-five potential investors in Haitian tourism, arts and crafts, agriculture, manufacturing, energy, and healthcare. Denis O'Brien, president of Digicel and the chair of the CGI Action Network, was Haiti's most consistent partner, financing all of the $12 million restoration of the old Iron Market, a key portion of the new Marriott hotel, and 175 new schools throughout the country. His example inspired others to join him.

In 2013, NRG Energy, thanks to David Crane, installed more than 400 kilowatts of solar power at small businesses, clinics, and schools, many with no previous access to electricity. In 2014, the CGI Action Network was helpful in bringing a $100 million Heineken investment in a Haitian brewery. And the Clinton Giustra Enterprise Partnership, which I'll talk more about later, launched Acceso, which trained farmers, increased and improved peanut production, and produced 900,000 lime, moringa, and mango seedlings for farmers to plant. They preserved topsoil and increased farmers' incomes about 40 percent.

In 2015, we inaugurated the new Marriott Port-au-Prince Haiti, a project jointly owned by Marriott and Denis O'Brien, employing 165 people and providing a new place for visitors and potential investors to stay.

In 2016, we worked with Haitian farmers to place moringa products and high-quality Haitian coffee in Whole Foods. The Kuli Kuli moringa products generated $400,000 in sales, more than Whole Foods projected. Our foundation's No Ceilings project helped support nine women-owned businesses and agricultural cooperatives with more than 4,000 farmers, mostly women, to increase their production and become more attractive to investors.

The Clinton Foundation also supported other agricultural operations, including the Haiti Coffee Academy, the Smallholder Farmers Alliance, and women-owned businesses like Kreyol Essence and Bèl Rèv, that use agricultural products like castor oil, moringa, and lemongrass, and SOIL, which provides toilets workers need and transforms the waste into compost for farmers. The agricultural delegation I led to Haiti attracted people who are still helping, like chef José Andrés and author and social business innovator Barb Stegemann.

In 2019, almost a decade after the quake, the CGI Haiti Action Network was still at it. One hundred thirty CGI commitments had been made, of which eighty had been completed and valued at $525 million. Twenty-eight ongoing commitments had received funding of $63.5 million. Amazingly, five more commitments were made in 2019 at our CGI meetings in the Caribbean.

What has the network done with almost $600 million?

- More than 65,000 farmers or small-scale producers received better seed, fertilizer, and other help, and gained access to more markets.

- More than 43,000 girls and women were supported through empowerment initiatives.
- More than 107,000 people gained more access to capital.
- More than 66,000 people got sustainable incomes.
- More than 60,000 people were engaged in combating climate change.
- More than 590,000 people got better access to health services, and more than 435,000 people participated in maternal and child survival programs.
- More than 11,000 people benefited from skills-based professional training programs.
- More than 100,000 children got to attend school, including those who attend 175 new schools built by Denis O'Brien and Digicel.
- More than $19.2 million was invested in small and medium-sized enterprises (SMEs).
- More than 4,400 acres of forest were protected or restored, with millions of new trees planted, 7.5 million of them by Timberland.
- More than $65 million was invested in public infrastructure.
- More than 8,400 new jobs were created.
- More than 125,000 metric tons of CO_2 emissions were eliminated.

There was also a lot that didn't go well. We never solved the land title problem and there's still no good nationwide mortgage system. The electric company still charges too much, serves too few, and requires too many polluting backup generators. Sae-A maintained its plant employing more than 10,000 people but is opening new plants elsewhere in the Caribbean and Central America—plants that could have gone to Haiti had the government kept its promises on electricity pricing (16 cents per kilowatt-hour, not 40 cents), on modernizing the port of Cap-Haïtien to save Sae-A time and money, on properly maintaining the transportation system for workers, and more. But the employees work hard and are intelligent. In a short time they increased their productivity by 50 percent! They deserve better from their government.

The biggest disappointment of the IHRC work was a housing expo, opened to great fanfare by President Préval in 2011, with dozens of models priced from $1,200 to $30,000, built by sixty companies from Haiti and many other countries which were selected in a competitive bidding process. Construction projects in the developing world can be difficult to manage under the best of circumstances—the temptation to get kickbacks from contractors is great, and not just in Haiti. The hundreds of millions in bribes all over Latin America paid by the Brazilian giant Odebrecht makes the Haitian dealings look like small potatoes. Our housing effort was designed to protect the donors, the builders, and the Haitians who could have realized a huge number of jobs (even the foreign companies had to commit to using Haitian labor). But the expo and its related projects were dropped not long after President Martelly took office, and the models that were built quickly deteriorated into squatter housing. The contractors who won the right to participate didn't even earn back the cost of their spec houses. Construction in Haiti reverted to being a piggy bank for the well-connected, or multiyear brick-by-brick building by people who couldn't get a mortgage.

After Martelly became president, he did succeed in keeping his biggest campaign commitment, imposing a tax on overseas calls, which he used to dramatically increase school enrollment. And after Laurent Lamothe was named prime minister, he worked hard to bring new investment to Haiti. It was pretty much downhill after that. Eventually, when Senate and local elections weren't held, Martelly had no parliament to deal with and spent his last year governing by decree.

Martelly left office in early 2016 and was succeeded by another newcomer, Jovenel Moïse, who also promised a clean start and real reform, but without any previous experience or institutional support in parliament or among the powerful families that dominate the country, he couldn't get much done. The country endured a long period of social unrest with increasing violence as rival gangs selling drugs moved in to fill the vacuum a functioning government should have filled, culminating in President Moïse's assassination in 2021 and the chaos that followed.

Along the way, there were a slew of baseless attacks on our work in Haiti. We were criticized for overstating the amount of money given by other countries. At least a billion dollars of Haiti's debt was forgiven by multilateral donors, and that was included in the total, though no new money came into Haiti as a result. On the other hand, the Venezuelan oil company Petrocaribe reportedly sent a lot of money to Haiti that bypassed the IHRC and not all of it was accounted for. That was beyond my control, as was the fact that not all the countries honored their full commitments after the IHRC was disbanded in 2011.

The most incredible accusation arising from the conspiracy promoters on the internet was that Hillary and I were somehow involved in the suicide of a former Haitian government official named Klaus Eberwein, just before he was to testify in front of a House committee about corrupt practices in Haiti. The mainstream media didn't pay it much attention, because neither Hillary nor I had ever met the man or even knew who he was, and there was no scheduled congressional inquiry. But that didn't stop the Trump campaign and other conspiracy theorists from flooding voters in South Florida on Facebook with the ridiculous claim.

Back in the real world, the IHRC did all the accounting and performance audits we could before our mandate expired. Then the World Bank, which had held all the donors' contributions in trust until the IHRC approved projects, began working with the Haitian government directly. I don't know how much the World Bank disbursed for particular projects and what commitments were never fulfilled, but the World Bank has the records.

In any case, not one of us at the Clinton Foundation ever touched those funds, and as I said we put 100 percent of the donations we received into projects in Haiti. I still believe the IHRC was a necessary institution because the earthquake killed 17 percent of the government's workforce, destroyed twenty government buildings, and collapsed the economy. But unlike the process set up in Indonesia, after the IHRC went out of business, no one in Haiti was put in charge with a mandate to account for all the incoming funds, how they were spent, and what the results were. That's what the IHRC was for, and I wish it had kept going longer.

Because of the frustrations with domestic politics and the dominance of entrenched elites, I came to believe that we could do more good by directly helping independent businesspeople and improving educational opportunities. They can still make a big difference.

So was it worth it? The thirty-eight trips, all the U.N. meetings, and the events to raise money for our partners' projects, the repeated frustrations, the false charges? To me it was, because of the way I keep score—a lot of people were helped and empowered to help themselves—and because I enjoy trying to make a difference in hard places. Measured by the real people who live and love and labor in them, Donald Trump was wrong; there are no "s__hole" countries. (It wouldn't be the last thing he'd be wrong about.) Yes, too many people are held back by government incapacity, corruption, and cronyism. But there are good people striving and dreaming everywhere. Demeaning their hopes and dreams is quick and easy. Actually helping them succeed is often long and hard work.

We live in an information ecosystem which prizes quick and easy. There are few quick and easy victories in Haiti. But two successive governments at least welcomed my efforts to help, even when I asked them to do things they couldn't or wouldn't do.

Of course, things can become so chaotic and lawless that it's all but impossible to make good things happen. Haiti is again spiraling out of control. The Best Western hotel is closed. The Iron Market burned and it had not been insured as promised. The Marriott is on life support with low occupancy. Sae-A chose to open new plants in Central America, where the governments are glad to have their jobs.

So many of Haiti's wounds are self-inflicted. Until it gets a government with more competence and the will to end corruption, business leadership more committed to growing the economy than to keeping control of one too small to give Haitians a shot at a good life, and now, outside support to maintain public safety and security operations, there will be too much suffering and too little progress.

As I finish this book, Kenya has agreed to lead a U.N.-backed mission to restore order and security. President Biden has pledged U.S. support for the effort, is encouraging other nations to contribute to it, and recently hosted the Kenyan president, William Ruto, at a state dinner Hillary and I attended. But to succeed, they'll need a new effort at development, free of corruption and full of accountability like the IHRC, if they want international support. Haiti's Transitional Presidential Council announced in late May that Dr. Garry Conille was its unanimous choice to serve as prime minister until new presidential elections are held. As I said above, Conille is a good, able, and honest man who can succeed if security is restored and the U.S. and other donors support him in establishing a transparent, honest government.

If you want an honest account of recent history and current events, read Jacqueline Charles's columns in the *Miami Herald.* She's a dedicated reporter who knows a lot about what's happening in Haiti and in the diaspora communities. Her Haitian-born mother advised her not to get involved because of all the problems, but she's drawn to it. I like being interviewed by her. She's asked me questions I can't answer and I have learned to say, "I don't know yet." She doesn't sugarcoat or take cheap shots, just goes for the story and disregards the storyline in her journalism. In 2022, she was honored by the National Association of Black Journalists as Journalist of the Year.

So, given all the built-in failure in Haiti, I still say "yes" to "was it worth it?" None of the problems negate the good that has been done—more jobs, more and better schools and healthcare, more empowered people. Again, your opinion on this depends on how you keep score and on your pain threshold for setbacks. Haiti remains full of good, talented, hardworking people, trying to live lives of dignity and decency, and leave their kids better off. Since there are challenges everywhere, you might choose to concentrate your efforts someplace else. But I'm glad I chose to work in Haiti because I became fascinated by its people, their gifts, and their potential on our honeymoon forty-five years ago and still am.

SEVEN

Hurricanes Hit Home, and Bush 41's Last Rodeo

In August and September of 2017, three big destructive hurricanes hit our part of the world in rapid succession. First, on August 25, Harvey made landfall in Texas, bringing massive flooding in the low-lying neighborhoods of Houston, with enough breadth to hurt a lot of other Texas communities and Louisiana, too. Then from September 6 to 10, Irma, a Category 5 hurricane, tore through the Caribbean, causing catastrophic damage to the unique ecology and the economy of Barbuda, devastating Saint Martin, and badly hurting St. John and St. Thomas in the U.S. Virgin Islands and several other Caribbean nations, before making its way north with enough power to hit Florida hard. Finally, on September 18, Maria, another Category 5 storm, hit Dominica first, then Guadeloupe, St. Croix, the third island in the U.S. Virgin Islands chain to be hit in two weeks, and Puerto Rico, causing the loss of power as the wind blasted power plants and crippled 90 percent of the electrical grid, including thousands of miles of transmission lines. Nearly 3,000 people were killed, with total economic losses estimated at $90 billion, and more than three quarters of the agricultural sector decimated.

On September 7, the five living former presidents established the One America Appeal to get more funds to Texas and Florida. Soon, we extended the effort to include the Virgin Islands and Puerto Rico. This was especially important because so many small donors had already given to help people in Texas and Florida, so the small-donor giving to Puerto Rico and the Virgin Islands was much less than it would have been had Maria hit first. It's hard to go to the well three times in a month.

We launched the appeal with a public service announcement that ran on the NFL opening game broadcast. All the funds would be placed in a special account in President George H. W. Bush's Library Foundation, with 100 percent of the donations going to already established funds in the states and territories. In addition to the NFL, the appeal was supported by the NBA, the PGA Tour, the Ad Council, Interstate Outdoor Advertising, and a number of big foundations, institutions, and wealthy individuals.

It was important to President Bush and his chief of staff, Jean Becker, for his team to take the lead on this. He and Barbara lived in Houston, and he had started his public career as a congressman there. Though he was confined to a wheelchair and was increasingly frail, he still wanted to serve. It was fitting that his last act of public service would help his neighbors.

The main fundraiser for the appeal was a concert on the Texas A&M campus, home of Bush 41's presidential library, on October 21, which was livestreamed on Facebook. "Deep from the Heart of Texas: One America Appeal" featured an all-star cast, most of them country artists, including Lee Greenwood, who sang his signature "I'm Proud to Be an American." But the night's surprise was Lady Gaga, who also was a big hit with the country-music-loving audience and made a large contribution to the fund.

George W. Bush ran the speakers program and told the rest of us—President Carter, President Obama, and me—to keep it short and sweet, and so we did. He didn't need to remind us that the focus of this night was on his father, who was sitting in the front row smiling and holding hands with Barbara. The concert and other efforts raised a total of $42,101,408 from more than

110,000 donors and we distributed it all by January 31, 2018. It was a fitting finale for George H. W. Bush. Soon both he and Barbara would be gone. But on this night, holding hands and looking up at their son as he kept the show on the road, they seemed at peace, grateful for their long run of life and love.

Texas and Florida were on their way to recovery. FEMA was doing its job. Houston, the hardest-hit city, had strong internal resources and capacity, and private donations were pouring in and being well spent. But for the Clinton Foundation and our CGI partners, the work in the Caribbean was just beginning. Meanwhile, I soon had the opportunity to apply what I'd learned about disaster recovery in the Caribbean. Two U.S. territories, Puerto Rico and the Virgin Islands, were hit hard, but the U.N. wasn't involved and the Trump administration didn't seem to care all that much, so the Clinton Foundation and our CGI partners tried to step into the gap.

The biggest challenge clearly would be Puerto Rico. I spent a lot of time on Puerto Rico when I was president, as did Hillary when she was a senator from New York, which has the mainland's largest Puerto Rican population. Most people think of Puerto Rico as San Juan and sandy beaches, but it's a big island with significant geographic and economic diversity and complicated politics.

As with Haiti, understanding Puerto Rico today requires a basic knowledge of its history. Puerto Rico is one of five remaining populated U.S. territories, along with the U.S. Virgin Islands and, in the Pacific, Guam, American Samoa, and the Northern Mariana Islands. Their citizens don't get to vote in presidential elections, and each territory has only one member in the House of Representatives, with limited voting rights.

Puerto Rico is by far the largest and most populous territory, with six times the landmass and nine times the population of the other four combined—its 3.3 million people outnumber the populations of nineteen American states. Today's politics began in 1950 when the largest party, the Popular Democratic

Party (PPD), asked that Congress make the island a sovereign commonwealth and Congress did so two years later. In 1967, a new party arose, the New Progressive Party (PNP), advocating Puerto Rico's annexation to the U.S. as a state. Since then the governor's office has shifted between the two parties, with the PNP winning eight elections and the PPD five.

There have been six votes on the status question since 1967, with commonwealth prevailing in the first two, in 1967 and 1993, the third in 1998 inconclusive, and statehood prevailing in the fourth in 2012, and the fifth, in 2017, but with a low 23 percent turnout. On November 3, 2020, there was a sixth vote and the first Yes or No referendum on whether Puerto Rico should pursue statehood. With a turnout of 54.5 percent of registered voters, those preferring statehood prevailed 52.5 percent to 47.5 percent. Clearly, the sentiment for statehood is growing.

Since 2000, no governor has been reelected. The bankruptcy of the island in 2017, the refusal of bondholders to grant any debt relief, and the iron grip of cronyism over the island's electric utility, which saddles Puerto Rico with rates much higher than anyone on the mainland pays, made governing difficult even before the storms. In the summer of 2019, Puerto Rico had another deep political crisis, with the resignation of the governor after two cabinet ministers were charged with corruption and a slew of emails were released in which the governor and other members of the political class ridiculed the Puerto Rican people and their problems. Then the governor's preferred successor resigned after the Supreme Court ruled he had not been properly confirmed by the parliament and the person next in the constitutional line of succession, a woman closely tied to the former governor, repeatedly said she didn't want the job, but then seemed determined to hang on to it. All this happened in a week!

So why should we help? First, the people need and deserve support. And Puerto Rico, with all its problems, still has great potential. It has a larger per capita income than most Caribbean nations, relatively high levels of education, takes care of its natural resources, and is full of hardworking people. There are gifted honest men and women in both parties willing to run for office and to work together to get things done. There's a good business base and able people working in healthcare, education, agriculture, ecotourism, green energy, and other fields. And Puerto Ricans in large numbers have served with distinction in the U.S. military. And, most important, they're American citizens, with skills that are a valuable economic asset to our country. So there's a lot of room for improvement.

The U.S. Virgin Islands was better positioned to recover quickly because the population is smaller, the government was functioning, and there were a lot of people both willing and able to help, led by Tom Secunda, a longtime partner of Michael Bloomberg. Tom and his wife, Cindy, have had a home on St. John for many years. They went to work immediately, and brought in people from the Bloomberg Foundation who provided valuable support.

In the immediate aftermath of the hurricanes, our foundation staff was in daily contact with first responders in the Caribbean, and we began coordinating with potential partners to meet requests for supplies and equipment. Our CGI partner Direct Relief quickly sent seventy-five tons of specifically requested medicine and medical equipment to Puerto Rico.

Soon, Prime Minister Roosevelt Skerrit of Dominica also asked me to help with their recovery. Dominica is a unique treasure. A tropical rainforest rising out of the sea, it's small enough that relatively modest investments can make a big difference, and is blessed with strong, able leadership. CGI members like Digicel, which serves Dominica, Team Rubicon, Direct Relief, International Medical Corps, and Airlink were on board. The Clinton Foundation began weekly teleconferences to help coordinate the transition from emergency relief to rebuilding and recovery work. On November 8, we launched Solar Saves Lives, a coalition of more than forty small innovative solar companies who pledged to work with our foundation, CORE, and others to deliver solar and solar storage technologies to regions in Puerto Rico and the Virgin Islands that needed them. I had seen how important solar lighting was in the camps in Haiti and knew this could help a lot.

During the rest of November, I met with Governor Kenneth Mapp of the U.S. Virgin Islands in New York, visited Puerto Rico at the invitation of the governor, Ricardo Rosselló, and the mayor of San Juan, Carmen Yulín Cruz, who were on opposite sides politically but seemed committed to get things done, and spoke at a U.N.-CARICOM donor conference in New York, which garnered more than $2 billion in pledges for the region.

In Puerto Rico, I toured a hurricane shelter in Canóvanas, a big marketplace in San Juan, and a large Direct Relief medical tent in San Juan. I met with Governor Rosselló, Puerto Rico's representative in the U.S. Congress, Jenniffer González-Colón, and the mayors of ten cities, listening to their litany of challenges.

Before I left, I took a walk in Old San Juan and ran into some utility workers trying to get the power back. They were from ConEd in New York and I had met some of them working in Chappaqua, where Hillary and I live, after we lost power lines in a winter storm. I mention this because America's utilities have had a longstanding agreement to help each other when big power outages occur outside their service areas. It was nice to see friendly faces reminding us that Puerto Rico is part of the U.S. and that this is one benefit they haven't lost.

On the last day of 2017, the One America Appeal stopped raising money and distributed all the funds, more than $42 million, including a few million to Juntos y Unidos for Puerto Rico, and to the Fund for the Virgin Islands. On January 31, 2018, our CGI Action Network on Post-Disaster Recovery got down to the business of building back better, with our first planning meeting in New York. More than one hundred people came.

In February, I went to the Virgin Islands to see the damage and some good projects on St. Thomas and St. John with Tom Secunda, Governor Mapp, and Congresswoman Stacey Plaskett, an impressive leader Hillary and I had gotten to know in Hillary's campaign. We visited the Regional Medical Center and brought $100,000 worth of supplies donated by our CGI partner Andrew MacCalla of Direct Relief. I noticed that the field of solar panels on the hospital grounds had been damaged and made a mental note to see if future installations could be made more hurricane-resistant.

After a brief stop on St. John with Tom and Cindy Secunda to view the damage to the Virgin Islands National Park and participate in a community meeting, I flew to Dominica. Prime Minister Skerrit had organized a full schedule, starting with a meeting with parliament, then with the prime minister and his cabinet to discuss both their most pressing challenges and their long-term goal to become the world's first climate-resilient nation. From there, we visited Pichelin, a town virtually destroyed by Maria, then drove an hour to visit a school so that I could talk to parents and children. Before I left, the prime minister and I announced a new partnership between the Clinton Climate Initiative and Dominica to develop an energy plan to achieve their climate resilience goal.

I left Dominica upbeat, believing they could make progress for two reasons. First, the country is small, only 290 square miles, with a unique ecological significance that's obvious when you see it. Second, it has capable leadership. When I first met him, the prime minister was only forty-five but he'd already been in office for fourteen years. He's a devout Christian who sees his mission in both moral and practical terms. In remarks to the U.N. he said he didn't have time to argue about climate change because he was too busy living it. Women are also playing a large role in the endeavor, led by Foreign Minister Francine Baron and Digicel's in-country CEO Nikima Royer. The British Commonwealth of Nations secretary-general Patricia Scotland is also a native of Dominica.

In April and August, we had the first two Action Network Meetings at the University of Miami with more than 350 members each that produced fifteen more commitments. After the meeting I went back to the Virgin Islands to announce a solar project with Bloomberg Philanthropies and CGI partner Expedia.

In late January 2019, Hillary and I went to Puerto Rico for the third Action Network meeting. This one drew six hundred people and garnered thirty-nine more commitments. Before the meeting started we visited small businesses who'd gotten support from the One America Appeal and an urban farm supported by chef José Andrés's World Central Kitchen, which provides fresh meals for people affected by natural disasters, conflicts, and poverty. The farmers, Franco and Natalia, were a knowledgeable, committed young couple who had used every bit of available land around their house to plant crops. They explained how there was a big market for homegrown food that would be both more nutritious and less expensive than the large amounts of food Puerto Ricans import every day.

Our second stop was a modern tree nursery where Para la Naturaleza is growing native trees to help reforest the island, replacing trees lost both to Maria and to earlier deforestation. The most fun we had was watching Lin-Manuel Miranda and a stellar cast perform *Hamilton*. Lin-Manuel and his father, Luis, are playing a big role in helping Puerto Rico recover. Luis and his wife, Luz, are longtime friends and supporters of Hillary's, and being with them to watch their son bring the crowd joy was a welcome respite from Puerto Rico's ongoing struggles. The next day we had dinner with Lin-Manuel and Luis, along with George Clooney and José Andrés. George, Lin-Manuel, and Nespresso had begun an effort to help local coffee growers recover from the loss of 80 percent of the island's coffee trees. The good news? Coffee yields returned to pre-hurricane levels in 2022.

Our next network meeting held in early June attracted more than four hundred people to the University of the Virgin Islands on St. Thomas. The 29 new commitments made there brought our total to 86, and the total number of participating organizations to 775. I got to see the work of Love City Strong, founded by Kenny Chesney. It's rebuilding houses on St. John and prepositioning materials in warehouses to minimize the damage and speed rebuilding after the next storm. And I visited an Early Head Start classroom run by Lutheran Social Services in St. Croix, and met with AmeriCorps members working throughout Puerto Rico. Both Early Head Start and AmeriCorps were started with Hillary's enthusiastic support when I was president.

As I write it's too soon to say whether the current upheaval in Puerto Rico will lead to more people shying away from a mess they think is unfixable, or to a new wave of energy for reform and better tomorrows. Regardless, good things are happening there, and the Virgin Islands is moving in the right direction. In Dominica, the forests are so thick that many trees weren't completely uprooted when the powerful winds blew them down. Amazingly, they are rising again on their own. Maybe it's an omen.

EIGHT

Family Life Goes On

Hillary and I were busy and happy at work, but even as we changed our day jobs, we remained devoted to our family as Chelsea began her own career, married, and had children of her own. In 2001, we went to California for Chelsea's graduation from Stanford. Hillary and I had loved our visits to Palo Alto, meeting Chelsea's friends and their families and a couple of her favorite professors. We also spent time with Steve and Laurene Jobs, who, during Chelsea's Stanford years, had been kind enough to let us use a house they had in the woods a few miles out of town so that we could have some private time when we visited her. It was a wonderful gift, as was his newest product, an iPod. I made heavy use of it for years. I loved the iPod because I could cluster my music. I had six versions of "My Funny Valentine" and eight versions of "Summertime." It's fascinating to see how gifted artists interpret great music so differently.

There's an old saying that seeing things differently makes politics and horse races. The challenge comes when there are changes in the rules, or one set of rules for the in-crowd and another for everyone else, or no rules at all. Navigating big challenges is also part of watching your children make their way into adulthood and start their own careers.

Chelsea was able to take a semester off during her senior year to help Hillary in her New York Senate campaign and fill in for her at the White House, including going with me on foreign trips. She did a good job in both roles, still graduated on time, and it was great having her with me those last few months.

In late January, after our White House years came to an end, almost three weeks after we watched Hillary being sworn in as New York's junior senator, Chelsea went back to Stanford to finish up. She only had to take one required course, but if she wanted to graduate with highest honors, she also had to write a thesis, and had just three or four months to do it. Most of her classmates had been working on theirs much longer. But she made the deadline, pulling a lot of all-nighters in the library, laying her head down on her worktable to get a little sleep.

The thesis was on the Irish peace process and my role in it: *A Convergence of History, Politics, and Possibility: The Story of How and Why an American President Intervened in Northern Ireland.* She wrote that I'd been interested in the Irish Troubles since 1969 when they broke out while I was studying at Oxford. But I made a big commitment to trying to solve the problem during the 1992 primary campaign in New York, which has our country's largest Irish American population, including many who were deeply involved in Irish issues. I needed their support to win New York and fend off the last serious chance to derail my nomination. As for my commitment to Ireland and peace, Chelsea didn't gild the lily; she wrote that it was rooted in both personal conviction *and* the hope of political gain. Thankfully, she added that the more I got into it, the more committed I became. "Dad, you took some real risks, had a good plan, and forged real relationships. You did a good job."

I just reread it. I know I'm biased, but it's well researched, well written, and balanced. After twenty years, it's aged well, still interesting and informative. Her advisor, the eminent historian Jack Rakove, must have agreed. She graduated with highest honors.

The graduation ceremony on the Stanford football field was on a perfect sunny day. In true Stanford tradition, most of her class didn't march straight to their seats, but jumped around, did somersaults, handstands, and other stunts, entertaining the families and friends in the stands. The ceremony was brief, with a speech from Carly Fiorina, a Stanford grad who had become CEO of Hewlett-Packard. Hillary and I were so proud of our daughter, who had gone far from home, made lifelong friends, learned a lot, and was eager for the next chapter of her life.

Chelsea had told us for years that she wanted to go to Oxford after she finished at Stanford. One night she called and said she had good news and news I might not like. She said Stanford had asked if she wanted to attend a meeting about a possible Rhodes Scholarship. She told them she was honored but thought she shouldn't be considered.

I asked her why. "Don't you want to go to Oxford anymore?"

"Yes, I do. Can you afford to send me?"

I said, "Yes, I'll be able to by the time you enroll."

"Dad, that's how I'd like to go. Winning a Rhodes Scholarship would be a great honor, but if I won, it would be because of the life I've already had, the places I've been, and the people I've met. It wouldn't change my life. The scholarship should go to a young person like you were, someone whose life it will change."

I had never been more proud of her. Chelsea enrolled as a Master's candidate in the fall of 2001, accepted by University College, Oxford, thirty-three years after I became a student there. In November 2002, in her second year, Hillary and I flew to England to celebrate Thanksgiving with her. She and her roommate, Jen Lee, a Harvard graduate and Juilliard-trained cellist, had moved into a small house in North Oxford for their final year and invited us to share a meal with more than twenty of their fellow students, including Americans who couldn't go home and British and other students who'd never celebrated the holiday.

We liked our daughter's eclectic collection of friends, including two U.S. Army officers soon to go on active duty, who invited me to join in a game of touch football the afternoon before dinner. One of them, Wes Moore, won the Maryland governor's race in 2022 and is one of our most promising young political leaders. The other, Seth Bodnar, is now the president of the University of Montana. A typical rainy Oxford fall morning had left the playing field slippery and muddy, but they were used to it. The conditions didn't hamper their enthusiasm or their efforts. I still had a pretty good throwing arm back then but the other team cut me no slack. I left the field covered in mud and a few bruises, glad to have survived.

The dinner was a great success, as we devoured the traditional Thanksgiving meal, tightly packed around tables in two small rooms, all the while carrying on vigorous conversations. I remembered how intimidated I was when I was a student at Oxford more than thirty years earlier whenever I was invited to tea at a women's college. Sitting through their conversations was like being the ballboy at a fast-paced tennis match as the verbal serves and volleys flew across the net. It was hard to keep up and not get hit. The women and the men were impressive this night, too, so I tried to draw them out and speak only to answer the questions they asked. Chelsea has had good judgment and good fortune in her friends, from her early years to today. I've always enjoyed spending time with and learning from them.

After Chelsea finished at Oxford, we moved Thanksgiving to our home in Chappaqua, where Chelsea began inviting longtime friends from New York and England to join us. They soon brought their spouses, significant others, and visiting parents. Before long, there were kids, too. We couldn't do it at all in 2020 because of Covid, had only a small gathering in 2021, but in 2019, we had forty-three people. About that many came to the restart in 2022.

Since that first celebration, everyone has been invited to say what he or she was grateful for. Some came just after or still in the midst of steep personal or professional challenges. Yet everybody always found something to be grateful for. In our family, the toughest task fell to Hillary after the 2016 election. She found her voice when most of us, me included, were still searching for ours.

In 2003, Chelsea finished her two-year stint at Oxford by completing the thesis required for her Master's in International

Relations on the Global Fund to Fight AIDS, TB, and Malaria—how it started in 2001, what it was supposed to do, and where it fit into the world's response to big global health challenges. She invited me back to Oxford to watch the last step toward getting her degree: a session in which she would answer questions about her thesis posed by academics and others in the room. She answered all the questions well, and afterward we spent some time with her principal advisor, Dr. Ngaire Woods, an impressive New Zealander who'd first come to Oxford as a Rhodes Scholar. She clearly liked Chelsea, believed in her promise, and would soon be encouraging her to get her doctorate.

In May 2014, Hillary and I went back to Oxford for the formal ceremony awarding Chelsea her doctorate of philosophy in International Relations, held in the university's old Sheldonian Theatre. She earned it with a thesis analyzing the impact of the first ten years of the Global Fund. It became part of a book she wrote in 2017, *Governing Global Health: Who Runs the World and Why?*, with her Oxford friend Devi Sridhar, a Florida native who is now chair of global public health at the University of Edinburgh, Scotland.

The eleven years between her two Oxford degrees were eventful for Chelsea personally and professionally. She worked at McKinsey and Company for three years, gaining experience in a wide variety of businesses. After McKinsey, she worked at Avenue Capital, analyzing possible investments in chemical companies, renewable energy, and new technologies. Then she went on to New York University, helping to set up its international programs and cochairing Of Many, a student multifaith group led by an American rabbi and an imam from Indonesia. She has been deeply committed to interfaith work for a long time. She read the Quran from start to finish in high school. I was always proud of her for her accomplishments and grateful and a little awestruck by the way she threw herself into things and kept going in the face of all the negative press and endless innuendo about our family. She determined early on not to let the daily news define her, to learn something from every good and bad thing that happened, and maintain her sense of poise, grace, and dignity.

After helping her mother in the 2008 campaign, she got a Master's in Public Health from Columbia, then she taught for a decade at the Mailman School of Public Health there. Over the last thirteen years, Chelsea has served as vice chair of the Clinton Foundation and the Clinton Health Access Initiative, and led several other important initiatives, all while teaching her course in public health in New York, taking care of her family, keeping up with friends working in innovative companies, and doing other things important to her, including writing a series of children's books and running in two New York City Marathons. She's been invaluable to our foundation work in more ways than I can count. A few years ago, I told her, "You know, for a short period in high school you thought you knew more than your parents did about everything. Alas, it's finally true."

Our biggest Chelsea day was July 31, 2010, when she married Marc Mezvinsky. She and Marc had been friends since they met at Renaissance Weekend in South Carolina when she was thirteen and he was sixteen. They stayed in constant touch, even after Marc later enrolled at Stanford. When Chelsea went there, too, their friendship thrived but they didn't date until 2005. How that morphed into marriage is a story for them to tell.

They had an interfaith wedding, attended by four hundred family and friends at the famous Astor Courts estate on the Hudson River near Rhinebeck, New York, a historic town where the oldest inn had hosted George Washington and other revolutionary leaders.

As I walked her down the aisle, I was nervous and choked up, reliving all the years that led to this day. I was afraid I'd lose it before the handoff, but it was her special day and I managed to do my part. She and Marc exchanged vows under a chuppah in a moving ceremony officiated by Rabbi James Ponet and Reverend Bill Shillady, a Methodist minister who is a close friend of ours. Chelsea, her mother, her grandmother, and her bridesmaids all looked beautiful. Marc's mother, father, and his ten brothers and sisters were there, all of them beaming. Afterward, we had a dinner full of toasts and dancing. I was so glad Hillary's mother, Dorothy, at ninety-one, had lived to see this day. Chelsea adored her, as did many of her young friends. I did, too. She had survived a rough childhood to become a wise, tenderhearted but tough-minded woman. I was so glad Hillary and Chelsea had her as a confidante for so long.

Just a little over a year later, Dorothy died after falling and hitting her head while climbing the stairs at our home. There's a small elevator that Hillary kept in working order for her, but she wouldn't use it, saying she had to keep moving. Hillary was devastated; her mother had been a rock. And Chelsea had lost her last grandparent, the one who had played by far the largest role in her life (my mother and Hillary's dad died when she was twelve and thirteen).

When we had a memorial service for Dorothy in the backyard of our home for family and friends, what struck me most were the wonderful things several of Chelsea's friends said about her. Dorothy Howell Rodham had been abandoned, cold-shouldered, and ignored by two generations of her family. She spent her life making sure her kids, grandchildren, and their friends knew she cared about them. And she kept growing. She forced herself to watch an hour of Fox News every day, saying, "Nobody's wrong all the time, and when they are, I want to have an answer." The day she died, she was reading Oliver Sacks's latest book. Hillary and I read the book in her honor, but it's still in the room where she was reading it, with the bookmark where she left it.

Hillary would suffer two more losses in the next decade. Her brothers Tony and Hugh have had lives full of adventures and misadventures. Hugh served as a Peace Corps volunteer in Colombia, and the tales he told about it would have made a great Gabriel García Márquez novella. In 1974, they both came to Arkansas to campaign for me when I ran for Congress. One night, four guys picked a fight with them over politics in a local bar and the police were called to pick the four tough guys up off the floor. They took two to the hospital and let Hugh and Tony go when the whole bar said they didn't start the fight. When they were in Arkansas, Hugh got a law degree and a doctorate in education. Tony went back to Chicago to work, and Hugh became one of the public defenders in Janet Reno's successful drug court in Florida, which kept first offenders out of prison. Tony soon joined him.

Tony wound up in Washington, and we hosted his 1994 wedding to Nicole Boxer at the White House, which produced our nephew Zach. Their marriage ended in 2001. Four years later, Tony married Megan Madden, a champion rugby player. They had two children, Fiona and Simon. They're in high school now, both good students, good athletes, and good people. After graduating from USC, Zach became a gifted writer, video producer, and content creator who now works for the Democratic National Committee. We've loved watching them grow up, going to their events, and cheering them on.

In 2012, at fifty-six, Tony's clogged arteries required bypass surgery. Then he had prostate surgery, which was successful, followed by hip surgery, which had to be redone. They all took a toll. In early spring 2019, he contracted a severe respiratory disorder, was hospitalized, and put on a ventilator and a cardio ECMO machine that cleaned and oxygenated his blood. His medical staff had all but given up hope he would recover, but miraculously he did, and was breathing normally after almost three months on the machine.

Then, on his way out the hospital door, he had a final checkup that revealed cancerous lesions in his liver. He couldn't mount another comeback, but he didn't waste energy complaining. Instead, he made the most of his remaining time, going to his kids' games and enjoying his family and friends. Tony died on June 7, 2019, facing the end with courage and grace, and a week later, in a local park on a beautiful sunny June day, his wife Megan, his three children, his brother Hugh, big sister Hillary and I, along with a lot of friends who still miss him gave him a loving send-off.

Sometimes family is more than blood. A month after Tony died, Hillary lost her best friend from childhood, Betsy Ebeling, after a ten-year bout with cancer. Betsy was the sister she never had. We often visited with her and her music-loving husband, Tom, as our kids were growing up. She cast the Illinois delegation's vote for Hillary at the 2016 Democratic convention and gave Hillary a wonderful parting gift, introducing us to the famed Canadian mystery writer Louise Penny. We had a wonderful trip with Betsy and Tom to Louise's home in eastern Quebec in 2017. We stayed in Hovey Manoir, the site of one of her murder mysteries, visited four more of them, and met friends who were models for her characters. We liked it so much we all went back three more times, and in the process became real friends with Louise, a terrific writer with endless imagination.

Betsy would have loved her own memorial service: a joyous, laughter-filled celebration of a fine woman, family matriarch, and gifted public servant, much loved and admired, brave and upbeat to the end. Hillary spoke tenderly about what a unique and wonderful woman Betsy was, saying she would miss her in irreplaceable ways. She still does.

Hillary and I both try to keep our family flames burning. Hugh has been semiretired for several years in Coral Gables while his Cuban American wife, Maria, keeps up her busy law practice. He was an early litigant in the tobacco cases, representing injured clients in the long-running case, which ended with most of the money going to state governments and their lawyers but earned him more than enough to retire, make profitable investments, and play golf with his friends. Then he developed complicated painful back problems, but he kept going, including refurbishing and improving the tiny house on Lake Winola in rural Pennsylvania, where he, Tony, and Hillary spent many summer days as kids. It's just south of Scranton, home of the Rodham clan. The little house is more than a hundred years old, with pictures and local landscape art that are as old or older.

In May 2023, Hillary and I went with Hugh and Maria back to the place I had first seen more than forty years ago, then without a bath or a shower, where the kids got clean by standing outside below the porch while a grown-up dumped a washtub of water on their heads. When you have more yesterdays than tomorrows, living in the present and for the future requires nurturing good memories and making peace with the less happy ones. But forgetting some things is also important. A couple of years ago, I read Scott Small's brilliant short book, *Forgetting: The Benefits of Not Remembering*, which explains why as we age, we need to free space in our minds to make better decisions. Like many older people, I forget where I put things I need and still remember things clearly that I need to let go of. But I'm working on it.

My family, besides Hillary, Chelsea, Marc, and my grandchildren, is my brother, Roger, and his son, Tyler, plus a raft of cousins in Arkansas and a few in Texas who've been a big part of my life for a long time. Roger's had a tough life, struggling with substance use disorder for decades, in and out of rehab with a brief stint in federal prison that saved his life. Thirty years ago, he moved to California and put together a house band that played for the audience during the filming of Harry and Linda Bloodworth-Thomason's TV shows *Designing Women*, *Evening Shade*, and *Hearts Afire*. Afterward, he worked intermittently, but he could never maintain sobriety. He kept using through his lost marriage, until he almost died on his birthday in 2017. He finally decided he wanted to live, went back to rehab, and stuck with it. As I write this, he's been sober for seven years. If you ask him, he can tell you the exact number of days.

In 2022, Roger moved back to Arkansas and bought some land outside Hot Springs, where he was born and raised. The five-acre lot in the woods has a big log cabin he's almost finished turning into a home, another log building he's turned into a guest/rental home, and about fifty yards away, a smaller building where he makes the healthy vitamin soap he's sold for a few years, mostly at farmers' markets and online. Now that he can produce sufficient quantities, he hopes to market it to hotels and other big buyers.

I think he's finally settled, grateful to be able to support himself, live in a place he loves, see his old friends, and know that the one thing he always tried to do right—to be a good father—resulted in Tyler growing into a fine man who loves his dad and his mother. I'm very proud of him and believe he will live out his life free to put his good heart and strong body to work on things beyond survival.

I'm proud of Tyler, too. After finishing high school and college at Loyola Marymount University in California, he moved to New York, got a job, and finished two years of acting classes at the Actors Studio. When Covid closed theaters and reduced TV and movie opportunities, he got another job managing the East Coast properties of a successful lawyer and continued to explore acting. He's made small films shown at movie festivals, and recently was nominated for best actor at one of them. We talk often, text more, and enjoy meals in New York and his visits to Chappaqua, where he plays with our grandchildren, which they all love.

We all have victories and setbacks in our personal lives and within our families, and we all experience good times and grief. Thankfully, for me there have been far more of the former than the latter.

PART II

Fighting Disease and Poverty Around the World and at Home

NINE

The Clinton Foundation and the Creation of CHAI

The early work I did as a former president was usually the result of requests from others. I incorporated the Clinton Foundation to take the initiative in trying to meet our challenges faster, better, and at a lower cost, particularly those in which we could impact the most lives. This section contains stories of the people doing that work, the dedicated donors who helped them, and the people whose lives they saved or improved.

From 2002 on, I invested more and more time in the work of the foundation, starting with efforts to be helpful to my neighbors, particularly small businesspeople, in Harlem. Our first foundation initiative there helped a wide variety of small businesses with consulting and equipment, including a hat store, a card store, a pharmacy, a dentist office, an insurance agency, a soul food restaurant, a video store, a plumbing operation, and two new florists. At its peak the initiative had more than one hundred experts helping small Harlem businesses.

But I also wanted to do more on the AIDS crisis. I was Arkansas's governor in 1984 when Ruth Coker Burks, whom I'd known since she was a kid and who would come to be known as the "Cemetery Angel," went to a local hospital to visit a friend and saw an AIDS patient obviously near death, alone. She went into his room and sat on his bed. He said he wanted to see his mother. The duty nurse told Ruth that his mother wasn't coming, that nobody came to see "them." She went back to his bedside and held his hand until he died. When she arranged for his burial, she learned that only one local funeral home would take him and then only for cremation. So she paid for that and buried his ashes in her little family cemetery west of town.

When word got around, other people with AIDS started coming to her, a white, straight, religious working mother revolted by the stigma, rejection, and fear being visited on her fellow human beings. Over the next decade, often with her daughter in tow, Ruth buried thirty-nine more people in her family cemetery, and consoled and supported hundreds of others. She wrote about it in her moving book, *All the Young Men*, a powerful reminder of what it was like during the early days of AIDS in the U.S. Hillary and I had lost close friends to AIDS in the 1980s. In the 1992 campaign, when I was confronted by AIDS activists in New York, I promised to work hard to fight stigma, increase care, and accelerate the search for effective treatment.

My 1992 Democratic convention featured the landmark speeches by AIDS activists Elizabeth Glaser and Bob Hattoy, both of whom were tireless advocates for more aggressive policies until AIDS claimed their lives, Elizabeth in 1994, Bob in 2007.

Another person AIDS brought into our orbit in the 1992 campaign was Magic Johnson, who endorsed me because he was determined to live a full life with AIDS and wanted others to have the same chance. It was the beginning of a lifelong friendship with Hillary and me, including his support in both her presidential campaigns.

I also met Ricky Ray and his family. He and his brother were hemophiliacs who contracted AIDS through blood transfusions. They were shunned at school. When I was elected, I called Ricky and invited him to my inauguration. Sadly, he died a few weeks before I was sworn in, but his family came in his honor and for eight years I kept a photo of Ricky in the hallway to my private study and dining room next to the Oval Office.

When I was president, we doubled funding for AIDS care

in the United States and increased support for the research and development funds that hastened the availability of the first antiretroviral AIDS medications, or ARVs, which by the mid-nineties turned the virus from a death sentence into a chronic disease. By early 1996, we had cut the FDA approval process from thirty-three months to just under a year, and the latest AIDS drug was approved in just forty-two days.

The story in the developing world was very different. We had tripled overseas funding and been active in all the groundwork to establish the Global Fund to Fight AIDS, Tuberculosis, and Malaria, which was formally launched just after I left office, but it wasn't nearly enough. We needed more money, less stigma, and an effective pushback against the organized interests and widespread myths that stood in the way of saving lives and slowing the epidemic.

The argument often advanced by those opposed to getting ARVs to people in poor countries was that poor sick people wouldn't figure out how to take three separate pills every day, even if their lives depended on it. Not true. In 2001, I visited the neighborhood AIDS clinic near my office in Harlem, where low-income patients took their medicine more than 90 percent of the time. Many lives were being saved, but it cost $10,000 a year, covered by Medicaid for the poor in the United States, but still far beyond the means of citizens or governments in developing countries. India was producing generic ARVs at a cost of $500 per person a year, but most low-income countries still couldn't afford anywhere near enough of them to stem the tide.

Also, the big drug companies were lobbying hard against the U.S. and other nations funding the generic versions of ARVs and allowing them to be sold outside the countries where they were produced, claiming that the countries with the largest numbers of people with AIDS lacked the trained staff and laboratory equipment to administer them effectively and to provide the necessary follow-up; that corrupt governments would sell the drugs back into the U.S. and other rich countries, undercutting the protection their patents gave for the large investments necessary to develop the medicines; and that generic drugs were much less effective than their original, patented products.

Even some people in the public health community seemed to agree that getting ARVs to people in poor countries where the epidemic was raging was a fool's errand. They thought the effort would fail because you can't just give people pills; you have to treat them, monitor their compliance, and have the ability to stay in touch and do follow-ups. A lot of experienced and caring people thought it couldn't be done.

Brazil had proven them wrong. Defying Big Pharma pressure, their domestic drug production facilities had begun to produce ARVs and successfully distribute them, even to remote tribes deep in the Amazon rainforest, with a remarkable coalition that included the government, the Catholic Church, tribal leaders, and other volunteers. About 180,000 people were receiving the medicine in color-coded cartons to remind them that they had to take three pills a day, every day. Soon they produced a study showing it was cheaper to keep people alive than to let them die in a local clinic or hospital, then have to bury them. Within three years, the death rate had been cut in half and hospitalizations of AIDS patients decreased 80 percent. But outside Brazil, fewer than 100,000 people in low-income countries were receiving medication.

The naysayers were also proved wrong in the Caribbean, where Haiti had the highest infection rate. Dr. Paul Farmer, whose clinic in the Central Highlands had gotten enough medicine to save a few hundred lives, spoke out forcefully against the inhumanity of providing treatment solely in the richest nations. So did Dr. Bill Pape, who had founded the world's first AIDS clinic in Port-au-Prince in 1982.

Soon after I left office, Sandy Thurman, who had led our White House AIDS office and was still active from her home base in Atlanta, asked me to join Nelson Mandela in cochairing the International AIDS Trust, a group of prominent citizens, including several former national leaders, who agreed to urge wealthy nations to devote much more money to fighting AIDS in poor countries by providing education, prevention, *and* treatment. I agreed to do it, hoping Mandela and I could raise more money and increase acceptance of the idea that treatment should expand beyond countries with good health systems and the money to pay for the medicine.

Three million people were dying every year. At least six million people were already so sick they needed medicine to survive. And an estimated thirty million people were already infected, most of whom weren't yet sick enough to know it. We had to do more. When Mandela and I were asked to speak to the biannual International AIDS Summit in Barcelona, Spain, in 2002, I had already given speeches to the National AIDS Trust in London and to the African AIDS Summit in Abuja, Nigeria, where I met Muammar Gaddafi for the first and only time.

Gaddafi was in an expansive mood and suggested we should arrange a marriage between his son and Chelsea and "launch a dynasty." Without laughing I explained that in our culture the decision was my daughter's, not mine, but that I would relay his proposal as soon as I got home. When I did, Chelsea, also straight-faced, said, "Dad, I think I'll pass."

In Barcelona, Mandela and I agreed to focus on the moral imperative of getting the ARVs to the people who needed them most. He said he would do all he could, especially in South Africa, where his chosen successor, Thabo Mbeki, seemed to be dealing with the world's largest AIDS population with a combination of denial and resentment. I liked Mbeki and hoped I could change his mind.

Regardless, Mandela said, for the sake of Africa and countries around the world without the resources and capacity to deal with the epidemic already well underway, I had to do more now while I still knew leaders personally and had their confidence and trust. That's exactly what I wanted to do. Remember, the Global Fund had just been established and not funded, and President Bush's PEPFAR program, the President's Emergency Plan for AIDS Relief, was not yet up and running.

On July 12, 2002, when Mandela and I walked on the stage to give the closing remarks to the biannual International AIDS Summit, 10,000 activists, health officials, and scientists cheered, glad to have our support, and wondering what we would say. I went first, saying we needed less stigma and denial, much more prevention and treatment. Now that lifesaving ARVs were available and being produced in India and a few other countries, we needed a lot more money and lower prices. I acknowledged my own error in opposing needle exchange programs in the U.S. and, until near the end of my term, the sale of generic ARVs outside the countries that produced them. I urged the big pharmaceutical companies to reduce prices to lower-income countries and said if they didn't, the affected nations should be able to get generic drugs from India and other producers with help from wealthy countries donating at least $10 billion to the new Global Fund.

Then I introduced Mandela, eighty-four and using a cane, but still full of passion. He spoke about a young HIV-positive woman from a Pacific island nation who was in the audience, saying that he had been so moved by her presentation at an AIDS meeting that he bought her the medicine to stay alive. Then he had her stand, living proof that everyone with HIV/AIDS deserved treatment "no matter where they live or whether they can afford to pay." This all sounds so obvious today. Then it was a radical departure from the consensus in wealthy nations that treatment was both unaffordable and undeliverable. Now that we knew it wasn't true, we had to deliver.

After our speeches, Denzil Douglas, prime minister of St. Kitts and Nevis, came up to me and said we were on the right track. He was a doctor and head of the eastern Caribbean countries' AIDS efforts, an important responsibility since the Caribbean had the second-fastest-growing AIDS rate after Africa. Denzil said, "We don't have a denial problem or a stigma problem. We have a money problem and an organization problem." I had a lot of respect for Douglas, so I asked, "Denzil, what do you want me to do about it?" He answered, "I want you to fix it." I immediately said, "Okay." I wasn't sure how to start, but it seemed to me that, rather than just asking for money for a fund with as many questions as answers, we should get to work in nations creating lifesaving operations worth investing in.

Ira Magaziner was also at the conference. When I was in the

White House, he had worked with Hillary on healthcare reform in my first term and led our effort to jump-start e-commerce in the second. We had already discussed my desire to do something on AIDS and he'd written me two memos suggesting how to do it, so I encouraged him to come to Barcelona. He did and had his own discussions with African and Caribbean leaders who were there. After we got back, Ira sent me a letter saying that I could have an impact in countries coping with AIDS—not just in Africa and the Caribbean but in other places where the AIDS problem was worsening rapidly, including Russia and Eastern Europe, China, India, and other countries in Asia—by raising money from nations, foundations, and individual donors to fund and set up effective treatment programs.

Ira said he would be willing to organize and lead our efforts for a while without pay to see what we could do. He had built a successful corporate consulting business so he had the knowledge, experience, and means to take on the challenge. I was glad he agreed to do it because I couldn't do it full-time with my other obligations to pay my debts, finish building my library and presidential center in Arkansas, and get the rest of the foundation going in New York.

We decided to work first on trying to get more ARVs at lower prices to countries that wanted us to help. I would ask a few donor nations to allocate $100 million over five years to help pay for medicines and strengthen programs in countries they would choose, and Ira would go to the Caribbean and to Africa to see who was most eager and able to ramp up their efforts.

Just a few days after we got back from Barcelona, Ira called to say that, in the Bahamas, a dedicated group led by Dr. Perry Gomez and Mrs. Rosa Mae Bain had been providing AIDS care since the early 1980s, and had raised private funds to put a couple of hundred people on ARVs. But they were paying up to $3,500 a year for generic drugs the Indian manufacturers priced at $500. The drugs they ordered were going through two middlemen who were charging exorbitant markups—that's how distorted and disorganized the market was.

As president, I had established good relations between the United States and India for the first time in thirty years and I knew the companies were pleased that Mandela and I were pushing their products. I was confident we could fix this. I asked Ira to try to convince the companies to ship directly to the Bahamas at $500 plus freight costs, which meant that with current spending they could greatly increase the number of people on ARVs, then fewer than two hundred. He did and they agreed.

I knew this would be our easiest win, but it set a pattern. I would raise money and open doors, and Ira would work with governments to set up operations and systems to get the best possible prices in the most efficient, least costly way. We agreed that he would hire good people, make sure they understood the mission, and let them do their jobs.

Ira's first trip to Africa resulted in agreements with Rwanda, Tanzania, and Mozambique, soon followed by Lesotho and South Africa. Our first donors were Ireland and Canada, whose prime ministers, Bertie Ahern and Jean Chrétien, were good friends of mine. I had worked closely with Bertie Ahern on the peace process in Northern Ireland, and with Jean Chrétien on ending ethnic cleansing in Bosnia and Kosovo, restoring democracy to Haiti, expanding NATO, and supporting a unified Canada in the run-up to the separatist referendum in Quebec. Soon Norway, Sweden, France, Australia, and the U.K. also had made generous commitments, as had other nations in smaller but much needed amounts.

From the start, all the donor governments' money went directly to the AIDS-affected governments to fund medicines, the necessary testing and equipment for it, and treatment clinics. What was then called the Clinton HIV/AIDS Initiative (now CHAI, the Clinton Health Access Initiative, a name we adopted as we took on more health challenges and one I'll use from now on) drew up the contracts, with strict accountability, transparency, and anticorruption requirements that we monitored. But I wanted the governments to handle the money, and in so doing to increase their capacity for honest, competent governance in healthcare and other areas.

We also depended on generous individuals, mostly from the

United States, Canada, the U.K., and in the Bahamas local businesspeople, to give us the money to operate. Our first major contributor to the Caribbean effort was a Chicago media executive, Fred Eychaner. He had been a supporter and a friend during my years in the White House, and he was enthusiastic in embracing this effort. In those first few years, we also depended heavily on volunteers. Within two years, we had forty full-time staff and more than one hundred volunteers in twenty countries, including the African nations I mentioned with more than 30 percent of the continent's AIDS population; thirteen Caribbean nations, with more than 45 percent of the region's cases; and India and China, with 90 percent of Asia's people with AIDS.

In 2003, we made our first major breakthrough in generic drug prices when the major Indian producers Cipla, Ranbaxy, and Matrix, and a South African company, Aspen, agreed to drop the sale price on all contracts from $600 to $169. As their volume grew, they reduced the price more, to $140, and eventually to $90, about 37 cents a day. The Indian companies welcomed our efforts to help them change their business model and lower their prices, not just by increasing their sales dramatically, but also by improving their production and delivery processes.

When we started working with the generic producers, the companies were selling the drugs, even at $500 per person per year, the same way an independent jewelry store operates: it was a low-volume, high-margin, uncertain payment business. Remember, at the time, in developing nations, there were fewer than 100,000 people outside Brazil—only 50,000 in sub-Saharan Africa—getting the ARVs. After South Africa, India had the largest AIDS population at 4.6 million and the Indian companies had already lowered the price there to about $365 per person, still too high for a nation with a per capita income of $500 per year. At the beginning, there were only a few international, government, or foundation funding sources led by the World Bank and the Bill & Melinda Gates Foundation, providing $95 million a year, bringing total spending in developing countries to about $24 per year per person infected. The massive funding from the Global Fund, President Bush's PEPFAR program, UNITAID, and others was yet to come.

As donor governments made the commitments, CHAI worked with drug manufacturers and the governments in Africa and the Caribbean to build a big supermarket-chain business model: a huge-volume, low-margin, certain and prompt payment business. By early 2004, we also had agreements reflecting that approach with the major European and U.S. companies providing the diagnostic testing and equipment essential to the effective administration and monitoring of the medicine. We also made agreements that enabled thirty more countries where we had no staff to buy medicines and tests based on our low-cost contracts. We never asked producers to lose money—that would have been unsustainable—but to make money in a way that would save the maximum number of lives, using the business model which CHAI would apply, over and over, in other settings and with other health challenges, to save lives by making the building blocks of survival available to more people more quickly at lower cost.

As of this writing, after more than twenty years, CHAI has grown into an amazing organization with a proud legacy. Today there are more than 1,000 people working all over the world. The central office started and remains in Massachusetts, but the senior management comes from around the world. Eighty countries buy their ARVs off contracts negotiated by CHAI, covering more than 28 million people, more than two thirds of the adults on treatment. More than 900,000 children are being kept alive by CHAI-negotiated ARVs, more than 80 percent of the children in the world on treatment. Along with HIV/AIDS, CHAI has taken on malaria, tuberculosis, and early childhood diarrhea; helped Dr. Paul Farmer and Partners in Health build a network of hospitals, including a cancer center in Rwanda, and organized two dozen partners to retrain and improve the healthcare workforce there; built hundreds of clinics in Ethiopia; reduced the threat of hepatitis C; improved women's reproductive health; and so much more, including brave service in Liberia during the Ebola crisis and providing valuable service to the World Health Organization and fifteen countries in Africa and Asia from the early days of the Covid pandemic.

All told, CHAI has offices in 37 countries, works with governments on specific programs in 39 more, and has negotiated price reductions for medicines, diagnostics, vaccines, and other lifesaving devices, products, and services now available in more than 125 countries. How this all happened is enough to fill a book, but I think you'll get a feel for it in these accounts of people serving and people saved.

TEN

The Activists, the Champions, and Bush 43's Fair Deal

In late 2003, I went to China to speak at its first public meeting on AIDS, a conference at Tsinghua University in Beijing. By then we had been working for nearly a year alongside our partner Dr. Eric Goosby and his NGO, the Pangaea Global AIDS Foundation, to develop treatment guidelines for the Chinese Ministry of Health. I had good meetings with former president Jiang Zemin and the new president, Hu Jintao, who understood the gravity of the AIDS threat and seemed willing to take it on. But the university session was the main event. Four senior Chinese government ministers were there, as was Dr. David Ho, a Chinese American who in 1996 had been named *Time* magazine's Man of the Year for his groundbreaking research on AIDS at the Aaron Diamond AIDS Research Center in New York, a cosponsor of the event.

The best part of my appearance had nothing to do with what I said. When I opened the floor for questions, a young AIDS activist who had already gained notoriety for his energetic, often disruptive public demands that China do more to combat the problem, stood up and started to talk. I was impressed by what he was saying, so I invited Song Pengfei to the stage to say his piece. He had quite a presence. His spiky hair and hip dress would have made him look right at home at an ACT UP event in the United States. He was also sharp as a tack as he made the case for China to abandon denial and embrace care and treatment. China had already moved a long way, as evidenced by the presence of the ministers at the conference and the speaking role given to a female physician, Dr. Zeng Yi, the first Chinese doctor to openly advocate for aggressive efforts to end stigma and begin care and treatment.

After Pengfei ended his remarks, I hugged him and took him to shake hands with the government officials. At the time, there was still a lot of fear and stigma surrounding AIDS in China and I knew this simple gesture might be worth more than tons of talk. About ten days after the event, Prime Minister Wen Jiabao had a meeting with several AIDS activists in his office, and within a few weeks President Hu was visiting AIDS patients in hospitals, shaking their hands. Both events were broadcast on Chinese television.

After the Beijing conference, our work really took off. The Clinton Foundation was one of the few international NGOs given approval to operate there. We were even given an office in the Chinese Ministry of Health and were operational by the spring of 2004.

At the time, China had essentially two different AIDS challenges. In the urban areas, most people with AIDS had been infected through same-sex contact with someone already infected, or through IV drug use with contaminated needles. In the rural areas, most people were infected by receiving blood transfusions using contaminated needles, then infected their spouses or partners, though there were also IV-drug-use-related infections. Often, small villages already had a shortage of working-age adults, because so many had moved to cities to earn a living and send money home to parents or children. Now, in village after village, the already fragile family and social structures were being decimated.

The Chinese government asked us to work on strengthening the national laboratory system for testing, getting them the best possible prices for ARVs and building comprehensive care and treatment programs, including needle exchange services and methadone treatment to move people off addiction. In 2005, I went back to China on an extended five-day trip that included stops in Zhengzhou, Kunming, Urumqi, Hangzhou, and Beijing. By then, thanks to a World Health Organization grant, CHAI was providing pediatric drugs and testing equipment for more than 2,200 Chinese children living with AIDS.

In Yunnan province, we helped treat more than 6,500 patients in fifteen prefectures and counties. The Gilead Foundation gave Eric Goosby the funds to train doctors and help AIDS patients, many also affected by TB and hepatitis, in drug detention centers, the first time non-Chinese health professionals had ever been allowed to work in them. Soon the Chinese government ranked Yunnan as the best province for HIV care and treatment outcomes.

I learned something about Chinese culture and politics on that trip. The health minister asked me to meet some of the patients and their families, to share a meal with them and play with the children. He said that rural people in China were more culturally conservative and less knowledgeable about AIDS, so both stigma and fear made them reluctant to interact with their infected neighbors. He said my presidential trip to China in 1998 had been heavily covered and I was still well respected, so if they saw me on television eating with families and playing with children infected by HIV, it could have a big impact on how their neighbors treated them. I ate a meal with the families at the clinic I visited and played on the floor with the kids. They were simple, straightforward people having a tough time, like a lot of the people I grew up with. I got more out of the encounters than they did and hoped the press coverage had the desired effect.

I also visited Urumqi, the largest city in the predominantly Muslim Xinjiang Uighur Autonomous Region in north China, near Mongolia and Kazakhstan. The Chinese government was concerned about a Uighur separatist movement, but the people I met were working together. At the large business gathering where I spoke, held in a massive warehouse full of consumer goods, we were entertained by a children's choir where the singers were roughly one third Han Chinese, one third Uighur, and one third fair-haired Kazakhs. Their uniforms appeared to be of Kazakh style, they were mostly Muslims, and they were singing in Chinese.

In 2006, with the support of the Chinese government, the foundation moved into the Xinjiang Uighur Autonomous Region and helped to increase those on treatment to more than 3,000, about 90 percent of the total identified AIDS patients. Our staff also helped set up an insurance program to help people deal with the costs of infection. The policy sold for about $100 per patient per year. It was popular and led to an increase in people on treatment. When the tensions between the two main ethnic groups, Uighur Muslims and Han Chinese, intensified as the government brought in more Han Chinese to weaken the Uighur separatist movement, CHAI's work was interrupted on occasion, but our people stayed on, arranged for children's medicine, and were never denied access to the facilities that provided treatment and training. I hoped the inclusive cooperation I saw would be able to withstand the underlying tension between the forces of Muslim separatism and the authoritarian response it was bound to provoke. Sadly, it did not, and by 2021, under President Xi, more than a million Uighurs were being held in detention camps.

We kept working in China until the end of 2010, when the Chinese government, with support from the World Health Organization, took over its HIV/AIDS program. CHAI's effort had been a big success, with more than 65,000 people, including 2,200 children, on treatment, triple the number in 2005.

Along the way, we were blessed by an ever-growing number of donor governments, foundations, and individuals, the largest of which, for the last several years, have been the Gates Foundation; the U.K.'s foreign development ministry (now called the Foreign, Commonwealth & Development Office); and one I had a hand in forming, UNITAID.

UNITAID was born with a unique crowdfunding idea developed by French president Jacques Chirac and foreign minister Philippe Douste-Blazy to do France's part in helping people in lower-income countries meet the U.N.'s Millennium Development Goals: a small one-euro tax on air travel in and out of France.

In July 2005, Douste-Blazy came to my home in Chappaqua to discuss his proposal and to ask me a simple question: "What should I do with the money?"

I recommended that he start by buying drugs to fight HIV/AIDS, malaria, and tuberculosis, and tell the drug companies he was prepared to buy in large volumes on multiyear contracts, but he wanted big discounts in return, making France's and its UNITAID partners' money go further. Even with all the money projected to pour into the then relatively new Global Fund and PEPFAR, large numbers of people would remain without life-saving medicine, especially children with AIDS who couldn't take the adult dosages and also needed nutritional supplements so their bodies could absorb the meds, and adults for whom the original ARVs no longer work when the virus mutates.

Because this occurs in only 10 percent of the infected population at any given time, the "second-line" drugs are much more expensive. So, too, were the children's AIDS drugs because they also were produced in much lower volumes than the adult pills. Prices for effective malaria drugs and TB meds were also still out of reach for many nations, even when manufactured by generic producers.

After we spent a couple of hours discussing the details, Douste-Blazy left Chappaqua with a pledge of my full public support and eagerness to encourage other nations to join. In September 2006, at the annual U.N. meeting in New York (and coinciding with the second meeting of the Clinton Global Initiative), I spoke at UNITAID's formal launch as the "International Drug Purchasing Facility." Brazil, Chile, Norway, and the U.K. joined France as founders. Soon, South Korea joined the UNITAID board, as did the Gates Foundation, the African Union, and the World Health Organization. The last board seat was given to a young French-Moroccan representative of ACT UP, to represent NGOs. Soon after that, thirty-nine more countries pledged to work with UNITAID, almost half with their own air-ticket levies. Even small, low-income nations with limited air traffic were excited and wanted to do their part to save lives.

The airline taxes had raised more than a billion euros by the end of 2012. To date, the partnership between UNITAID and CHAI has reduced pediatric ARV prices by 80 percent, enabling more than 900,000 children to access treatment, up from 70,000 in 2006. The price of second-line HIV medicine came down 75 percent, providing treatment to 130,000 adults in twenty-five countries, and $539 million worth of drugs, diagnostics, and therapeutic food for children had reached forty countries.

UNITAID has grown and taken on more health projects with several other NGOs. I'm just grateful for the chance I had to help it get started. Douste-Blazy said our conversation gave him the idea he needed to make a difference—combining innovative funding with innovative spending. It's still working.

Starting in 2003, I began taking annual summer trips to Africa, always with a group of supporters and timed to be in South Africa on or near Mandela's birthday, July 18, so that I could be with him and do something to support his foundation, too. In each country, I'd meet with the leaders, our delegation would visit CHAI projects and other foundation efforts, and I'd thank the CHAI staff and partners who were doing the work. These stories come from some of those trips.

Ireland was the first nation to commit to spending $100 million over five years on care and treatment in Africa. In the end, Irish Aid, with the strong backing of Prime Minister Bertie Ahern and his ministers, exceeded its commitment in time and money in support of our lifesaving work in Mozambique and Lesotho. In 2006, I went to Dublin to announce that Ireland would commit to extend its work through 2010. By then, there were more than 23,000 patients in Mozambique receiving ARV treatment, including 2,334 children, as well as more coverage in rural areas and a special pediatric facility in Beira, the fourth largest city in the nation, with Mozambique's highest infection rate.

Lesotho, a small mountainous nation of 1.8 million completely surrounded by South Africa, then had the world's second highest infection rate, with more than 500,000 infected and

300,000 in immediate need of care. CHAI started working there in 2004 and I went in July 2006 to inaugurate the country's first pediatric AIDS clinic. Within a year and a half CHAI had substantially increased the number of people getting ARVs, eventually reaching 85,000 adults, including 4,400 kids, by 2012. But with so many new people getting infected and others needing medicine to stay alive, there was a lot more to do.

The government of Lesotho was all in on the mission, with a policy to test everyone in the country twelve or older and to involve people with AIDS in the effort to reduce stigma as they increased treatment even in remote mountain villages not accessible by any wheeled transportation.

Perhaps the most remarkable of these foot soldiers was Tsepang Setaka, who was ten or eleven years old when she was abducted on her way home from school, held captive for several days, and sexually attacked before she could escape. Years later, after falling ill with tuberculosis, she was tested and learned she was also HIV positive because of her rape. She received treatment at a clinic opened when Lesotho began buying drugs under Clinton Foundation agreements, and quickly regained her lost weight and strength.

Tsepang then became an "expert patient," helping to nurse and counsel fellow patients and receiving a small stipend from CHAI. In early 2006, she was chosen to join the "Know Your Status" campaign, going to villages to convince people to get tested and doing counseling. She was doing all this in a country where, at the time, there was stigma in having AIDS, even stigma from having been raped, and skepticism about whether these strange drugs could make a difference. But this small young woman, still in her teens, was determined not to be defeated by others' perceptions and above all not to be a victim. Her story got people's attention and her strength and confidence were infectious.

Rwanda also wanted CHAI's help to increase treatment for AIDS patients. I was eager to do it. Hillary and I first went there in 1998, four years after the genocide claimed an estimated 800,000 lives in just ninety days. The horrendous slaughter in Rwanda inflicted by leaders of the majority Hutu tribe on the minority Tutsis and their Hutu sympathizers occurred in April 1994, at the same time as the NATO bombing campaign in Bosnia, a pivotal step in ending the genocide there. I ordered the evacuation of all Americans from Rwanda and sent troops to guarantee their safety, but we were so preoccupied with Bosnia, with the memory of Somalia just six months old, and with strong opposition in Congress to military deployments in faraway places not vital to our national interests, that neither I nor anyone on my foreign policy team adequately focused on Rwanda. Also, someone in the State Department or the White House told our U.N. officer to oppose Canada's proposal to lead a force of 10,000 to halt the slaughter, which we shouldn't have done. I didn't know about that before the vote and tried to find out who was behind it, but no one would take responsibility.

But even with most of the killing already well underway, with just those few thousand troops, and making allowances for the time it would have taken to deploy them, we could have saved a lot of lives. The failure to try to stop Rwanda's tragedy became one of the greatest regrets of my presidency.

In 2002, when I went back to finalize our partnership to fight AIDS, the country had already made impressive social and economic progress under President Paul Kagame, who was determined to build a sense of national unity, not by denying the past but by making sure it was understood, then promoting a culture of personal and community responsibility, not victimhood, and a commitment to reconciliation without revenge. Kagame had convinced a large majority of Rwandans that was the only way to move beyond the past into the future.

Kagame's been criticized for cracking down on his critics, especially those who want to bring back tribal politics, barring them from running for office, even arresting them and going after them across Rwanda's border with the Democratic Republic of the Congo. That's fair enough. But if you compare Rwanda's before and after with other African countries, in today's environment of divisive tribalism, alternative facts, and relentless blaming, what the Rwandans accomplished looks even more impressive.

The consequences of Rwanda's choice were already being felt

by 2002. Although the country's per capita income was still less than a dollar a day, the streets were clean, as were the sidewalks, because all adults volunteered a few hours a week to clean them up. President Kagame wanted his people to be proud of their capital and he wanted visitors to see that poverty and cleanliness could go hand in hand. He believed that clean streets would send a clear signal to people from other countries that Rwanda was full of hardworking, future-focused people worth investing in.

A reporter traveling with our group took a taxi from the airport to the hotel. On the way, he asked the driver if he resented my coming to help Rwanda now when as president I had done nothing to stop the genocide there. The driver responded that he didn't. He said that the slaughter was homegrown, that no one made them kill each other, and that as far as he knew, I was the only leader who had come to Rwanda and apologized. Now, he said, they needed all the help they could get, and he was glad I was there.

I heard a similar message at the Genocide Memorial outside Kigali, a museum that abuts a hillside containing the remains of more than 300,000 victims. I got a tour from a young man who appeared to be in his mid-twenties, handsome in his dark suit and tie, and very well spoken. I asked him if he had lost relatives in the carnage.

He replied, "Yes, my parents and a brother and lots of aunts, uncles, and cousins. All told, seventy-three of us were killed." I said it must be very hard for him to take us through this. He replied, "No, it's therapeutic. President Kagame says we have to face the past so we can let it go." I told him he reminded me of a woman I had met with a group of survivors when Hillary and I came to Rwanda in 1998. When the machete-wielding killers had come to her village, her Tutsi family had been betrayed by Hutu neighbors whom they considered friends, having shared meals and celebrations and seeing their kids play together. After the attack, she woke up in a pool of her own blood to find her husband and her six children lying near her, all dead. She told us, "I cried out to God in anger that I had been spared. But I realized it must be for a reason and it could not be something as mean as vengeance. So I do what I can to help us begin again." What she did was to find adoptive homes for orphans, without regard to their tribal roots.

When I told the young man this story, he smiled and said, "I should remind you of her. She's my aunt."

After I left the genocide memorial, I visited Ndera, one of the "reconciliation villages" established by President Kagame to provide homes to survivors, returning refugees, families of victims, and families of perpetrators. They got the land to build a house on for free if they were willing to live side by side with someone from the other side. I was greeted by the local mayor and the provincial governor, both women. Since 85 percent of the victims of the genocide were men, having more women in office was a necessity. Kagame embraced it as an opportunity. At the time, 49 percent of the parliament were women, then the highest percentage in the world. Today it is just over 61 percent.

I'll always remember the people I met in Ndera. First there was a joyful welcome dance by a group of local children, Hutu, Tutsi, and Twa, a tribe small in population and physical size. After that, our group gathered in the yard of a Hutu woman lovingly caring for two bedridden Tutsi orphans with a congenital malady that would claim their lives. Standing in the yard were people who told their stories, including a young Hutu man who fled to the Congo after being part of the killing spree. He told me he came home when President Kagame said people like him could return if they confessed their crimes and submitted themselves to the community courts, called *gacaca*, which imposed sentences of community atonement service. I also spoke with two women who lived next to each other and who were holding hands. The Tutsi woman had lost her husband and brother. The Hutu woman's husband was in prison awaiting trial before the International Criminal Tribunal for Rwanda because he was alleged to have played a major role in the genocide. But there they were together, neighbors holding hands, a living symbol of escape from the bloody past into a future based on their common humanity.

Soon the CHAI team was providing AIDS medicine and training Rwandans to treat patients. In July 2005, I returned with a year's supply of pediatric ARVs for 2,500 children. At the time Rwanda was providing treatment to only 260 children.

Then, in July 2006, I visited the Rwinkwavu district hospital, built by our partner, Dr. Paul Farmer's Partners in Health (PIH). By then Paul and Didi had two more children, a daughter Elizabeth and a son Sebastian, as PIH built more hospitals and clinics and trained more health workers.

In 2008, Paul, Chelsea, and I also broke ground on the new Butaro Hospital, in Burera, on a beautiful hilly site near the Ugandan border. Until then, Burera had been the only district in Rwanda without a hospital. PIH was the main contractor, with the MASS Design Group creating the plans and supervising construction. The partners had met each other at the Clinton Global Initiative and MASS Design's commitment there saved a lot of money and improved the project.

It was all fascinating to me, but my most indelible memory from that 2008 trip is of a stop back in Rwinkwavu to see a cassava field and visit a small village that was connected to the health system only by a traveling community health worker. By then, the country had a network of hospitals in the large cities, clinics in larger towns, and health workers who visited the smallest places. They made sure people were taking their ARVs, helped pregnant women, and evaluated those who were sick to see if they needed to go to the nearest clinic to be treated or, if seriously ill, sent on to the regional hospital. This was the model Paul Farmer and PIH built in rural Haiti and what President Kagame wanted for all Rwandans.

On that day, I met the village's community health worker, Beatrice, and her patient, fifteen-year-old Jean-Pierre, along with his nineteen-year-old sister, Eugenie, who had raised her brother (and herself) for several years after they lost both their parents, probably to AIDS. By 2005, Jean-Pierre's HIV infection had developed into an advanced stage of AIDS. His legs were covered with open sores, and he was near death when Eugenie brought him to the Rwinkwavu hospital. PIH treated him, gave him the lifesaving drugs, and provided food for him and his sister, who had eked out a living for them for years as a farmworker. When he recovered enough to go home, he and Eugenie moved into a small house PIH had built to get them out of what had been their home, a tiny, sweltering mud hut that I could barely stand up and turn around in.

Best of all, they gave him Beatrice, the community health worker who became a friend and mentor to Jean-Pierre and his sister. When we met, I asked them what they wanted to do with their lives. Though AIDS had stunted his growth and kept him out of school for years, Jean-Pierre was bright-eyed, upbeat, and looking to the future. He said he hoped he could become a doctor so he could help children before they got as sick as he had been. Eugenie, who had been caring for her brother and putting food on the table since she was nine, said she wanted to open a village store so her neighbors wouldn't have to walk for miles to buy simple things. Both were worthy dreams.

So many people were still dying. Beatrice was determined to save as many lives—and dreams—as possible. She was strong, committed, and kind. I'm so glad she and others like her were on the front lines of the battle.

In 2012, Chelsea and I joined Paul Farmer and the legendary race car driver Jeff Gordon at Butaro Hospital to inaugurate the Cancer Center of Excellence. He had committed at CGI to build the first comprehensive cancer care facility in East Africa, able to provide treatment, including chemotherapy, and connected to cancer centers throughout the world, including the St. Jude Children's Research Hospital in Memphis, which puts all its advances in research into the public domain. The Cancer Center is still there, doing even better, thanks to a new medical school, the University of Global Health Equity, that Partners in Health built just across the valley from the center.

In 2013, Chelsea and I returned to Rwanda to visit one of CHAI's new Human Resources for Health clinics in action. The basic idea behind HRH was to provide high-quality training for all the doctors, nurses and midwives, dentists, and hospital administrators, and to get more of them, to meet the government's goal of being completely independent of foreign assistance for its healthcare operations by 2020. When HRH started, Rwanda had only 633 doctors and 6,970 nurses with little training for a population that exceeded 10 million. Before HRH there had been lots of healthcare training programs in developing countries, but nothing on this scale, with this goal. It would cost around $30 million over several years, but if it worked, Rwanda would have a sustainable healthcare system with the ability to provide top-quality training for new medical professionals from Rwanda and other African nations.

USAID committed to financing HRH for a couple of years, enough money to do the job, but only if there was a dramatic change in the way foreign assistance was funded. For decades our government had allowed U.S. NGOs which won contracts for work abroad to claim about 25 percent of the money allotted as overhead and 25 percent or more in administrative costs, so that often less than half the taxpayers' money was spent on direct programs.

We wanted to change that so that the vast majority of our foreign assistance, at least in healthcare, was spent on its intended beneficiaries. It wasn't easy. These groups were largely run or represented by people who had worked for members of Congress in both parties. The groups usually did good work but at a cost that couldn't be justified, especially since the United States spent a smaller percentage of its national income on nonmilitary foreign assistance than any other wealthy country. Several universities, eager to work on HRH because it was a unique, exciting opportunity to make basic health operations self-sustaining, agreed to a dramatic change in the foreign aid formula: they would charge nothing for overhead and only 7 percent for administrative costs. Among other things, the savings allowed the Rwandan HRH program to invest $15 million in medical equipment to upgrade their hospitals' training capacities and service delivery.

The Rwandan Health Ministry received the U.S. aid money and contracted with the U.S. schools. CHAI received none of the money; our own donors funded our advisory work. Eventually, CHAI helped Rwanda form partnerships with twenty-five medical, nursing, and dental schools and healthcare management programs. As of 2019, more than one hundred faculty members had delivered more than 80,000 hours of clinical training time.

One final point on the power of more money to leverage lower prices. Every time CHAI succeeded in driving prices down for countries based on our negotiated contracts, both before and after UNITAID, everyone else's prices soon dropped, too. It was no longer morally defensible, politically possible, or economically necessary to charge other buyers of generic drugs much higher prices than those CHAI negotiated. The higher aggregate demand dropped the prices, and any remaining differential could only be justified based on the buyers' relative financial reliability and promptness of payment. Soon, countries funded by the Global Fund, but not served by CHAI, also got the benefits of falling prices.

Thanks to George W. Bush, PEPFAR-funded countries did, too, whether or not CHAI also worked there. When he was president, W and I would talk once or twice a year, whenever he had the time to call. He was busier than I was and whenever I needed to run something by the White House, I worked with his staff. Today, when we do speeches together, he sometimes remarks that one thing that built trust in our relationship is that I never leaked our conversations. We had some good ones because he knew he didn't have to edit himself for fear that what he said would appear in the press, in or out of context.

With his permission, I decided to depart from my policy to recount one of our conversations here, because President Bush deserves it.

In April 2005, when Pope John Paul II died, President Bush asked me to join the American delegation to his funeral, along with the first lady, his father, Secretary of State Condoleezza Rice, White House chief of staff Andy Card, and New York mayor Mike Bloomberg. The pope had met with all five American presidents who served during his papacy, beginning with President Carter. President George W. Bush and I had met with him three times each. I saw him in Denver, Newark, and

St. Louis on his American trips. He also called me early in my first term to urge me to do more to stop the killing in Bosnia. Many of the victims were Croatian Catholics, but by far the largest number were Bosnian Muslims. The pope thought they were all God's children. He disagreed with both President Bush and me on one big issue each: with Bush on the Iraq War, with me on women's reproductive rights. He always made his position clear, then moved on to areas where we stood on common ground. I liked and admired him and was glad to be asked to go.

On the flight to Rome on Air Force One, Bush invited me up to his office for a talk. His PEPFAR program had been approved in 2003 and started in 2004, with an initial five-year budget of $15 billion. He asked me to explain what the Clinton Foundation was doing. At the time, PEPFAR was in fifteen countries, including several in which CHAI also had operations and, according to the CHAI staff, they had a very productive, cooperative relationship. After I described CHAI's operations, I complimented him on the work they were doing and thanked him for continuing, as part of the PEPFAR budget, American support of the Global Fund, which provided the funding for a lot of the medicine bought by nations in our purchasing group.

Then I ventured into a delicate area. I said for all the good PEPFAR was doing, it could still save many more lives for the same level of spending if he would allow—not require but just permit—the governments that PEPFAR was supporting to use the funds provided to buy generic drugs. At the time, PEPFAR required them to purchase Big Pharma–patented ARVs. Although they were given steep discounts from prices charged in the United States, the cost was still about ten times higher than what our partners paid for generics.

I knew this was not an easy issue for him. Many of the U.S. drug companies were big supporters of his party, especially after Al Gore had said, late in my second term (and I agreed), that poor countries should be able to buy generic medicine under the international agreement to relax patent protections for life-saving medicine in emergencies. Bush could have responded to me by saying that he'd done more than I did, by passing PEPFAR through a Republican Congress, with strong support from Christian evangelical groups. In doing so, he had already kept his promise to be a "compassionate conservative."

But he didn't say that. Instead, he kept the decision on the merits. He said his people had told him the generics weren't nearly as effective as the Big Pharma drugs. I replied that they had been approved by respected international panels. But I knew that wouldn't be enough to sway him. So I asked, "What if I referred every drug we use to the U.S. Food and Drug Administration for approval? If the FDA says they're safe and effective, would you tell the countries PEPFAR supports they could buy them if they wanted to?"

Without a blink he said, "That sounds like a fair deal."

And what a deal it turned out to be. CHAI submitted twenty-four drugs to the FDA. Soon twenty-two of the twenty-four were approved, and the fifteen countries served by PEPFAR were notified that they could use the U.S. aid to buy them. Eventually more than 95 percent of PEPFAR funds allocated to buying AIDS medicines were used to buy generic drugs and the savings allowed PEPFAR to move into more countries, more than doubling its impact.

When he took office, President Obama supported and expanded PEPFAR. Hillary, as secretary of state, worked with Dr. Eric Goosby to figure out how to cover more people. After the 2016 election, President Bush worked with Republican leaders to preserve PEPFAR funding. It survived President Trump's proposed budget cuts. All American taxpayers should be proud of the lives our nation saves.

CHAI is still growing in 2024, and is pursuing an ambitious four-year strategy recently approved by the board. The organization remains decentralized, fast, and adaptable. The vast majority of the staff operate in-country with the support of global teams to obtain the lowest prices and the best supply chains and with relatively small centralized management, finance, and human resources teams. But the mission is broader than ever: to save even more lives by reducing the burden of all major causes of premature death in low- and middle-income countries, while increasing their capacity to create and sustain high-quality health systems until they can operate without CHAI's assistance.

If CHAI's past is prologue, the staff will have to achieve these big goals with 80 percent of its time. Typically, 20 percent of the time is spent responding to partner governments' requests for help with serious problems that come up. In 2008, Cambodia ran out of medicine necessary to contain a dengue fever outbreak. Within a week CHAI got the medicine from our Indian suppliers and shipped it to Cambodia, saving thousands of children's lives. In 2013, Malawi faced a serious shortage of several drugs. CHAI worked with the government to create an inventory of and a forecast for shortages, located the medicines in other African countries, helped pay for them, and shipped them to Malawi. In 2014 and 2015, Liberia was engulfed by the Ebola epidemic. With support from Norway and CGI partners who donated and delivered one hundred tons of medical equipment to Liberia and other affected countries, CHAI helped organize and distribute emergency protective gear to health workers and coordinate the government's healthcare response. Our full-time staff never left Liberia during the outbreak but thankfully were never infected. In 2020, CHAI was asked to work with the WHO to develop its strategy to deal with COVID-19 in Africa and to support our partner nations' governments in responding to it, and especially in India to alleviate a severe oxygen shortage.

Dealing with these emergencies is an essential part of CHAI's work. You can't build a better house while it's on fire: first you have to put the fire out. The cost of the Covid fire has been great enough to put a lot of our other goals at risk.

This brings me to the last and perhaps the most crucial point. CHAI is able to work with governments and in many countries with private sector supporters to set and achieve remarkable goals because of generous funding from foreign governments and well-endowed foundations. However, these sources, with a few notable exceptions, led by the Gates Foundation, UNITAID, and PEPFAR, have begun to flatline or decline for a number of reasons, including the financial stress of Covid, rising nationalism in donor countries reducing support for all forms of foreign assistance, and shifting priorities in foreign aid spending. CHAI has continued to grow by garnering a larger percentage of the donor pie, based on its high performance, low-cost delivery, and creative flexibility.

Healthcare still remains the best-funded of all international aid efforts. The initiatives I have covered in this chapter have attracted support from more than sixty governments, international organizations, NGOs, and individuals in amounts ranging from a few thousand to tens of millions of dollars. But the economic contraction triggered by the coronavirus, as well as the increased urgency of addressing climate change, food insecurity, and extreme poverty in poor rural areas, demonstrate why the current model of funding global health needs strengthening at the grass roots. Even when new funds were increasing every year, in most CHAI partner countries, citizens' own out-of-pocket payments were already the largest funder of health, and there were still severe shortages of essential healthcare workers because governments can't afford to train or pay them.

So over the next ten to fifteen years, CHAI is going to try to help a significant number of African and Asian countries build their own universal health coverage systems to assure access to basic health needs without severe financial hardship. It won't be easy, but we have to find a way. Meanwhile, if you're an American, don't forget that in many parts of the United States there is also a shortage of trained, well-paid workers doing essential public health work and, with government Covid spending tapering off, too many hardworking people who still don't have access to quality, affordable healthcare.

I'm very proud of what CHAI's done and confident that it will keep doing great things as we continue to build more health capacity and, hopefully, work ourselves out of a job someday. But the enduring legacy will probably be the millions of lives we saved with the drastic cuts in pricing for lifesaving medicine, beginning with our work with the generic AIDS ARVs, and extending to other AIDS-related testing devices, the drugs for tuberculosis, malaria, and other lifesaving treatments. There's still a lot of potential for more progress.

ELEVEN

CGI: Reinventing Philanthropy, One Commitment at a Time

Nestled high in the Swiss Alps, Davos, Switzerland, is a beautiful little village with great skiing that is most famous for hosting the annual World Economic Forum. For fifty years, the founder and chairman, Klaus Schwab, has brought together leaders in politics, business, and philanthropy from all over the world to discuss the state of the world's economy, and its most pressing political issues. Corporations pay hefty fees for their leaders to attend, both for the public programs and for the receptions, meals, and meetings which give the attendees a chance to hear about and discuss issues important to them.

To its critics, Davos symbolizes what is wrong with globalization—a lot of rich people pretending to care about poor people, with no intention of doing or paying for what it would take to make a real difference. That may apply to some of the attendees but not to all. Many of them have done a lot to help improve health and education, raise incomes, and reduce the threat of climate change. Leaders of NGOs also come to discuss their work and seek support. And people who disagree about globalization as practiced are given a platform, including Joe Stiglitz, a Nobel Prize–winning economist, former member of my Council of

Economic Advisers, and a fierce critic, who is usually there to argue his case.

My first visit was on January 29, 2000. With about a year left in my second term, I brought five cabinet members with me to the gathering, both to support the benefits of our growing global interdependence and to warn of its dangers. In my speech, after making the obvious point that the new technologies which power positive globalization were also available to the world's bad actors, including terrorists, narcotraffickers, and organized crime syndicates, I said our interdependence would continue to pose new challenges, including the speed with which new diseases spread, the rapid increase in economic inequality and insecurity, and the likely return of ethnic, racial, and religious tribal conflicts. As the United States continues to wrestle with COVID-19 and growing racial disparities in economic opportunity, healthcare, law enforcement, and other aspects of our lives, I wish I had been wrong about all of that more than twenty years ago.

When I first spoke at Davos, despite large numbers of people moving out of poverty and improvements in access to healthcare, half the world still lived on less than $2 a day, a quarter had no access to clean water, 130 million children never went to school at all, and 10 million of them died every year of preventable diseases and conditions like diarrhea. Even in wealthy countries, including the United States, the rapidly changing economy was damaging communities and dislocating workers, particularly older workers without college degrees, who lost their jobs and couldn't find work paying anywhere near their previous incomes.

While the opening of new markets across the world had indeed lifted millions out of poverty, by 2001 it had been clear for years that too many people were being left out and left behind while global financial giants and multinational corporations enjoyed enormous profits. As the chief beneficiaries of globalization, they have a responsibility to dramatically reduce the burdens on those whose lives and livelihoods are hurt by it and to increase the number of people able to participate fully in its benefits. Twenty-plus years later, the imperative is clearer and the consequences of continued neglect more dire.

To reduce damaging conflicts rooted in racial, religious, tribal, and cultural hatreds, people need to believe they and their families can build better futures in a time of rapid economic and social change. Otherwise, they will feel trapped in stagnant waters, seething at being looked down on or forgotten, desperate for any lifelines, including ones woven from fibers of racial, religious, and cultural divisions, driving people to the false conclusion that authoritarian dictators can take care of your group's anxieties by keeping the "others" down and out.

The Davos crowd gave me the polite reception you would expect them to give to the U.S. president, but I could tell most of them were convinced that the new order was doing far more good than harm, and that national governments, not corporations, were mostly responsible for doing something about the excessive inequality and insecurity the modern world had wrought.

Now as a former president starting a new foundation, I no longer had the power and resources of the executive branch to build more inclusive prosperity, but my foundation's early successes lowering the price of AIDS medicine and reducing the calories in drinks served in public schools had shown that partnerships between the private sector, nonprofits, and governments could go a long way toward solving big problems no single group had been able to tackle successfully on their own.

For the next decade, I continued to go to Davos when invited, to speak and meet with political, business, labor, and NGO leaders. I especially enjoyed the forum offered to Israeli president Shimon Peres and me for a couple of years, a late-night conversation with a question-and-answer session that highlighted Peres's brilliance, eloquence, and foresight as we tried to convince people they had to and could do more to humanize globalization.

I enjoyed the World Economic Forum, but no one was ever asked to commit to do something about all the problems we discussed, and when projects were announced, there was no system to help those who made them succeed in keeping them and no required report on progress or lack of it.

After I got home from Davos in 2004, I started talking to my staff about whether we could hold a similar meeting during the annual United Nations General Assembly week in New York in September when key world leaders would already be in town. Some of my advisors thought it was a great branding and fund-raising opportunity. I said it might be, but the world didn't need another talkfest, so I'd do it only if we asked every attendee to make a concrete commitment to action in the U.S., their home country, or region of their choosing, and report on their progress in keeping it. Would people actually pay to come to a meeting which required them to spend even more time and money to help save the world? I had a hunch that a lot of people, especially those who didn't go or weren't ever invited to Davos, might be open to the challenge.

So our foundation team began to design what would become the Clinton Global Initiative, a forum to bring people together who wanted to make positive change, and give them the chance to do it. I hoped to create a diverse community of doers, including heads of state and other government officials, leaders of NGOs, philanthropic organizations, business, labor, and finance, artists and athletes, and other citizens hungry to make a difference and advance causes they believed in. Many of them routinely attended conferences within their separate sectors—gatherings of similar businesses, philanthropies, and NGOs—but I thought they could do so much more together and I hoped that beginning with a commitment in mind would get attendees to move beyond talk to specific actions that would create more opportunities and solve more problems.

We announced the first CGI Annual Meeting at Davos late in 2004 and began to prepare for September 2005. Our small staff was led by Ed Hughes and Mary Morrison, both of whom had worked with me in the White House and were eager to accept the challenge. Ed worked on developing the programs, Mary handled membership and logistics. Our largest angel investor was Tom Golisano, a no-nonsense businessman from Rochester, New York, who founded Paychex, which provides payroll and other services to companies. In those early years, Tom was the difference between life and death for CGI. He remained our lead sponsor for eight straight years. Finally, when he knew we could make it without him, he went on to pursue his deep interest in helping people with intellectual disabilities, including supporting the Special Olympics. We were so lucky to have him as long as we did.

We spent a lot of time not just on what topics would be discussed and who would speak at the plenaries and on the panels, but on what to name the gathering. Publicis Events helped us with the branding. I'm not too good at that, but I know a good brand when I see it. Publicis suggested fourteen possible names. Two of them had the word I was looking for—Initiative. Not a Meeting. Not an Exchange. Not a Summit. Initiative implies action, which requires commitment. And since we were asking people from all over the world, we settled on the Clinton Global Initiative, CGI. It's turned out to be a good call.

The inaugural meeting and all those that followed through 2016 would be held at the Sheraton in midtown Manhattan, which had the right mix of meeting space and a central location far enough from the United Nations to be relatively free of the normal General Assembly traffic gridlock. From the very first, Ed Kane and the Sheraton staff went the extra mile to help, including bailing us out of early problems with registration.

The first registration period was chaotic and the commitment process was rudimentary to say the least. People just wrote down the commitments on cards, which we used to organize follow-ups. But year after year, we worked to improve the process, helping members design their "Commitments to Action," giving them a commemorative certificate, encouraging them to network with like-minded members from another sector or discipline, and facilitating and supporting those interactions however we could. For instance, if a nonprofit needed funding, we would help them find a corporation or philanthropist with similar interests and join forces to launch a project, and give them tools to manage the commitment.

There were a lot of positive responses to our invitations in the months leading up to that first September meeting, but as the date approached, I still had no earthly idea if anyone would show up for the three days of plenary sessions and programs, let alone if it would work. Along with the requirement to make a commitment, we had instituted a membership fee of $20,000 to help cover the cost of the conference. It was modest by Davos standards and often waived for people and groups who were doing good work but barely able to afford the travel and lodging costs. Still, who had ever heard of charging people to brave the New York traffic in U.N. Week to make commitments to spend more time and money?

But people did show up, at first nearly overwhelming our hardy staff and hardworking volunteers. King Abdullah of Jordan, British prime minister Tony Blair, and Secretary of State Condoleezza Rice participated in our first plenary session, and were joined in the audience by current and former heads of state, including the presidents of South Africa, the Dominican Republic, Turkey, Nigeria, and Ukraine; heads of international and multinational companies such as Coca-Cola and Dow Chemical, as well as nonprofit leaders and social activists from around the world. More people attended in the subsequent days, including U.N. secretary-general Kofi Annan and the leaders of Rwanda and Norway. The plenary sessions were open to all and people chose which issue panels they would attend.

Somehow it worked. Those in attendance made more than $2.5 billion worth of specific commitments, including the construction of two wind energy power plants in the Dominican Republic, millions to bolster microfinance projects of the Grameen Bank, and a $100 million Africa investment fund.

From start to finish not all our commitments were large, but they all made a difference to those who kept them and to those who received their benefits. At the second meeting in 2006, a New Jersey businessman, Barry Segal, said he wanted to donate $100,000 and asked our staff about projects where it could make a real difference. They introduced him to Sustainable South Bronx, an NGO then managed by Majora Carter. In 2006, the South Bronx included the poorest congressional district in the United States, with more than 40 percent of its population at or below the poverty line and an unemployment rate in the high double digits. The population, two-thirds Latino and one-third Black, had an obesity rate of 27 percent, and a severe asthma rate seven times the national average. People lived surrounded by manufacturing operations, four power plants, and dumps with 40 percent of New York City's garbage, with the smallest amount of open space in the city, less than one-half acre per thousand people.

Carter grew up in the neighborhood. When she moved back in with her parents to go to graduate school, she organized a drive to beat back another waste facility, started a job-training program in waste cleanup, and established Sustainable South Bronx to create green jobs and a healthier, happier neighborhood. The city gave her the funds to create an eleven-mile greenway network in Hunts Point, with tree-lined streets connecting open parks. But she had no money to hire people to maintain the parkland, to train people to care for the trees on the streets, or to involve young people in maintaining the greenway. Barry Segal was so impressed he committed $100,000 a year for three years to hire Greenway Stewards to do that work. They soon found more neighborhood partners, increasing their impact and that of the Segal Family Foundation gift.

A lot of good things happened in CGI's second year. More than 1,000 leaders of nongovernmental and charitable organizations, business, labor, and government, including fifty current and former national leaders, came. During the first session, First Lady Laura Bush announced the first of more than two hundred commitments, a joint pledge of $16.4 million from USAID, PEPFAR, and the Case and MGT Foundations to bring clean water systems to 1,000 villages in sub-Saharan Africa.

I was so glad Laura came. It was important to me to establish CGI as an inclusive, nonpartisan community of people who do things. And Laura Bush cared about a lot of things that mattered, including the fate of Afghan women and girls and poor people in African nations who needed clean water to survive and thrive. She was clearly a big influence in the White House. And she doesn't miss much. Two years earlier, when she and George came to my library dedication, they joined his parents, President and Mrs. Carter, and the other first family members for a brief reception in the apartment built atop the library. It's a nice space full of artifacts from Arkansas history, memorabilia from our family's years there, arts and crafts from the collection Hillary put together in the White House, and a large selection from my personal collection of books, many dating back to my college days. Ever the librarian, Laura took some time looking over the books, then came up to me and said, "The books are organized by subject area, then put in alphabetical order by author. Who did that?" I smiled and said, "I did. Hillary says I've spent years organizing our books." She deadpanned, "Pretty impressive," and walked away. Laura Bush is a "still waters run deep" woman. The more I saw of her, the more I appreciated the deep caring that drives her life.

After the first two meetings, it was clear that we were on to something special, with real potential to do good, so we needed someone who could run CGI full-time, find more sponsors, and properly staff the commitment-making.

Bob Harrison, a former Goldman Sachs executive, had decided to devote himself to charitable work. He was chairman of the Cornell University Board of Trustees, and for the previous eighteen months had served as the executive director of the Alliance for a Healthier Generation, our partnership with the American Heart Association to combat childhood obesity, which I'll talk more about later. The alliance's work was important, but I was confident that we could find an able public health expert to keep it going. We needed Bob at CGI. Thank goodness, he took the job and stayed for a decade.

Although CGI's format and some areas of concentration changed over the years, as the changing world required, the core elements of the CGI Annual Meeting remained from start to finish: we celebrated doers, empowered every attendee to be one or become a better one, and fostered partnerships among people who didn't normally work together. We never figured out how to get small donations to the commitments, other than by streaming the meeting every year, so we featured crowdfunding sites, especially Kiva.org, an organization where you can make small business loans of $25 or more, and when they're repaid, you can keep your money or reloan it. To date, Kiva has handled more than $2 billion in loans by 2.2 million lenders in eighty countries with a 96 percent repayment rate. It's an amazing operation.

The commitments department soon became the largest unit of CGI, filled with young, knowledgeable, and energetic people, who were always on the lookout for rising stars in the NGO world. Whenever possible, we began to include three other elements into every aspect of our work: first, an emphasis on the empowerment of women and girls as central to advancing all our other goals; second, the nonpartisan aspect of our work; and third, the necessity of creating market-based solutions to problems to assure their sustainability, essentially to operate like B Corporations in the U.S., companies that tell investors on the front end they're working on a longer time frame, committed to the well-being of their customers, suppliers, employees, and communities as well as their shareholders. Believe it or not, from the 1930s until the early 1980s, that was what corporate law was supposed to require. (In 2019, Doug McMillon, president of Walmart, urged the Business Roundtable to embrace the stakeholder position again.)

Over the years, President George H. W. Bush, Senator John McCain, and Governor Mitt Romney came. In 2008, as the Republican nominee for president, McCain announced at CGI that he was suspending his campaign to return to Washington to work on the financial crisis. After Superstorm Sandy, we gave Governor Chris Christie a plenary session to discuss the challenges New Jersey faced in rebuilding.

Of course, the Democrats were always well represented. Barack and Michelle Obama came, as did John Kerry and several other members of Congress, governors, and mayors. Foreign leaders were invited and attended, including King Abdullah of Jordan and Indian prime minister Narendra Modi soon after he took office. Hillary also attended while she was secretary of state. In 2010, she spoke at CGI to announce the formation of the Global Alliance for Clean Cookstoves, a more than $60 million public-private partnership, coordinated through the

United Nations Foundation, to create a thriving global market for clean and efficient household cooking solutions. Because the primary means of cooking and heating for three billion people in developing countries was and still is traditional stoves and open fires, nearly two million people, mostly women and young children, died every year from illnesses related to breathing smoke and other cooking gases. Since its founding, the alliance has helped more than 600 million people gain access to clean cooking fuels and technologies, which not only improve their health, but reduce harmful emissions, and its efforts have sparked new investment in the technologies, totaling more than $200 million in 2022. Hillary is still supporting the project.

One of the most interesting parts of CGI for me was responding to the long action memos on choosing main topics and picking the speakers and moderators for each panel and plenary session. Chelsea and I joined Bob Harrison and the CGI staff for hours of poring over the options for topics and participants. Often, Chelsea and the staff knew more than I did about what people were doing on a given subject and I learned a lot from and usually deferred to them.

Chelsea was also instrumental in CGI's focus on initiatives to help girls and women, including the creation of a permanent track on women and girls at CGI. In 2022, she did panels with young activists and led the tribute to her mentor and friend the late Dr. Paul Farmer. She dedicated our Public Health Equity initiative to his memory and announced we were naming it for him, saying we intended to do our part to carry on Paul's work by working to expand and support the global healthcare workforce, following the example of his beloved Partners in Health.

Every year, we kept working to improve the CGI model. For instance, we noticed that several of the commitments we announced on the last day of each meeting had been sparked by spontaneous conversations in the hallways after sessions or some other event. Members were finding partners with shared interests who needed complementary skills, had or needed funding, or just wanted to join forces. One of many examples of this was the unlikely meeting in the hallway at the Sheraton of Zainab Salbi, the founder of Women for Women, an NGO that supports women in war-torn areas, and Richard Adkerson, the CEO of Freeport-McMoRan Copper & Gold, an international mining company. As the two of them started talking, Zainab mentioned that Women for Women was trying to expand in Congo, where Adkerson's company had operations. Soon she had a partner to support her efforts there.

To foster more of these spontaneous partnerships, we began to schedule time and space for networking at our meetings and added technology to make it easier for like-minded partners to find each other. We also added a smaller midyear meeting to touch base with members and chart progress on commitments, and added working groups to combine commitments for specific target areas, such as the Haiti Action Network, which is still active and doing important work amounting to more than $500 million in committed aid so far.

In 2007, CGI hosted the first Clinton Global Citizen Awards to recognize leaders from civil society, business, the arts, and government for their contributions to society. The ceremonies, which included appearances by Alicia Keys, James Taylor, K'naan, Juanes, Angélique Kidjo, the Roots, Janelle Monáe, Tony Bennett, Ben Stiller, Seth Meyers, Elvis Costello, and Diana Krall, among others, served as uplifting moments for our attendees after what were often busy days. One of the most moving moments at CGI came when Andrea Bocelli performed with the Voices of Haiti youth choir his foundation supports.

Philanthropically minded celebrities who wanted to use their gifts and success to do something for society also did much more than just perform at CGI. Matt Damon, who learned about global development at a young age from his mom, came to CGI to learn what he could do to help millions of people with a scarcity of water. He met Gary White, a brilliant sanitation engineer, and they formed Water.org, which has now helped millions of people get access to safe, clean drinking water. Jon Bon Jovi, Ben Affleck, Ashley Judd, and others joined us to raise the profile of their work and explain it to a wider audience.

Also in 2007, I wrote a book called *Giving*, which covered the different ways other-directed people of all ages across the United States and around the world were trying to make a difference in local, national, and global issues. It was full of stories of real people doing amazing things, some of whom were involved in CGI, and I hoped it would inspire others to give it a go. It sold well for a book of its kind and still sells a few copies every year.

In response to a growing demand from people who couldn't make the trip to New York or wanted to involve more local partners in their region, we held three meetings overseas. The first, in 2008, was in Hong Kong. CGI Asia was a new experience for many Asian businesspeople, but it did result in $185 million in commitments to help some 10 million people in the areas of education, energy and climate change, and public health. Commitment-makers included the BAIF Development Research Foundation, Boeing, WWF, Credit Suisse, and the World Food Programme. I was especially honored that Minister Mentor Lee Kuan Yew, the founder of Singapore, came and participated as well.

We put our international meetings on hold while Hillary was secretary of state, because we needed foreign sponsors to pay for them and didn't want to raise conflict-of-interest questions. We started up again in Rio de Janeiro in 2013, where leaders from across Latin America and around the world met to find ways to carry Latin America's social and economic progress into the future, with a focus on developing human capacity, designing for green growth, and harnessing innovation and technology in the region. Chelsea led a Day of Action at a community day care center in Rio's Morro do Vidigal neighborhood. Although Hillary, Chelsea, and I had to leave early to fly to Nelson Mandela's funeral in South Africa, we later announced twenty-seven Commitments to Action valued at more than $222 million, with the expectation they would help more than 500,000 people.

Our third international meeting was held in Marrakech, Morocco, in 2015. CGI Middle East and Africa focused on investing in youth; securing access to energy, food, and water; and expanding infrastructure for communities throughout the region.

One of the best things we did with the CGI model was to extend it to college students in the United States and around the world. The Clinton Global Initiative University (CGI U) was announced at Harlem's Apollo Theater in 2007, an event we held with MTV and featured Bono, Alicia Keys, Chris Rock, and Shakira, who were all active in philanthropy. The first CGI U, at Tulane University, brought together students from more than 250 colleges and universities, representing almost every state and continent except Antarctica, to make commitments focusing on energy and climate change, global health, poverty alleviation, and peace and human rights. Each annual meeting of CGI U included, in addition to the plenary sessions and programs, a day of service to the community hosting the meeting. For example, in Nashville in 2023, 530 CGI U students provided groceries to families alongside a local food bank, prepared supplies for schoolkids, and cleared land for an upcoming Native American cultural center.

After Tulane, we went to the University of Texas in Austin; the University of Miami twice, in 2010 and 2015; UC San Diego; Washington University in St. Louis; Arizona State University; UC Berkeley; Northeastern University; and the University of Chicago. We were scheduled to have our first international meeting in 2020 at the University of Edinburgh but had to substitute online events because of Covid. Howard University, Vice President Kamala Harris's alma mater, hosted our 2021 CGI U online and she participated in our discussion about creating opportunities in a more inclusive economy and eliminating the economic and health disparities made even clearer by the COVID-19 pandemic. We did another online CGI U hosted by the American Association of Community Colleges in 2022, then had a great in-person return at Vanderbilt in 2023.

The Commitments to Action the students made ranged from on-campus clean energy programs to U.S. and international efforts to advance health, education, and economic conditions. In 2013, Donnel Baird, then a student at Duke University, formed a group called Bloc Power to finance and market energy efficiency and retrofit efforts in 1,000 churches, charter schools, small businesses, and other nonprofits in U.S. urban areas. In

2019, I met him in an old Brooklyn church with the pastor and community leaders who had improved not just the church but several buildings on their block, providing lower energy bills and a cleaner environment. Bloc Power is still going strong.

In 2009, two Vanderbilt University students, Chanukya Dasari and Birju Solanki, committed to open the first no-cost vision clinic in Kansas City, where the low-income population relied on free and lower-cost health facilities that didn't offer eye care. By recruiting medical students and other volunteers, each clinic can treat several hundred patients and provide vision screenings for many more, on an annual budget of $2,000–$4,000 after the diagnostic equipment is purchased. Fifteen years later Birju still runs the clinic, and you can see for yourself how successful they have been at KCFreeeyeclinic.org.

All told, there have been more than 7,000 of these commitments, made by more than 10,000 students from 160 countries. Many of the students raised their own money for the projects, but the CGI U Network, a group of schools, companies, and foundations, have also provided more than $4 million to help.

Chelsea led the CGI U service days that were an important part of every meeting. After Superstorm Sandy, she helped raise more than 1,000 volunteers in eight hours to participate in a service day in the Rockaways in Queens, one of the hardest-hit areas. They spent the day picking up debris from streets, doing basic house repairs and cleaning, handing out disaster relief supplies and coats, and clearing a new playground on the beach buried in a mountain of sand. Chelsea's friend Zach Iscol, then out of the Marine Corps, enlisted the veterans' disaster relief organization Team Rubicon to help organize the day, guided by a software program developed by a young Egyptian American. They knew exactly how many people were needed to complete the assigned work in each area, meet their goals in the allotted time, finish all the houses, and clear the last of the sand mountain off the playground. And Zach is now New York City's Emergency Management commissioner.

One of the most exciting innovations to come out of Chelsea's involvement with CGI University was the CGI U Codeathon, a two-day competition in advance of the annual meeting that challenges student teams to develop technology platforms to address a specific significant problem with a proposed effective technological response. The event culminates with students pitching their ideas to a panel of judges to determine the winners. In recent years the Codeathons partnered with Clinton Foundation initiatives like the Health Matters Initiative and the Clinton Climate Initiative to focus on digital solutions to address mental health on college campuses, energy efficiency, and disaster recovery.

The Codeathons continued through the coronavirus shutdown. In 2020, for the second year in a row, IBM sponsored the Call for Code Global Challenge, supporting nearly 59,000 students through training and a series of hackathons to find the most innovative proposals to reduce the risks of climate change or the adverse impacts of the COVID-19 pandemic. The five semifinalist projects included: an online portal to provide small farmers in developing countries with the latest weather forecasts and crop water requirements based on the type of crop and the farmer's location; a one-step site for small businesses in Australia that provides information on all available relief programs for small businesses hurt by the Covid shutdown and a simple process to apply for help; a browser plug-in that makes it easy for online shoppers to buy carbon credits to offset the emissions that come from transporting the goods they order; an app that replaces physical lines with virtual ones for shopping and voting; and an app designed by a working mother with two school-age children and a toddler that synthesizes what schoolwork is to be done each week in any home school, public school, private school, or other lesson-based entity like a drawing or martial arts studio. The information is securely distributed in a format easy for parents, grandparents, and guardians to understand.

You never can tell where one of these coding ideas will catch on. Fifteen years ago, Ashifi Gogo developed an online app that can be used to check the integrity of drugs shipped to developing countries. At the time, more than 25 percent of them were diluted, contaminated, or outright phony. The app, called Sproxil, works with unique labels that are attached to products and can be scratched to reveal a code, which is looked up using the app. It has worked so well that the company has expanded its focus to other kinds of counterfeit goods, including bottled and canned beverages. It's still going strong, still a private company run by Ashifi, the very embodiment of CGI's culture of possibility.

Despite the seriousness of the subject matter, CGI U was also a lot of fun, as students often chose to spend part of their spring break with us. They seemed to value the opportunity to meet other students from around the world in person they otherwise would have never met. We were grateful that many of the most creative and big-hearted people in entertainment and sports also chose to spend time with these students: Jon Stewart, Usher, Alonzo Mourning, Pharrell Williams, John Oliver, Natalie Portman, Conan O'Brien, Jimmy Kimmel, and so many others joined us through the years.

One of my favorite moments was when Stephen Colbert joined us in 2013 at Washington University in St. Louis. He did a special episode of his show from CGI U, including announcing his commitment to launch his own CGI—the Colbert Galactic Initiative—because simply solving the earth's most pressing challenges wasn't ambitious enough!

While the students may have been comfortable joining the global conversations online, I had been reluctant to join in, although I knew I should, since we were missing an opportunity to amplify important issues and our work. My staff conspired with Stephen and his team to accelerate it. As part of his interview with me during our closing plenary, Stephen surprised me by announcing that he had launched an account for me on what was then called Twitter as @PrezBillJeff. Over the next couple of days we traded tweets before he handed the account and the audience back to me to become @BillClinton. So I have Stephen to thank—or blame—for welcoming me to social media.

By 2010, I knew I wanted to do more to help the United States recover from the Great Recession that had struck hard in the fall of 2008, with the effects lingering for years. I wrote a book, *Back to Work*, which laid out some of the things I thought both governments and NGOs could do to boost the economy in the short and long terms, and decided to hold special annual CGI meetings to bring people together to focus on creating jobs and driving economic growth in the U.S. In June of 2011, we convened the first CGI America meeting in Chicago, to which we'd return twice more, followed by two meetings in Denver and the final one in Atlanta. We had good local experiences in cities with active, effective mayors who worked hard to ensure success. The six CGI America meetings from 2011, to 2016 produced more than six hundred Commitments to Action, which improved the lives of more than 4.9 million people in the United States.

Two big programs came out of CGI America. First, the AFL-CIO pledged $10 billion to jump-start large-scale construction of our public infrastructure, including retrofitting existing buildings to become energy-efficient. Much of that investment came from teachers' and other public employees' union pension funds, and the effort included training hundreds of thousands of men and women to qualify for good union jobs as the clean energy and green building markets increased. I first raised the idea with AFL-CIO president Richard Trumka in Davos in 2011, and he brought in Randi Weingarten, the president of the American Federation of Teachers, which was looking to invest, and the Building Trades Unions, which wanted the jobs. Randi drove the effort and by the end of their five-year commitment, they had exceeded their goals, eventually growing the fund to $16.5 billion, the largest private infrastructure fund in the country then. The fund's projects have already created more than 100,000 jobs nationwide, including 18,000 in the modernization of LaGuardia Airport in New York. I hope they'll keep at it. The union pension funds earn a good return on projects that agree to hire other union workers. New jobs are created and the pension funds of building trades workers, who have been underemployed for too long, are strengthened.

The second one was a Carnegie Corporation commitment to fund 100,000 new STEM teachers for our public schools. President Obama had called for them in his 2011 State of the Union address, but the Republican Congress wouldn't provide the money. After the Carnegie Corporation made a CGI America commitment to fill the gap, the number of partners, originally twelve, more than doubled. A full-page editorial in *The New York Times* said the commitment, named 100Kin10, was the most important effort in STEM teacher preparation in the country. In November 2021, they announced that they had exceeded their goal by adding more than 108,000 STEM teachers to our nation's classrooms in ten years, and re-upped in 2022.

In advance of the 2014 CGI Annual Meeting, our tenth, we decided that it would be a good idea to do an independent review of our commitments, find out how many had been successful, and see if we could determine a pattern in which projects had gone well and which hadn't. The results were intriguing and in many ways reflected what we wanted CGI to be. The raw numbers were encouraging, with around 80 percent of the nearly 2,900 commitments completed or still actively pursuing their goals at the time of the survey. The rest were either inactive, stalled, or unsuccessful, not a bad record for what were in many cases bold and innovative projects in very challenging environments like public health and international development. Most of the projects that failed did so because they couldn't raise the necessary funds, or changing conditions made the work too difficult to execute.

But what was most interesting to us was that the commitments most likely to succeed were true partnerships, where people from different sectors brought distinctive talents and resources to bear on a common problem. Taken as a whole, the partnership projects actually exceeded their goals. It appeared that what I had seen in countless examples across the world as president was also true in philanthropy: that cooperation beats going it alone nearly every time.

What did all the commitment-making and -keeping amount to? From 2005 through 2016, more than 3,600 commitments improved the lives of more than 435 million people in more than 180 countries. Here are three examples:

In June 2012, Procter & Gamble made a CGI commitment to save one life an hour every day by 2020. Through Flash Flood for Good, a partnership with a Christian relief organization, World Vision, dedicated to serving people in need regardless of religion, race, ethnicity, or gender, P&G produced a water purification packet that can quickly turn ten liters of dirty, unsafe water into clean, safe, drinkable water. The packet eliminates waterborne viruses, bacteria, and disease-carrying microorganisms and reduces diarrhea in developing countries by up to 90 percent. World Vision is one of P&G's hundred partners in fifty countries, helping distribute 200 million packets a year at a cost of 10 cents a packet.

In 2013, on a visit to a small village primary school in Rwanda, Chelsea and I poured filthy, fetid water into two large containers, filtered only through a white cotton cloth to get the largest chunks out. Then we added the purification packet and stirred. The water began to clear almost immediately. After a few minutes we put glasses in the water, filled them, and drank. The water was delicious, clean, and safe, a potential lifeline for countless millions of poor people who don't have access to something that life requires. As of 2024, P&G's partners have provided more than 22 billion liters of clean water to people in more than one hundred countries.

Wings to Fly, a partnership between the Kenyan Equity Bank, led by James Mwangi, and the Mastercard Foundation and its president Reeta Roy, provides scholarships to bright, underprivileged children in Kenya to attend secondary school. Wings to Fly has given scholarships to 10,000 students, with 98 percent of the scholars graduating secondary school and 94 percent continuing on to college. In 2015, Chelsea and I spoke to 5,000 of them in a large indoor stadium in Nairobi and listened to four of the young people tell their stories, including a young man I met who talked about how he used to intentionally get arrested so he could spend the night in jail with a roof over his head and food to eat, and a young Muslim woman in a majority-Christian nation who thanked her fellow students for supporting her desire to get an education and to contribute to society. Her classmates high-fived her after she finished her talk. The students in Wings to Fly are all asked to become instructors to others who follow in their footsteps.

In July of 2012, Chelsea and I visited the Building Tomorrow Academy of Gita in Uganda. At the CGI Annual Meeting the previous fall, Building Tomorrow had committed to build and staff academies for 15,000 primary-level students by 2016. We met teachers and students in classrooms and greeted hundreds of community members thrilled with their new school and the opportunities it brought.

Founded by Joseph Kaliisa and George Srour, Building Tomorrow works with the Ugandan government to build the schools in rural communities and partners with more than twenty-five colleges and universities internationally to involve young people, mostly American college students. When a community is chosen, local citizens commit to volunteer over 20,000 hours to construct each school. When construction is completed, the building is leased to the local government to manage day-to-day operations and the Ugandan Ministry of Education funds teachers' salaries and other long-term operating costs. Currently, more than 200,000 students are enrolled in Building Tomorrow programs across Uganda, including more than 2,000 with disabilities.

We can't include all the stories I'd like, but here are some figures that show CGI's impact:

In energy and the environment:

- Nearly 2.7 billion metric tons of CO_2 were cut or abated.
- More than 401 million acres of forest were protected or restored.
- More than 8 million people gained skills to cope with environmental stress and natural disasters.
- Nearly 4 million clean jobs were created.
- More than 37 million people became actively engaged in efforts to promote climate change solutions.

In economic empowerment:

- Nearly 78 million people got improved access to financial services or capital.
- More than 13 million girls and women were supported through empowerment initiatives.

- More than $1.6 billion was invested or loaned to small and medium-sized enterprises.
- More than 50 million farmers or small-scale producers gained access to better inputs, like seed and fertilizer, better supports including more systematic planting and harvesting training, and up-to-date knowledge of fair market prices.

In education:

- More than 5.9 million girls were reached with efforts to increase female enrollment in schools.
- Nearly 35 million people obtained access to information technology.
- More than 52 million children received a better education.

In health:

- More than 114 million people had increased access to maternal and child health and survival programs.
- More than 33 million people got access to safe drinking water and sanitation.
- More than 36 million people received treatment for neglected tropical diseases.
- More than $318 million in research and development funds were spent on new vaccines, medicines, and diagnostics.

Over the twelve years that we convened CGI meetings in New York, there were many unforgettable moments, both onstage and behind the scenes, including a live conversation with astronaut Reid Wiseman aboard the International Space Station and a televised conversation between Archbishop Desmond Tutu, always a popular guest, and Aung San Suu Kyi, who was then under house arrest in Myanmar. (She's now in tighter confinement again, in spite of her good-faith efforts to work with the military.) And on the final afternoon of each meeting, I announced the tallies of commitments made during the previous days, and sent our members off with a few words of thanks.

In 2016, we held what we thought would be the final Clinton Global Initiative Annual Meeting in New York, having bested our original commitment by two years. It was a bittersweet event, especially for Chelsea and me, not long before the end of a bitter, divisive election, but we had to do it. If Hillary won the election, we couldn't take foreign sponsors and even U.S. companies would be accused of getting involved in order to influence the White House. If Trump won, he would go after anyone who supported us, foreign or domestic.

In my final remarks I tried to explain how CGI was an outgrowth of my other foundation work and my desire to get others involved, to help those already doing good things increase the impact of their work, and to encourage our partners to press on in the face of the ferocious headwinds of divisive tribalism at home and around the world.

After reviewing the history of CGI and highlighting some of its remarkable contributors and their work, I tried to address the current moment:

> Don't be disheartened. Don't be deterred. Or in the wonderful words of my tradition, "Do not grow weary in doing good." Deal with the headlines, but never forget the trendlines. The trendlines are better than the headlines. Good news about what's going right in the world is a hard sell today, but look at the trendlines. More than a billion people have been lifted out of extreme poverty since 1990. We have dramatically reduced the number of people dying from tuberculosis and malaria on all continents. Infant mortality is going down. The gender gap in global primary school enrollment has virtually been eliminated.
>
> Don't ever give up what brought you here. . . . The next thirty years could be the time of greatest discovery and possibility and creativity the world has ever known. . . . But only if we get up tomorrow knowing that if we just get caught trying, and we do it with somebody else, chances are it'll work out better than we ever dreamed.
>
> CGI worked out better than I ever dreamed—thanks to you. God bless you.

Although we halted the annual meetings between 2016 and 2022, we kept the CGI model going. Our Action Network on

Post-Disaster Recovery for victims of the 2017 hurricanes in the Caribbean brought together over 750 organizations in several meetings that produced more than eighty-five new, specific, and measurable plans that advance recovery and promote long-term resiliency across the region. As I described earlier, the Haiti Action Network is alive as well.

Experts recognized how CGI had helped transform the possibilities for philanthropy. Matthew Bishop, who cowrote *Philanthrocapitalism* and served as U.S. business editor for *The Economist*, observed in *Politico*, "In providing a marketplace where these partnerships could be forged, Mr. Clinton put CGI at the heart of a new movement in international problem-solving. . . . If for some reason CGI does have to stop, it would almost certainly be necessary to invent something else like it."

Not everyone agrees, of course. In 2018, Anand Giridharadas, former foreign correspondent and columnist for *The New York Times* and contributor to *The Atlantic*, *The New Republic*, and *The New Yorker*, published *Winners Take All: The Elite Charade of Changing the World.* The book is a blistering critique of the growing inequality in the United States and around the world and the global elites who have claimed an unfair and unsustainable share of the world's wealth while "pretending to care" about the people they had shafted. The book holds up Davos for special scorn, but also criticizes CGI and me personally for letting big corporations and the super-wealthy off the hook by giving those he dismissively calls "globalizers" a forum to look good and do very little. He has the same criticism about the Robin Hood Foundation, which raises over $100 million a year to help poor people in New York by holding a gala dinner to raise the money.

Unlike Peter Schweizer's *Clinton Cash*, which I'll discuss later, this is not a piece of political propaganda designed to help elect far-right wolves in populist clothing. Instead, Giridharadas argues that inequality keeps increasing because the principal architects of the global "winners take all" economy do try to do some good, but never propose anything that will make a significant difference because doing so would reduce their wealth and power.

There's something to it. I've seen people set up tax-exempt foundations with high overhead costs that didn't fund charitable operations as fully as their contributions would permit. The author interviewed Darren Walker, the president of the Ford Foundation, who was candid in admitting he worried about the same thing. I like and admire Walker. He's brilliant, energetic, and committed to improving lives.

The book's main argument is that real change will only come when we change the power structure in the United States and the world from the bottom up. That would certainly make a big difference, but as the 2020 and 2022 election results show, it's not easy or quick work in a deeply divided country. The United States has suffered two severe meltdowns in the new century—the 2008 crash and the Covid-driven collapse in 2020. Both required much more government investment at the national level to rebuild the economy and, in the meantime, to help people pay their bills and keep businesses afloat. For a while it looked as if the deficits produced by this spending were manageable, but the return of higher interest rates on our national debt of $33 trillion and our low savings rate show that it's not a sustainable policy.

So should we all stop what we are doing and just work on redistributing wealth and power at the grass roots? It's a compelling argument in theory, but in practice I'm convinced that in the messy real world, where markets play a big role in the allocation of goods and services, working people worry a lot about high interest rates, and the struggle to make all of it more effective and more fair has faced stiff headwinds, we'd be worse off without people like Bill Gates, Melinda French Gates, MacKenzie Scott, Susie Buffett, and Laurene Powell Jobs trying to save lives, empower poor people with better healthcare and education, strengthen global and national health systems, and incentivize governments in developing countries to build their capacity and eliminate corruption.

With large government donors keeping their donations flat, or pulling back to deal with COVID-19's economic damage in their own countries and other pressures, we'd better hope NGOs, businesses, philanthropists, and crowdfunding groups keep stepping up, especially when it comes to global health and climate change. I hope the examples offered here will persuade you to support that position.

Better health and thriving children give families the chance to be more productive workers and better, more involved citizens. Doing that work hasn't stopped Bill Gates from opposing the repeal of the estate tax, supporting good climate policy, or advocating other progressive issues. CHAI only works in countries where it's invited and always tries to help countries improve their ability to take care of themselves with less corruption and more capacity. CGI America worked with the labor movement to establish a $16 billion infrastructure program, but the unions didn't stop working for more progressive economic policies, including President Biden's much larger infrastructure program, which thankfully finally passed in early 2022.

Would we really be better off if all those CGI commitments were never made and kept and all that money had been spent on local politics in the U.S. to counter the gains made by the antigovernment forces in Congress and state legislatures all over the country? What about the work in developing countries? We didn't turn them into Scandinavia, but millions of people are better off.

Of course, politics and government policies matter everywhere in defining how much people can reduce inequality, increase incomes and social mobility, and improve the quality of life. But politics, as Max Weber said a century ago, is "a strong and slow boring of hard boards." There are times when big changes can be made, but most times require hard work to make modest progress and protect existing gains. And, as I've painfully learned, there are no permanent victories or defeats in politics. We had repealed Reaganomics in 1993, substituting an "invest and grow" model designed to grow the middle class, reduce poverty, and raise incomes across the board. This approach produced the most widely shared prosperity in a generation, but when the GOP later won the White House and Congress, they still went back to trickle-down economics. Meanwhile life goes on and those without direct political power have to decide what to do with each new day.

I believe the right approach is to be active in politics, supporting policies more likely to achieve shared economic prosperity and more inclusive communities; to push large corporations to act in the interests of *all* their stakeholders—their shareholders, *and* their employees, suppliers, and communities; and to back nongovernmental activities that bring as many positive changes and help as many people as possible by filling the gap between what the government does and the private sector provides, doing so faster, better, at lower cost, and doing it whenever possible in cooperation with both the public and private sectors. This kind of creative cooperation may be a lot to ask in today's polarized business and political climates, but there's plenty of evidence that working together to solve our problems works better than constant conflict.

TWELVE

The Widow Farmer and the Spice Traders

I wasn't born on a farm, but in the summer before I started the second grade, we moved from Hope, Arkansas, to one my uncle owned outside of Hot Springs and stayed for more than a year. We raised cattle, sheep, and goats on about four hundred acres. I enjoyed helping with the animals, and have many fond memories of that time, with two exceptions: the outdoor toilet, cold in the winter and attractive to snakes in the summer, and getting butted over and over again by an angry ram unhappy that I'd hopped the fence into his territory. Before then, when I was a small child and my mother was away in New Orleans studying to be a nurse anesthetist, I lived in town with my grandparents. My grandfather was a kind, hardworking man who ran a small grocery store, and supplemented that modest income with a job as a night watchman at a sawmill, where I spent a couple of happy starry nights, climbing on the large sawdust piles and sleeping in the backseat of his car. While there was enough money for essentials, there wasn't much left over for extras.

I'm telling you this now because in addition to CGI and CHAI, I was always looking for more ways to form productive grassroots partnerships, starting with our work with small businesses in Harlem. Some of the most interesting and rewarding ones have helped men and women—who work small plots of land and scrape by without the money or other resources to do more than just that—get by from day to day. One of the difficult truths of our newly interdependent world is that intelligence, ability, and the desire to work hard are equally distributed, but opportunity is not. Much of what we in wealthier countries take for granted in our modern systems of health and sanitation, education, transportation, communications, and government aren't available to people in poor countries striving for better tomorrows for themselves and their children. As a result, many bright, industrious people, no matter how hard they work, can't rise above a subsistence living, pay for an education for their children or even make modest improvements in their own situation.

During my presidency we tried to help spur growth in and trade with Africa by passing the African Growth and Opportunity Act and forgiving the debts of poor countries if they used the savings to invest in economic development, education, and health. We also funded two million microcredit loans a year in poor villages through USAID. After I left the White House I wanted to keep working on these problems, helping many more farmers, ranchers, and fishermen and -women who were vulnerable to bad weather and inefficient supply chains. In theory, most African countries were capable of feeding themselves and producing crops for export. In practice, most farmers were just hanging on, leaving too much land fallow or poorly farmed, unable to afford good feed, seed, and fertilizer, and too often paying half their incomes to someone with a wagon to take their crops to market. Unless this changed, I was convinced that more and more poor farmers would keep flooding into cities already dealing with unmanageable growth and many more governments would yield to the inevitable temptation to sell or lease land to nations with lots of money but without the ability to feed themselves, including China and Saudi Arabia.

In the early years of the foundation, I met Sir Tom Hunter, a Scottish businessman and philanthropist. Hunter started with nothing but an idea: selling sports shoes out of his minivan. After he grew his idea into a $500 million business and expanded into other areas, Tom began working to improve economic literacy and entrepreneurship in Scotland. When I asked him to work with me to help small farmers in Malawi and Rwanda, he eagerly embraced the challenge. In 2005, at our first Clinton Global Initiative meeting, we announced the Clinton Hunter Development Initiative (CHDI) to work with small farmers to improve their yields and their access to markets for their crops.

Over the years the focus of CHDI would shift—as later the name would, to the Clinton Development Initiative (CDI), after Tom Hunter's foundation shifted its focus to other projects—but the central idea remained economic empowerment for small farmers and their communities. We wanted to help the farmers' own bottom lines by improving their seed stock, fertilizers, and other inputs, showing them alternative planting techniques, helping them get their harvests to market at lower cost, and once there, helping them negotiate for better prices—very similar to what cooperatives and county extension agents do for U.S. farmers.

CHDI emphasized programs that could be expanded, replicated, and sustained, with costs borne by local governments and communities, instead of long-term reliance on foreign donors. We had learned a lot from our experiences with CHAI and knew that a big part of making the program sustainable was the ability to increase farmers' incomes quickly. In the same way we needed manufacturers of AIDS medicine to still make a profit even when selling their products at much lower prices, we first had to help the small farmers succeed in the existing market for their goods to achieve long-lasting and replicable benefits.

In the beginning, CHDI had four major pillars—helping smallholder farmers to boost agricultural outputs, bolstering education in their communities by helping to build schools, improving water and sanitation by digging wells and building washing stations, and, in a joint program with Partners in Health, improving healthcare.

By 2007, CHDI had made good progress on its goals. Twelve hundred farmers in a local cooperative association received a $65,000 loan from the Malawi Rural Finance Company to purchase improved wheat seed and fertilizer. CHDI built the sanitation system and developed the piped water supply for the Neno District Hospital in Malawi that Partners in Health had built, and helped the government of Rwanda organize the largest purchase of fertilizer in the country's history, increasing farmers' yields and incomes.

I met a widow with a thirteen-year-old boy whose plot was only a quarter of an acre. The year before she joined CHDI, her income was $80. I don't know how she made it. But with better inputs and the ability to get her crops to market at dramatically reduced cost, she earned $320, then above the country's median income, and was able to send her son to school for the first time.

Two thousand eight was a pivotal year for CHDI when it launched its first experimental "anchor farm" in Malawi. Through donor contributions, CHDI bought a commercial farm to anchor smallholder farmers in the surrounding area. The initial anchor farm was able to buy seeds, fertilizer, and other inputs at bulk prices and share those savings, as well as its access to markets, with 250 smallholder farmers. Along the way the anchor farm became a central clearinghouse for instruction in higher-yield and sustainable farming techniques, such as encouraging the farmers not to burn the previous years' stubble but to plant beneath it, using the decaying organic matter as a natural soil enhancement. The anchor farm model proved so successful that by 2020, CDI operated anchor farms in Malawi, Rwanda, and Tanzania supporting more than 105,000 farmers.

In 2013, Chelsea and I visited one of the anchor farms in Santhe, Malawi. The farm was impressive, with modern tractors and an energetic, well-trained staff. So was a conversation I had with one of the smallholder farmers, a woman who had been doing so well since participating in the program that she was able to send two children to school with the additional profit she had made from her small plot of land. She had managed to plant something on every bit of it surrounding her house.

I also met a group of women at the farm practicing planting in ways that both would save more soil in dry weather and better endure hard rains, and remember one of them in particular. I doubt she knew who I was, other than someone with white hair who had come a long way to visit the farm. Understandably skeptical of my knowledge and interest, she asked me if I thought I could do the planting she was doing with her small spade. I said I could. She seemed unconvinced, so I took her spade and seeded a bit of the row she was working. It had been a long time since I'd done that, but I was able to make my way down the row without too much trouble. When I handed the farmer back her implement, I'll admit I was nervous to see if my work was up to her standards, and relieved when she nodded in satisfaction. It wasn't a speech to the U.N. but it was a big deal to me. At least she knew we were on the level. Chelsea and our in-country staff got a kick out of it, too.

The anchor farms were only a part of CDI's work supporting economic empowerment in Africa, but they serve as a good example of what I spoke of earlier in terms of building systems that are replicable and sustainable. Since the farms, and the farmers they support, are integrated into the local economies, they're much more sustainable than those relying on a constant influx of outside capital. They don't solve every problem faced by smallholder farmers, but they do provide supports that allow a hardworking family enough income to rise above a purely subsistence living. Best of all, the land stays with the local population. They don't have to labor in futility or flee jobless to the cities while their land is given over to outside interests and its harvests exported.

Two other Clinton-Hunter projects supported Rwandan coffee and soya growers. CHDI had begun working with 6,500 Rwandan coffee farmers in 2007 to expand their operations and increase sales, and in 2008 created two organizations, the Rwanda Farmers Coffee Company (RFCC) to advance the fledgling Rwandan coffee industry, and Mount Meru Soyco Limited, a soya-processing partnership with a Tanzanian company that produced cooking oil for the Rwandan market and for export. RFCC began by securing better returns for coffee growers and promoting the sale of premium beans overseas, especially in the U.K. It soon became apparent that the industry needed a centralized roasting and packaging facility in Rwanda instead of relying on foreign companies and the overhead they added.

With the right kind of factory to roast and package Rwanda's high-quality coffee for local, regional, and international markets, they could capture maximum value for the coffee and return a higher percentage of it back to Rwandan coffee farmers. RFCC, with the Rwandan National Agricultural Export Development Board, began the process of designing and building the facility in Kigali with our support. After some construction delays, it opened in 2014, with the capacity to process 3,000 tons of beans a year, potentially benefiting more than 50,000 smallholder farmers. The coffee was good.

The soya-processing facility also opened in 2014. Like the roasted coffee beans, the soya processed at Mount Meru was grown by the smallholder farmers CHDI was working with, providing a market for nearly 100,000 of them. The facility itself provided more than 200 others with jobs. By 2015, it was estimated that Rwanda produced approximately 25,000 metric tons of soya per year, much of it by its small farmers.

In 2005, while raising funds for the South Asian tsunami, I met Frank Giustra, a Canadian who had been successful in mining and movies and wanted to expand his philanthropic work beyond his home base in Vancouver. Frank began to support the foundation financially and in 2006 announced that he wanted to give away half his money, principally to help increase incomes and reduce inequality in Latin America. The Mexican businessman and a friend of mine, Carlos Slim, was so impressed that he joined Frank and me at the June 2007 kickoff in New York and pledged $100 million to support the effort. We agreed to focus on helping small entrepreneurs, fishermen, farmers, tradespeople, and artisans to raise their standard of living in ways that others could adopt.

At our third annual CGI meeting later that year, we announced the Clinton Giustra Sustainable Growth Initiative, or CGSGI. In Peru, at the government's request, we worked with Carlos Slim's foundation to perform more than 50,000 cataract surgeries, ahead of schedule and under budget. In Colombia we helped six Cartagena hotels purchase 20 percent of their goods and services from 150 local suppliers; provided a professional nutritionist, health monitoring, and more than 3,243,000 healthy meals to children in schools operated by Shakira's Pies Descalzos Foundation; and in Bogotá supported successful vocational training and jobs for more than 5,000 disadvantaged young people.

In 2012, CGSGI changed its name to CGEP, the Clinton Giustra Enterprise Partnership, to reflect its new strategic focus on farm and business opportunities that could make a profit and support themselves. Over the next few years, CGEP started a lot of new businesses, including a peanut supply chain enterprise in Haiti, a produce seedling supply chain enterprise in El Salvador, and beyond Latin America, similar efforts in India and Indonesia.

In 2014, we refined our approach and doubled down on our most successful pilot, Acceso, a demand-driven model that provides small-scale farmers a path out of poverty into sustained economic mobility. Acceso bridges the gap between small-scale farmers and commercial buyers and acts as an intermediary, taking farmers' products at guaranteed prices, aggregating, processing, and then selling to the best market channel. Farmers benefit from increased agricultural productivity, financing, fair prices, and sustainable access to high-value markets, which improves their livelihoods. Buyers benefit from competitive prices, stable supply, high product quality, and the opportunity to impact low-income communities by purchasing local products.

Since 2016, Acceso has grown its seed-to-market model to serve farmers in three countries: Colombia, El Salvador, and Haiti. In early 2020, CGEP transferred out of the Clinton Foundation to continue its work within Acceso, which is supported by Frank Giustra and the Giustra Foundation. Since 2007, the project had helped more than 600,000 people through its social enterprises and health programs in Latin America, the Caribbean, Asia, and Africa, with more than $42 million generated for smallholder farmers and fishers.

As of 2024, Acceso works with more than 26,000 farmers in Colombia, El Salvador, and Haiti, has bought over 54,000 metric tons of products from small-scale farmers, and has generated an average increase in income of 250 percent for farmers and food system workers, with expansion plans underway in Guatemala, Honduras, and the Dominican Republic.

Frank Giustra made a promise to himself and others back in 2007 that sustainable development would be his life's work and he's kept that commitment and will continue to do so as long as he's able. He's donated more than $100 million, not for personal acclaim, but to ensure that Acceso earns a significant social return on impact by helping smallholder farmers and their families embark on a lasting path out of poverty. I'm very grateful that he kept his commitment to give so much. The smearing he took in 2016 as part of the radical right's campaign to perform reverse plastic surgery on the foundation made me sick, but Frank believed in his work and forged through it, including staying on the Clinton Foundation board until 2020.

The Clinton-Hunter and Clinton-Giustra partnerships embodied important features of effective NGOs: a) the ability to try new innovative approaches and build on successes, and b) if projects don't work, to learn from them, keep working to improve, or move on. Of course, you have to be careful with your donors' funds and carefully account for how and why a project didn't meet expectations. While not every project succeeds, you won't know unless you give it a try.

With both the Clinton-Hunter and the Clinton-Giustra partnerships, as well as other projects in the United States and abroad, many of our efforts were unqualified successes, but in others we came in with good intentions, solid research, and relevant experience, but still found ourselves taking a different course when our efforts didn't prove to be sustainable and replicable. Anyone who works in the nonprofit sector has had the same experience—it's humbling, but you can often learn more from failing than you realize. Over the years when we've met with other like-minded organizations, offering and soliciting advice on projects, the hard-won knowledge about what didn't work and why was often as valuable as the success stories.

I'll give you a couple of examples. One of my favorite Clinton-Giustra projects was with the TANA organization, which supported Afro-Colombian women entrepreneurs in a remote part of Colombia. They grew organic spices from perches in trees to protect them from floodwaters of the Atrato River, which flowed through their community. CGSGI worked with the women to increase their productivity and to help them sell more of their spices in Cartagena and elsewhere. At first the effort succeeded in increasing the spice women's incomes. Then, for reasons beyond our control, the market for the spices flattened out, and even with the support of our initiative and the spice growers' increased productivity, the project wasn't expandable.

I also loved our Chakipi project, in which native Peruvian women were provided backpacks full of basic consumer goods like soap, toothpaste and toothbrushes, and other products not available in small Andean villages. The women would go from village to village until the supplies or the demand ran out, return with their cash, and be paid the difference between the base cost of the products and what they sold them for. For most of the women, it was the first steady income they'd ever earned. Soon they were going in pairs to larger towns with a folding table to display their wares. Eventually they set up a store in Lima to cater to lower-income neighborhoods there. When Clinton-Giustra moved into Haiti, Chakipi went there, too. In the end, sadly, the project proved to be unsustainable. But I'll never forget it, and I'm still not sure that the "Avon in the Andes" project wouldn't work if it were part of a larger consumer products organization with steady financial support.

We had similar experiences with other initiatives. Of course, in many cases, particularly with CHAI, we had the opposite experience—our success in a particular area, reducing the price of HIV/AIDS medicines, testing, and equipment, was the key to expanding into other health challenges like malaria, TB, hepatitis, and chronic illnesses.

The biggest obstacle to breakout success in agriculture is that small farming and essential food production don't receive anywhere near the level of support from donor governments, international organizations, and philanthropists that healthcare does, so we keep trying to fund scalable solutions against higher odds. The German government actually gave us $3 million to support our farming work in Africa for a couple of years so they could determine whether it could be scaled. It helped a lot of people but not for long enough. Thankfully, others are working on this problem, too. The Norwegian government funded our tree farmers in Malawi, who earn carbon credits for the investments. That did work and I'll say more about it in the next chapter. In Nigeria, businessman and industrialist (and CHAI board member) Aliko Dangote personally supports aid to 180,000 small farmers, and the American philanthropist Howard Buffett has worked successfully for years for a comprehensive effort to lift the incomes of African farmers he supports. The right answer, I believe, would be an organized funding effort to expand all these and other successful efforts until four or five million farmers in developing countries can get good seed, fertilizer, proper skills, and efficient access to markets. It would be a tremendous boost to agricultural productivity, food security, and rural incomes. Remember the woman who quadrupled her income on a quarter of an acre? With the right help, there can be many more like her.

THIRTEEN

Supporting Health and Opportunity at Home

One of the "fringe benefits" of the modern presidency is being roasted on *Saturday Night Live.* I generally got a kick out of the show's portrayals of me by Phil Hartman and Darrell Hammond. One of my favorites was the skit in which I ended one of my Washington, D.C., jogs at a fast-food restaurant, where I proceeded to explain my policy decisions to patrons while swiping French fries from their trays.

It was funny because there was some truth to it: I started running in law school when Hillary urged me to. I ran five or six days a week after going home to Arkansas, three miles a day during the week, often longer on the weekend. I kept it up in Washington, usually running right out of the White House to the Mall, then up to the Capitol or down on the Potomac. I also ran at Fort McNair or West Potomac Park, which the Secret Service preferred because they were easier to secure. But I preferred the Mall. It was quicker and gave me the chance to talk to interesting people, from members of Congress to visiting tourists.

Two things happened to change that. In October 1994, a man came from Colorado and sprayed the White House with bullets to protest the recently passed Crime Bill's ban on assault weapons like the one he was using. After that the Secret Service pleaded with me to give up running in the open, saying they couldn't protect me with fifty agents. So it was down to Fort McNair and West Potomac Park, which, depending on traffic, would add twenty to thirty minutes to the running time. Then, in March 1997, after running three miles, doing fifty push-ups, and playing golf, I tripped on the steps outside Greg Norman's house in Jupiter, Florida, fell backward trying to regain my balance, and tore 90 percent of my right quadriceps. It hurt like the devil and the recovery took months, but thanks to two fine U.S. Navy physical therapists, my leg recovered. I actually lost weight using an upper body cycle, and then, when I was able, swimming up to a mile a day.

But I never really changed my traditional Southern diet or checked my love of the wonderful creations of the White House dessert chef, the late Roland Mesnier. So when I left the White House, I had a high cholesterol count and was taking medicine to keep those numbers in check. In 2001, I started jogging again but found I couldn't run much more than a half mile without slowing to walk a couple of hundred yards, then picking up the pace again. Although I lost a fair amount of weight in a hurry and was in better shape by Chelsea's graduation from Stanford in the spring, I still couldn't cover much distance without stopping. By early 2004, even on treadmills or walks in the woods, I'd often have to stop on steep inclines, catch my breath, then go on. I thought the cause was exhaustion from the long hours spent to finish *My Life* by the publisher's deadline, but I was in for a rude awakening: the decades of poor eating and family genetics had caught up with me.

For the last months of 2004, I had a full schedule planned, including stumping for Senator John Kerry's bid for the White House and the opening of the Clinton Presidential Center. In late August, Hillary was already headed to the New York State Fair in upstate Syracuse, an annual tradition since her 2000 Senate campaign, and I was looking forward to joining her, the one thing she asked me to do as her Senate spouse, because I knew a lot about farming and rural development, had visited countless county and state fairs, and loved being with people who made their living directly and indirectly from the land.

Then, on September 1, as I got off the plane after a trip to

New Orleans promoting *My Life*, including a big Louisiana meal, I felt a tightness in my chest. It was the first time it happened when I hadn't been walking in the hills near our house with Hillary, or on the treadmill at a steep incline. I wasn't overly concerned because a recent checkup at the Mayo Clinic in Phoenix showed my cholesterol levels had improved, although the examination also showed I had enough calcium buildup around my heart to put me in the top third of people at risk.

I called our family doctor, Lisa Bardack, the next morning and she advised me to get a treadmill stress test at a small clinic near our home. The test showed no signs of a cardiac event. Nevertheless, the doctors urged me to get an angiogram, which would look for blockages of the major coronary arteries, the leading cause of heart attacks, by injecting dye into the bloodstream and imaging the resulting blood flow to the heart.

Early the next morning I drove to get the test after calling Hillary to say that I'd join her at the State Fair as soon as the angiogram cleared me. It was not to be. The imaging showed blockage in all four of my major coronary arteries, two of them at 90 percent. While I had not had a heart attack, I'd come about as close as a person could. Although the physicals didn't pick it up, given my inability to run distances, I'd probably had some blockage since 2001, or before.

With blockages this severe, bypass surgery was the only option, and it needed to be done without delay. Instead of going to the State Fair, I was taken directly to New York Presbyterian Hospital in upper Manhattan, not far from my Harlem office, and was soon joined by Hillary. Chelsea, who was in Paris at the time, came as quickly as she could.

After the news became public, I received thousands of encouraging messages from friends, colleagues, and folks from all over the country and the world. I was also grateful to see that the news coverage included some much needed information about heart disease prevention and cardiac care. My surgery, while serious and not without risk, is quite commonplace in the United States, performed several hundred thousand times a year. I was hopeful that people taking an interest in my case would examine their own health and that those who needed to would take preventive steps or seek treatment before it was too late.

The surgery was performed on September 6 by Dr. Craig Smith, a gifted cardiac surgeon whose skill and calm demeanor were a blessing to me and my family. In 2020, when the coronavirus engulfed New York and filled its hospitals, Craig Smith was the chief surgeon at New York Presbyterian. He wrote a series of updates to the staff, designed both to inform and inspire them. Full of literary and historical allusions, powerful writing, and deep humanity, they are works of art that will be read a hundred years from now. You can read some of them in his memoir, *Nobility in Small Things: A Surgeon's Path*. It's honest, chronicling both his successes and failures while praising his colleagues, and is beautifully written.

What I most remember while going under anesthesia was a swirl of images, first of dark faces like death masks, which flew at me, were crushed, then were followed by circles of light containing the faces of Hillary and Chelsea and others I loved, which also flew toward me before floating off into a bright light not unlike the sun. What this meant, if anything, about my own mortality I don't know. I wasn't afraid of dying, but I didn't think my work here on earth was finished just yet, and I wanted to be around to support Hillary and Chelsea in whatever way I could. They were with me as I came out from under the anesthesia in the early afternoon in good spirits. Hillary said later that I looked so peaceful, with not a line on my face, as if I'd had the first restful sleep in more than thirty years.

And so began my recovery, including what eventually became a different and much more healthy relationship with food. I had an amazing medical team, led by my cardiologist, Dr. Alan Schwartz, a brilliant, dedicated man who practices what he preaches. He's almost as old as I am, still runs thirty miles a week, and when I gain weight tells me I have to eat less and move more. Dr. Bardack put up with my complaints about the regular blood drawings to make sure all was going as planned. Both doctors are still with me in spite of my occasional resistance to their entreaties. They've kept me going for twenty precious years I've shared with family, friends, and work that all keep me hungry for more life.

The first days and weeks were painful as my body recuperated, and I started slow walks. I especially appreciated the advice and fellowship of others who had gone through the same or similar procedures, and was grateful for the frank advice and specific guidance on how to make sure I didn't revert to bad habits. Many people told me they were sad and frightened for a few days after their surgeries, even breaking into tears. That didn't happen to me. Because of my family history, I benefited from a long acquaintance with my own mortality, was glad to have another chance at life, and enjoyed the extended time to read, listen to music, and watch movies and sports, especially the baseball playoffs and the World Series. By early November I was in good enough shape to do a couple of campaign stops with John Kerry, including a large rally in Philadelphia, and a few weeks after the election, to welcome thousands of well-wishers to the opening of the Clinton Presidential Center and Library in Little Rock.

The surgery was by all measures a success, but I had to have two more procedures in the next five years. About 10 percent of those who have bypass surgery have fluid buildup around the lungs, and about 10 percent of those don't lose the fluid on their own. I was one of the unlucky one percent. The fluid contains a pulpy substance which settles into a rind that holds the fluid in and impairs lung function. I had it checked when I noticed difficulty on longer walks on steep inclines. In 2005, Dr. Josh Sonett pried open my ribs to create enough space to reach the rind, pare it away, and let the fluid drain away from my lungs.

Then, in February 2010, as I was about to leave on an overseas trip, I noticed my coloring was paler than usual. I called Dr. Schwartz, who said, "I think you dropped a vein. It's no big deal but you need to go get it fixed now." It's a fairly common occurrence, because veins used in modern bypass surgeries are thinner and weaker than arteries. So I went back to the hospital to have two titanium mesh stents inserted to open one of my blocked arteries. The doctor gave me the option of anesthesia or staying awake and watching the procedure on a screen near my head. "I'm not going to die, am I?" I asked. "No," he replied. "Then I want to watch." It was fascinating, and I skipped the postoperative anesthesia hangover.

Although what happened was not life-threatening, I finally realized that no amount of exercise could rid my body of its vulnerability to bad cholesterol and its consequences. So, with the help of Hillary and my longtime aide Oscar Flores, who had served on the Navy staff in the White House Mess before joining us in Chappaqua, I finally adopted a mostly plant-based, dairy-free diet.

Besides my recovery and my new relationship to food, the most positive outcome of my heart incident began with an outreach from Cass Wheeler, the president of the American Heart Association (AHA). Cass asked me if I would consider using what happened to me as a teachable moment for America, in particular for our kids. Because of the *Saturday Night Live* routines and other things, he said, only half joking, that I was the "poster child for bad eating habits." He thought that if I got together with the Heart Association in promoting heart health, we could make significant progress in fighting the high and still growing rate of obesity in America's young people, which until the explosion of the opioid epidemic, was our number one public health problem.

More and more children were reporting high cholesterol, high blood pressure, and type 2 diabetes, which had formerly been found mainly in adults. Obesity-related annual hospital costs for children had more than tripled between 1979 and 1999, and overweight children and adolescents had an approximately 70 percent chance of becoming overweight adults, increasing their risk for heart disease or other conditions leading to a lower overall life expectancy. This last statistic rang true to me, as I had more or less kept the eating habits I had developed as a chubby boy, with all of the health risks they entailed.

We had tried to address this looming epidemic during my administration as part of the overall healthcare reform effort, and when that was defeated, as part of the State Children's Health Insurance Program, or SCHIP, which provided healthcare to millions of children in the largest expansion of health insurance since Medicaid was enacted in 1965. I wanted to help, but not by just making public service announcements or talking about my own experience. That was fine, but America needed a long-term commitment to changing not only children's lifestyles and diets, but also changing the business practices that made it too easy for kids—and profitable for companies—to make unhealthy choices, even in their schools. To do that, the schools, the food and beverage industries, healthcare providers and insurers, the media, and the entertainment industry had to join the effort.

In May of 2005, eight months after my bypass surgery, the Clinton Foundation joined forces with the AHA to launch what would become the Alliance for a Healthier Generation at Public School 128 in New York City. I asked Arkansas governor Mike Huckabee to serve as a cochairman because he had developed an aggressive effort to combat childhood obesity in the schools of our home state, and had lost a lot of weight himself to encourage others. Governor Huckabee and California governor Arnold Schwarzenegger, who took over for him in 2007, were both Republicans, and their early involvement forged a bipartisan relationship with state governors that became a valuable part of the alliance's ongoing work. The alliance hit the ground running and developed good vehicles for reaching young people, including Nickelodeon's award-winning show *Let's Just Play*, which featured kids engaging in healthy activities.

In 2006, aided by a grant from the Robert Wood Johnson Foundation, the alliance instituted the Healthy Schools Program, which became a pillar of our work, with clear goals for participating schools: improving the nutritional value of food and drinks served in and out of cafeterias and vending machines; increasing physical activity during and after the school day; providing classroom lessons on healthy lifestyles; and promoting school staff wellness. The first year's goal was 200 participating schools. By 2007, that number had risen to 1,000. At last count, the Healthy Schools Program has helped 30.8 million children in 52,000 schools, districts, and out-of-school sites, building healthier places of learning, and expanding that work to the larger community.

For several years, we held an annual meeting at the Clinton Presidential Center to honor schools we recognized for outstanding progress in school nutrition and exercise programs. Hardworking educators from all over the country were recognized for advancing the health of their students and staff. At one meeting we featured a thirteen-year-old refugee from Katrina who had relocated to Little Rock, lost thirty-six pounds, and inspired his mother to do the same!

Perhaps our most significant accomplishment was a partnership with beverage companies to provide healthier alternatives to the drinks supplied to school cafeterias and vending machines. This was a very profitable area for the companies, so the challenge was to find a way for them to help the kids and still make money.

Led by Pepsi, Coke, Cadbury Schweppes, and the American Beverage Association, the companies agreed to switch their offerings in thousands of schools from high-sugar drinks to alternatives like flavored waters, diet soda, fat-free milk, and less sugary fruit juices. By 2010, full-calorie beverages had been removed from all the participating schools, and total calories from all drinks shipped to schools had dropped by 90 percent. The companies were still making a profit, and their youngest customers were much better off.

We tried and still try to do the same thing with snack foods, but with less success, partly because the snacks providers are more numerous and less well organized. We had more success in reducing the calories and increasing the nutritional value of food provided by contractors to schools that no longer prepared meals in the cafeteria. Later, as we focused on out-of-school eating, McDonald's made changes to its Happy Meal program to cut fat and sugar in those items that are primarily eaten by children and increased offerings of fresh fruit and salad. Since then, about five and a half billion servings of fruit, low-fat dairy drinks, and water have been sold in Happy Meals.

We still need to do more. In recent years the alliance has expanded the Healthy Schools Program to include juvenile justice facilities, tackling stress and trauma in classrooms, and promoting healthier out-of-school time. We've also had some success in getting insurance companies to include coverage of visits to doctors and dietitians for overweight children of their employees. In 2017, the alliance spoke out against the Trump administration's efforts to roll back school nutrition standards, garnering more than 98 million media impressions through placements on MSNBC, National Public Radio, Healthline, and many more. We also participated in Michelle Obama's Let's Move! initiative, one of the efforts she made as first lady to get kids and their families to eat healthier and exercise more.

On February 19, 2017, when I was seventy years and six months old, I became the longest-living person in my family for three generations, since my great-grandparents. They lived out in the country, went to bed with the sun, got up with the sun, ate sparingly, and didn't drink or smoke. I never saw my great-grandfather out of overalls and hobnail boots, or my great-grandmother in anything but simple cotton or wool clothes. Our world is very different from the one they lived in. It has brought us many benefits including medical advancements like the ones that saved my life, but if we're going to build a healthy society, we need to help our children make good choices while they're still young enough to create healthy habits for life.

And as for us adults, it's never too late to make healthier decisions about diet and exercise. If I can do it, anyone can.

I first met Bob Hope in Arkansas as a young governor when he came to do a show at the University of Arkansas in Fayetteville. He was in his late seventies, still busy and as funny as ever. I asked him how he stayed in such great shape and had the energy to maintain his schedule. He told me that as he had gotten older, he made sure to walk for an hour a day, every day. If he finished a show at 11 p.m. and hadn't walked, he'd do it then, and no matter the weather. He always traveled with rubber boots and a big umbrella.

In February of 1995, during my first term as president, I played golf with President Ford and President George H. W. Bush in the Bob Hope Desert Classic near Palm Springs. The tournament raised money for local charities, most importantly the Eisenhower Medical Center, which was built with funds from the event. Bob, then ninety-one, played a dozen holes with us, could still swing his driver parallel to the ground, and that day hit the ball much straighter than the three presidents did! A few years later, he called to say he was coming to Washington and asked me to take him to play nine holes. At ninety-four, unable to see more than a few feet in front of him, he still made par on a 173-yard uphill hole, missing a birdie by less than six inches. I wasn't a bit surprised when he lived to be one hundred.

In 2012, I was intrigued when a longtime friend, Tim Finchem, then the commissioner of the PGA, contacted me to see if the Clinton Foundation would serve as cohost of the 2012 Bob Hope Desert Classic. Bob had passed away nearly a decade before. Without his presence, with television viewing habits changing, and with competition from a new tournament in the Middle East which paid some players just to come, the tournament had to change to survive and continue its support of the local hospital. I agreed and our team, skillfully guided by Terry Krinvic and Hannah Richert, embraced the challenge and dove in.

In 2012, the PGA reduced play from five to the standard four days, with amateurs playing just the first two days, but the organizers wanted to keep the emphasis on health with the Humana insurance corporation and its CEO, Mike McCallister, as lead sponsor. McCallister was familiar with our work fighting HIV/AIDS in the developing world and addressing childhood obesity at home, and strongly supported the Clinton Foundation's getting involved and providing a day of health-related programming alongside the golfing. The foundation cohosted the Humana Challenge for the next four years.

It was a big success in its new format, with a good mix of young and veteran pros and celebrity players. I still enjoyed golf and was grateful for the chance to help save Bob Hope's tournament and to advance our health agenda.

We held the health and wellness summit on the Tuesday before the golf started. Health Matters: Activating Wellness in Every Generation was a fitting tribute to Bob and his lifelong dedication to his own health and to raising money for the Desert

Classic Charities organization, which supported health and wellness in the surrounding Coachella Valley. The event brought together more than two hundred stakeholders from healthcare, public policy, business, education, individual wellness, and sports to identify strategies to promote and improve individual healthy lifestyles in the home, the community, and the workplace.

We wanted to stress how entire communities could create better health outcomes for families across the economic spectrum, and the Coachella Valley was a perfect microcosm. Some of California's poorest and wealthiest families live there. It had the resources and will to improve public health. I was especially impressed by Dr. Raul Ruiz, the son of Coachella farmworkers who earned his medical degree and degrees in Public Health and Public Policy at Harvard. He then came home to work as an emergency room doctor at the Eisenhower Medical Center and also helped open a free clinic for underserved communities in the valley. In 2010, he started the Coachella Valley Healthcare Initiative, bringing all the stakeholders together to address the crisis in local healthcare. It became the model for the work we would do in other communities across the country. I was thrilled when Raul was elected to Congress in 2012, where he's become a strong voice for public health and infrastructure improvements.

When we started our work around the golf tournament, I didn't know how deeply the foundation would become involved in community-based health, but it was clear that, even with significant support from national groups, government, philanthropy, and the nonprofit sector, making real change in health outcomes required a group effort with the community, a message that still drives the foundation's public health work today.

As soon as the summit ended, we knew that we wanted to create a new entity to build on the ideas and strategies discussed at the conference and the models we had developed in other countries to help communities with health challenges across the United States.

There were too many places like the Coachella Valley with extreme disparities in healthcare access and outcomes, depending on family income. People who could afford good healthcare got it, but for too many others, chronic—and preventable—

conditions like diabetes and heart disease were a painful and growing reality. In the absence of universal healthcare coverage, which Hillary and I had worked hard for in the 1990s, long-term commitments by community stakeholders provided the next best alternative.

In the second year of the Humana Challenge we held health and wellness events for the community, and during the Health Matters Summit Dr. David Satcher, who had served as my surgeon general and founded the Satcher Health Leadership Institute at the Morehouse School of Medicine in Atlanta, led a panel on the mental health and the addiction epidemic all over the U.S. in communities large and small. One of the panelists was my friend Vin Gupta, whose eldest son Ben was enrolled in George Washington University's Law/MBA program and interned for Hillary at the State Department, when he drank a few beers with his girlfriend, then took a prescription opioid to "get a buzz." The combination can kill, because together they deaden the part of the brain that keeps the body breathing while sleeping. Ben Gupta fell asleep and never woke up. The same thing happened to three children of friends of ours. Vin wanted to do something and gave us the seed money to launch our efforts to prevent opioid overdoses and treat addiction.

In 2015, after Mike McCallister had retired as Humana's CEO, the company stopped sponsoring the golf tournament, and the PGA Tour selected CareerBuilder, the human resources and employment company, to succeed it. In 2016, we worked with them to fulfill our five-year commitment to the PGA, then handed the philanthropic reins over to California native Phil Mickelson and his wife, Amy, whose charitable causes included breast cancer research and a veterans support effort, Birdies for the Brave. We had helped save the tournament, but Phil was better positioned to sustain it.

After our tournament role ended, we kept working on critical community health issues in the Coachella Valley and in other communities with diverse problems and priorities, but we were caught in a painful paradox. As medical advancements provided more effective drugs and better treatments, Americans should have been getting healthier and living longer. Instead, lower- and middle-income Americans were dying from chronic diseases at increasingly high rates that were for the first time *lowering* life expectancy for some groups.

To have any chance of improving the situation, we needed to identify the differences in communities' problems, capacities, and attitudes, and accept that a program that might work for one might not for another. If one community had an active grassroots volunteer presence, but a less engaged or undermanned and underfunded local government, our approach would need to be different than if we had committed government partners and less active citizens. Communities with a nearby university or an engaged philanthropic sector would have greater possibilities than those without either.

So our Health Matters people worked with local leaders to tailor our efforts to their specific needs. After the Coachella Valley, we first added programs in central Arkansas, then expanded to Northeast Florida, the Mississippi Delta, Knox County, Illinois, and Houston. In each new community we started with what we called a Community Health Transformation Process. We worked with local stakeholders to chart a Blueprint for Action tailored to their specific needs and strengths, then helped them to implement it. In a way, we were trying to bring the lessons of CHAI and CGI home to America.

As I visited and talked to the people who were doing the work on the ground, it was clear that the drop in life expectancy for white working-class men and women was being driven by more than rising rates of diabetes, heart disease, suicide, and fatal overdoses, and for women, smoking. Underneath those challenges was a sense of hopelessness. A lot of those people were dying of a broken heart. They had lost their sense that they mattered, so before long the rest of America didn't matter to them.

Although the economy began to grow again during President Obama's second year in office, and accelerated more strongly in his second term, it meant nothing to those who didn't feel part of it. They were ripe for rage-based tribalism, something that as a white Southerner I was all too familiar with.

All societies are tribal, but the best of them are also inclusive: proud of their group, but welcoming of others. Rising resentment rooted in economic stagnation, social disrespect, and personal powerlessness is fertile ground for a polarized society, "us vs. them." We count, they don't. Today we are awash in the divisive tribalism I have opposed since I was a child. Growing up in Arkansas, I saw a lot of it, culminating in George Wallace winning my home state in the 1968 presidential race. The GOP had already begun its efforts to swing more Southern white voters to its banner, the people President Nixon called the "silent majority." There were enough of them to beat Vice President Hubert Humphrey in 1968 and Senator George McGovern in 1972. And of course, Trump lost the popular vote both times but prevailed in the Electoral College in 2016 and barely lost it in 2020. I'll talk more about how this has affected our politics later. From a public health perspective, it's important to realize how it's also affected our personal health and happiness by making it harder to build strong, cohesive communities.

The picture was most stark when it came to the opioid epidemic. Tens of thousands of overdose deaths had gutted families and left far too many vulnerable children without parents. These absences left holes not only in families but also in their communities—the houses of worship, the businesses, the entire social fabric. In nearly every community a leader would tell us, "Look, prevention is ideal and that's great. But I've got people dying every day in my town, and I need to stop the overdose deaths. I can't do any prevention, I can't do any planning, I can't do anything until I literally stop the bleeding."

We convened top leaders who were working on the epidemic who also said that in addition to our commitments to establish effective prevention and treatment efforts, we should immediately work to stop fatal overdoses by the best means available. An injectable drug known as naloxone had been used for years to treat opioid overdoses, allowing victims to survive long enough to get emergency treatment. Then, an Irish company, Adapt Pharma, had developed a nasal spray version called Narcan, which could be administered by just about anybody, giving the overdose victim precious time to get to a hospital. We began discussions with Adapt Pharma and by the time Narcan was approved for public use by the FDA in November of 2015, we had an agreement to help them distribute the nasal spray devices at a discount to group purchasers such as law enforcement, firefighters, first responders, departments of health, local school districts, colleges and universities, and community-based organizations. Through partnerships with Adapt Pharma and local philanthropic organizations, tens of thousands of doses of Narcan have been made available at a discount or free of charge, including a commitment by Adapt to provide every college campus in the U.S. with five doses of Narcan.

We're still working to increase that number, and we've broadened our work by partnering with faith organizations to build roads to recovery, thanks to support from the states of Georgia and California. Faith leaders receive training in overdose prevention, become certified in Mental Health First Aid, learn how to speak about substance use disorders from the pulpit, and develop comprehensive guides on local prevention, treatment, and recovery resources for their communities.

Unlike most American issues, the opioid crisis has crossed the partisan divide. It's an equal-opportunity scourge, sparking broad coalitions committed to reducing death and destruction. For example, in 2018, I accepted an invitation from GOP congressman Hal Rogers, who's represented Eastern Kentucky for forty years, to participate in the seventh annual National Rx Drug Abuse & Heroin Summit. His district has been ravaged and he wanted the government to do more to deal with the epidemic. We have to do this together.

One thing the coronavirus didn't destroy was the opioid epidemic. It got worse, as people in recovery were shut out of their usual support systems, while being even more vulnerable to the isolation, economic devastation, and other pressures that affected all Americans. In 2020, the Clinton Foundation partnered with Direct Relief International and other nonprofit and addiction groups to deliver 155,000 doses of Narcan, donated by Pfizer, to recovery residences in five states, the first step in what we hope will be a fifty-state effort to distribute the million doses Pfizer has pledged nationwide.

In the past few years, we handed over our community work to local leaders and ramped up our work on college campuses. We have a lot of challenges facing us, and if I've learned anything from the Clinton Foundation's public health work, whether it's getting lifesaving HIV/AIDS drugs to people who need them, combating obesity in our youngest citizens, or working with community stakeholders to improve health and reduce opioid deaths, it's that we're all in this together, and there's no time to waste.

FOURTEEN

Women and Children First

In 1995 at the U.N.'s Fourth World Conference on Women in Beijing, Hillary electrified the audience and women the world over with the declaration "Women's rights are human rights, and human rights are women's rights." Her fifteen-year-old daughter was one of the young women paying close attention. So I wasn't surprised when Hillary, after four years as secretary of state, wanted to join the foundation and work with Chelsea on projects to support women and girls, families, and childrearing.

In 2014, they launched No Ceilings, a partnership with Melinda French Gates and the Gates Foundation to collect, analyze, and publicize data on the status of girls and women since 1995 and to identify actions that could produce more rapid and measurable progress. I had seen Melinda working with women on health issues in a small African village. Her ability to listen to, communicate with, and move them was impressive. So was her willingness to invest in this project which could educate and motivate a large number of others to join her crusade for empowerment and equality.

A year later at the Best Buy Theater in New York, Melinda, Hillary, and Chelsea released the results of their work. *No Ceilings: The Full Participation Report* was an analysis of 850,000 data points on the status of women and girls over the past twenty years in 190 countries. The report showed remarkable progress in health and education, with maternal mortality cut almost in half since 1995, and the gender gap in primary school enrollment and completion almost eliminated. It also showed much less positive change in women's security, economic opportunities, and presence in public and private leadership roles. Not surprisingly, it revealed in specific terms what we all know: that the gains had not been equally shared because of natural and human barriers, including geography, income, age, race, ethnicity, sexual orientation, disability, and cultural norms.

Perhaps the most important thing No Ceilings did was to make its findings understandable and interesting to a much larger audience. Even though the *Full Participation Report* was available for download in six languages, only already knowledgeable and committed people were likely to read it. So an easily accessible website, NoCeilings.org, was designed to reach anyone who was interested, with clear visualizations of the information and compelling videos of stories of women and girls across the globe.

The announcement event showcased national and community leaders who were working to advance full participation of women and girls, including two female presidents and other women trailblazers working all over the world. The event generated a lot of press coverage for the report and its companion, *The Full Participation Plan*, with policy priorities for leaders and activists. There was also a lot of interest in the ad campaign released at the same time, showing all the ways in which women were "Not There." One hundred thirty-two people per minute accessed it on release day and eventually there were 283 million impressions on Twitter alone.

From 2014 through 2016, No Ceilings forged new partnerships and specific commitments through the Clinton Global Initiative. In 2014 the focus was on increasing educational attainment through high school and beyond. Hillary and the lead partner, the Collaborative for Harnessing Ambition and Resources for Girls' Education (Girls CHARGE), led by former Australian prime minister Julia Gillard, announced that thirty partners had committed $600 million to the effort. For example, Nepal committed to giving girls bicycles to make sure they could get to and from school safely. BRAC, the huge Bangladeshi NGO with 90,000 employees in twelve countries already helping more than 100 million people gain access to healthcare, education, and microfinancing, promised to establish 8,000 clubs to provide safe spaces for adolescent girls. The Clinton Foundation's job was putting folks like this in touch with big companies and other donors who could help them reach their goals.

In 2016 at the CGI Annual Meeting, Chelsea announced that No Ceilings, along with thirty NGOs, private sector and charitable partners led by Vital Voices and WEConnect International, would invest $70 million to help 900,000 women and girls in sixty countries to improve economic and leadership opportunities and reduce violence against women and girls. Our foundation had been working since 2015 to test this model in Haiti, with a Women's Economic Participation project providing services, market opportunities, and investor prospects to help women-owned small businesses and agricultural cooperatives with more than 3,000 members. In late July, Chelsea took a delegation of potential investors and buyers to Haiti for a tour of the businesses we were supporting and a larger meeting to visit more potential partners.

Another of Hillary's and Chelsea's initiatives, Too Small to Fail (TSTF), was launched long before its formal beginning. In 1972, Hillary took a fourth year in law school to work at the Yale Child Study Center and immersed herself in early childhood education programs in the U.S. and other countries. Her first job out of law school was with Marian Wright Edelman and the Children's Defense Fund. Then, when I became governor, she brought to our state an ambitious preschool program from Israel, Home Instruction for Parents of Preschool Youngsters, or HIPPY, an effort to give parents the instructions and materials to be their children's first teachers. Hillary was convinced it could help develop children's brains so they could start school with the skills to succeed, and independent evaluations proved that it did. By the time I ran for president, Arkansas had the largest HIPPY program in the country, serving 2,400 mothers and their children. We loved going to the graduation exercises where the kids showed their skills and the mothers were proud of their children and themselves.

By 2013, Chelsea, who was looking forward to becoming a mother herself, wanted to work with her mom to do more. And more had to be done. Almost 60 percent of U.S. children started kindergarten lagging behind their peers in critical language and listening skills. This slow start in brain development was graphically captured by the so-called word gap, the estimated 30 million fewer words that children from low-income, low-education households heard by the time they started school.

The simple idea that drove Too Small to Fail is the ability of all parents and other caregivers to change that by talking, reading, and singing to kids from infancy onward. TSTF's job was to get that message to as many people as possible, along with the provision of basic instructions, learning materials, and easy opportunities to do it. I was amazed at how many partners Hillary and Chelsea found to help. In 2013, they brought together a large group of entertainment industry executives to encourage them to integrate messages about early brain and language development in their programs. Millions of viewers saw parents, often in tough circumstances, including incarceration, finding ways to talk, read, and sing to their kids.

In 2014, Univision, then owned by our friend and foundation supporter Haim Saban, joined the effort in a big way, across all its television, radio, and online media, and through the community outreach activities of its local affiliates. Their efforts reached tens of millions of Spanish-speaking viewers. The next year, *Sesame Street* joined in with a unique text-to-parents program with the free health information service Text4baby, which reached more than 820,000 parents.

Two thousand fifteen also brought some unique new partnerships. Shane's Inspiration and Landscape Structures agreed to integrate TSTF's "Talk, Read, Sing" message on panels and signs in their playgrounds. In 2017, I went to the dedication of a beautiful one at Sollers Point, in Dundalk, Maryland, near Baltimore. The park was located next to a branch of the Baltimore County

Public Library and I had a nice visit with two opening day visitors, Danielle Gonzalez and her three-year-old daughter, Isabella. She told me that she visited the library at least twice a week and she was thrilled the park gave them a fun place to play and read. She told her story with quiet dignity, saying she married in her late thirties and had Isabella in her early forties. She and her husband decided they would both raise her to value learning and vowed both would read to her daily. Then, a few months earlier, her husband had passed away in his sleep. She knew she had to raise their daughter for both of them, and loved choosing books to read with her. She told me they read eight to ten books a day and smiled when she said she thought her husband would be proud. If every parent did half that, there wouldn't be many kids unprepared to start school.

The second partner I got to see in action was the Coin Laundry Association. It started by providing customers with parent tip sheets and other materials in 5,000 laundromats, then offered free laundry days for parents to bring their kids to get the tip sheet, child activity pages, and books. Then a hundred of the laundromats built "Family Read, Play & Learn" spaces for parents and kids to use while the wash was tumbling. I visited two of them, one in New Orleans and the other in Deer Park on Long Island, New York. The laundromat owners had never imagined they could be in the child development business, but were clearly proud and a little amazed at how much it meant to the parents and the kids. Families that couldn't afford an in-home washing machine were now able to spend time on something both profoundly important and fun. The Coin Laundry folks expect to have 500 more onsite play-and-learn spaces soon.

Over the last couple of years, TSTF's appeal and obvious benefits generated more support. The American Academy of Pediatricians pitched in to provide books to families that came to their offices. Tulsa, Oklahoma, and Oakland, California, did their own outreach in places where parents spend time—including grocery stores, hospitals, and houses of worship. Miami launched its efforts in 2016 at a joint event cohosted with the White House and Invest in US to support the development of young dual-language learning. Now there are at least thirty-five cities and two states, New York and Michigan, doing their own version of very early learning.

Since its inception, TSTF has distributed more than 1.4 million books to families who need them, almost 200,000 through diaper banks alone. More than thirteen hundred literacy-themed parks have been launched. Univision's campaign has amassed more than 800 million audience impressions and reached thousands of families directly through community events. Tens of millions of people have seen the Talk, Read, Sing messages in the TV shows that wrote them into the scripts. Sixteen independent academic studies have validated TSTF's positive impact on children's learning. It's all part of the village, as Hillary said long ago, that can help parents in raising children to thrive.

FIFTEEN

Skyscrapers and Trees to the Rescue

In *My Life*, I recounted the first time I laid eyes on the Empire State Building, in 1964, during my freshman year at Georgetown. I played saxophone in our college band, which was invited to give a concert at St. Joseph's College for Women, in Brooklyn. After the concert and the mixer, I accepted an invitation from one of the students to walk her home, meet her mother, and see what it was like to live in a small apartment in a big building surrounded by others just like it. During the brief visit I tried to imagine what it was like for them, and how nice it must be for them to have a small balcony overlooking the well-cared-for grounds connecting the four buildings that bordered it. It was a long way from Arkansas.

After our short visit, I hailed a cab and asked the driver to take me back to Manhattan and drop me off at Times Square, where I spent the next few hours taking in the bright lights and the packed crowds and listening to the conversations people were having in a Tad's Steak House. Then I walked the eight blocks to see the Empire State Building, in all its Art Deco grandeur. To my wide-eyed eighteen-year-old self, it embodied New York's bright promise. I remember a lot about that long-ago night when I fell in love with New York—its sights and sounds, and the Empire State Building.

So you can imagine how intrigued I was when in 2009 my foundation joined a partnership to retrofit the Empire State Building—to make it as energy-efficient as possible while keeping its original character and structure unchanged. The partners included our new Clinton Climate Initiative and the C40 organization, a global group of large cities committed to lowering carbon emissions and increasing energy efficiency in existing and new buildings; the building engineering company Johnson Controls; Amory Lovins and the legendary Rocky Mountain Institute, an energy think tank that emphasizes market-based solutions to lowering carbon emissions and increasing energy efficiency, with whom I had first worked more than thirty years ago when I was Arkansas's attorney general; the commercial real estate company Jones Lang LaSalle; and most importantly the building's owner, Anthony Malkin, the CEO of the Empire State Building Trust. Malkin made and kept a commitment to make the grand building the most energy-efficient office tower built before World War II and to do it with transparency so that other building owners, especially those with other older properties, would have a solid, successful model to follow.

The work done on the beloved landmark included the replacement of all 6,514 windows; the installation of insulation in key areas throughout the building, including behind all radiators; new state-of-the-art chiller plants; and sophisticated new temperature and lighting controls for all the building management systems. The room lights were completely changed to LED bulbs, which were not only more energy-efficient and longer lasting, but also capable of doing elaborate lighting displays to mark important events, holidays, and the like. The Empire State Building is visible from my foundation office in NoMad, and I never tire of seeing it rising majestically above the city.

It is a terrific example of the upsides of retrofitting existing buildings. First, the energy savings: after the bulk of the project was completed in 2010, the building's energy bills dropped by $4.4 million a year, and the ninety-year-old landmark is consistently ranked in the top 20 percent or better in energy efficiency of all buildings nationwide. It's the oldest one to receive an LEED Gold rating from the U.S. Green Building Council. The cost of the project was approximately $106 million.

That's a daunting figure, but due to the yearly energy savings, other incentives, and revenue from new tenants attracted by the idea of the iconic address coupled with state-of-the-art facilities, the project team calculated the retrofit paid for itself in about three years. And remember, that $106 million wasn't just sent off into the ether. It was used to buy materials and equipment, including the new windows from an Indiana company and the modern air chillers from a Wisconsin company. The local jobs it created for contractors, engineers, carpenters, and many others were good, high-paying ones, about 275 of them working in the building for several months. Those jobs and materials also generated tax receipts and other benefits. Those workers bought a lot of lunches and coffees over the years! And that's not all. The Empire State Building began reducing its greenhouse gas emissions by an estimated 115 tons over fifteen years, about 40 percent, proving building retrofits should be a major part of any plan to meet global emissions targets.

There's plenty of room to replicate what was done with the Empire State Building. At that time, 80 percent of New York City's energy was consumed by its over 900,000 buildings, with the largest 20 percent of those properties responsible for 80 percent of that consumption. Reducing the largest NYC buildings' energy use by 40 percent, as the Empire State Building did, would reduce total energy use in New York City by 25 percent, bring the economic benefits of all that work, and lower electric bills.

On April 21, 2022, I was back at the Empire State Building with Tony Malkin and his new supporters, Mayor Eric Adams, Governor Kathy Hochul, and Doreen Harris, the CEO of NYSERDA, the New York State Energy Research and Development Authority, to launch the *Empire Building Playbook: An Owner's Guide to Low-Carbon Retrofits*. It outlines the pathway, step-by-step, for commercial buildings to reduce carbon emissions, lower electric bills, and make a good profit on the investment. It's an updated version of what Malkin did with the Empire State Building and several other properties, and demonstrates how emissions can be reduced in existing buildings 75 to 90 percent through building upgrades and a renewably sourced grid.

This is one of those very big deals we don't talk enough about. Globally, 70 percent of carbon emissions are from cities which occupy 2 percent of the land. Today 70 percent of New York's emissions are still from buildings already standing. If every building owner followed the technical and financial steps in the *Playbook*, we could meet a lot of our climate goals quickly, save businesses and tenants money, create of lot of good jobs, make our buildings healthier places to live and work, and protect the future for our kids and grandkids.

At CGI in 2023, Tony Malkin gave an upbeat report on the large number of companies that have executed the playbook. Although many companies have already joined the parade, we need many more. You can get the playbook free online. It's updated in real time with new case studies, technology, and practices as Empire Building Challenge Partners complete and implement their plans.

We can also make a significant difference by organizing a large number of smaller, less expensive projects. The view from my personal office in Harlem looks out over blocks and blocks of century-old brownstones, the narrow but deep three- to four-story townhouses with flat roofs and stone façades. When we first opened our office in 2001, I noticed that most of the brownstone roofs I could see outside the windows were black, the color of the roofing materials and the tar used to seal them. I noted in a *Newsweek* article in 2011 that if those roofs were simply painted white, they'd reflect much more of the sun's rays and the buildings would be naturally cooler in the hot New York City summers, made worse by what's known as the heat island effect that can raise temperatures in the city as many as ten degrees over the surrounding suburbs.

Painting black roofs white was something I'd been touting before that article and haven't stopped—it's cheap and effective and can pay for itself in a single year. Mayor Mike Bloomberg did a lot of that, with much of the work being done by young people in a summer jobs program. The white roofs reduced air-conditioning costs by 25 percent and emissions by about 20 percent. I'm happy to report that in the ten years since, I've seen a significant change in my view—many of the townhouses and commercial buildings outside my window have white or silver roofs now. Large numbers of small efficiencies like these can also add up, particularly when they number into the thousands or millions. Every painted roof, every energy-upgraded home, every energy-efficient appliance installed makes a difference.

I want to switch coasts and mention a variation on this idea. If, like me, you've flown at night into Los Angeles, part of the fun of having a window seat is to glimpse the vast expanse of the city and its suburbs reflected in thousands and thousands of tiny lights stretching into the darkness as far as you can see, including streetlights laid out in grids tucked within the valleys and along the coast. The sheer number of lights is part of what makes the view so awe-inspiring.

In 2009, the Clinton Climate Initiative began working with Mayor Antonio Villaraigosa on a five-year project to retrofit more than 140,000 L.A. streetlights, replacing the standard yellow-tinted halogen bulbs with modern LED bulbs. In the same way that replacing the incandescent bulbs in your home reduces your electricity bill, the new bulbs, once installed throughout the city, reduced L.A.'s annual bill of $15 million by 63 percent. The cost of the project was funded through a $40 million loan from the city utility department, to be repaid in seven years through energy and maintenance savings, after which the city will pocket almost $10 million in savings a year.

As with the Empire State Building project, it's important to note the other benefits. The LED bulbs installed as part of the energy-saving upgrade generally last more than twice as long as the bulbs they replaced, saving labor costs and the amount of time a particular stretch of street is dark due to a burnt-out bulb. They're also brighter, providing greater safety at night.

The lights installed in Los Angeles reduced carbon emissions by more than 47 metric tons a year. In 2013, when the project ended, Mayor Villaraigosa said it was a significant factor in Los Angeles's nearly 30 percent reduction in overall emissions, which was larger than any other city in the nation at the time. One roof at a time, one streetlight at a time, one building at a time, the benefits add up, not only in helping stave off climate catastrophe, but also in jobs and economic growth.

Earlier I mentioned the C40 organization. What eventually became the C40 was started by London mayor Ken Livingstone in 2005 with representatives from at that time eighteen megacities, the world's largest energy-using urban centers, who agreed to cooperate on reducing climate emissions by taking quick, concrete, and market-based action to adopt climate-friendly policies. The following year the network grew to forty, and the new Clinton Climate Initiative, through our CCI Cities program, took on the role of delivery partner. Just as he had with CHAI, Ira Magaziner took a leading role in the climate change effort in the beginning, working on the Empire State Building retrofit through our Clinton Climate Initiative Cities program. In the beginning, Ira also put together teams with diverse skills to begin work on projects, including zero-emissions buildings, that could lead to a large reduction in greenhouse gas emissions. Big-city mayors of Toronto, New York, Rio de Janeiro, Paris, Los Angeles, and others have done some amazing work to that end. Michael Bloomberg, personally and through his foundation, has been especially active from the start.

Over the first few years, as the C40's delivery partner, CCI Cities assisted Houston, Chicago, and New York with retrofits, and overseas supported successful projects in the U.K., South Africa, Australia, Thailand, Mexico, and India. CCI Cities and the C40 helped Lima install over 6,000 LED traffic lights and worked with partner cities to reduce their transportation systems' carbon footprints in Bogotá, Rio de Janeiro, Lima, and Houston. The partnership also worked with cities around the world to promote large "climate positive" real estate projects, where CO_2 emissions for entire developments are at or even below zero, meaning their heating, cooling, and power systems don't add any additional greenhouse gases to the atmosphere and in some cases have a negative footprint. Successful development projects were completed in South Korea, Canada, India, the U.K., South Africa, Sweden, and here in the United States.

The Clinton Climate Initiative's Cities program merged with C40 in 2011. When Mike Bloomberg left the New York City mayor's office, he took charge of the entire effort. I really enjoyed the C40 work, especially all the carbon-neutral or -negative projects we were supporting, but I was glad to have Mayor Bloomberg take it over. He believed in the work, CHAI was growing too rapidly for Ira to manage both efforts, there was no comparable public financing available for the energy work, and Bloomberg could properly fund it in a way we couldn't. We were able to run CHAI, CGI, and the Alliance for a Healthier Generation as large projects because we had dedicated funding sources. Without them, we didn't have the capacity to do justice to all the C40 projects. Bloomberg was in a better position to give and raise the necessary funding, and was eager to take the reins. In this case success was a good start and worthy handoff. The C40 now represents nearly one hundred megacities across the world.

In 2009 the Clinton Climate Initiative worked on increasing the availability of funding for home energy retrofits, including one in Arkansas that was personally important to me, the Home Energy Affordability Program, or HEAL. It was created by CCI program manager Martha Jane Murray, who was inspired to develop it while leading the foundation's Hurricane Katrina recovery programs in New Orleans. She saw firsthand how energy-efficient home renovations benefited low- and moderate-income homeowners, and designed a program in which employers could use the cost savings from the retrofits of their own buildings to fund the same work for their employees' homes.

HEAL's partnership with the French cosmetics company L'Oréal's Maybelline plant in North Little Rock reduced the plant's energy consumption and greenhouse gas emissions, saving L'Oréal more than $80,000 a year. HEAL educated L'Oréal employees and their families about the importance of environmental responsibility in the workplace and helped them apply that knowledge to their own homes. With their HEAL savings, L'Oréal was able to provide its employees with home energy assessments and financing or loans for retrofits. With proof the HEAL model worked, we began to expand it to other states so that employees there could share in the benefits that their employers reap from retrofitting company buildings. As of this writing, more than 5,600 people are benefiting from energy efficiency audits and retrofits, totaling more than $2.4 million in residential energy efficiency investments.

C40 wasn't the only initiative to support large-scale retrofits. Launched in February 2011, the Better Buildings Challenge was a partnership between President Obama's Council on Jobs and Competitiveness, labor unions, and more than sixty organizations from the public and private sectors to support job creation by promoting private sector investment in commercial and industrial building energy upgrades. The goal at the outset was to make America's buildings 20 percent more efficient over the next decade, reducing energy costs for American businesses by nearly $40 billion and creating tens of thousands of good-paying jobs.

President Obama asked me to a White House meeting with the business leaders supporting the effort and to accompany him to a retrofit project in a D.C. office building to rally support for the initiative. By 2013, the Departments of Housing and Urban Development and Energy expanded the program to include multifamily housing, and the Obama administration challenged federal agencies to expand their use of performance-based contracts to upgrade government buildings at no cost to taxpayers. The administration also launched an accelerator program to promote energy-saving initiatives by state and local governments.

President Biden set substantial retrofit goals at the outset of his administration, including a net-zero emissions target for the entire portfolio of federal buildings by 2045, with significant new funding through the Inflation Reduction Act passed in 2022. Technological advances are providing more efficient retrofits with quicker payback than ever. Making buildings more efficient has always been an underutilized opportunity and should be a major part of any national infrastructure program. We should have been leading the energy efficiency parade for forty years. Now with evidence of climate change all around us, we have to do it. It will bring more shared economic and environmental benefits than we know.

Of course, while it's vital to limit the amount of CO_2 pumped into the atmosphere, it's not the only way to fight climate change. Fighting deforestation, which I touched on in the Haiti section by noting the 7.5 million trees planted by Timberland, can make a big difference. It's estimated that the world's forests are responsible for sequestering nearly 20 percent of the earth's carbon.

In 2008 CCI started its Forestry program to combat deforestation in Indonesia, Kenya, Tanzania, and Cambodia. We also began an important partnership in Guyana, with support from the Rockefeller Foundation, which focused on monitoring and reporting forest change, improving the strength of their government agencies, and promoting ecotourism and sustainable agriculture. CCI worked closely with President Bharrat Jagdeo and the Guyanese government to build a monitoring system by providing access to satellite data, and donated software and training. CCI also facilitated a performance-based contract between the governments of Guyana and Norway that provided payment to Guyana based on how much forest they protected each year. By 2014, Guyana had received a total of $125 million from Norway, which they used to continue low-carbon development. In subsequent years, the CCI Forestry program expanded into India and Vietnam. There are no more efficient trappers of carbon than trees, and replacing deforested ecosystems is not only good for the climate and the overall environment, it's an economic opportunity for local communities.

One of the best examples of that I've seen is the Trees of Hope program in Malawi, which was one of the projects the Clinton Hunter Development Initiative supported. Beginning in 2007, Trees of Hope worked with smallholder farmers and community groups in the Dowa District north of the Malawi capital, Lilongwe, to plant hardwood and fruit trees as cash crops. The Dowa District, like much of Malawi, was once covered by forest, but since the 1970s had been cleared and converted to farmland, and most of the people who live there work the land as best they can to produce a marketable crop. It's also one of the hottest parts of the country. By planting fruit trees for food and fast-growing hardwood trees to be sustainably harvested for home-building materials, the farmers also contribute to improved soil fertility, erosion control, watershed protection, and reforestation, while generating additional income by selling carbon credits.

In 2010, I visited one of the Trees of Hope projects, a nursery where farmers were growing mango and citrus seedlings for their own planting and for distribution to other small farmers throughout the region. Then I went to an open space for a meeting with the entire village. People of all ages came, with schoolchildren packed together up front, the adults next, and the oldest citizens gathered around in the shade of their other planting project—very fast-growing hardwood trees, chosen by the villagers because they could be harvested every few years to replace their baked-mud huts, which were very hot and uncomfortable most of the year. The trees grew six feet or more every two years. The village elders welcomed both the shade and the extra income provided by companies in the developed world, which paid the villagers for planting the trees to offset the impact of the companies' emissions elsewhere.

In most African countries, there is no private ownership of land outside larger cities. The villages own it in common. The villagers I met were so excited by what they were doing that they voted to keep only 55 percent of their carbon credit earnings, sharing the other 45 percent with nearby communities so they could set up their own planting operations. Over the next couple of years, the project was handed over to farmers and community groups who have planted millions of trees that absorb hundreds of thousands of tons of carbon dioxide.

Planting trees is like retrofitting buildings. The good news is anyone can do it. The bad news is that it's challenging to do on a scale large enough to halt, then reduce, total global emissions. That's what the Trillion Tree Challenge is trying to do by uniting governments, companies, NGOs, and youth movements to plant a trillion trees. The movement has the enthusiastic backing of Marc Benioff, founder and CEO of Salesforce and publisher of *Time* magazine, and renowned conservationist Jane Goodall. It's doable. Today the earth has about three trillion trees, but just a hundred years ago there were almost twice that many. A grassroots effort in every nation to plant its fair share and preserve existing trees is probably the most cost-effective thing we could do to reduce emissions and restore fertile topsoil. Many efforts are underway, but it will take time and a determined effort to protect existing forests for them to work. A trillion more trees actually standing could capture 200 gigatons of CO_2 in a few decades, an amount equal to two thirds of the world's emissions increase since the dawn of the Industrial Age.

More than forty years ago, as a young governor, I read an article in the Sunday *New York Times Magazine* about the annual deforestation of the Amazon rainforest, then amounting to an area the size of Kansas. I thought that governors should each take a pledge to replace a portion of it based on each state's size and planting capacity. We couldn't replicate the unique biodiversity but we could replace the capacity to absorb CO_2. I got no takers, but we did it in Arkansas, organizing efforts among schoolchildren, garden clubs, and small landowners who worked with the state forestry program. By the time I left office, our forest cover had increased from 48 percent to 53 percent, notwithstanding clearcutting by the big timber companies.

Besides retrofitting buildings, fighting deforestation, and planting new trees, we also have to find new ways to produce the energy we need without adding more carbon dioxide to our atmosphere. At our 2013 CGI America meeting, seven Sioux tribes in South Dakota announced the Oceti Sakowin Power Authority, or OSPA, to take advantage of their abundant wind resources by developing wind farms and transmission facilities. Through OSPA, the seven tribes—the Cheyenne River Sioux, the Crow Creek Sioux, the Flandreau Santee Sioux, the Oglala Sioux, the Rosebud Sioux, the Standing Rock Sioux, and the Yankton Sioux—will own all of the energy infrastructure and when the facilities are completed will distribute the power, eventually more than 1,000 megawatts, enough to power hundreds of thousands of homes, to its member tribes and make the excess power and energy credits available to outside entities.

Thanks to Apex Clean Energy and Apple, the project is in its final planning and development stages, and its most recent testing had determined that the project will produce even more power than previously thought, with some of the strongest and most consistent winds in the United States—a boon to the Sioux tribal communities, which are among the poorest in our country. The tribes could eventually produce more than a gigawatt of wind energy, generating enough revenue to revolutionize their economic, education, and health prospects. I'm hoping tribes to the south, in Wyoming, Utah, New Mexico, and Arizona, will follow suit. They could all be self-sufficient and sell excess power to California to meet its ambitious renewable energy goals. Besides the vast areas of the country that are ripe for wind power development, there are enormous swaths of the United States and its neighbors that are bathed in sunshine and perfect for solar energy production, the price of which has fallen about 80 percent over the last decade.

In 2012, the Clinton Climate Initiative launched the CCI Islands Energy program to transition small island nations, primarily in the Caribbean, from diesel to clean energy. With abundant sunshine, these island nations are prime candidates for energy self-sufficiency—and even energy export—but too often lack the institutional commitment and capital to make real progress in replacing their reliance on high-carbon and expensive imported diesel fuel.

In late 2017, CCI, along with the Solar Foundation (now merged with IREC), Direct Relief, New Energy, and Operation Blessing, created the Solar Saves Lives partnership to address the ongoing energy crisis in Puerto Rico. Its initial focus has been to bring solar power to resource-strapped community medical clinics, some of which are geographically remote and operate under the constant threat of outages, which cripple their ability to serve their patients. To date the partnership has installed solar services and battery backup systems in fifteen of these clinics, totaling 1,800 kilowatts of power, the equivalent of 2,200 metric tons of carbon, and saving the facilities over $800,000 in utility bills. Solar Saves Lives has also provided 1,700 LED lights to the Río Piedras indoor market in San Juan and distributed 50,000 SolarPuffs, lightweight inflatable solar lanterns made by the Solight company, cofounded by entrepreneur Alice Min Soo Chun. Her work with Haiti after the earthquake convinced her of the need for individual solar lighting in disaster relief situations. SolarPuffs have helped reduce crime, including sexual assaults in refugee camps. In 2022, Alice brought them to Ukraine to help people who live in buildings damaged by Russian attacks on them and on the electrical grids that serve them.

In 2018, I attended the official opening of a 3-megawatt solar farm in Vieux Fort, St. Lucia, that was developed by its government under Prime Minister Allen Chastanet and the local utility company, with the assistance of CCI. The solar farm is the first utility-scale renewable energy project on the tiny island nation, which like its neighbors gets 99 percent of its power from diesel-generated electricity, with all of the fuel imported. At its capacity, the project will generate enough electricity from the sun to power 3,500 homes in St. Lucia while offsetting over 3,800 metric tons of carbon dioxide every year. They're connecting the farm to a battery-based energy storage facility nearby, an important part of any solar-based system, since the need for the power generated by the panels doesn't go down when the sun does.

Despite the severe consequences of climate change we're already living with and more extreme events almost certain to follow, I believe we can still pull ourselves back from the brink, but we have to quit fooling around. It's now accepted by most climate scientists that four of the five great extinctions in our planet's long history—massive die-offs that wiped out most of the prevailing species alive at the time—had their roots in extreme climate change, at least one by massive amounts of carbon dioxide released into the air, probably by volcanic activity. These events not only wiped out 90 percent of life on land, they also killed the majority of life in our oceans, due to the extreme acidification that accompanies high amounts of carbon in the atmosphere.

We're nowhere near those levels now, but we're getting there faster than our planet has ever traveled before. Eighty-five percent of all the carbon we put in the air above preindustrial-era levels has come since the end of World War II, 50 percent of it since 1990. The oceans, as vast as they are, have taken up some of the slack by absorbing more carbon and as a result are becoming more acidic, with unknown consequences to the enormous ocean ecosystem that covers 70 percent of the planet and to the more than a billion people around the world who get most of their protein from fish. Besides becoming more acidic, oceans are hotter than ever in recorded history, one reason 2020's Atlantic hurricane season concluded with Iota, the season's thirtieth named storm, and 2023's Hilary generated the first Tropical Storm Warning ever for California. In October of that same year, Otis went from a tropical storm to a Category 5 hurricane in just fourteen hours, then slammed into Mexico near Acapulco, doing a lot of damage.

The big difference between the five prehistoric climate calamities and our impending one is that our problem is manmade and we know there are economically beneficial options to slow and eventually reverse it. If we choose wisely, we can build fairer, safer, healthier, and more sustainable economies everywhere on earth. If not, we'll pay a terrible price.

The climate projects that CCI and many CGI partners have done offer just a few examples of what we can do to slow and eventually reverse the buildup of greenhouse gases in our atmosphere. There are plenty more. We just have to find the will, creativity, and resources to do whatever it takes to make progress before it's too late to avoid consequences far worse than those we're living with today.

Even though we're a long way from 1997 when Vice President Al Gore flew all the way to Japan to help save the first global climate agreement, the Kyoto Protocol, only to have the Senate vote against it 95–0, there is still a lingering belief that a dramatic reduction in greenhouse gas emissions kills more jobs than it creates and shrinks local and national economies.

That's not true, but the transition period does present real challenges to areas dependent on high-CO_2 energy sources and carbon-intense activities. It will take diligent and determined efforts to create enough new jobs to replace those in areas where traditional energy jobs are now. We would fix a lot of that if we stopped treating this as a partisan political issue and instead dealt with it as both a profound threat to our security and daily lives, and an unbelievable economic opportunity, with real practical short-term problems that have to be addressed so that the hard-working people in carbon-producing industries, and their families, are not forced to bear the burden of problems we all caused and the cost of making changes we all need.

There are far more profits, businesses, and jobs to be had from the fight against climate change than by holding on to the status quo. Many private companies have already figured this out. My friend, college classmate, and Clinton Foundation board member Rolando Gonzalez-Bunster founded InterEnergy Holdings, an energy supplier in the Caribbean and Central and South America and now the largest clean energy supplier in Central America. One InterEnergy subsidiary is expanding solar and wind energy in Punta Cana, in the Dominican Republic, converting its entire fleet of service vehicles to electric power, and investing in high-efficiency thermal energy for some of its hotel industry customers, all of which reduces emissions while helping its bottom line and those of its customers. Another InterEnergy operation has built wind and solar facilities in Panama that provide 260 megawatts of power, enough to meet 20 percent of Panama's power needs.

In late 2022, Rolando's company brought solar energy to the Samaná Peninsula on the northeast coast of the Dominican Republic. Its beautiful beaches surround the peninsula and attract more than a million tourists a year. But the permanent residents who provide local craftworks and food and beverages to the visitors had no electricity. InterEnergy brought solar power to every home and business and gave every resident an electric cookstove, safer and less expensive than the old way, with stoves fired by imported propane. I recently visited the little paradise. I didn't see any whales, which are a big draw that time of year, but the happy grateful people made up for it.

There are many more examples. It's simply not true that fighting climate change is a job killer with no upside. As I said, we have to deal with embedded legacy costs of the old energy economy and offer energy companies and dependent communities a reasonable transition period to embrace clean energy options and the business and employment opportunities they bring, but we can do it. The climate change investments in President Biden's Inflation Reduction Act will help a lot, and I hope the GOP representatives who are attacking it don't succeed in cutting its investments, which will generate more revenue than they cost in just a few years. But much of this work can and should be done by the private sector now. Making our buildings more efficient and producing more clean energy are already profitable, while the costs to the United States and the entire global economy of doing nothing are already high, and could be catastrophic for our children and their children if we don't act now.

We all have a moral obligation and, as demonstrated by Russia's invasion of Ukraine, a vital national security incentive to move into a carbon-neutral and eventually a carbon-negative economy, and to do so while the opportunity to avoid the worst climate consequences is still available to us. If we do it right, we will build a fairer, cleaner, healthier, more sustainable, and more prosperous economy. So I'm going to keep doing what I can as long as I can, and I hope you will, too.

I'm very grateful for the opportunities the Clinton Foundation, through CHAI, CGI, and our other operations, has had to work with governments, the private sector, and other nonprofits to have a positive impact in the United States and all over the world. We can all accomplish so much more, but it will require us to work together to solve these problems and create new opportunities. To do that, we need to find ways to beat back the prevailing political tides, which prize conflict over cooperation, division over inclusion, breaking over building. The dysfunction that weakened our political institutions is a powerful reminder that, as the old saying goes, most of our wounds are self-inflicted. It's to that vexing dilemma I now turn.

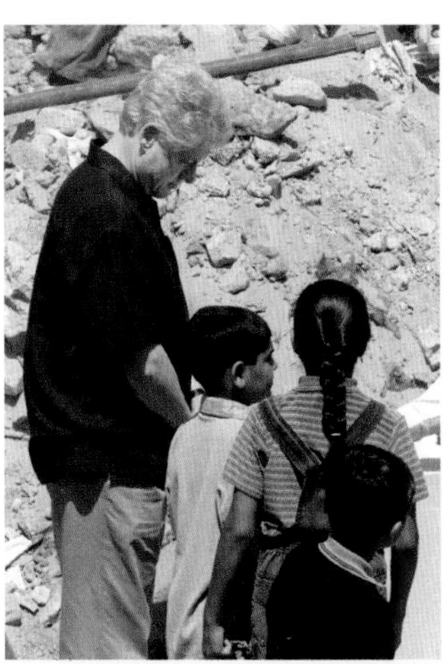

Visiting with children in Anjar, India, who survived the 2001 earthquake

Celebrating independence with East Timor's president-elect Xanana Gusmão in 2002

With President Andrés Pastrana and Queen Noor being serenaded by Los Niños del Vallenato in Colombia, June 2002

With Nelson Mandela at the 2002 International AIDS Conference in Barcelona

My first '04 campaign event after my heart surgery with Senator John Kerry in Pennsylvania

Four damp presidents at the rainy opening of the Clinton Presidential Center and Library in Little Rock in November 2004

President Bush and I were incredibly moved by the children's drawings we were given on our tour of tsunami damage in Sri Lanka.

Early drawings were fraught with emotion, but the later drawings showed renewed hope, with sunny skies and flowers.

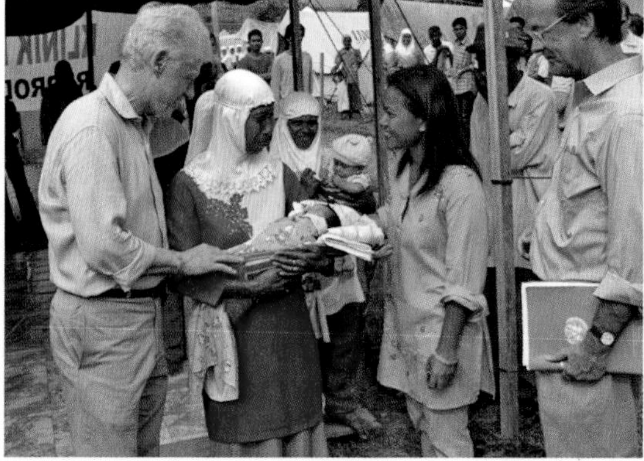

Meeting baby Dawn for the first time in Banda Aceh in 2005 in the wake of the devastating tsunami

Launching the Healthy Schools Program at the Alliance for a Healthier Generation in 2006

With Tony Blair, L.A. mayor Antonio Villaraigosa, San Francisco mayor Gavin Newsom, and London mayor Ken Livingstone in 2006, as the Clinton Climate Initiative becomes the implementing partner for the C40 group of cities

A new friend I met visiting our HIV/AIDS work in Phnom Penh, Cambodia, in 2006

Meeting the workers building a new hospital in Neno, Malawi, in 2007

Helping Hillary celebrate her 2008 Pennsylvania primary victory with her mother, Dorothy, and Chelsea

With Hillary, Secretary-General Ban Ki-moon, and Haiti President Préval at the U.N. International Donors' Conference in 2010 after the earthquake

Safely back from North Korea with Euna Lee and Laura Ling as they're welcomed home by Al Gore and their families in 2009

Planting a tree with a Malawi farmer in the Clinton Development Initiative's Trees of Hope program to reforest and reap carbon credits

With Jean-Pierre and Beatrice in Rwinkwavu, Rwanda, in 2008

Chelsea and I joining Paul Farmer and race car driver Jeff Gordon at Butaro Hospital to inaugurate the Cancer Center of Excellence in 2012

With Chelsea and volunteers at the 2023 CGI U Day of Action in Nashville

A wonderful visit with Malawi president Joyce Banda after touring some of our HIV/AIDS work there in 2013

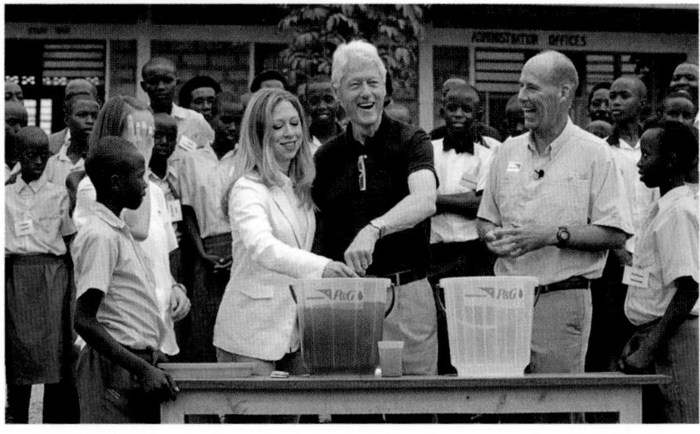

Chelsea and I demonstrating CGI partner Procter & Gamble's water purification tablets in Rwanda in 2013. Yes, they really work!

Chelsea and I pitching in to help City Year volunteers in South Africa paint a playground outside of Johannesburg in 2013

A shopkeeper in Dar es Salaam, Tanzania, who had been helped by a CGI program in 2013

Dawn, no longer a baby, and his family in 2017

Melinda French Gates, Chelsea, and Hillary at the release of *No Ceilings: The Full Participation Report* in 2015

Visiting Morehead State University in Kentucky during the 2016 campaign and holding a nanosatellite made by students there

President George W. Bush and I celebrate with the 2016 class of Presidential Leadership Scholars in Little Rock.

In Medellín, Colombia, in 2017, amazed at the changes to Comuna 13. Once ruled by drug lord Pablo Escobar, it's now a tourist attraction.

Lady Gaga and five former presidents at the George H. W. Bush Library in Houston as part of the One America Appeal for hurricane relief in 2017

Hillary and I, along with World Central Kitchen founder chef José Andrés, visiting the home of a Puerto Rican couple after Hurricane Maria

World Central Kitchen working with the Clinton Presidential Center in Little Rock to distribute meals during the worst of the Covid lockdown

President Volodymyr Zelensky of Ukraine joins us virtually at the 2022 Clinton Global Initiative annual meeting.

Receiving the Czech Republic's National Order from President Petr Pavel on the twenty-fifth anniversary of its joining NATO in 1999

PART III

Politics, Rewriting History, and Reviving the Foundation in a Still Uncertain Future

SIXTEEN

An Old Story in New Clothes

Though I've worked hard to put my postpresidential work beyond politics, working whenever possible with both Republicans and Democrats, I have been involved with campaigns for Hillary, and when asked, for President Obama and President Biden, as well as other candidates for Congress and state and local elections. I still like meeting people at rallies, on the street, in diners, bookstores, you name it, and talking through issues with them. I enjoy a good argument, though I don't like it when hecklers turn down my offer to take the microphone, have their say, and let me respond. That shows they're not completely on the level or afraid they're wrong.

Before 2014, I rarely had hecklers, but by 2016, they'd become a regular fixture. Well before that, I had to get used to people recording my answers on cell phones, often held by someone from the opposition or from a social media site, hoping to catch me in a careless remark they could make hay from.

From the 1980s on, and especially since the 1994 elections gave us the Congress led by Newt Gingrich, we have become more and more polarized in our politics, with a brief period of unity after 9/11, broken first by the Iraq War, with the pace picking up after the financial crash in 2008, then intensifying in 2010 with the rise of the Tea Party. By 2014, divisive tribalism was raging like a wildfire through our civic discourse. I've been in hard-fought campaigns, starting with my first losing one for the House in 1974, when I was a twenty-eight-year-old law professor running against a popular four-term Republican in a district where, just two years earlier, Nixon had trounced McGovern 74 to 26 percent.

But people still talked and listened to each other. Over the years, as campaigns got more heated, I tried to listen hard to people and to respond with a positive suggestion when they expressed anger, resentment, or frustration about a problem. I also cautioned people not to jump too quickly on the bandwagon of a candidate who fed their anger without any reasonable proposals to make their problems go away, or at least make them easier to deal with.

From 2010 on, such reasoned talk became rarer and rarer as the campaign rhetoric and social media propaganda shed more heat than light, creating a real market for candidates who inflame grievance, promise benefits they can't deliver, and skewer their opponents as tools of the "establishment." The right wing has been richly rewarded for making every contest a battle in an endless culture war. I grew up in the segregated South of the 1950s and '60s, so I was raised on this stuff and know its power. It gave us the reactionary period after Reconstruction ended in the late 1870s, with the Jim Crow legislation, lynchings, and violence; the anti-immigration fever in the early 1900s; the Red Scare in the 1920s; the pro-Fascist America First movement in the 1930s and '40s; McCarthyism in the 1950s; and more of the same in every decade since. The QAnon fantasies of today prove that now you can sell completely manufactured conspiracies. Artificial Intelligence will make it even easier.

Politics has always been a contact sport, and the lure of power has always been addictive, so it's tempting to disqualify your opponent by assassinating his or her reputation. It's catnip to the political press and saves politicians the effort of coming up with real solutions. It's all about branding, sticking a label on your opponent that makes him or her an untrustworthy one of "them," sticking it to the poor, beleaguered, righteous "us." The far right is brilliant at this sort of branding, hyping our racial, ethnic, gender, regional, religious, and cultural differences and denying our common humanity. If it's done skillfully enough, and not fought effectively, the people get saddled with the no-holds-barred tribalism we have today, a culture war on steroids. There are no facts, only opinions: the truth is whatever helps you. If facts hurt you, they're lies.

In his book *The Revenge of Power*, the Venezuelan journalist Moisés Naím says that in many nations today, who has power is determined by what he calls the "3 Ps": divisive Populism, political Polarization, and a Post-fact information ecosystem. The author says this toxic combination can destroy any democracy. It has put ours in peril. And nobody does it better than Donald Trump, at least rhetorically.

In the face of all this, if you want to do something that will actually benefit people, you have to figure out how to defend yourself, counterattack, and still offer a positive message to the people you want to empower, including those whose "3 P" identity makes it hard for them to listen. The diminishing number of people who can go either way still need a reason to move in your direction.

How did we get so divided, and what do we do about it? I'll try to answer the first question by recounting some telling things I saw on various campaigns over the last two decades, then suggest what we can do to save our democracy and regain some balance. It won't be easy, as President Biden has discovered. He and Congress have done some very big good things, including the massive recovery act, the infrastructure and CHIPS bills, and the Inflation Reduction Act, which has finally let the federal government negotiate for lower drug prices for Medicare and Medicaid as the Veterans Administration has done for its hospitals for years, and invest billions in fighting climate change in ways that create a lot of jobs and lower energy bills.

But inflation, especially in gasoline and food prices, crime, and trafficking immigrants to the border are real issues for millions of people. So are extreme inequalities, areas of enduring economic stagnation, wildfires and other natural calamities, racial and gender discrimination, and the frontal assault on democracy in the United States and abroad.

The hard right has continued their "3 P" strategy of divisive populism, political polarization, and post-fact communication because it's been working for them. That's partly because independent voters often show higher tolerance for the GOP's most right-wing extremists in Congress than for the Democrats' much smaller number of left-wing members. There's far more agreement on the Republican side in denying the 2020 election results and what happened on January 6, 2021, than there is in the Democratic caucus on the left's most sweeping proposals. And only a very small minority of House Democrats favor defunding the police, while 100 percent of the GOP House members voted to make a leading election denier their new Speaker in late 2023.

Why does this happen? Partly it's because extreme positions get more media coverage, resulting in the votes of 85–95 percent of House Republicans who can fairly be labeled as far right and the 8–10 percent of House Democrats who could credibly be characterized as far left being treated equally in the media in search of "balance." Democrats have to do well in the suburbs with voters who have worked hard for the lives they have, and cut their losses in more rural areas. These voters can be frightened by the Republicans' genius for branding Democrats as the embodiment of the GOP's definitions of wokeness, critical race theory, and contentious transgender issues.

That works a lot better for the GOP than actually doing things. When they tried to repeal the Affordable Care Act, their promise to do it without raising costs for people with preexisting conditions was exposed as a fraud, and they got beat. When they gave us the most right-wing Supreme Court in at least a century and took away a woman's right to choose, they lost again in the 2022 midterms, giving the Democrats and President Biden the best outcome a president's party had achieved in their first midterm in forty years.

Between 2014 and 2017, I gave four speeches at Georgetown University on the four most important pillars of good public service: People, Policy, Purpose, and Politics. Each is fundamental to a successful, healthy democracy, and we've argued about them as long as we've been a nation. The far right that dominates the Republican Party today believes the purpose of politics is getting power and using it to preserve a social order in which they are the dominant caste. They want government to do less to empower people and more to control their lives, except when it comes to guns and dark money in politics.

The polarizing strategy is designed to make as many people as possible feel fear and loathing for "the other," while reducing the power of our increasing diversity by redrawing voting district lines for state and federal elections to hamper the chances for Democratic candidates and moderate Republicans. Then they hammer hot-button social issues to get over the finish line.

Today's struggle is just the latest manifestation of the old "us vs. them" fight, dressed in the shiny new clothes of sophisticated technology. It's one that has to be fought by those in every generation who believe in every person's right to opportunity, dignity, and freedom, in Lincoln's credo that the government must do things for people that they cannot do for themselves, and in the conviction that we'll all do better acting together. This idea was first embodied in our national motto *e pluribus unum*, "out of many, one," and was adopted for our Great Seal in 1782, thanks to John Adams, Ben Franklin, and Thomas Jefferson, who had plenty of disagreements but thought what we have in common matters more. It was easier then, I suppose. Women and Black Americans couldn't even vote, much less have a seat at the table. Nevertheless, the founders still fought like cats and dogs with a highly partisan press slanting or making up the news. Still, they put their trust in "We the People" to form "a more perfect union."

What follows is my take on what's happened to the United States since I became a private citizen again, especially since 2008. As you read it, ask yourself how this or that move affected *people* in their daily lives. Did government make a meaningful difference, positive or negative, with a change of *policy*? What was the *purpose* of a given action—was it to empower all our people or to consolidate power for one group at the expense of the rest of us? And how has *politics* changed for better or worse with new technologies, unlimited big money, shortened attention spans, the calculated effort to get guns, especially assault weapons, into as many hands as possible, the loss of locally owned newspapers, radio, and television stations, and the growing economic, political, and psychological pressure on the mainstream political media to sell a simple storyline instead of telling the full story?

Early in President George W. Bush's first term, the neocons in his administration said that leaders like Colin Powell, Brent Scowcroft, and me, all living in the "reality-based world," had kept America from being truly great after the Cold War by not leveraging our ability, as the sole remaining military, economic, and political superpower, to remake reality to our own ends. When I was asked about being trapped in the reality-based world, I just smiled and said, "I grew up in an alcoholic home. I spent half my childhood trying to get *into* the reality-based world. I like it here and want to stay." I admit that I tried to use our soon-to-be challenged dominance in a very different way: to build a world I wanted American children to grow up in when we were no longer the only big dog on the block—a world with more partners and fewer enemies. China was growing, Europe was coming together, Latin America was on the verge of prosperity if it could keep improving its politics, and India's cities were beginning to spur real growth. I believed then and still believe that to make the future work better for them *and* for us we have to build a world with as much shared prosperity, shared responsibility, and social inclusion in as many places as possible, including in the United States.

The presidential election of 2004 was the closest reelection contest since Woodrow Wilson's in 1916, before our entry into World War I. It was also the first time provisional ballots were in use, partly in reaction to the controversies surrounding the 2000 election. The polls were closely monitored by both Republican operatives looking for evidence of virtually nonexistent fraud and their Democratic counterparts making sure eligible voters weren't kept from the ballot box. Even then, many Republicans were convinced there must be rampant fraud in hotly contested places where Democrats outvoted the GOP. The Republicans believed that after President Reagan's victory, they had found a formula for generational dominance of the White House—painting the Democrats as urban-dwelling, overeducated, out-of-touch elites who were weak on defense and crime, committed to putting more people on welfare and taxing hardworking middle-class voters to increase minority voters' dependence on government.

From 1980 through 1992, it worked. The GOP had a 45 percent base vote advantage compared to the Democrats' 40 percent, which meant we had to get a large majority of the nonbase voters to win. President Reagan was a great storyteller and many of his best ones were designed to show that the government would mess up a two-car parade. By the 1980s, confidence in government to do the right thing had dropped dramatically.

I won in 1992 with a campaign of positive populism, asking the wealthiest Americans to help finance an economy that would increase the incomes of the middle class and help more poor people work their way into it. And I rejected the idea that issues like fiscal responsibility, crime, welfare, teen pregnancy, adoption, strong families, and a strong national defense were "Republican issues."

By 2000, our successes in promoting peace, security, and broadly shared prosperity, along with changing demographics, had given both parties a base of about 45 percent, creating a huge incentive for the GOP to win the persuadable public by seeming principled but less extreme and more practical. That was the genius of George W. Bush's "compassionate conservativism" slogan. Essentially, the message was, "You can have the same prosperity you have with Clinton and Gore, but with a smaller government and a bigger tax cut. Wouldn't you like that?"

To win more conservatives, Bush also offered specific proposals well to the right of his slogan, including a return to trickle-down economics, embodied in his big tax cut proposals.

Although he lost the popular vote by 500,000, it worked well enough to get him into the Supreme Court and a 5–4 victory in *Bush v. Gore*, which stopped the recount in Florida and reinstated the Election Day count, a 537-vote edge for Bush. Bush's Electoral College win also got a big boost from Ralph Nader, who got 97,000 votes in Florida and 22,000+ in New Hampshire, votes that according to post-election surveys would have gone to Gore by more than four to one.

In the 2002 midterms, given Bush's surge in popularity after 9/11 and the ongoing military operations against the Taliban and al-Qaeda in Afghanistan, the Democrats did pretty well, losing only eight House seats and a net two in the Senate, which shifted control from a one-vote Democratic majority to a one-vote Republican one. In the governor's races, twenty states changed parties, with a net gain of three for the Democrats. The GOP effort to nationalize all elections along the cultural divide hadn't yet succeeded in turning every election into an "us vs. them" conflict.

Several of the winning Democratic candidates would go on to long careers, including Jennifer Granholm, who won the Michigan governor's race and is now the secretary of energy; Jeanne Shaheen, who became governor and is now a senator from New Hampshire; and Tammy Baldwin, then running for Congress in Wisconsin, now the first openly lesbian senator. I was especially proud of our only Senate pickup, as Arkansas attorney general Mark Pryor, whom I'd known since he was a boy, defeated incumbent senator Tim Hutchinson.

There were losers, too. None hurt me more than the defeat of Georgia senator Max Cleland, a decorated Vietnam veteran who lost both legs and one arm to a grenade. He was defeated by Saxby Chambliss, who ran ads with images of Max with Osama bin Laden and Saddam Hussein after Cleland refused to support the GOP legislation creating the Department of Homeland Security, because, in merging several agencies, it stripped tens of thousands of federal employees of job protections, even those who had no access to classified information or technology.

In 2004, I wanted to do what I could to support John Kerry and looked forward to the Democratic convention in Boston in July. Kerry had won the nomination after a hard-fought primary campaign dominated by Democrats' determination to make history with the first defeat of a sitting president when American troops were at war. Kerry had a chance. He was a decorated Vietnam veteran who opposed that war, an expert on foreign policy and environmental concerns, with a solid record on economic issues.

The convention being in his hometown didn't hurt and Kerry made a smart opening move against the divisive slash-and-burn campaign being run against him by the Republicans and their right-wing surrogates. He assigned the keynote address to the same state senator and Democratic nominee for the Senate from Illinois Hillary and I had campaigned for earlier in the year. Barack Obama knocked it out of the park, starkly contrasting the divide-and-conquer attacks on Kerry by saying, "There's not a liberal America and a conservative America . . . not a Black America and white America and Latin America and Asian America; there's the United States of America." He described how his life and Kerry's embodied that idea, and more important, how Kerry's philosophy and policies would help all of us move closer to it.

The theme was almost as old as the Republic. In Jefferson's inaugural, he said, "We are all Federalists, we are all Republicans." I gave it a try in 1992 by saying the Republicans always ran on "us vs. them." I wanted an America where "there is no them, there's only us." It was always effective, but Obama's speech was especially good, beautifully written and even better delivered.

Hillary and I spoke on Monday night, July 26. She got a great ovation and spoke movingly of her work for New York and the nation after 9/11 and her confidence in Kerry after seeing him at work in the Senate. Then she introduced me to speak for "the next great Democratic president."

My job was more direct: to make a strong, fairly specific case for Kerry and in the process to rebut the scurrilous Swiftboat attacks on his military service. Instead of attacking the president and the Republicans as bad people, I said they really believed in what they'd done. We believed in a different course and people should decide which direction to take, based on the clear evidence that our way worked better than theirs.

Then I went after the Swiftboaters. When the Vietnam

War raged, I said, "neither the President, nor the Vice President [Dick Cheney], nor I served . . . but John Kerry said, 'Send me!' " When the Navy wanted boats to go on dangerous trips up the Mekong River and draw fire, not dodge it, "John Kerry said, 'Send me!' " Ever since, whenever there has been a job to do to advance our founders' charge to form a more perfect union, John Kerry has always said, "Send me!" The crowd was shouting the words with me now. Then I told them that for the next hundred days, it was our duty to help him win, our turn to say to John Kerry—and the crowd roared—"Send me!"

By late October, I had recovered enough from my heart surgery to do a huge rally with Kerry in Philadelphia. He won there, but came up three million votes and thirty-five electoral votes short, making President Bush the only Republican to win the popular vote in the thirty-six years and counting since his father did so in 1988.

For all our differences, in President George W. Bush's second term, our democracy seemed to be holding together. In 2006, Congress passed a twenty-five-year extension of the Voting Rights Act of 1965 that, among other protections for minority voters, required places with a history of racial discrimination in voting to get advance approval, or "preclearance," for changes in voting laws likely to have racially disparate impacts, including the number and placement of polling places. The House passed the extension by a vote of 390–33, the Senate approved it unanimously, and President Bush signed it at a packed ceremony on the White House South Lawn attended by members of both parties of Congress, civil rights leaders, and family members of those who had died for the cause. It seemed as though all Washington agreed that it was important to protect and increase voter turnout in the United States.

Shortly afterward, in the 2006 midterms, Democrats won majorities in both the House and Senate, due to the weakening economy, the growing unpopularity of the Iraq War, the federal government's troubled early response to Katrina, and the Democrats' successful effort to recruit good candidates. Democrats picked up thirty-one House seats and six in the Senate—and six governorships to boot. Nancy Pelosi became the first woman Speaker, and Harry Reid was the new Majority Leader. Hillary won reelection easily with strong support statewide, including a good showing in traditionally Republican rural areas and small towns in upstate New York. While midterm contests generally favor the party out of the White House, 2006 seemed to signal more, a return to "reality-based" politics and policies. It was also a good omen for the 2008 presidential election, so good that it presented a real challenge to the best-known potential candidate, the junior senator from New York.

SEVENTEEN

The Senators Face Off

I loved doing events for Hillary, though once she won her Senate seat in 2000, she didn't need much help. Her work spoke for her—securing aid to help New York recover from 9/11; supporting the families of those who were killed and the survivors, some with agonizing injuries; serving on the Armed Services Committee (the first New Yorker ever to do so), where she helped to ensure better care for wounded servicemembers, especially those with traumatic brain injuries, secure safer vehicles and more protective gear for our forces in combat zones, and save defense operations based in New York. She was also the only senator the Pentagon asked to serve on a special commission to recommend how best to reorganize our military for the twenty-first century.

One day I was walking out of the Hart Senate Office Building after giving testimony to the Foreign Relations Committee as a young Army officer was coming in. He shook hands with me and said, "Mr. President, you don't know me, but I represent the Pentagon on Capitol Hill. I think you should know that the general consensus at the Pentagon is that no member of the Senate or House from either party knows more about our issues than Senator Clinton. And she really cares about the men and women in uniform. We don't always agree with her, but we always listen because she's always straight with us. And she never takes a cheap shot in the press."

I was proud but not surprised. Almost everyone who really knew her felt the same way.

Her work on domestic issues struck the same chord. She worked with upstate New York businesses, from big ones like Corning to a small manufacturer of fishing rods, to expand their markets. The rod company got online and tripled their sales, all to buyers in Norway, and quadrupled its workforce from three to twelve. She helped the wineries and farmers upstate and on Long Island to increase their sales in New York City markets and restaurants. She saved three hundred jobs at a Defense Department data processing center in Rome, which had been scheduled to close, and even persuaded the department to increase its workload there, adding four hundred more jobs. That's a lot in a small town in a rural county. Finally, she became an active member of the Senate Alzheimer's task force and a new one focused on autism, where she worked to raise awareness on Capitol Hill of the large number of families with children all along the autism spectrum who needed help to give their kids the best possible future. And she kept working to support 9/11 survivors struggling to get their lives back.

In 2006, she coasted to reelection, with ads featuring New Yorkers talking about what she had done to help them and how she made them feel. All I had to do was show up at the State Fair, visit the farmers and the artisans in the pavilions, and eat Dinosaur Bar-B-Que at their mobile unit, a fixture at the fair. I also did a number of fundraisers so she could spend more time in the Senate and on the campaign trail.

In December of 2006, Hillary and I took a short vacation to the small Caribbean island nation of Anguilla, to the home of our friend Bob Johnson, the founder of BET, the Black Entertainment Television network. We took long walks and talked about her running for president in 2008. When she asked me what I thought, I said the Democratic nominee would almost certainly be elected, because of the increasing opposition to the war in Iraq and the already clear weakening of our economy, thanks to the return of trickle-down economics and the lack of oversight from the SEC and federal bank regulators over increasingly risky derivatives trading, especially in real estate. Besides, it's always hard for any party to win three presidential elections in a row.

Primary elections and caucuses are about culture and conditions; candidates and their campaigns; the calendar, because early victories tend to give winners a bigger boost than later ones; and the coverage, because how the political media decides to cover campaigns determines what voters not directly involved know or don't know. Social media was beginning to play a role in 2008 as a means to communicate with and mobilize small donors and other supporters, but its role was nowhere near as dominant as it became in 2016 and 2020.

Although the likely field of Democratic primary candidates was large and strong, I told Hillary I thought only she or Senator Barack Obama could win. She had a national following built from eight years as first lady, six as senator, and twenty years of work before that from law school to Boston to Washington to Arkansas fighting on behalf of children and families, especially to improve education and healthcare for people without regard to their race or income. And she had a strong record on security issues, which generated a lot of support from the military, veterans, and national security communities.

Obama was a successful community organizer and an effective state senator, and had served two years in the Senate, making friends at work, learning more about national issues and the legislative ropes, cosponsoring legislation with Republicans, and planning his campaign. Most important for 2008, as a state senate candidate in 2002, he had delivered a clear statement of why the United States shouldn't invade Iraq, followed by a powerful keynote speech at the 2004 Democratic National Convention. And he knew that in a new era increasingly dominated by sound bites and storylines, having a lot of experience was somewhere between a wash and a net negative in a presidential campaign, because no matter how much good you've done, there are votes or statements that can be used against you. Better to strike while you're still new and the iron's hot.

I thought Obama was the only candidate who could beat

Hillary for several reasons. First, he was more than talented enough to pass the first presidential test: you could imagine him being president. Second, his running would mean two historic candidacies—one Black, one female—both with a chance to be elected president, and I thought most Democrats would probably see breaking the race barrier as more important than the gender barrier, although the latter, too, had proven to be deeply embedded. Third, he was the only candidate who could prevent Hillary from winning the lion's share of the Black vote. Fourth, he was from Illinois, where Hillary was born and grew up and still had great support, but no chance to win against their own popular senator. Fifth, Illinois was next door to Iowa, the first state to vote, in a caucus, and Obama had sent people there to lay the groundwork not long after taking office in the Senate. And finally, he had the advantage of being new, always a plus in the Democratic primaries and one which had helped me win the nomination in 1992.

Hillary's story would be that after decades of service she was ready to be president on day one, with a commitment to the well-being of ordinary Americans, a clear grasp of the national security issues, and decades of standing up for civil rights, women's rights, and human rights, and getting results in education, healthcare, and economic development. Obama's story was that he represented real change, a chance to empower ordinary people at home and abroad by moving beyond the red state/blue state divide to unite America with hope and change. Exhibit A was his opposition to the Iraq War and Hillary's vote to authorize it.

It was critically important for Obama that the political press adopt a "storyline," a frame of reference for organizing the information that comes fast and furious at campaign reporters every day, that was as close to his storyline as possible. If he could do that, it would create a lot of groupthink that would affect the print, social, and television media and Hillary would have to counter it, as much as possible, by disciplined messaging, good performance in the debates, strong campaigns in the states, and paid advertising.

His strategy was to run a fifty-state campaign designed to

flood all the states with organizers and to ring up big victories in the caucus states by generating strong support among those most likely to caucus, college students and white liberals. Her strategy was to do as well as possible in the early primaries in January and in the big vote- and delegate-rich states from February on, as the calendar grew more favorable to her.

The first big issue of the campaign was their respective records on the Iraq War. It was a big issue because there was a disconnect between lawmakers and their constituents: while most Democrats strongly opposed the war, many Democratic members of Congress had voted to authorize President Bush to use force in Iraq if Saddam didn't cooperate with the weapons inspections looking for large, unaccounted-for stocks of biological and chemical weapons that were left over from the first Gulf War.

Hillary was a sitting senator in 2002 when the Iraq War vote came before the Senate. Barely a year after 9/11, with troops in Afghanistan still hunting for bin Laden, President Bush had asked Congress for authority to attack Saddam Hussein to remove the threat of any weapons of mass destruction he might have. In a few days, Hillary would have to cast a vote on his request, as well as an alternative offered by Democratic senator Carl Levin of Michigan which essentially said, if Saddam doesn't cooperate with the inspections and the U.N. authorizes an attack, come back to us and we'll support it. The decision was presented to the American people in stark terms: If you think Saddam has weapons of mass destruction and is supporting al-Qaeda in the war on terror, vote for the resolution. If you don't think he has any WMD, see no evidence that his secular dictatorship has anything to do with radical Islamic jihadism, and think it's a mistake to shoehorn another war into the battle against the 9/11 killers in Afghanistan we haven't won yet, vote against it and for the Levin alternative.

The real dilemma was more complicated. After the first Gulf War in 1991, Iraq's records of Saddam's WMD caches and missiles were uncovered, then matched against what was known to have been destroyed, with the rest assumed to be still in Iraq. The U.N. authorized an inspection program to find the remaining stocks and destroy them. The inspections continued in fits and starts until 1998, my sixth year in office. Most of the items on the list were discovered, a lot of them thanks to the cooperation of one of Saddam's two sons-in-law, both of whom defected to Jordan for a while in the mid-1990s. The one who had overseen the stockpiles gave us a lot of good information that led inspectors in the right direction. Unfortunately, Saddam lured them back with offers to kiss and make up and soon they were both killed.

In 1998, Saddam kicked the U.N. inspectors out, allegedly because he was angry that the sanctions hadn't been lifted after years of cooperation. Then I authorized, in concert with Prime Minister Tony Blair and the U.K., a bombing campaign for four days on targets our intelligence agencies had identified as the likely storage sites of any remaining WMD stocks. We hit the targets, but since the inspectors weren't allowed back in, no one knew for sure what the impact of the bombing was.

After 9/11, there was broad agreement that the inspections had to resume, because again, according to verified U.N. records, there were substantial unaccounted-for stocks of biological agents aflatoxin and botulinum and chemical agents VX and ricin, as well as some Scud missiles. No one thought Saddam would use them and guarantee his own destruction, but there remained a risk that they might be stolen, sold, or given to terrorist groups. So the U.N. authorized the inspectors to resume and Saddam accepted them. The head of the inspection team, Hans Blix, a tough-minded Swede, took on the challenge methodically and vigorously. When he thought the work was being stalled, he said so and got the access he needed.

So why, if Blix was on the job, did we need to give President Bush the authority to go to war? And why would Blix, who would become one of the strongest critics of the Iraq War, support the Bush resolution? Because Blix knew that Saddam only did the right thing on the inspections when he felt forced to. And he knew Saddam was caught in a bind rarely discussed in the United States: he wanted the West to believe he no longer had any WMD and wanted Iran to believe he did. Saddam had fought a bloody eight-year war with Iran which ended in a stalemate in 1988, and ever since, he had feared his much larger neighbor remained a threat to his survival. He thought the possibility that he had WMD was a deterrent to another conflict he might not survive. After 9/11, Blix agreed that the world needed to know whether he had WMD stockpiles or not, and if he did, they had to be destroyed. He thought if President Bush was serious about letting the inspectors do their jobs, the threat of imminent attack from the United States for noncooperation would push Saddam to cooperate.

That's what the vote came down to: Was Bush committed to letting Blix finish the job? On the negative side, the administration was full of neocons, clustered around Vice President Cheney and Defense Secretary Rumsfeld, who thought they could use America's position as the world's only military, political, and economic superpower to remake the world in our image. And they wanted to start in Iraq, which they thought presented a bigger problem and greater opportunity than dealing with al-Qaeda, even after 9/11. They believed it would be easy to depose Saddam, then establish a functioning government supported by most Iraqis, and leverage the example to spark a movement toward more open democratic societies in the Middle East. If President George W. Bush listened to the neocons, he would start a war before the inspectors finished, rather than run the risk that there was nothing to find.

On Monday, October 7, just a few days before the vote, President Bush gave a speech in Cincinnati, laying out the case against Iraq and its WMD that the neocons were pushing. But he left the door open to allowing the inspections to run their course and avoiding war. I listened very carefully. Twice he said that Iraq could avoid conflict by declaring and destroying all its weapons of mass destruction and complying with other U.N. resolutions. One quote: "I hope this will not require military action, but it may."

So Hillary was in a quandary. For a Democrat in a Democratic state, the safe vote was no, but New York had been attacked, so feelings were more scrambled. Regardless of how she voted, the force resolution clearly had enough votes to pass both the House and the Senate, and Senator Chuck Schumer, Hillary's fellow

New Yorker, was voting yes. On the other hand, if WMD were found and not turned over, or if Blix finished and found nothing but said he'd been kept out of places where remaining stores might be located, there could be another vote. Just a few years earlier, several Democrats had voted against the first Gulf War authorization, which was popular from beginning to end, and none of them were badly damaged by it.

She was torn, because she was a New Yorker up to her ears in 9/11 work, ably serving her country and state on the Armed Services Committee, and deeply immersed in both the needs of the men and women in the armed services and what needed to be done to enhance our defense against new threats. She had forged a constructive relationship with the president and was inclined to give him some flexibility as commander in chief, especially since he had honored his commitment to her to support $20 billion in aid to New York after 9/11 when some congressional Republicans were opposed. Finally, she thought her vote for the resolution might increase both Saddam's cooperation and Bush's willingness to let the inspectors finish, in spite of the unrelenting pressure of the neocons and his own hatred for Saddam, who had made a clumsy, poorly concealed effort to kill his father in Kuwait after the elder Bush left office. Also, the Levin alternative wasn't real, because it required the support of the U.N. Security Council before any attack could take place. Germany and France were leading the opposition to war in the U.N., with support from China and Russia, to veto any force authorization in the Security Council regardless of what the weapons inspectors found.

When Hillary asked me what she should do, I said the resolution was going to pass regardless, and if we went to war, she would have a lot to do to support the troops, whatever happened. Given how it played out, I should have screamed, "*Just say no!*" Instead, I think my response helped to trigger her responsibility gene to enter a field in which the ideologues had already captured too much ground.

On October 10, the House approved the resolution 296–133, and the next day, the Senate followed suit, 77–23. Hillary voted with the majority. Then we all watched for five months as the

United States prepared for war, Blix raced against time, and Bush held the stopwatch.

On March 8, 2003, I went to England to give the annual Churchill lecture at Blenheim Palace, the Churchill family's magnificent ancestral home in Oxfordshire, then drove to Chequers, the official country residence of the prime minister, to see Tony Blair. He had one last idea to avoid war. By then, a majority of Americans had accepted the neocon claims that Saddam most likely still had WMD and may even have offered support to al-Qaeda before 9/11. Virtually no one outside the U.S. believed the latter or thought it made sense to start a war with Blix so close to the finish line. Blair's idea was to get the U.N. to adopt its own stopwatch: a U.N. resolution setting a deadline for finishing the inspections on a timetable Blix said he could meet.

Blair knew that opposition to war had hardened in Europe and elsewhere in response to Bush's buildup. Like Hillary, he was in a quandary, torn between the opposing arguments and his competing objectives for the U.K.: to remain America's strongest ally and to support the European Union, in which the U.K. could play a leading role, in part because of its special relationship with the U.S. He hoped his idea could prevent him from burning either bridge. Blair knew trust was in short supply and it would be difficult to persuade a majority of the Security Council to cast a vote that could be characterized as even conditional support for the invasion. But he was a good vote counter and it was a good argument: How can you start a war with uncertain consequences when you'll know the answer to the WMD question in a few days?

Tony said the only way to pass a resolution Germany and France were working against was to get the support of Chile and Mexico, who were serving two of the rotating terms on the Security Council. He asked me to make the case to their presidents, Ricardo Lagos and Vicente Fox, because I had good relationships with them. Ordinarily I would have cleared the request with the White House, but time was short and the request was consistent with President Bush's most recent speech in Cincinnati saying Iraq could avoid war by complying with the U.N. resolutions. Bush still hadn't said he was going to war regardless of the inspections, and Blair was by far the most important ally Bush had left. I was sure Bush was aware of Blair's effort and would know he asked for my help.

So I flew home to make the calls, knowing it was a hard sell. I got through to Fox first. He was friendly but forthright: 85 percent of his people opposed invading Iraq under any circumstances. He also believed that, even if Saddam had WMD, he wouldn't use them. And any deadline resolution could be portrayed as conditional support from Mexico for an invasion. Lagos, whom I knew much better, said the same thing. He was leaving office with a 76 percent approval rating, which he was using to support his chosen successor, Defense Minister Michelle Bachelet, who if elected would become Chile's first female leader. He said he couldn't risk turning Chile upside down in a cause he felt was already lost. Still, a few days later, he and a couple of other leaders did float the possibility of a thirty-day extension, which the White House, locked and loaded, quickly shot down.

On March 20, just twelve days after I met with Blair, the Iraq War began. Saddam was quickly deposed, captured in December, and tried, convicted, and executed three years later. The war continued for more than eight years, until late 2011, then returned on a smaller scale in 2014 when the U.S. and other forces helped the Iraqis reclaim land lost to ISIS, another vicious terrorist group trying to control part of the still fractured country. More than 4,500 U.S. troops lost their lives there, about 3,400 in combat, and about 33,000 were wounded. Most of the casualties were in the first three years. Of course, many more Iraqi combatants and hundreds of thousands of civilians were also killed.

No weapons of mass destruction were ever found. When the Iraqi who oversaw the WMD stocks was captured and interrogated, he said his government had destroyed those we didn't hit in the 1998 bombing, but Saddam had ordered his people, on pain of death, never to acknowledge it, fearing Iran would move against him.

When the statue of Saddam in Baghdad came down, the cracks in Iraq's foundation came out. As the 9/11 Commission later stated, terrorism came to post-Saddam Iraq with a vengeance, and took a deadly toll on the lives of soldiers and civilians there.

Saddam played his Iran card too long by not telling the truth from the very start, and not doing everything possible to speed up the inspections to prove it. And the U.S. sacrificed the almost unanimous sympathy and support of the world after 9/11 on the altar of the neocon dream by not letting Blix finish his job.

In early 2005, a bipartisan commission cochaired by Republican Court of Appeals judge Laurence Silberman and former Democratic senator Chuck Robb, a highly respected Marine officer and Vietnam combat veteran who did not support the Iraq War, issued a report on the intelligence failures at the root of most of the arguments for war. The report found that the Intelligence Community was dead wrong in almost all of its prewar judgments about Iraq's weapons of mass destruction, especially the evidence of a dangerous new bioweapon, saying, "This was a major intelligence failure." Still, the Commission found no indication that the Intelligence Community "distorted the evidence" about Iraq's WMD program. They said "what they believed. They were simply wrong."

The Intelligence Community also found no evidence that Iraq had anything to do with or any advance knowledge of 9/11. They were right about that. The commission's official report was issued in a classified version with seventy-four recommendations, and an unclassified one containing sixty-eight of them. In Chuck Robb's memoir *In the Arena*, he says President Bush honored his commitment not to interfere with the commission's independence and accepted 95 percent of its recommendations.

I tell this story not to change your mind about the Iraq War, but to explain why Hillary and some others voted as they did, and why the caricature of Blair as a warmongering accomplice to U.S. policy, for which he was pilloried for years in the U.K., is oversimplified. Of course, when the war started, and he chose to stay with the U.S., he was all in, as you have to be when you send troops into harm's way. But until the war bell rang, he was trying to find another way.

It's also worth noting that after the invasion, in fits and starts, many Iraqis did try to lift their country out of Saddam's dark shadow, the wreckage of the war, and the destruction of governing capacity by the early U.S. decisions to disband the Iraqi army and to keep experienced Ba'ath Party members from participating in any new government. Millions voted in competitive elections for the first time; the Shia Iraqis didn't all become puppets of Iran; the Kurds kept performing well; and serious people tried to put a functioning representative government back together. But the cost was great in lost and damaged lives, including many U.S. soldiers with lost limbs and brain injuries who would not have survived in earlier wars; in the loss of confidence in American politicians and intelligence agencies at home and abroad; and in speeding up the polarization already well underway in the U.S.

For Hillary, and for me, it was a lesson hard won. Sometimes you can't stop a freight train or move it to a better track. You just have to step away and wait for another chance to make a difference.

Back to the 2008 primary. The state-by-state chronicle of the contest between Obama and Hillary has been well documented elsewhere. First, Obama won in Iowa. Hillary and John Edwards had good organizations, but Obama's, aided by a large influx of people from Illinois, was better. His Iowa victory earned the usual 18-point bump in the polls in New Hampshire, with Obama going from 5 points down to 13 ahead just five days before the New Hampshire vote and only two days before the only debate on Saturday night. This was a huge break for him because usually the Iowa Caucus and the New Hampshire primary were eight to twelve days apart, giving more time for the impact of Iowa to ebb. It wasn't unusual for Iowa and New Hampshire to have different winners. This time New Hampshire had moved its date up a week to stay ahead of Michigan and Florida, who were opposed to the permanent Iowa/New Hampshire monopoly on the first and second contests, and had moved their primaries up in violation of the Democratic Party calendar. So Hillary was 13 points behind just five days before the New Hampshire vote.

She did well in the televised debate, and Senator Obama made a rare error. When asked by the moderator why some people didn't seem to like her, Hillary, with good humor, brushed it off, then Obama interjected, "You're likable enough, Hillary." However it was meant, it came off as a putdown. The next day she had an encounter with a voter which brought her to tears. The episode aired on the evening news. It was a raw, real rebuttal of the cartoon characterization of her as robotic and ruthlessly ambitious.

Hillary also ran only positive ads and benefited from the support of a large number of old friends and a remarkable array of New Hampshire women, including several highly influential legislators. That's especially important in New Hampshire because there are so many of them, 400, each representing only about 3,300 people, so they know virtually all of their constituents and can make a real difference if they're organized and committed. She won New Hampshire by 3 points, moving up 16 points in just two and a half days with an entirely positive campaign. I had never seen that happen before and haven't since. The race could have been over had Obama won. Now it was back on.

A week later came the Michigan primary. Hillary had a 10-point lead over Obama in the most recent poll, with Edwards several points behind him, and she had good, well-organized support there. The party's rules said all the candidates could run in Michigan and Florida but could only visit to raise funds. No campaign events or advertising. In Michigan, Obama and Edwards took their names off the ballot, a smart move designed to minimize the impact of Hillary's likely win. Instead, longtime Michigan congressman John Conyers and his wife, who were leading Obama's campaign, ran radio ads urging people to vote uncommitted, which they said did not violate the DNC rules against advertising since Obama was not on the ballot. Hillary got 55 percent of the vote to 40 percent for Uncommitted, mostly Obama and Edwards supporters.

On the nineteenth Hillary won the Nevada caucus 51–45, overcoming a stiff challenge from Obama, who had the strong support of the union representing the hotel workers. Thank goodness the mostly female, mostly Latina workforce supported her and showed up anyway. Hillary's Nevada campaign was led by Clark County commissioner Rory Reid, who put together a great organization and got good help from, among others, Dolores Huerta, legendary for her leading role in starting the farmworkers union with Cesar Chavez, actresses Eva Longoria and America Ferrara, social activist Elsa Collins, and others who all worked the hotel staff in the cafeterias and break rooms like seasoned pros. And she got favorable coverage and a wonderful endorsement from the publisher of the *Las Vegas Sun*, Brian Greenspun. Brian, once a moderate Republican who had recoiled at his party's move to the right in the 1980s, had been critical to my carrying Nevada twice. He, his wife, Myra, and daughter Amy are close friends of ours. Brian thought she'd be a great president.

Next up was South Carolina. After losing Iowa, Hillary had won New Hampshire, Michigan, and Nevada, and was well ahead in soon-to-vote Florida, so some in Hillary's campaign thought she shouldn't contest a race in South Carolina she had no chance to win. Given the way it played out, they might have been right.

Congressman Jim Clyburn, the state's most powerful Democrat, didn't publicly endorse Obama, but after Iowa was clearly heading in his direction. Obama was waging a vigorous campaign, as was John Edwards from next-door North Carolina. Hillary had a lot of supporters there, too, including popular former governor Richard Riley, who compiled an impressive record as governor and secretary of education in my administration for all eight years.

The most critical thing I thought South Carolina would tell us is how well Hillary could do with Black voters in a place where both she and Obama put on a full-court press. If she could only get 10 percent in states with a heavy Black vote, she couldn't win the nomination. If she got 30 percent, she could.

The political press turned sharply negative in South Carolina, saying that I was Hillary's attack dog, playing the "race card" on Obama. They accused me of saying his campaign was a "fairy tale" in New Hampshire. After the life I'd lived, it hurt to be accused of playing the race card. I should have seen it coming. With Hillary's big wins, the press narrative was in danger. The difference between coverage in today's hard-right-wing media and in the mainstream political media is that the latter prefer not to say anything that's demonstrably false. They just omit information that contradicts or blunts the impact of their storyline.

I was speaking at Dartmouth College just before the New Hampshire vote and was asked about Hillary's Iraq War vote and Obama's opposition to the war. I said that when Senator Obama was asked at the Democratic Convention in 2004 about how he would have voted on the resolution, said the case hadn't been made to the public but he hadn't seen all the intelligence, so he didn't know for sure. I also told the audience something else they likely didn't know, that both he and Hillary had cast more than eighty votes on Iraq in the Senate, differing only once, when he voted for confirmation of a new military commander and she voted against him because she disagreed with the prevailing strategy. So the "fairy tale" was not a reference to Obama and his impressive campaign, but to the storyline that there was a big difference between them on Iraq. Stating facts in defense of my candidate was not an attack on him but a disagreement with the storyline.

In fact, my respect for Obama was growing. One night when all the candidates were out of state for a debate, all the press still stuck in South Carolina had to cover was a rally where I spoke for Hillary. There were several hundred people there. After I made the positive case for her, I opened the floor for questions. A young Black man stood up. He said he was a minister who had recently moved to the state to start a church. He then said that he liked Senator Obama, but the Democrats had to win in November and he had decided to support Hillary because she had a long record of supporting civil rights, had been a fine senator and first lady, and he didn't think the country was ready to elect a Black president. I thanked him for his support, but said I disagreed with him about whether Obama could win, saying that since he had won Iowa and was running a good campaign, he could win the nomination, and if he did, I would do everything I could to help elect him. (This account is confirmed in the book *For Colored Girls Who Have Considered Politics* by Minyon Moore, the director of the Public Liaison office during my administration and one of the authors, who was in the audience and saw the event unfold.)

When it was over, I was afraid of the headline, "Even Clinton Admits Obama Can Win!" I needn't have worried. There wasn't a single mention of it, perhaps because it contradicted the "Clinton Plays the Race Card" storyline.

It's true that I compared Obama's coming victory in South Carolina to Jesse Jackson's in 1988, but not in a derogatory way. Early on election morning I went to work at a polling place with two congressmen who were supporting Hillary. A young man with a local radio station came up and asked what we were talking about and I said the history of South Carolina primaries. He asked if I thought Obama would do well and I said I did. I said we had just discussed how well Jesse had done in 1988, putting together an impressive coalition of Black and working-class white voters in his home state. Immediately the press and Obama supporters were howling that I had shown disrespect to Obama and his supporters, insulting his Black supporters by suggesting that they would vote for him because of his race, and his well-educated liberal white supporters by comparing them to the poor working-class whites who had supported Jesse. I thought Jesse had run a great campaign in 1988 and I called him to explain what happened. He laughed it off, saying he understood what they were up to. Somehow the press reports forgot to mention that the two Hillary-supporting congressmen with whom I was talking about Jesse were both Black, Greg Meeks of New York and Kendrick Meek of Florida.

Barack Obama won South Carolina with 55 percent to 27 percent for Hillary and 18 percent for John Edwards. He received about 80 percent of the Black vote and a good number of white voters, just as Reverend Jackson did in winning 55 percent in 1988. Hillary, with strong Black leadership and a record on issues important to grassroots leaders, like not loading up Black neighborhoods with toxic waste dumps, managed to get about 20 percent of African Americans to support her, right in the middle of the gap between the road to defeat and a path to victory. I'll always be grateful to Hillary's South Carolina cochairs, three respected African American legislators, Senator Darrell Jackson, Senator Robert Ford, and Representative Harold Mitchell. Because they supported her, they all drew primary opponents in the coming election, but all three won handily, by 65 to 72 percent, showing that most African Americans who voted in the primary liked both Hillary and Obama. That was the real story, and what made the primary so fascinating.

Shortly after New Hampshire, Hillary had to make some changes in her campaign. She brought in Maggie Williams, who had been her chief of staff in the first lady's office; Minyon Moore, who had run the White House constituent outreach and political affairs operations when I was in office; Cheryl Mills, who had served in the White House Counsel's office and defended me brilliantly before the Senate; and Tina Flournoy, a gifted political maven then with the American Federation of Teachers. All four were strong, accomplished Black women, and the headquarters operation got a lot better. Their unprecedented prominence didn't get a lot of coverage.

Three days after South Carolina, Hillary won Florida 50 percent to 33 percent for Obama, and 14 percent for Edwards. They were all on the ballot this time. So it looked better heading into February—losses in Iowa and South Carolina, victories in New Hampshire, Nevada, Michigan, and Florida.

She was also ahead in the popular vote, though it was rarely reported. She was hurt badly by Michigan and Florida going against DNC rules and holding their primaries before February 5, a choice she had nothing to do with, and was hurt even worse by what the DNC did to punish the two states, and how the political press covered it.

In both states the Republicans handled the arrangement as provided for in their party rules, counting the votes but allocating only half the delegate votes they otherwise would have received. The Democratic Party rules would have produced the same result. But after Michigan and Florida voted, the DNC's Rules Committee decided, by a secret one-vote majority, to change their rules to strip all the delegates from both states, while saying they might decide to allocate them with half votes at a later date. It was obvious they were going to do that. Otherwise they would have had to pretend the primary never existed.

Still, the political press declined to include in their reports of the vote totals those that Hillary won in Michigan and, even more indefensibly, in Florida, where Obama and Edwards were on the ballot, saying they could be included later when the DNC decided what to do with the delegates.

If that one member of the Democratic Party Rules Committee had done the "democratic" thing and voted to seat the delegates but cut their votes in half, which of course they later did, the political press would have had to report the totals showing Hillary ahead in the vote count. The political press's decision, using the secret Rules Committee vote as an excuse, not to report her vote totals in the two states that jumped the line were daggers that undermined her big-state strategy and the case she was making to the superdelegates, mostly elected and party officials who were made voting delegates by the party rules.

Heading into February, it was clear that Obama had done and would do better than Hillary with African Americans, younger voters, in the caucuses, in the Democratic Rules Committee, and in the political press coverage. By contrast, Hillary had done and would do well with working-class and older voters, Latinos and voters with military and national security ties, and would shine in the debates, in the big state primaries, and in other states that rejected caucuses in favor of more democratic primaries. The pattern held in the contests to come.

The national coverage was so biased, it was laughable. At least the press, unlike in 2016, didn't pretend otherwise. For example, *The New York Times* sent a reporter into all the stores in Chappaqua to ask if the people working there had anything negative to say about Hillary or me. I learned about it in Lange's Delicatessen, which was probably his last stop. The employees and owner were chuckling about it. When the reporter learned our neighbors liked us, there was no article. It didn't help with the storyline.

Obama's best decision was to start his campaign early with a full fifty-state strategy, something Hillary's campaign had to develop after she strengthened her leadership team in February, but she never really caught up. He also had an early, aggressive, and effective effort with the superdelegates, helped by much more positive press coverage for him than for Hillary, including the omission of her vote totals in Michigan and Florida.

By February, it was clear that Hillary's best chance was to maximize her strength on the stump and in the debates, her command of the issues, and her determination to make the economy, healthcare, and education accessible to people who were working hard and needed more opportunities. Meanwhile my best use was to reinforce her message and stay under the national media radar by focusing on meeting voters in medium- and smaller-sized communities, at university events, and in overlooked urban neighborhoods. All told, I did about three hundred events, including thirty-nine in Pennsylvania, thirty-one in Indiana, and twenty-something each in Ohio, Texas, and California. The state and local media coverage was straightforward and fair. She won them all.

From February through to the end, Hillary did well, finding her voice and, when she had a good local organization, often doing better even in states where the established state politicians had endorsed Obama. My favorite was Massachusetts, where Senator Ted Kennedy, Senator John Kerry, and Governor Deval Patrick all endorsed Obama and Hillary won by 15 points, thanks to a vigorous campaign, her longstanding ties to many people in the state, and the extraordinary efforts of Representatives Richie Neal, Jim McGovern, Steve Lynch, and Barney Frank.

She also won in New York's neighbor New Jersey. And she won Pennsylvania by 9 points, thanks to strong support in Pittsburgh and the rural counties of Western Pennsylvania, in Northeast Pennsylvania where her father grew up, and in Philadelphia, thanks to former governor Ed Rendell and the city's Black mayor, Michael Nutter. In a national television interview, Nutter was pressed on why he wasn't supporting a man who could become the nation's first Black president. He said he was Black and was also the husband and father of two strong women who liked Hillary, but his job was to support the person he thought would be best for Philadelphia. That's why he was supporting Hillary. The Black mayor of Trenton, New Jersey, Doug Palmer, said the same thing.

In late May, West Virginia and Kentucky went for her by 40 and 35 points. Ironically, she was actually helped by the political press saying the remaining primaries were meaningless and she should just drop out. People in states that hadn't voted yet appreciated that Hillary wanted their voices heard and felt she owed it to them to finish what she had started. By then, a lot of remaining mostly working-class voters thought the press's overt preference for Obama made him the establishment's choice and that Hillary cared more about them.

South Dakota and Montana were the last two states to vote. I had gone to South Dakota several days earlier to do stops, one of which was at the local American Indian college where the president, Tom Shortbull, had put together a small meeting of tribal leaders. He introduced me by saying why he thought it was important to support Hillary. He said when he was a state senator, she had come to Pine Ridge Reservation as first lady, then persuaded me to come. Then I came with a delegation committed to improving opportunities for one of America's poorest communities. He then mentioned the good things that happened after our trips and ended with a question: "If we listen to the party leaders and walk away from the only candidate who's actually done something for us, why would anyone ever support us again?"

I didn't need to say a word. After the event I went to a pay phone in the parking lot and called headquarters, telling them that if they'd let me do a two-day swing through small towns, and if Hillary would come once or twice, she'd win. I made the stops, eighteen of them, often forty or fifty miles apart, and loved every one. I still often drink my morning coffee out of a Webster, South Dakota, mug. She came, got the endorsement of the state's largest newspaper, and even carried the University of South Dakota community. Outspent by more than four to one, with every prominent Democrat in the state endorsing Obama, Hillary won by 10 points.

But it was too late. On the last day, Obama carried Montana by 15 points, in part because he had organized early. I went there and first worked the eastern part of the state, where Hillary was doing well, but when I got to Missoula, home of the university, I knew we were toast. One guy in a bar told me he liked Hillary but, as with other states, Obama's campaign had been working there since early 2007.

On June 7 in Washington, Hillary made her concession speech to a large crowd of supporters. She said she had fought hardest for people who needed a president who would help them, and mentioned several examples. Then she congratulated Obama on the "extraordinary race he has run" and said, "I ask all of you to join me in working as hard for Barack Obama as you have for me." More than half of the speech was about Obama and the importance of electing him. The rest was a clarion call to women and girls not to give up on their dreams. It was a brilliant speech and it went a long way to unite the party. She always showed up when it was pouring rain, demonstrating again why she would have been a great president and making those of us who love her very proud.

Obama soon named Joe Biden as his running mate, a smart move that added experience to the ticket, especially in foreign policy and fighting crime, something I had seen firsthand when I worked closely with Senator Biden on the Crime Bill and on Bosnia, Kosovo, and several other foreign policy issues. Then Obama had a successful convention in Denver, where Hillary spoke for him and persuaded her most die-hard supporters, who called themselves "The 300" (in reference to Leonidas and the 300 Spartans who fought the massive Persian army to the last man at Thermopylae), to join in making his nomination unanimous. John McCain won the GOP nomination, and in an attempt to unite a Republican Party whose right wing didn't think him right-wing enough, named Alaska governor Sarah Palin, later a Tea Party favorite, as his running mate.

In late September, the housing bubble, blown up by financial machinations which left banks massively overleveraged, burst, placing the entire financial system at risk and in effect ending the election. I always thought Obama would win, but now it wouldn't be close. As a senator, Hillary had gone to Wall Street and warned them that their overleveraged trading in housing derivatives and other poorly collateralized debt obligations would lead to disaster if they didn't stop. Wall Street ignored the warning and kept raking in the cash.

President Bush had to spend the last months of his presidency dealing with the financial crisis and the Great Recession it triggered. He knew he had to provide federal assistance to avert a depression, but he hated giving massive sums to the very institutions that had caused the crash. Congress felt the same way.

The first vote on the $700 billion Troubled Asset Relief Program (TARP) bill, aka the bank bailout, was held in late September 2008. The legislation failed in the House 205–228, with Democrats in favor 140–95 and Republicans 133–65 against. When the stock market reacted to the vote by dropping 777 points, a slightly revised version of the bill passed the House and Senate a few days later, and was signed into law by President Bush, still with more overall Democratic votes than Republican. Without the Democrats in Congress backing the Republican president, there weren't enough votes to pass the bill. The GOP members loved feeding at the trough but didn't want to plug the holes when it leaked.

The most extraordinary aspect of the bank bailout was that everything happened in the teeth of the 2008 presidential election, with both candidates voting for the bill, although McCain would later say that he regretted his vote, claiming the money was misspent, a position many of the GOP supporters of the law would take in later elections to placate the right-wing media and the antigovernment voters they'd need to keep their seats.

I felt for McCain. He was an old-fashioned conservative who believed in honorable compromise and respectful treatment of his opponents. He enjoyed working with Hillary in the Senate and called me during the 2008 campaign, asking how he could speak out against Russia's attempts to undermine the former Soviet republic of Georgia's increasingly open, effective democratic government without looking like a warmonger in a country increasingly opposed to the Iraq War. Later I spoke at a dinner in New York for his foundation, hosted by our friend Lynn Forester de Rothschild, who was a supporter of both Hillary and McCain. Two thousand eight was just not his year. He might have done better in 2000, but lost the primary to George W. Bush after a brutal takedown in South Carolina from which he never recovered.

Almost all economists believe the aggressive fiscal measures taken by Bush and later by Obama were necessary and largely effective in halting the disintegration of the financial sector and the larger economy, but the facts wouldn't make it more palatable, especially when several Republican members of Congress blamed homeowners for the crash and, over the opposition of most Democrats, had given them less help than they gave the banks that had reeled them into risky mortgages and shaky trading offerings.

In the last weeks of the election, the Obama campaign asked me to make campaign stops in several states where Hillary had done well in the primary, and where polling had indicated Senator John McCain was close or leading down the final stretch. I did a couple of events in Florida, including one in Orlando with Senator Obama, then went to Pennsylvania, Ohio, and West Virginia. Kerry had won four years earlier in Pennsylvania 51 to 48 percent, but he had lost the other three. Obama needed to do better, and I was glad to help.

Though Hillary made far more appearances than I did and had a much larger impact on the outcome, I tried to make sure that people knew that Obama and the Democrats understood Americans were hurting, with declining incomes, job losses, foreclosures, maxed-out credit cards, unaffordable healthcare, rising food, utility, and gas costs, and increasing poverty and inequality, and that he had good, realistic plans for how to improve their lives and their children's futures. Most voters were eager for a new leader and a new direction. They had given Congress to the Democrats two years earlier and decided to give Obama a chance to do better.

I was happy about his victory but concerned that the same forces that had guaranteed Obama's election could prove his undoing. The serious financial crisis he had inherited would last longer than typical economic downturns, and when things didn't improve quickly, voters might blame the new president before he had a chance to make things better, or at least before they could feel the upturn.

And lurking not far from the surface was an even more profound problem. Another, more radical "us vs. them" America had been making its case at least since 1994 with the rise of the Gingrich Republicans, and it hadn't gone away. During a McCain town hall in Minnesota, an audience member accused Obama of being a terrorist, and later on a woman, when asking McCain a question, said Obama was an Arab and insinuated that he wasn't one of "us." The people at the town hall didn't invent those fantasies that night; right-wing media had been raising spurious questions about Obama's birthplace for months. To his credit, McCain took the microphone from the woman, pushed back forcefully, and continued to run a hard-fought but fair campaign. But in his choice of Governor Sarah Palin as his running mate, he had also reached out to the growing segment of his party that focused on cultural grievance and divisive populism, with relentless attacks that often were clearly false.

The Republican right apparently believed that protecting democracy in an increasingly diverse country didn't work for them. After all, they voted to extend the Voting Rights Act in 2006, then promptly lost both houses of Congress. In a more normal time, the GOP would have tried to broaden its appeal. Instead they chose to double down, to Just Say No to the president, purge their party of as many moderates as possible, and try to win enough white working-class voters outside the South to carry the Electoral College, which is heavily tilted in favor of less populated, more culturally conservative states.

This was a preview of what was to come in the years after Obama took office. Senator Mitch McConnell, who was Republican Whip during the election, became Majority Leader when the GOP won the Senate back in the 2014 midterms. In his memoir, McConnell said he'd voted for President Johnson and supported the Civil Rights Act, but as he rose to prominence in the Senate, he became a master at partisan politics, both at home and in Washington. After President Obama won in 2008, he said his number one priority was to make him a one-term president.

I saw the Republican strategy working in Arkansas in 2008, when four former Democratic governors joined Governor Mike Beebe on a campaign swing for Obama: Jim Guy Tucker, Senators Dale Bumpers and David Pryor, and me. All of us had approval ratings between 55 and 70 percent, with Beebe leading the pack. We made stops all over the state and had a great time. Dale was so excited that he said at the last rally that he thought Obama might win Arkansas even though many Arkansans were disappointed he didn't come to the state, just to show respect to Hillary. I told Dale I had loved being with him, but we were about to get the hell beat out of us. The only people at the rallies were young people, both Black and white, who liked Obama, and our tried-and-true friends, who were older then and not as active as they used to be.

Sure enough, Arkansas was one of John McCain's best states. He won by 20 points. An exit poll showed Hillary would have won by 15, but I doubted that enthusiasm for her would last either, as time, distance, and the loss of locally owned rural newspapers and radio stations—with the rise of Fox News and more politically strident evangelical churches filling the spaces they had once occupied—took their toll.

Those factors didn't translate into political victory for Republicans nationally in 2008, but they would come back with a vengeance. Still, Obama won the election handily, with a big Democratic turnout and a strong showing with independents, who were tired of the Iraq War, furious about the financial crash, and eager to make a new beginning. The hard-right base of the GOP, because they were also turning against the Iraq War and opposed the bank bailout, was less enthusiastic in its turnout, despite McCain's selecting Palin as his running mate.

Two Americas were emerging with very different stories. Those represented mostly by Democrats believed that our growing diversity was a source of strength, not decline, and the right path for such a diverse nation was to fight inequality through shared opportunities and shared responsibilities, and equal treatment in our local, state, and national institutions. As I noted in the introduction, the other America, represented primarily by the Republican Party, saw that same diversity and the economic stagnation in more rural areas as a sign they had lost control over our economy, our social order, and our culture, and grew even more determined not to lose control over our *politics*, through which they could regain control over the other three. Millions of them were not the howlers we saw acting out at the rallies, or storming the Capitol on January 6, 2021. They just thought they didn't matter anymore, that America had said to them, as the title of Fiona Hill's brilliant book about her small hometown in rural pro-Brexit Northern England puts it, "There Is Nothing for You Here."

EIGHTEEN

Our First Black President and the Resurgence of the Hard Right

In a highly polarized time, serious policymaking often takes a backseat to name-calling designed to distract voters from considering the actual consequences of what the candidates are proposing. In Obama's first term, the most glaring example of this was the furious battle over the passage and implementation of the Affordable Care Act. It was fought with dueling storylines: a clash of fantastic claims of catastrophe on the right competing with President Obama's and the Democrats' efforts to increase coverage, lower costs, and improve healthcare quality.

When I first ran for president, the Republican storyline was that all Democrats were free-spending liberals and that middle-class incomes were stagnant because everyone had been so crushed by the burden of the welfare state. The antitax, anti-government sentiment was so baked into their storyline that President Bush 41 felt forced to say at the 1992 Republican convention what a big mistake it had been to sign the Democratic Congress's budget bill with modest tax increases and restraints on spending and he would never do such a terrible thing again.

My 1993 economic plan disproved the storyline. As I mentioned earlier, we replaced "trickle-down economics" with an "invest and grow" plan to both reduce the deficit and increase

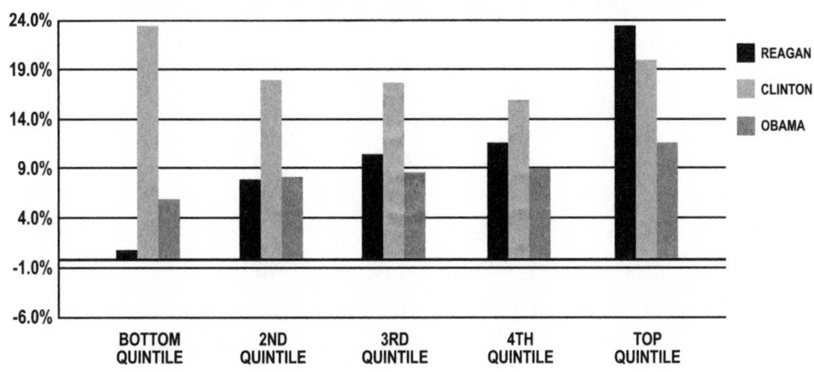

Source: U.S. Census Bureau, Current Population Survey, Annual Social and Economic Supplements

critical investments. The plan contributed to the big Democratic losses in the 1994 midterm elections because no one yet believed that employment was going up and the deficit was going down, but more jobs were created than ever before, millions more than under President Reagan, with a higher percentage of them private sector jobs, and even more important, incomes increased across all income groups, not just for the top earners.

In 1996, I was reelected by a margin of more than eight million votes, with 379 electoral votes. In my second term, we balanced the budget, something unheard of when I ran for president and predicted by no pundit or politician at the time, ran two surpluses, left a third for my successor, and still had large increases in investments to support education, the environment, research and development, and working families. Interest rates were historically low, and our cities, large and small, were gaining new life. The Crime Bill worked, too, as crime, especially violent crime and the numbers of mass shootings, dropped eight years in a row. Public approval of the federal government rose dramatically.

But Democrats paid a high price for reversing trickle-down economics and giving us the lowest crime rate in twenty-five years, the lowest murder rate in thirty-three years, and the lowest gun homicide rate in forty-six years, thanks to the Brady background check law, the Crime Bill's 100,000 new police officers, the assault weapons ban, and the ten-bullet limit on ammunition magazines. When I left office, both houses of Congress were in the hands of Republicans. Our lower turnout in 1994, their brilliance at "branding," and the preference of the political press for oversimplified binary choices sent many of our finest members into retirement, including the Speaker of the House, Tom Foley, and Jack Brooks, a committee chairman from Texas, who previously had always had the support of the NRA. They both warned me this would happen. These losses would be the canary in the coal mine of the divisive tribalism ahead.

In the early days of the Obama administration, we were still in the teeth of the Great Recession, and the prevailing Republican storyline that government overreach was the root cause of all ills had been damaged, but not destroyed. They chalked up the mortgage crisis to the old saw of "too much government." The main culprit, they argued, wasn't excessive risk-taking by banks, and big-money contributions to members of both parties in Congress, but the relaxation of lending requirements to satisfy the Democrats' push to get more low- and middle-income Americans into homes they owned, not rented, even if they couldn't afford them.

Republican leaders and some bankers hated the Community Reinvestment Act (CRA), a sensible law on the books since the 1970s, but rarely enforced before I took office. It simply requires banks to make loans in communities where they take deposits. By the time I left office, more than 95 percent of all CRA lending, almost a trillion dollars, had occurred during my terms, thanks to the efforts of Gene Ludwig, the comptroller of the currency, to encourage local lending and to enforce the CRA. And after the crash, an independent study by the nonpartisan Congressional Budget Office showed that banks that complied with the law were actually *less likely to fail* than banks that packaged mortgage-backed securities and sold them far and wide.

The storyline against the auto bailout under Obama tracked the TARP attacks: it was just another terrible big-government boondoggle that would send good money after bad, and it would all be wasted anyway by fraud and misuse before it even got to an autoworker's bank account. That wasn't true, either. Even the auto companies that didn't take the bailout money supported it because it kept their suppliers in business and saved a lot of manufacturing jobs in America.

The right-wingers made the same attack on the $800 billion economic stimulus bill and Vice President Biden's implementation of it. First, they said it was too big. It wasn't. The crash had blown a $3 trillion hole in the economy and we needed to speed up job creation. Second, they made a lot of hay out of a relatively small part of the package that made loans to new companies with promising technologies because one of the early ones, Solyndra, failed, costing the taxpayers just under $600 million. That was true, but it was also true that within a few years the overall program of which Solyndra was a part turned a profit for the taxpayers and has created a lot of new jobs to boot. Sadly, the early loss got a lot more coverage than the net profit and its economic benefits.

So the old antigovernment, antitax storyline never went away, but it did need new voices. Increasingly alienated, mostly white working-class voters were still angry with the GOP establishment because of the Great Recession, the bailout, and trade deals with lax enforcement, but also were opposed to the Democrats' commitment to inclusive social policies and politics and language that spoke of entitling, not empowering, lives. They were looking for new faces, unburdened by experience or willingness to compromise, and eager to champion divisive tribalism and grievance arguments.

The Tea Party formed to fill this need, and its effect on our politics was stark, in large part because of its fanatical opposition to the Affordable Care Act. Its members stormed local town halls and ginned up the same "government will take away your doctor" scare tactics they'd used to scuttle the universal healthcare efforts that Hillary had led in my administration. Those attacks, plus others, including those by reality television show host Donald Trump that trumpeted doubts about Obama's citizenship, pushed the parties and those who supported them further apart. The Tea Party, which would later morph into the Republican congressional group known as the Freedom Caucus and eventually drive GOP party leaders like Eric Cantor and John Boehner out of politics entirely, began to demonstrate its clout, calling for protests in 2009 and 2010 that devolved into shouting matches and epithets. In one instance Congressman John Lewis and his chief of staff were accosted by Tea Party members on the steps of the Cannon Office Building, using a barrage of racial slurs that prompted Lewis to remark that it reminded him "of a different time."

With the clock running out before the 2010 midterms, the Obama administration and a Democratic-led Congress under Speaker Nancy Pelosi put the final touches on the Affordable Care Act and the president signed it on March 23, 2010. The bill was both a triumph of policy-driven government and a prime example of the tradeoffs necessary to advance major new social legislation in America. Some of the tradeoffs weren't pretty, affirming Mark Twain's observation that the two things people should never watch being made are sausage and laws. There was another problem: it would take time to get the healthcare benefits up and running, so the GOP could continue their negative attacks without cost until enough people benefited from them.

Still, like the creation of Social Security in the 1930s, Medicare and Medicaid in the 1960s, and the Children's Health Insurance Program in the 1990s, the government had established a far-reaching new program in the Affordable Care Act, and like those earlier programs, passage was just the first step. There were many adjustments to be made in the implementation process and court battles ahead, some of which we are still fighting more than a decade later.

Even without the Tea Party and the battles over the Affordable Care Act, the 2010 midterm was going to be a bruising battle, if for no other reason than the historical tendency of the party in the White House to lose congressional seats in the first midterm after winning the presidency. To make matters worse, Democratic turnout in midterms had been falling from presidential election levels more than Republican turnout, which had led not only to losses in Congress, but also in state and local races, most of which are held in nonpresidential years. Democrats and their funders had also neglected to focus on local elections, which are crucial in building the base of the party and mobilizing voters concerned about issues close to home.

The lingering job losses from the Great Recession, which had technically ended in the fall of 2009, nine months after President Obama took office, hurt too. In the fall of 2010, the unemployment rate was still 9.6 percent, very close to its peak the year before. Worse, because this was a financial crash, not a normal downturn, the average time a worker remained unemployed was thirty-five weeks, months longer than in previous recessions.

I campaigned heavily for Democrats in the summer and fall of 2010, presenting the facts about what Obama had done to right the financial ship and pushing back against the Tea Party attacks on those efforts and on the Affordable Care Act. Joe Biden was out there, too, essentially making the same argument. But it was a hard sell. A full-court press on the healthcare plan—even one based on a plan originally proposed by the conservative Heritage Foundation and instituted in Massachusetts by then-Governor Mitt Romney—wasn't the top priority for voters most concerned about high unemployment and homes lost to foreclosure. Also, it was easy for Republicans to demonize "Obamacare" because people hadn't felt its benefits yet, as they hadn't felt the job-creating effects of the stimulus bill or saving the automobile industry.

It was 1994 all over again, when voters hadn't yet felt the benefits of our bill repealing trickle-down economics or the Crime Bill, so we were vulnerable to attacks on both that increased their turnout and depressed ours.

Meanwhile, the Tea Party was raging through the Republican Party, with its Always Say No program: to be a real Republican you had to favor repeal of what they derisively called Obamacare, deny the existence of climate change, question Obama's birthplace, and believe whatever you saw on Fox News.

The story that best captured 2010 to me was the Republican primary for Congress in South Carolina between Trey Gowdy and the incumbent Bob Inglis. Inglis was a conservative, devout Christian who had served three terms during my presidency, voted to impeach me, and retired in 1999 after his third term as he promised he would. He ran for his old job again in 2004, won 85 percent of the primary vote, and was easily reelected twice. But in 2010, he faced a tough primary contest from four challengers, including the Spartanburg district attorney Trey Gowdy. Inglis was attacked for supporting the TARP bill in 2008, opposing the Iraq War surge, and advocating for free market approaches to climate change while the Tea Party demanded denial. He also rebuked a GOP congressman who had shouted that President Obama was a liar during his address to Congress on healthcare. Inglis told his constituents that he had had an epiphany during his prolonged absence from the House while he healed from a fall. He had been touched that both Republican and Democratic colleagues had reached out to him and resolved to treat all of them with respect. He said he would still oppose Obama most of the time, but the president was a Christian born in the United States who loved his family and his country and Republican efforts to stoke hatred of him were bad for the country.

Believing in climate change and being decent to the president were nonstarters. You didn't belong in the new GOP with those positions. In spite of Inglis being endorsed by the NRA and the National Right to Life Committee, Gowdy beat him 71–29 and went on to lead the Select Benghazi Committee, organized in 2015 to attack Hillary.

It was a harbinger of things to come. In 2010, the Republicans gained sixty-three House seats, the largest switch since 1948, and seven Senate seats, just two short of a majority. They also won six governorships and control of twenty state legislatures, which would be a big plus in the once-a-decade redistricting that follows each census.

The storyline of big-government overreach, of all its benefits going to the undeserving "them" and not the worthy "us," had roared back with a vengeance, contrary to all the evidence. In fact, the largest number of beneficiaries from saving the auto jobs were working-class white men and the largest number of winners from expanding healthcare coverage were working-class white families, especially those with preexisting conditions or with children who now could be covered up to age twenty-six, and those whose previous coverage was so meager it was often useless. Sadly, too many of them were in denial, and that, plus the fact that Democrats were still slow to learn that the midterm elections were just as important as presidential ones, made the midterms in both 2010 and 2014 a nightmare.

Bob Inglis wrote me in 2011, asking if he could come to Harlem to see me. On October 13, we had an extraordinary encounter. I congratulated him for what he said about President Obama and for his advocacy of a free market response to climate change. He thanked me, but said he hadn't come for that. He said he had come to Washington in the Gingrich Congress of 1994 full of self-righteous anger and so determined to impeach me for any reason that he asked to be on the Judiciary Committee. He said Gingrich had sold him and the rest of the large GOP freshman class on a strategy of constant attack and he didn't realize how wrong it all was until he came back to Congress and lived with the continued evolution of hate-based fact-free politics. Gingrich gave the new members and lots of others a copy of his version of Mao's Little Red Book, with more than a hundred negative words like "weak," "pathetic," and "treacherous" that he wanted them to use as often as possible whenever they talked about Democrats. When we lost the 1994 midterms, he started his reign as Speaker by calling Hillary and me the "enemies of normal Americans."

Inglis said it might be too late, but he hoped I'd forgive him. I happily agreed and encouraged his bipartisan work with Liz Patterson, the incumbent Democrat he defeated back in 1992, to bring Democrats and Republicans together in South Carolina to find things they could agree on and work for them. He's still at it, penning an October 2, 2023, article in *The New York Times* urging the Republicans in the House to "grow up" and turn away from the "authoritarian separatists who reject pluralism—a founding American principle that expects disparate groups to come together to keep the government functioning." So far, he doesn't have many takers, but at least he's trying.

Obama's reelection campaign in 2012 came at a tricky time. Unemployment had fallen and the country was well on its way to bringing back the jobs lost from the recession and adding more. But too many people still didn't feel it. It was one thing for economists to say that financial downturns take up to ten years to recover from and Obama was ahead of the curve; it was quite another for a working person or someone running a small business or farm to feel it, and regain their confidence that tomorrow would be better than today.

Eventually Mitt Romney won the GOP nomination and chose conservative young Congressman Paul Ryan to be his vice presidential running mate. Even though Romney had abandoned many of the moderate positions he had once held—including a government-run health insurance marketplace—he would never be a darling of the Republican right, and his successful career in finance made him both more acceptable to comfortable, economically secure voters and more vulnerable to losing voters in the culturally conservative, economically populist white working class.

As the Democratic convention approached in early September, President Obama asked me to give the nominating address. I knew I had to address the public's lagging confidence in the country's economic recovery, Obama's impressive record under great duress, and my conviction that Obama would be far better for America in the next four years.

I worked on the speech while on vacation on Long Island, and was several drafts in when I arrived in Charlotte on the convention's opening day. Obama's team and people who had served with me offered helpful advice to strengthen the case I had to make: Obama's policies had put a floor under the crash and were bringing us back with a stronger, more inclusive recovery, and it was a mistake to go back to trickle-down economics that had failed in the past and would do so again if Mitt Romney were elected. I ended the speech with a reminder that those who had bet against America in the past had lost, that we'd come through every test stronger, and that Obama was by far the best choice for us to continue that progress.

It was for the most part a straightforward comparison of records and proposals, but it did have some pretty good punch lines. Here are a few of my favorites:

"And by the way, after last night [when the first lady had given her own powerful speech], I want a man who had the good sense to marry Michelle Obama!"

"Since 1961, for 52 years now, the Republicans have held the

White House 28 years, the Democrats 24. In those 52 years, our economy has produced 66 million private sector jobs. So what's the job score? Republicans 24 million, Democrats 42."

I reminded them that Romney had opposed the auto bailout, which had saved the whole parts supply chain. "So here's another job score. Are you listening in Michigan and Ohio and across the country? . . . Obama 250,000, Romney zero."

"The Republican argument against the President [at their convention] was actually pretty simple and snappy. It went something like this: 'We left him a total mess, he hasn't cleaned it up fast enough, so fire him and put us back in.' . . . They just didn't say much about the ideas they have offered over the last two years. They couldn't, because they want to go back to the same old policies that got us into trouble in the first place."

Anyway, the speech was well received in the hall and in the press. I even got the title of "explainer-in-chief" from President Obama. I've spent a fair amount of time with him over the years, beginning with my already mentioned trip to Houston, where he, Hillary, and I visited with Katrina survivors. I came to deeply respect him and his amazing wife. I appreciated it when he visited me in Harlem and later shared a great lunch in lower Manhattan on one of his trips to New York.

And it was always an honor to be invited back to the White House, particularly once in late 2010 when he decided that I should accompany him to an impromptu joint press conference to explain and promote the bipartisan tax agreement he'd just struck with Senate Democrats and Republicans. But the press room was locked for the White House holiday party that had just started, and he had to ask someone to open it up. After the conference started, Obama stayed only a few minutes before announcing that he had to attend the party or Michelle would be mad, so he left me there to face the reporters, many of whom I knew well. I figured I'd get a lot of ribbing from the press, and I did, but I stayed and answered questions and had a good time doing it.

I also enjoyed playing golf with President Obama. On the first round we shared, he was new to the game, but by the second time we played, he had gotten a lot better, and was three strokes ahead of me, although I was closing the gap, when he said he had to leave the Army Navy golf course to get back to business. I kidded him that the rules were still working for him.

And of course I'll never forget the visit in 2013, when he awarded me the Medal of Freedom. I've often said presidents shouldn't get other awards, because the privilege of the job is reward enough. But it was a true honor, one for which I and my family, who were all there, will always be grateful.

I'm also thankful for the chances I've had to be around Michelle. One memory stands out in particular. When Sargent Shriver died at the ripe old age of ninety-five, the first lady represented the White House at his funeral. The family asked me to speak because I'd known him since the 1972 presidential election when, as George McGovern's vice presidential running mate, he spent the last weekend of the campaign in Texas, where I was working for the ticket. And I'd shared a couple of wonderful dinners in Florida with him and his son Anthony. I really admired Shriver, what he stood for and how he lived his life. When I rose to speak about him, my words came straight from the heart. I went back to the pew, emotionally spent and on the verge of tears. Michelle sensed it, and just quietly reached over and grabbed my hand and squeezed. We didn't know each other that well, but it was an act of uncommon grace and kindness I'll never forget.

The 2012 race was a dead heat coming into the convention, but the president got a good 5-point convention bump and, a couple of weeks later, was helped again by the release of a video of Mitt Romney at a small fundraiser for big donors saying 47 percent of Americans would vote for President Obama because they are dependent on the government and believe they are victims who think the government has a responsibility to care for them.

It fed into the storyline that Romney was an out-of-touch rich guy, and rallied our troops. In the end, President Obama was reelected 51–47. The Democrats even picked up two Senate seats and eight House seats. Through his economic recovery investments, overseen by Vice President Biden, the automobile industry rescue, overseen by New York businessman Steven Rattner, and the success of the Affordable Care Act, Obama had demonstrated that government could actually work for people.

But it was a false dawn. The new Republican base didn't really love Romney. After all, as governor of Massachusetts, he had worked with Democrats to pass healthcare reform. For the Republican right wing, cooperation that made government work didn't help them. And it sure didn't advance their "us vs. them" storyline. Instead, House Republicans voted more than fifty times to get rid of Obamacare, without ever offering an alternative and without ever paying a price. And the Senate blocked virtually all of President Obama's nominees to the U.S. Court of Appeals, until a bipartisan deal ending the filibuster for judicial appointments below the Supreme Court was struck by fourteen senators, seven Republicans and seven Democrats.

At the state level, Republicans ramped up their efforts to make it harder to vote, including cutbacks on early voting, repealing of Election Day registration, and requiring specific types of government-issued photo identification to vote. Florida even cracked down on nonpartisan voter registration drives, forcing the League of Women Voters to close down its operations. To reduce the Democratic vote in college towns, North Carolina passed a law requiring college students to go home to vote or their parents would lose their state tax deduction for dependent children. Texas required a state-issued photo ID to vote, but with two exceptions: a photo ID from a state college or university didn't count, and a state-issued concealed carry permit with no photo did!

The voting restrictions and gerrymandering were beginning to have an effect. The Koch brothers deserve a lot of credit for this. For years they had been funding candidates for the state legislatures, arming them with proven attack lines designed to paint Democrats as godless, anti-American aliens, and providing them with model legislation undermining environmental regulations, denying climate change, privatizing schools, attacking unions, resisting tax increases, weakening the Affordable Care Act, restricting voting options, and much more. Anonymous corporations provided much of the money. It worked, moving state governments to the right. Democrats had no organization to counter this. Our major donors like giving money to presidential candidates and hadn't yet done what the Republicans do so well: make the system and the rules work better for them.

For example, in 2012, although President Obama narrowly lost the state, Democratic candidates for the House in North Carolina narrowly won the total vote 51–49. But thanks to gerrymandering, there were still nine Republicans and four Democrats in the North Carolina House delegation. Thankfully, throughout the 2012 election cycle, courts both state and federal, including both conservative and progressive judges, had blocked or blunted Republicans' most extreme actions.

Then, in 2013, the Supreme Court moved sharply in the other direction. In one of the most radical departures from legal precedent in my lifetime, the Supreme Court decided in *Shelby County v. Holder* that the Voting Rights Act had been so effective in blocking discriminatory voting practices in areas with a history of discrimination that a lot of Black candidates had been elected to office, so it was no longer fair to hold those places to a different standard. The majority found that the formulas determining these preclearance jurisdictions were outdated, even though Congress had renewed them by overwhelming margins just seven years earlier. In her dissent, Justice Ginsburg warned that weakening the Voting Rights Act because it was working was "like throwing away your umbrella in a rainstorm because you are not getting wet." Soon we were all getting wet as Republican legislatures across the country rushed to change laws in ways they believed would reduce turnout in heavily Democratic areas.

It worked. In early 2024, the Brennan Center for Justice released the results of a multiyear voting file showing that in the counties formerly covered by the preclearance provisions of the Voting Rights Act, the racial gap in voting had grown almost twice as fast than in other parts of the country with similar demographic and ethnic profiles. The 2014 midterms were another disaster for the Democrats. With increasingly shrill attacks against the Affordable Care Act, GOP Senate candidates who sounded less crazy than their counterparts in 2010, and the fall-off again greater among Democrats than Republicans, the Republicans picked up nine Senate seats and thirteen more in the House, assuring them of majorities in both houses of Congress.

I could see it coming in Arkansas when I got a call from Senator Mark Pryor, who was being challenged by Congressman Tom Cotton, a Harvard Law grad, decorated Army officer who served in Iraq and Afghanistan, and an articulate, aggressive member of the far-right House Republicans. I thought Pryor was in a good position to withstand the coming fire because he was a genuine moderate who had worked with Republicans on a number of issues and had friends in every county. He did have one problem in a state where more and more voters watched only Fox News: he voted for the Affordable Care Act. In 1996, in his early thirties, he'd had a rare cancer and survived, even though his insurance company had initially tried to decline coverage. He knew what it was like to be sick and dependent on insurance, and he didn't want anyone else to get sick with no insurance or worry about losing the insurance they'd paid for when it was most needed.

In April, more than six months before the vote, Mark called and said, "I know you're trying to help me. I'm picking up your tracks all over the state. But it's no use, I'm going to lose." I asked how he knew that when he was still 10 points ahead in the polls. He said the lead was meaningless, because his name recognition was still more than 20 points higher than Cotton's and the gap would soon disappear.

So I said, "Tell me what happened." In our small state, personal encounters often mean more than polls. Mark said he'd just been in a rural county in northeast Arkansas and had run into an old friend. "I've known this guy for years and knew he had some health problems. When I asked him about his health, he said, 'Oh, Mark, I'm so happy. I got on the internet and found a policy that covers more and costs less than my old one. And it's so much better than Obamacare.' When I asked what the website was and he told me, I said, 'That's the Affordable Care Act site! I voted for it to help people like you.' This guy just put his hand on my shoulder, shook his head, and said, 'Mark, you know I love you, but I watch Fox News. I know nothing as good as my policy could have come out of that piece of crap.' "

I wanted a second opinion, so I called an old friend who lived on the northern edge of the Ozark Mountains in northwest Arkansas. Levi Phillips is rarely out of jeans and boots, has white hair and a white beard. He looks like a character out of *Duck Dynasty*, but he's more liberal than most people reading this book. And a friend for fifty years. When he picked up the phone, I asked, "Levi, can we save Mark Pryor?" He answered, "I don't know, it's gonna be hard. Want me to find out?" I said I did, and he hung up, knowing exactly what I was asking him to do. He got in his pickup and drove down into the heart of the Arkansas Ozarks, to a tiny place with about fifty people in the southwest corner of one of our most rural counties. On election days, a couple hundred more people come in out of the woods to vote at the general store. The man who owns it is whip-smart and is a better barometer for his people than any poll or focus group.

When Levi walked up the steps into the store in 2014, I hadn't run for state office in twenty-four years and hadn't been in the store since the 1980s. The man looked up and said, "Hi, Levi. Clinton sent you, didn't he?" Levi said, "He did. He wants to know if we can save Mark Pryor." The man answered, "Well, let's get the preliminaries out of the way. You know I always supported Clinton. He was a good governor and a good president. And I really like Mark Pryor. He's worked hard and is fair to everyone. But we're gonna give Congress to the Republicans." When Levi asked him why, he said, "Well, I'm not a fool. I know the first thing the Republican Congress will do is something to help rich people." (He was right about that. Their first effort was an attempt to weaken Dodd-Frank, the bill passed to prevent a rerun of the financial crisis.) "But Obama's been there six years and the Democrats haven't done anything for us, either. At least the Republicans will leave me alone. The Democrats want to take my rifle and make me go to a gay wedding."

How could this man think I was a good president? He knew I passed the assault weapons ban and the ten-round clip limit in the Crime Bill. He knew I had appointed openly gay people to important positions. But he was smart and fair-minded enough to know a president had to care about people and problems that were rare to nonexistent in his small remote corner of the Ozarks.

By 2014, though, he thought our party as a whole didn't care about them anymore, thanks to the clever divisiveness of Fox News, readily available false information on the internet, relatively rare coverage of rural America in the mainstream media, and, to old-fashioned ears, the condescending judgmental language of some of the more liberal commentators. If Fox, *Breitbart*, and the other right-wing outlets were "their" outlets, the others must be "ours."

You may be thinking, so what? Democrats still had the demographic edge. In theory, yes. In the real world, not unless you show up at the midterms as Democrats did in 1998, 2006, 2018, and 2022, when Democrats and moderate independent voters showed their anger at the hard right and their "post-fact" power plays. But when our enthusiasm wavered, they were always there, lying in wait, as they were with a vengeance in 1994, 2010, and 2014. By the last two weeks of 2020, and in Virginia and New Jersey in 2021, they had also found a strategy to erode our advantage with suburban and Hispanic voters. More about that later.

NINETEEN

Hillary Steps Down and In

Hillary had always planned to leave the State Department after the 2012 election. When President Obama had asked her to be secretary of state, she told him the truth—she loved being a senator from New York, wanted to go back to it, and he had other good options for State. He asked her to think about it. I thought in the end she'd have to do it, and when I talked to the president-elect, I told him to be patient; she didn't make big changes lightly. I said she didn't say yes when I asked her to marry me until she'd said no twice. I think something that swayed her was that she, like all Democrats, wanted him to succeed, and if she didn't say yes, it might undermine the respect and cooperation she'd earned from her Senate colleagues. Finally, Hillary said if she accepted, she wanted to make sure she could choose her top staff and meet the president for lunch weekly when they were both in the country. He agreed and she said yes.

She had loved the job more than she'd expected to, but after four years of endless travel and high-stakes work, she was exhausted. Previous secretaries of state had been known for high-profile efforts to resolve crises or make peace. Only a few had also earned a reputation for making the most of "the building," meaning the several hundred operations and more than 70,000 employees on the organizational chart of the State Department. Hillary was determined to do both: to travel the world to solve problems, reduce tensions, and advance the president's agenda, and to help the State Department's workforce be seen, heard, respected, and effective. She believed our world leadership depended on Defense, Diplomacy, and Development. She had done backbreaking work to support the first, advance the last two, and deal with the big crises. She needed a break.

President Obama urged her to stay on. He had developed a close relationship with her and had come to trust her in tough situations. She was loyal to him and kept whatever differences they had on policy between the two of them. She was on track to end her tenure with sky-high public approval ratings, and unusually good working relations with the Pentagon, the intelligence agencies, and Congress, including many Republicans who weren't yet too afraid of their right wing to say what they thought. She'd also received thorough, fact-based coverage in the media, including Kim Ghattas's excellent book *The Secretary*.

Then came Benghazi. On September 11, 2012, Ambassador Chris Stevens and Information Management Officer Sean Smith were killed in an attack on the U.S. diplomatic compound there. Hours later, two CIA contractors who were former Navy SEALs were slain in the second of two attacks on a still officially secret CIA compound about a mile away.

The U.S. and the U.K. had joined France, other NATO allies, and Arab League members in providing U.N.-approved air support to the uprising against Muammar Gaddafi in early 2011. In October 2011, he was found hiding in his hometown and was killed by fellow Libyans. A new civilian government was established in Tripoli, the capital, but after decades of dictatorship holding together a complex web of tribal alliances, the government was fragile, with limited ability to control the many militia groups who had begun quarreling among themselves after Gaddafi's demise.

Chris Stevens, an experienced diplomat, became the U.S.

ambassador to Libya, where he had served before, and got to work trying to bridge the differences. He traveled around the country for meetings, which is why he was in Benghazi. Stevens spoke Arabic fluently, had met alone and unarmed with tribal leaders, and worked well with them. He was probably the most popular foreigner in Libya. But not with everyone. Ansar al-Sharia, an extremist group, claimed credit for the attacks.

When the assault on the diplomatic compound occurred, a security officer immediately took Stevens and Smith to a steel-reinforced safe room where they remained until the attackers withdrew, setting fire to the buildings on the way out. There was an escape route, a ladder that led to the roof. The security officer got on the ladder and beckoned Stevens and Smith to follow. They didn't, either because they were too weak from smoke inhalation or didn't hear or couldn't find the ladder. Smith's body was soon found. Stevens was found later by a group of Libyans walking in the ruins of the compound and taken to a hospital. After attempts to revive him failed, he, too, was declared dead by smoke inhalation.

The terrorists then staged a separate attack on the CIA facility, killing the two contractors before being driven off. Soon tens of thousands of Libyans poured into the streets of Benghazi to mourn Chris Stevens, and another group stormed the headquarters of Ansar al-Sharia and ran several of their members out of town.

How did this happen? Could it have been prevented? Hillary accepted responsibility whenever something went wrong involving those 70,000+ State and USAID staff at more than 270 posts around the world. She quickly appointed an Accountability Review Board, as required whenever State Department personnel lose their lives overseas. It happens more often than people think. It was the nineteenth such investigation since 1988. (You may be surprised by the big number. The others took place when Congress didn't exploit tragedies to make political hay.)

The five-member board was led by the highly respected Tom Pickering, a recently retired foreign service officer who had led many challenging embassies, including El Salvador during its civil war, Israel during the first Intifada, and Russia just after the fall of the Soviet Union. His lead partner was recently retired

Chairman of the Joint Chiefs of Staff Admiral Mike Mullen, a well-liked and very able straight shooter.

The Review Board did a good job identifying problems in handling diplomatic security and coordinating with the people working with local governments and those in the State Department hierarchy charged with giving them the support they needed. The board's report found too much reliance on Libyan security contractors and called for more support from Congress for the State Department's needs, which the board pointed out "constitute a small percentage both of the full national budget and that spent for national security." The report contained twenty-nine recommendations to fix the problem. Hillary and her team handed out assignments designed to implement all of them and she pledged not to leave her job until the changes were underway. After the president's reelection, she kept working, testifying about Benghazi for five hours before Senate and House committees and preparing a long memo for President Obama with her recommendations for the next four years in foreign policy, soon to be overseen by incoming Secretary of State John Kerry.

Hillary's last day was February 1, 2013, and the State Department gave her a rousing sendoff, grateful for her leadership, from urging the president to approve the mission to get bin Laden, to securing the votes in the U.N. imposing tough sanctions on Iran, to flying all night from Asia to broker a cease-fire in Gaza between Hamas and Israel, to her wide-ranging efforts to educate and economically empower women and girls in the poorest countries, and to make the countries she visited feel important to the United States.

After she left the State Department, Hillary joined Chelsea and me at the Clinton Foundation, and for the first time since I lost reelection as governor of Arkansas in 1980, we were both out of politics. Sort of.

The congressional hearings on Benghazi, which had started just before Hillary left office on February 1, 2013, continued on, eventually producing five separate reports from House and two from Senate committees. All the committees were chaired by Republicans, all found no wrongdoing by Hillary, and all generally supported the recommendations of the Accountability Review Board she had appointed and which she had already begun implementing. In the end, the GOP-led committees played it straight and because they did, predictably earned precious little press coverage.

The Republicans knew Hillary was their strongest political opponent in 2016. They had to discredit her. So when the regular Republican majority committee hearings didn't get the desired result, the House Republican leadership, on May 2, 2014, formed a "special committee" on Benghazi headed by Representative Trey Gowdy, the former prosecutor who had defeated Bob Inglis in a Republican primary after Inglis refused to deny climate change, question President Obama's birth in the U.S., or foment hatred of the president.

The new Benghazi committee, officially labeled the Select Committee on the Events Surrounding the 2012 Terrorist Attack in Benghazi, was purely political, set up to attack Hillary. Republican leader Kevin McCarthy even bragged about it on Fox News on September 29, 2015, saying, "Everybody thought Hillary was unbeatable, right? But we put together a Benghazi Special Committee, a select committee. What are her numbers today? Her numbers are dropping."

By then, Hillary had been a presidential candidate for five months, announcing first with a video designed to showcase the people she wanted to help. Three months later, on June 13, 2015, in a rally on a beautiful summer day in the Four Freedoms Park on Roosevelt Island in New York City's East River, she gave a kickoff speech to thousands of people and talked more about what she wanted to do for our country.

On October 22, 2015, more than one hundred days after she launched her campaign for president, Hillary testified for the second time about Benghazi. She was grilled for more than eight hours in an eleven-hour stretch between 10 a.m. and 9 p.m.

McCarthy was right that more than a year of Republican attacks had driven her poll numbers down. But at the hearing, she handled herself, the tragedy, and her record in a way no other man or woman in public life could have matched. She was strong, direct, and calm, displaying the qualities that would have made her a great president. People who watched it live or saw the straightforward coverage and commentary on television and in print media were impressed, and her campaign got a needed boost of enthusiasm.

When it was finally over in 2016, the Benghazi committee investigations, six in the House, two in the Senate, had cost taxpayers $7 million and gone on longer than congressional probes into 9/11, Watergate, the assassination of President Kennedy, and the attack on Pearl Harbor!

Long before that, the headlines had forgotten Ambassador Stevens and the other three Americans who lost their lives, and glommed on to the fact that Hillary had used her personal email to conduct business as secretary of state and that the emails eventually were stored on a private server in our house. Most of these stories were written as if the inquiry that produced them was sparked by a suspicion that she violated the law. Even today, most people still don't know how it started.

In 2014, more than a year after Hillary had left the State Department, Congress changed the Federal Records Act to require that records still in possession of current and former government employees be included in official government files within twenty days, and to require the use of government devices when doing business. Before that, the State Department rules allowed her and other State Department employees to use their private email devices, as long as their business-related emails were saved and turned over when the career employees in charge of archiving and retrieving records asked for them.

In October of 2014, the State Department record-keeper asked all former secretaries of state to check their emails and copies of any documents they still had to see if there was anything that should be part of the department's official records. Colin Powell said he had deleted all his emails years before. Madeleine Albright said she didn't email, as did Condi Rice, although her top aides did and they complied with the request. Hillary called in her lawyers and asked them to go over her emails and resolve all doubt in favor of the State Department request. They already had more than 90 percent of them because they were sent to other State Department personnel using their government-issued email accounts which automatically stored them. The State Department reviewed all the ones she submitted and returned more than a thousand, judging them not to be related to her work.

As for the server, that's on me. Well before the emails became an issue, the team handling my communications concluded that the company whose server we were using was doing a less than stellar job and that we could get better service and more security if we just bought a server and installed it at our house, where the Secret Service is on duty around the clock. The Secret Service approved the move and even asked to be able to use the server, too. So, I gave the go-ahead.

The email story became the biggest story of the 2016 election. It would get 20 percent more coverage than all Trump's negatives combined. It was at the core of a reputation-destruction campaign that was also aided in early 2015 by the publication of Peter Schweizer's book *Clinton Cash*. At the time, the author was on the payroll of GAI (the Government Accountability Institute), funded by the right-wing billionaire Robert Mercer and working closely with Steve Bannon, the white nationalist head of the right-wing social media site *Breitbart News*. The essential argument of the book was that Hillary and I and the Clinton Foundation had gotten a lot of money by using her position as secretary of state to give access to the State Department to our supporters, including donors to the Clinton Foundation, though even Schweizer admitted he had found no "smoking gun" evidence, just questions.

It took about two days to discredit the book for its attacks on the foundation. Some of the errors were so obvious that even the publisher, a Rupert Murdoch company, demanded several changes in the text to continue printing it. But the book achieved its larger purpose when, amazingly, *The New York Times* and *The Washington Post* joined Fox in signing "exclusive" agreements to use the book as a "resource" for the campaigns, knowing full well whose payroll the author was on and his past work as a right-wing propagandist.

Gene Lyons, an Arkansas journalist who had earned the ire of the political media in the 1990s with his book *The Hunting of the President*, coauthored with Joe Conason, wrote a column blasting the *Times* and the *Washington Post* for teaming up with Fox on the "exclusive" arrangement with Schweizer, saying "he makes his living vilifying Democrats" and referred to a "long list of withdrawn or retracted stories under his byline." He also quoted the British *Sunday Times*, finding that "facts that are checkable do not check out. Individuals credited for supplying information do not exist or cannot be tracked down. Requests to the author for help and clarification result in further confusion and contradiction."

Nevertheless, *The New York Times* praised Schweizer's "meticulous reporting," as the basis for its first "Uranium One" story, implying that as secretary of state, Hillary sold out the national interest by helping a Russian company to buy a Wyoming-based enterprise for a few million dollars in contributions to the Clinton Foundation. Lyons destroyed the story piece by piece. He said, "The Clinton Rules are back: all innuendo and guilt-by-association." The story was so bad that the *Times* and the *Post* essentially reversed field and conceded that Hillary was not involved, my supporter and Clinton Foundation board member Frank Giustra was not involved, and the charges were false. But besides hurting Frank, airing the charges had hurt Hillary, me, and the Clinton Foundation. It was a "three-fer" for *Breitbart* and the political press.

What was going on? The political media needed a close race, and Hillary was still a big favorite, so, ignoring the warning of the 2014 midterm results, they decided they wouldn't get a close race without damaging her reputation. Then they contracted the work of finding ammunition to a source they knew to be biased and unreliable and never publicized the fact that how she handled her emails was explicitly allowed by government regulations. *Read that again:* government regulations explicitly allowed Hillary to use her own device and said she had to save any business-related work until the State Department people in charge of archiving records asked for it. No matter how closely you followed the 2016 election and how many email stories you read, I'd be surprised if even 3 percent of the voters knew that, or about those multiple Republican-chaired Benghazi committees that had found no wrongdoing by her.

Meanwhile, Hillary had a campaign to run. Like I said earlier, elections are about culture, conditions, candidates, their campaigns, and coverage on television, social media, radio talk shows, and in print media, which often drives what the television networks and other outlets cover and talk about. The press treatment in 2015 and 2016 would turn out to be the worst in my lifetime and made a bigger difference in the election than any coverage I'd ever seen. With the political press's inexplicable obsession with the false email narrative and the sensationalizing of the *Clinton Cash* falsehoods, the ultimate effect was that their coverage, along with Comey's unprecedented violation of decades of FBI policy—plus an assist from Putin—tipped the Electoral College in Donald Trump's favor.

I lived through Whitewater and the political media's breathless coverage which continued even after Hillary and I were cleared of wrongdoing in 1995. The Republicans kept on going, though, with Ken Starr's crowd eventually becoming the first special counsels to lose their bogus cases in court. I didn't believe it could get any worse. But, boy, did 2016 prove me wrong. We may never know the political press's motivations for its coverage of Hillary's campaign—personal animus, power lust, the extra income driven by clicks and retweets, or some combination of all three and other factors—or why most of the mainstream media hasn't acknowledged its impact on the most critical election of my lifetime.

But I do know this: the media is indispensable to our democracy and is one reason our republic has survived as long as it has. The good news is that by and large, they've tried to mend their ways and find a way back to objective reporting. But with the exception of a few brave truth tellers, they've done so without acknowledging what they did in 2015 and 2016.

When we first began discussing the possibility of her running for president again, Hillary was clearly the Democrats' best choice to beat the third-term jinx if she concentrated on what her administration could do to make people's lives better: from expanding eligibility for healthcare coverage under the Affordable Care Act; to making it easier for working parents to take care of their children; to moving the green energy economy to a more sustainable job-producing model; to implementing a big infrastructure program to create lots of jobs, bring clean water to communities with dangerous rusting pipes, and get affordable broadband, education, and training within reach of every American, especially in economically stagnant areas; and to being more aggressive in confronting China's clear abuses in trade policy and currency manipulation.

She had to demonstrate how she would be different from Obama without being disloyal or separating herself from the achievements she strongly supported and wanted to build on. It was a tough task. She made many efforts to do so, including going to places with problems not being dealt with early in her "listening tour" mode.

Hillary's main primary opponent was Vermont senator Bernie Sanders, who had been elected to the House in 1992 as an independent, a label he kept when he moved on to the Senate in the 2006 midterm sweep. Sanders thought President Obama had not been far enough left in his proposals for healthcare, taxing the rich, and providing easier access to college, and he opposed all trade agreements, thinking they hurt more Americans than they helped. He considered running against Obama for the nomination in 2012, but didn't, in part because he was up for reelection, and he wanted to keep his seat.

In 2016, he had nothing to lose, and he sensed a growing frustration among working-class and younger voters who felt things had to be shaken up for them to get a fair shake. It didn't seem to occur to these voters that if they had voted in the 2010 and 2014 midterms as they did in 2008 and 2012, Obama would have gotten a lot more done and they'd have been less frustrated.

Bernie was vigorous, decisive, and sure of the righteousness of his cause. He told voters what would be different if they elected him. His pitch paid off in the army of younger voters who showed up to work for him and the large number of small contributors who financed the lion's share of his campaign.

Hillary campaigned on a platform with specific progressive goals and realistic methods for achieving them, including how to pay for them. Bernie's platform had bigger promises but fewer specifics on how to achieve them, much less how to pay for them, especially given the fact that Congress was still in Republican hands.

Essentially, he said we needed to become a bigger version of Denmark with lots of free things. Except they wouldn't be free and if we only taxed the wealthiest Americans, it wouldn't be enough to pay for his priorities. He did acknowledge that the middle class would pay more in taxes for healthcare but said they would more than make up for it by not paying for health insurance. In theory, that's true. We spend way more than any other country for healthcare. But Bernie never talked about how to make the transition, how long it would take to win back the House and Senate with enough votes to pass his proposal, and what would happen to the hundreds of thousands of people who worked for insurers whose jobs would be lost, or the fact that Denmark taxes its people up to 53 percent of annual income, much higher than the United States, with lower defense expenditures per capita, leaving much more money for social programs.

But it sounded so good. Bernie convinced his supporters that Hillary was almost reactionary for not supporting dismantling the Affordable Care Act and replacing it with a single-payer system, guaranteeing free college for everyone, and raising the minimum wage to $15 an hour immediately in all fifty states, regardless of the differences in the cost of living. His troops shouted that if you weren't as far left as he was, you were an inauthentic pawn of the establishment. Hillary was allergic to promising something no president could deliver, and since her platform was the most progressive yet realistic one ever offered, she believed she could sell it, unless people stopped listening. That's exactly what the Republicans and the political press were hoping to accomplish by keeping her tied up with the emails as long as possible.

Hillary narrowly won in Iowa, but it felt like a landslide, given what had happened there in 2008. In New Hampshire it was the reverse. She lost by a lot, in spite of having a good campaign staff and all her longtime supporters. I lost New Hampshire in 1992 to Paul Tsongas, whose hometown in Massachusetts was just five miles from New Hampshire's narrow southern border. Vermont borders the entire west side of New Hampshire from north to south, so Bernie was a constant media presence for those who watched Vermont television. Hillary's campaign leaders urged her not to contest an unwinnable race, but she said it would be disloyal to all the people who had worked so hard for her for so long. She went to New Hampshire, made her pitch, and sent her message: you might leave me this time, but I will never leave you.

I supported her decision on the merits and because I knew what was coming next: South Carolina. The vote there revealed how Black voters really felt about her and also revealed the dark underbelly of the Sanders campaign: the "Bernie Bros," who were very active on social media in bashing Hillary in brash, often brutally sexist terms, and in going after people who supported her. Their social media strategy had kept them under the mainstream media's radar screen for a good while, until just a few days before the South Carolina primary, when they went after Congressman John Lewis for endorsing Hillary.

Hitting Lewis was a big mistake, because he was a wonderful, brave man who repeatedly risked his life to advance civil rights and because virtually all of South Carolina's prominent Black elected officials, led by veteran Congressman Jim Clyburn and the impressive young mayor of Columbia, Steve Benjamin, were already for her and used the Bernie Bros against him. She won 73 percent of the vote, better than I did twenty-four years earlier and better than President Obama did in 2008. Then she won Nevada again. After that the Southern states rolled up big numbers for her: Georgia, Alabama, North Carolina, Virginia, Mississippi, Louisiana, Arkansas, Florida, and Texas. She also won almost all the big states outside those in the South: New York, Pennsylvania, New Jersey, Ohio, Illinois, and California.

But many of the white working-class voters who had supported her so strongly in 2008 were defecting, lured by Bernie's promises and reacting to all her bad press. His numbers didn't add up, but nobody cared until he did an interview with the New

York *Daily News*, virtually the only publication that gave him the close scrutiny Hillary was used to. They gave major, largely negative coverage to answers he gave—or couldn't give—to the questions they asked by simply printing a transcript of his interview and giving Hillary a rousing editorial endorsement. It went a long way toward dashing his hope for an upset in New York, where he'd grown up.

I wasn't surprised that the Northern states of Minnesota and Wisconsin went for Bernie. The primary and caucus electorates were very liberal, and he was more to the left on everything but gun safety, race, women's and children's rights, and protecting the Dreamers (schoolchildren of undocumented immigrants). And although in an older body, he was a new face, looking rumpled but real. He also won states that went big for her in 2008, including Oklahoma and West Virginia, and he almost won Kentucky.

In many places, Hillary's county-by-county map looked like Obama's in 2008. But she still had her staunchest supporters, including Latinos, and had added the Black voters who had liked her all along, and knew she cared about their kids because of her long history of support for civil rights, her work with Marian Wright Edelman at the Children's Defense Fund, her support for Mothers of the Movement, a group who had all lost unarmed children to gun violence or encounters with police officers, and her outreach to young Black Lives Matter leaders.

I wasn't worried about Illinois, which she barely won, because her primary campaign had become a proxy for the fierce battle over local issues in the Chicago area, which Bernie's supporters smartly played to the fullest. I was sure they'd come home in the general election. But I was worried about Michigan, where she had won decisively in 2008 but lost by 2 points this time (I'd gone to the Labor Day Parade in Detroit in 2015, and it just felt flat); Pennsylvania, where I got more heckling on the Crime Bill (which Bernie had voted for!) than anywhere else; and Wisconsin, where Governor Scott Walker had won both houses of the legislature and fended off a referendum to remove him from office by stirring up a firestorm of rural and small-town resentment against the university towns, unions, and urban Black Americans who he said were gobbling up all their hard-earned tax dollars to advance a dangerous left-wing agenda. In her prescient 2016 book about Wisconsin, *The Politics of Resentment*, Katherine Cramer tells the story of the rising rural backlash against "liberal elites" as a major factor dividing America. People in economically stagnant areas were tired of waiting for the benefits of globalization while more populous, more diverse, and more highly educated and trained areas were thriving.

The larger and more troubling issue was that Hillary at the start of the 2016 campaign was a different person to the voters than she was in 2008. She wasn't the senator from New York who had warned the big banks they were endangering the economy, worked to increase the incomes of small businesses and farmers in traditionally Republican areas, improved security for our troops and healthcare for our veterans, and was the first person to put support for families with autistic kids high on the national agenda. She wasn't the first lady who had worked to get healthcare for millions of children, reached across party lines to dramatically increase adoptions, including for kids with disabilities, and advised me not to sign NAFTA unless first we had congressional approval of the money necessary to replace the jobs that would be lost and to train the displaced workers to do those new jobs. She wasn't the first lady of Arkansas who had put improving healthcare for families and better education for all kids, especially in poor underserved rural areas, high on our reform agenda.

Now she was either a former secretary of state who had been really effective on issues large and small but not those at the forefront of voters' concerns in 2016, or an establishment figure running for Obama's third term who'd mishandled her emails. She had even given paid speeches after leaving office, including to Wall Street groups, although she gave more than two thirds of the money to the foundation to fund the work she was involved in, and, as I said, she, not Sanders, had gone to Wall Street while still a senator in 2007 to warn them about their dangerous trading practices. More important, her coverage since leaving office was relentlessly negative. If she was seen as running for Obama's third term, burdened with more negative coverage than any Republican would get, that was a big problem.

In all the books about her, I wish more attention had been paid to what she did for people in her Senate career, how popular she was, and how much support her hard work generated in New York. It's a textbook example on how to build a world of shared opportunities, responsibilities, and communities from the ground up. And if voters had been allowed to hear it, along with her positive proposals for the future, I think she would have won.

On the other hand, compared to 2008, Hillary was much better organized from the start, did well in the debates, and despite Bernie's well-organized and vigorous campaign and the media's email beatdown, she won the primaries by 3.7 million votes, 55 to 43 percent, a much better result than in 2008, when she'd won the popular vote by 100,000 votes and lost the nomination in the caucuses and the superdelegates. This time, she earned enough delegates in the primaries and caucuses to be nominated and then added to that an enormous lead in the superdelegates, some of whom were perplexed by why our party would even allow someone who wasn't a Democrat to run for the nomination. Nevertheless, Bernie complained a lot about the Democratic National Committee, especially the rule providing for superdelegates, although he liked the rules that worked for him, like the one allowing lots of caucuses and permitting them to apportion all the delegates even in states that also held primaries. For example, Hillary won the primaries in Nebraska and Washington and Bernie won the caucuses, but while the primaries had almost three times as many voters as the caucuses, the caucuses controlled all the delegates.

I had a good time campaigning for Hillary in the primary, doing what I had done in 2008, fundraisers so she could stay on the campaign trail, and going to places in key states like Nevada and Ohio where the campaign thought I could make a difference.

There was one event that gave me some hope that we could begin to put the country back together. In the spring of 2016, I visited Morehead State University, a college in easternmost Kentucky, about forty miles from the West Virginia border, to tout Hillary's plans for rebuilding the economy in rural America, including the area around Morehead, which had once been a center of coal mining.

Kentucky had voted for me twice, in part because I had done a lot of work to get coal miners in Arkansas black lung benefits after the Nixon administration tightened the eligibility rules so much that people who were obviously disabled couldn't get any benefits at all. As president I had done all I could to make sure the miners got their due, but I also tried to heal their communities by maintaining benefits for miners and getting new job-creating investments there. By then coal mining in the eastern United States had already been in decline for more than thirty-five years, displaced first by lower-sulfur coal from the West, then by natural gas.

In 1999, I went to Hazard, Kentucky, on a sweltering hot day to promote the New Markets Tax Credit, my last major bipartisan initiative, which gave credits up to 39 percent for investments in poor areas. Hazard was hurting. When I went back in 2016, the place was reborn, but not enough had been done to give other places like it a new future.

That's what Hillary wanted to do and the case I was trying to make when I visited Morehead State. She had voted consistently in the Senate to help the miners and was familiar with their problems, not only in Arkansas, but also in New York, which had its own coal legacy issues. In 2015, she proposed to invest $30 billion in coal country to maximize their ability to attract and perform the work of today and tomorrow. Sadly, that didn't get much coverage.

When I visited the campus, I got a good reception from a large group of students the campus Democratic Club had raised. And before the rally, the university president, Dr. Wayne Andrews, invited me to tour its Space Center's nanosatellite program, an initiative that had grown out of the first $500 million nanotechnology bill I'd strongly supported late in my second term with broad bipartisan backing. As I recall, the program then had six grad students, four from the Midwest and one each from Ukraine and Vietnam, and a dozen undergrads, all from Eastern Kentucky. The satellites they were making weighed eight pounds and cost a million dollars, and had many of the capabilities of traditional communications satellites that weighed on average two hundred pounds and cost more than $200 million. The students in the program design and make the components, and assemble the nanosatellites. They now also make larger microsatellites that weigh twenty-four pounds in a partnership with NASA and major tech companies.

I visited a lab where a nineteen-year-old undergraduate from Eastern Kentucky was carefully placing a small nanochip in a tiny container designed to protect it in space. When I asked him what the container was made of, he said, with a nice Appalachian twang, "Tungsten. Tungsten does real well in outer space." I asked where it came from and he said, "I made it here with a 3D printer." Then, as I was about to leave, he stopped me and said, "President Clinton, don't let them make fun of Hillary for saying she'll put up a half a billion solar panels. Actually, I think she's a little low." When I asked him why he thought that, he said, "Because before you know it, we'll be making solar panels with 3D printers, too. They'll be cheap as dirt and just as good. Then we'll all be free."

I wasn't sure he was right on the timetable, but I wanted to jump for joy. A little more than six months from an election in which the American people had been told over and over that the emails were the most important issue since the end of the Vietnam War, here was someone too smart and future-focused to fall for the campaign coverage.

As of 2020, the Morehead State Space program, Eastern Kentucky's first engineering school, had helped Kentucky rank second in the U.S. in exports of aerospace products and parts. They've become the state's number one manufacturing export, increasing 183 percent over the last five years to $15 billion a year. Nine thousand three hundred people work for the space cluster of which Morehead is the hub, and it supports 21,000 more jobs, with a payroll of $1.46 billion.

While Hillary and Bernie were duking it out, on the GOP side Donald Trump was eating everybody's lunch. The first time I saw him in Florida onstage with all the other candidates in early 2015, I told the group I was with that I thought Trump could win the nomination. Most of them rolled their eyes. They either didn't come from "flyover" country or had lost touch with their roots. Trump was a genius at turning legitimate concerns into rage-fueled resentment by convincing deeply alienated people he had mastered a system they hated and would change it to benefit the working class, especially in culturally conservative, economically stagnant areas, and hurt those they blamed: college-educated, socially liberal, upper-middle-class voters. And he didn't mess around with surrogates—he did his own dirty work.

Here was his essential message: The Republicans have been treating you like a cheap date for decades. They tell you what you want to hear about the Democrats, but when they get elected, they're in the tank for big banks and big companies on globalization, bad trade deals, and immigration, costing us millions of good jobs and holding down wages for the working class. All these people on the platform with me are just retreads—Low Energy Jeb, Lying Ted, all of them—they're so boring and anti-change. Elect me and I'll actually do something for you. I'll build a border wall on the Rio Grande to keep the illegals out. They're just a bunch of murderers and rapists, anyway. I'll send the illegals already here back home, and you can have their jobs. And I'll make the Mexicans pay for the wall! I'll stop the Chinese from cheating us, keep their products out, and you can make that stuff here. I'll repeal Obamacare and give you something better and fill the courts with rock-ribbed conservatives. And I'll hate all the same people you do. That's how we'll Make America Great Again.

Trump rode that message to victory in the primary. Besides the rallies, he did a lot of media interviews. He always said provocative things, many of them crude, false, or both. But his strategy had a dual benefit. First, it kept his base excited, and second, it gave the political media so many things to hit him on that they couldn't focus on any one thing long enough for it to impact the public remotely as much as their endless haranguing about the emails. From 2015 until the conventions, the political media actually gave Hillary more negative and less positive coverage than Trump. The emails were "trumped up" in more ways than one.

The two conventions were a week apart in July. They were very different, but both were interesting and revealing. Trump opened in Cleveland, named Mike Pence as his running mate, and ran a longer, slightly less rambunctious version of his big rallies. It was much darker in tone and substance than most conventions, but in the deeply polarized environment, it worked better than I thought it would. He got a modest bump of about 3 points and the Democrats started in Philadelphia just four days later with the race extremely close, just the result the political media wanted.

Hillary's convention was very good for her. It was upbeat, positive, and focused on an impressive group of people who were supporting her and why they did. The speakers embodied a broad cross-section of America, with a good representation of union workers, small business owners, farmers, teachers, and several students—who were white, Black, Latino, Native American, and Asian American, male, female, and members of the LGBTQ+ community. There were people with disabilities and people who were injured on 9/11. President and Mrs. Obama, Vice President Biden, and Bernie Sanders all spoke and made the case for Hillary. President Obama was especially effective when he pointed out that she was the best qualified candidate in his lifetime, better qualified than either he or I had been, to be an effective president on day one. Bernie Sanders cut to the chase, saying of course he and Hillary had differences, but that's democracy. He said she had opened the party to his supporters and their influence was evident in the platform. He also said she would be a fine president, which was important, given the continued grumbling among his supporters whose behavior at the convention showed they couldn't believe they'd been beaten.

Her nomination of Senator Tim Kaine of Virginia as her running mate was well received. An impressive former governor, lieutenant governor, and mayor, he also spoke fluent Spanish as a result of his volunteer work with Jesuits in Honduras as a young man. His wife, Anne, had served in Governor Terry McAuliffe's cabinet and her father had been a moderate, progressive Republican governor of Virginia before his crowd became an endangered species. She had made good in her first "presidential decision."

Hillary's campaign leaders asked me to make her more "real" to the country. I did my best to describe the woman I had known and loved for more than forty years with stories that both pushed back on the cartoon coverage but also were relevant to the lives of voters.

The speech started, "In the spring of 1971, I met a girl," which probably made some young women cringe, but proved a good way to start the story of our first years together, leading up to our marriage and Chelsea's birth. I gave examples from every stage of her life, showing that from a young age to her service as first lady of Arkansas and in Washington, as a first lady, New York senator, and secretary of state, whenever she got involved in something, she always made it better. And she did it while always being a mother first, staying close to her family, keeping her friends from childhood and adding to them every step of the way. "Ask the people who know her and you'll see. She always makes things better." I said there's a big difference between talking about change and making it, and Hillary was the best changemaker I'd ever known.

The next night, Chelsea gave an eloquent, loving, and persuasive account of what it was like to be Hillary's daughter. Then Hillary gave a really upbeat speech about how she wanted to make things better for Americans. She looked great all dressed in white, in honor of the women who crusaded to give women the vote almost a hundred years earlier. And she talked about what she wanted to do in clear, strong, compelling language. The person people learned about from seeing her and others who knew her and had served with her was very different from the relentless ridicule she'd been through. She was the happy warrior with whom I'd shared more than half my life.

Thanks in part to Donald Trump, perhaps the most notable speech of the convention was given by Dr. Khizr Khan, whose family had come to the United States from the United Arab Emirates and whose son, U.S. Army Captain Humayun S. M.

Khan, had been killed in Afghanistan in 2004. When a bomb-laden truck had driven toward Captain Khan and his men, he immediately ordered his troops to draw back, then took ten steps forward before it exploded, killing him. Captain Khan was posthumously awarded the Bronze Star and the Purple Heart. When Dr. Khan spoke about his son's patriotism and his belief in America's promise of equality and opportunity for all, his voice trembled as his wife leaned into him.

Then Dr. Khan, who would later be awarded the Presidential Medal of Freedom by President Biden, said his family wouldn't be welcome in Donald Trump's America, with its proposed Muslim ban and endless slurs against immigrants, and that Trump, unlike his late son, had never put himself in harm's way or sacrificed for America. He said he wondered if Trump had ever read the Constitution and pulled out his copy, held it up for all to see, and offered to lend it to him. The effect of the Khans, standing close on the stage and lifting up their son as the best of our country, was breathtaking.

But not to Trump, who had plenty of breath left to take a shot or two, saying he had sacrificed a lot in building his businesses. He even dissed Mrs. Khan for remaining silent. It hurt him and reinforced the power of Khan's message.

Hillary got a bigger bounce out of her convention than Trump did because it was positive, with all kinds of Americans talking about what her election could mean for them, including a 9/11 victim she'd supported through multiple surgeries and a painful recovery, and a first responder who said that after 9/11, Hillary had done everything she promised to do when the cameras were off. He liked her for being "a workhorse not a show horse." She left Philadelphia with the wind at her back, and I thought if she did well in the debates, it would work out.

The coverage even became more balanced, though the press still wanted a name-calling brawl. The first warning sign came when Hillary was about to give a speech of what she wanted to do. A member of her traveling press corps told one of her staff that Hillary's proposal to improve the lives of working people living in areas of the country with low economic growth was impressive, but they'd been told that she wouldn't get any TV coverage unless she attacked Trump. That's the storyline the political press wanted—Trump screaming "Lock her up" to frenzied crowds, and Hillary taking him on. Good for their ratings, but bad for persuadable voters who wanted to know what Hillary would do for them. It was the first time since the email flood that I'd seen her discouraged, but she kept going.

After the convention I went back on the road. The campaign felt the most effective way for me to spend my time, apart from fundraising, was to travel to critical states, fire up the local campaign staff and volunteers, then go to crowded places, shake hands, answer questions, and take selfies. Apparently such spontaneous encounters garnered more social media coverage and saved the campaign the cost of holding events. The only problem with it was that there was nothing substantial for the local media to report and the only way to get Hillary's positive message out was to advertise and to shine in the debates. In 2008, the blizzard of front-porch rallies I did was very inexpensive but got extensive local coverage on what she actually wanted to do for people. Selfies posted on social media were largely useless for that, but the campaign had saved $100 million to run a positive and comparative ad blitz in the last ten days or so. And the debates would have a big effect. I knew she would work hard to prepare with a very able team. So I stayed on the road and with the program.

There were three instances in my travels in the general election that showed me vividly the ways our country was both coming together and breaking apart. The first was an encounter on a bus trip through Ohio, talking to people in small and midsized towns who were mostly concerned about the opioid crisis and the need for more local drug treatment, and more jobs. On the way into Marietta, I saw a Black pastor standing alone by the side of the road. He was well dressed and wearing a large cross embossed with red stones.

I stopped the bus and got out to shake his hand. He said, "Mr. President, I'm Bishop Stewart and I'll save you some time. I'm for Hillary. I was even for her in the 2008 primary, just as I always supported you, because I am the proud grandson of Luther Black of Hope, Arkansas."

I was pretty sure what he was going to say next, but I wanted to hear it. "When you started running for president," he continued, "my grandfather called me and said that for a few years after World War II, he got his groceries from your grandfather's store across the road from the cemetery in Hope. One day your grandfather saw my grandfather just staring at the food and he said, 'Luther, you need to buy food for your family but you don't have any money, do you?' He answered, 'I don't, Mr. Cassidy. I worked this week but I didn't get paid. I always work but sometimes I get paid a week or so late.' So your grandfather said, 'Luther, any man who works deserves to feed his family.' He told him to take what he needed, sign for it, and pay when he had the money. And my grandfather said he did the same thing for a lot of customers who were hard up."

Reverend Stewart continued, "Then he said, 'You have to support Governor Clinton. If he's half the man his grandfather was, he'll be a great president.'" He said his grandfather was right about me, and based on what he had seen Hillary do as first lady, in the Senate, and leading the State Department, he thought she would be great, too. Trying to hold back tears, I agreed with him about Hillary, thanked him, and headed for the barbershop in Marietta.

The second instance was the polar opposite of that first encounter. Closer to the election, I was on a tour of North Carolina and stopped at East Carolina University in Greenville to shake hands. Most of the students who came to visit and mentioned me on their social media sites were young women supporting Hillary, but I noticed a blond, blue-eyed young man who obviously spent time pumping iron standing at the back of the crowd, staring at me with a hostile glare. I made my way back to him and shook his hand. He said, "Can I ask you a question?" I told him to ask away. "How did it feel to take $50 million out of your foundation?" I replied, "I don't know. That's a lot more than I'm worth. Hillary and I give money to the foundation. I have donated about 10 percent of my speech earnings to the Clinton Foundation, Chelsea donates all of her speech income, and since Hillary joined us, she's given 70 percent of her speech earnings to cover the costs of foundation programs she's worked on. And we've put millions more from our family foundation into it. You don't have to take my word for it, because unlike Bernie and Trump, we've released thirty-eight years of our tax returns."

He sort of sneered and said, "Yeah, you can do that when you control the establishment."

For all his body muscle, his brain had been fried by falsehoods he probably read on the internet. Senator Daniel Patrick Moynihan once said, "Everyone is entitled to his own opinion, but not to his own facts." We're a long way from that now. In a post-fact world, everything asserted is just an opinion, including the earth is flat, vaccines are ineffective and dangerous, two plus two equals five, and of course the emails were a scandal.

The third instance was a visit that reminded me of why politics, business, and nongovernmental organizations all matter. On one of my last trips before the election I was in Florida, in the small town of Immokalee in Collier County, also home to Naples, one of the wealthiest cities in the nation, and the Big Cypress National Preserve. In 2016, Immokalee had just over 24,000 residents, of whom 71 percent were Latino, 18 percent African American, and 3.2 percent white. Many were migrant agricultural workers. More than a third of families lived below the poverty line, and just under half of the residents were under the age of eighteen.

The Coalition of Immokalee Workers is an internationally recognized human rights organization whose work includes the Fair Food Program, an innovative partnership among the workers and growers from Florida to the Northeast, as well as retail buyers, including Walmart, Subway, and Whole Foods. All the partners benefit—the workers with better working conditions and a fair wage; the growers with a more stable workforce and decreased liability risk; and the retailers with higher-quality products whose valuable brands are untainted by workplace abuses, because CIW fights beside them, especially against human trafficking and slavery.

CIW embodied the message Hillary wanted to send in the last days of the campaign: government should help all workers get better working conditions, better pay, and protections from abuse by unscrupulous employers. The CIW had proved that if they worked together, both workers' lives and the corporations' bottom lines would improve.

This window into how politics can advance the lives of real people was too often shut and locked in 2016. The politics of subtraction and division, of resentment and tribalism, leads to power for those who stoke the most fear and anger. But when we face unprecedented challenges from a global pandemic, excessive inequality at home and abroad, a warming planet, homegrown extremists, culture clashes, and authoritarian countries dedicated to weakening or destroying our democracy, we need a different approach—more addition and multiplication. As Hillary said, we have to be stronger together. We all know how boring the media thought that motto was in 2016, but it was and remains true.

TWENTY

Comey and Putin Get into the Act

After the conventions, the candidates moved into the debates. They were all interesting. A record 84 million people watched the first one. Ironically, Hillary wore red and Trump wore blue. She was in great form and he was clearly uncomfortable trying to fit his vitriol into the format. It was a clear, big win for her. The second debate was far more contentious, with questions from an audience of undecided voters. When Trump stalked around, then stood behind Hillary as she answered a question about the Affordable Care Act, she managed to keep her cool. Hillary later said that she probably should have told him, "Back up, you creep. Get out of my space." It certainly would have been better TV. In the end, Trump's stalking around sort of worked for him, as he lost the second post-debate surveys by less than the first.

The big story in the third debate was Trump's refusal to say he'd concede if he lost the election. Although his hard-core base liked his refusal, the post-election surveys said most people disagreed, with 80 percent of the electorate saying they would accept the results. The biggest plus for Hillary in the debates, especially the third one, may have been the simple fact that millions of voters got to watch her talk about the issues for the first time.

According to Gallup, she won them all, by 34, 18, and 29 points respectively, and among independents, by 29, 19, and 23 points. She did much better with women than men, who still rated her the winner by 20, 11, and 19 points. Her biggest edge was in being "more presidential" by 32, 29, and 38 percent of the viewers, and "having a good understanding of the issues" by 36, 31, and 37 percent. She also got more "likable" as the debates progressed by 19, 28, and 28 percent.

In the third, most substantive debate, moderated fairly by Chris Wallace with 72 million viewers, she led Trump by an average of 15 points as the better candidate to deal with immigration, Social Security, Russia, and the Supreme Court. The most troubling number was her small 4-point margin on the economy, showing the strength of Trump's economic arguments against trade. Of course, these numbers were better for her than the head-to-head polls because not all voters watched the debates. Still, with three weeks to go, it would take something truly astonishing to beat her.

That's exactly what we got. We were already in the throes of the release of thousands of Hillary's emails to and from her campaign chairman, John Podesta, about the campaign. WikiLeaks had gotten them from Vladimir Putin and released them on October 7, right after the Trump *Access Hollywood* "groping" story broke, hoping to change the storyline back to Hillary's emails. Tom Friedman of *The New York Times* read them all and wrote a column entitled "WikiHillary for President," saying the email trove, including her speeches to big-bank audiences, showed "someone with a vision, a pragmatic approach to getting things done and a healthy instinct for balancing the need to strengthen our social safety nets with unleashing America's business class to create the growth required to sustain social programs."

Of course, most people only read or heard about campaign gossip. Putin gambled that our political press would only cover that because it produced more clicks and retweets than the more substantive ones showing how much more ready to be president she was. Putin was right: he did blunt the Trump groping story, which had already blunted the announcement by the Director of National Intelligence and the Secretary of Homeland Security that the Russian government was interfering in the election to help Trump. It got good coverage for about thirty minutes. All that happened in eight hours on one day!

Although Putin's interference helped Trump by blunting the groping story, it didn't hurt Hillary much. With less than two weeks to go, she was holding her own with a lead between 5 and 6 points, with $100 million in positive and competitive ads on order showing how the election would affect the voters and their kids.

Then, just eleven days before the election, Jim Comey got into the act again, announcing that he was reopening the email investigation he had closed in July, because some of her emails had been found on the laptop of Anthony Weiner, a former New York congressman and the estranged husband of Hillary's personal aide, Huma Abedin, which had been seized as a part of the unrelated investigation into him. Once again Comey violated many decades of FBI policy, followed during Republican and Democratic administrations alike: the FBI didn't comment on an ongoing investigation within sixty days of an election unless someone was being indicted.

Back in July, he'd broken the policy that the FBI didn't comment *at all* when an investigation concluded with no charges being filed. Comey concluded that "no reasonable prosecutor" would bring a case against Hillary because she had been honest in her interview and none of the disputed emails she received and forwarded were marked classified. But he also smeared her and three hundred other State Department employees for being "extremely careless" in handling classified information, saying the material should have been classified because the intelligence agencies "owned" it and they classified it, and it was "possible" that hostile actors gained access to Hillary's computer.

Translated into plain English, he was saying that the State Department and the intelligence agencies had always had different classification systems. The Intelligence Community Inspector General Chuck McCullough, an ardent Republican, after failing to persuade the forty-year State Department veteran who was responsible for classifying material to adopt McCullough's classification position, asked Comey to look into it, and Comey appointed himself the ultimate judge, not his superiors in the Justice Department, and not President Obama. Finally, Obama made a statement that Hillary didn't do anything to endanger national security, but it didn't get much coverage.

Thanks to the late Representative Elijah Cummings, who pushed the Department of Justice to retrieve the relevant emails, we also know Colin Powell, who had also used a personal computer at the State Department with its data stored on a commercial server, had advised Hillary to use her own device and server, because he believed the State Department server was not secure. He was right. While Hillary was secretary of state, the department's files were hacked, along with those of other government security agencies. But hers weren't! Comey couldn't bring himself to say that.

McCullough's real beef seemed to be with his own intelligence agencies, not the State Department, which had consistently followed its own rules. Shouldn't he have reported to Congress on the intelligence agencies' lack of concern for its own classification problem? No, because McCullough had targeted the State Department and its leader.

How did this happen? After Hillary left the State Department, someone decided it would "look better" to change the way inspectors general had been appointed since the position was created in 1978. Up until then, the IGs were nominated by Congress but the White House had to approve them, to solve the constitutional issue of letting the legislative branch force the executive branch to hire people who report directly to Congress and who might be heavily biased, especially when the president and the congressional majorities are of different parties. Now, for no apparent reason, the inspectors general would be okayed not by the White House but by a "nonpartisan" review board. Soon there were people with clearly partisan backgrounds "swearing on a stack of Bibles" that they would never politicize the inspector general's work. Some got through the interview process and proceeded to do just that. That's how we got to McCullough and to Comey usurping the title of classification chief.

If the political press really believed these different classification systems were a big problem, why didn't they ask the heads of the intelligence agencies why they weren't trying to fix it? Why didn't they say there should be one authority on classification covering all the agencies? Why didn't they demand that the one person who could mandate a fix, the president, bring all the agency heads, CIA, DOD, NSA, DIA, State, and any others with classification systems, into the Situation Room and keep them there until all these problems were ironed out? These are all the logical things you'd do, if you were on the level. Why did Comey put himself above the president, who said Hillary didn't do anything to endanger national security? And why didn't the press give Obama's assessment a lot of coverage?

When Comey said that Hillary was "extremely careless," he was really saying, "She didn't send any of these emails but whenever she forwarded one to appropriate staff, I counted it against her, just as I did when others did the same thing." All these people, dealing with dozens of emails every day, overlooked Comey's definition of their highest duty: to be classification clerks for the overtly partisan inspector general of the intelligence agencies.

Hillary received more endorsements than any previous candidate from people who'd spent their careers in intelligence—including Republicans and independents as well as Democrats. Now Comey and his allies in the press were basically saying she was careless. They knew better.

Here's an example of her lack of carelessness. On the evening of May 2, 2011, after the success of the bin Laden operation, President Obama called all the former presidents to tell them.

When I answered the phone, the president said, "Bill, we got him!"

"Got who?" I asked.

"Bin Laden. Hillary didn't tell you?"

I laughed and said, "Mr. President, you told your team not to tell anybody, didn't you?"

He chuckled and said, "Yes, but . . ."

"Mr. President, she didn't tell anybody."

Although I still had a security clearance, I had no need to know. On the raid, the president made the right call and she was right to urge him to do it and right not to tell anybody, including me.

What about John Kerry, who used his personal email in his first year as secretary of state until the rules changed in 2014, requiring him to use a State Department device? In May 2016, a State Department Inspector General report said Kerry had "primarily" used a State Department device before 2014, Kerry's second year, when the department changed the rules and required the use of a State Department device, and he complied. Before that, would Comey say Kerry was "extremely careless" in using his personal device, too? Couldn't do that. He wasn't the target and it blurred the storyline.

It later came out that Comey himself used his personal email for official business in clear violation of FBI policy. So Comey's position was that it was careless of Hillary to follow the State Department's rules but okay for him to break FBI rules. The rules apply to the target but not to the shooter. Brian Fallon, who did a lot of television interviews for Hillary, said, "I don't know whether to laugh or cry."

Now, eleven days before the election, Comey decided he had to tell the "special" Select Benghazi Committee about it, the very committee that Kevin McCarthy had told the world a year earlier was just a political operation set up to hurt Hillary after *five* other Republican-led House committees had cleared her of any wrongdoing. Comey knew full well what would happen. There's a reason the FBI has followed a policy of not commenting on anything short of an indictment close to an election. Even J. Edgar Hoover, with all of his backstage shenanigans, didn't do that.

Comey later justified his breaking this "norm" by saying he'd promised the committee that he'd notify them if there were any new developments, and he thought she was going to win anyway and didn't want this to undermine her legitimacy. My first reaction, after gagging on his "not wanting to undermine her legitimacy," was, he didn't know there was a new development. Huma was Hillary's personal aide, not someone in a line position, so the chances that there was a relevant new email were very remote. Second, he hated to be criticized; he wasn't afraid of being sacked by the attorney general, the deputy attorney general, or the White House, but he was getting heat from a cadre of ultraconservative current and ex-FBI agents in New York with close ties to Rudy Giuliani, Trump's attorney at the time. And third, Comey was a Washington Republican masquerading as a master of the moral universe. He may have thought Hillary was going to win anyway, but there is no way he didn't know that his breaking longstanding FBI policy would hurt her badly, and that the political press wouldn't punish him for doing it.

In Hillary's polls, she dropped 5 points overnight. I had never seen anything like that. In the next ten days *The New York Times* gave the Comey move ten times more coverage than it had given to the differences between Hillary and Trump on the issues that would affect voters' lives in the previous sixty-nine days. They had to cover it, but they knew it was highly unlikely to lead to anything and should also have given at least equal coverage to the issues that would affect voters and hit Comey hard for violating FBI policy. I was on the road and basically said this to everyone I could. At least it seemed to reassure and motivate Hillary's hard-core supporters.

Back at headquarters, they did the polls and focus groups and decided Comey's intervention had damaged Hillary so badly that her positive ad campaign would fall on deaf ears, so their only option was to pull the positive ads and double down on hitting Trump. Essentially the message was "No matter what Comey says, Trump is far worse for America." Trump's last ad rush took the other side of the coin, "What have you got to lose?"

Sure enough, early Sunday morning before the Tuesday election, the FBI completed its review but waited for several hours, until all the talk shows were over, to say, "Nothing new there." I had no idea how many votes it would change. Many people had voted in the nine days since Comey made his announcement, so a lot of damage had already been done. And of course, Trump cried foul—the establishment had won again—which riled up his "Lock her up" crowd even more.

Hillary won the popular vote by just under 2.9 million votes, with narrow margins in New Hampshire and Minnesota, and losses of less than 1 percent in Michigan, Wisconsin, and Pennsylvania, and 1.2 percent in Florida, more than enough to cost her the Electoral College. We live in the only country in the world where you can win the election and still lose the job.

Election night was like a death watch. I just tried to be there for Hillary, to help her get through it with Chelsea, Marc, Charlotte, and baby Aidan. I thought back over all the years we'd been together, how I quickly decided when we were in law school that she was as gifted a leader as I'd ever met. She inspired confidence in people and made them believe they could and should make a difference. In all the work she had done since, she devoutly followed the instruction of Methodism's founder, John Wesley: "Do all the good you can, by all the means you can, in all the ways you can, in all the places you can, at all the times you can, to all the people you can, as long as ever you can."

She would have been a great president.

I was heartsick for her and for our country. I knew she wouldn't be broken by this. But the country might be.

The next morning Hillary suited up—literally. With millions of people still in shock, she took the stage in a dark, purple-accented pantsuit and gave a proper concession speech.

In a steady voice, Hillary said, "Last night I congratulated Donald Trump and offered to work with him on behalf of our country. I hope he will be a successful president for all Americans. . . . This is painful and it will be for a long time. . . . But I want you to remember that our campaign was never about one person . . . it was about building an America that is hopeful, inclusive, and big-hearted. We have seen that our country is more divided than we thought. But I still believe in America and I always will. And if you do, we must accept the results and look to the future. Donald Trump is going to be our president. We owe him an open mind and the chance to lead.

"Our constitutional democracy enshrines the peaceful transfer of power and we don't just respect that, we cherish it. It also enshrines other things: the rule of law, the principle that we are all equal in rights and dignity, freedom of worship and expression. We respect and cherish these values too and we must defend them. I am so grateful for our country and for all it has given to me. I count my blessings every single day that I am an American. And I still believe as deeply as I ever have that if we stand together and work together with respect for our differences, strength in our convictions, and love for this nation, our best days are still ahead of us."

Compare that to Trump's whining response to losing in 2020, his support for the January 6 insurrection, his refusal to attend Biden's inauguration—the first president to do that in 152 years—and his attempt to persuade Vice President Pence and his congressional allies to refuse to certify the 2020 election. Hillary's concession speech provides a telling contrast in what each of them believes it means to be an American with real devotion to our Constitution and the essential requirement that we all live under the same set of rules.

Hillary's "best days still ahead of us" had already started for her and her family, and for all the people who had worked hard for her. Those who had hoped they might serve in the coming administration had to find something else to do. And Hillary got to work right away trying to help them.

We also resumed our long walks in wooded areas in and around Chappaqua, and Hillary went to work on turning the little house next door into a proper guesthouse for our family and old friends. She did a nice job, opening the entry to the living room to make it more welcoming and full of light, and hanging paintings, photos, and mementos that meant a lot to us. Marc and Chelsea had given us an amazing gift, two flags made from bed linen, tablecloths, and other cotton items, cut and sewn into a U.S. flag and a Union Jack by citizens of Paris who waved them to welcome the American and British soldiers when they marched into the city after running the Nazis out in World War II. It reminded me of what my country was capable of doing when we were faced with an overwhelming challenge so great that denial was impossible and democracy and freedom were on the line.

Meanwhile, all kinds of people were running around trying to claim credit or shift the blame for Trump's victory. Trump and his crowd were happy. The Mercers were happy. Putin was happy. Fox and *Breitbart* were happy. But Jim Comey and the political media's first priority seemed to be avoiding any responsibility for the outcome of the election they had done so much to bring about.

Still, Comey and the press got the lion's share of the blame. Nate Silver, a respected political analyst, said Hillary's net 3-point drop in the polls, including a larger 4.5 percent drop in the swing states, was "media driven." He later said, "You really have to twist yourself into a pretzel to conclude that the impact wasn't large enough to cost Clinton the election." For the first time in years, his opinion got virtually no coverage in the political press, and he had to make his case on social media.

A different but persuasive "Comey Did It" case was made by Brad Fay, whose company, Engagement Labs, does interesting research on consumer product brands, polling thousands of people every day, asking them online about what they're saying offline in face-to-face conversations about various brands. Since 2008, they've asked questions in presidential election years to pick up daily conversations about presidential candidates. According to Fay, Hillary opened a clear lead over Trump after the first debate that persisted until Comey's statement on October 28, when there was an immediate 17-point drop in net sentiment for Hillary and an 11-point increase for Trump, a 28-point change "in the word-of-mouth standings . . . much greater than the traditional opinion polling revealed."

In addition to the political press coverage and Comey, Putin also had something to do with it, barraging Bernie voters with false charges—Hillary was part of a cabal that was running a child trafficking ring out of a pizza parlor in Washington, she was sending arms to ISIS, she was deathly ill, and the pope was for Trump—and telling them that if they couldn't vote for Trump, to vote for a "real progressive," Green Party candidate Jill Stein, or stay home. In December of 2015, when General Michael "Lock Her Up" Flynn, Trump's national security advisor, had gone to Moscow to see Putin, Russian TV showed footage of the dinner Putin hosted for him.

Guess who else was there? Jill Stein, sitting at Putin's table.

The Russian meddling worked. Jill Stein doubled her vote from 2012, enough to change the outcome in Michigan and Wisconsin and to virtually tie the vote in Pennsylvania, where the "don't vote" angle was effective enough with younger Black voters in Philadelphia to do the rest.

The campaign to discourage young Black voters from turning out centered on rewriting the history of the Crime Bill and Hillary's comment back then that gang killings of young Black and Latino boys was predatory behavior, was led by the man who did the same job for Bernie before he went to work for Trump. That explains a lot of the heckling I got in Philadelphia and why the hecklers wouldn't take me up on my offer to take the microphone and make their case, then allow me to respond.

The Russian campaign had an impact, but Trump wouldn't have been close enough to benefit from Putin's efforts without the much larger impact of Comey and the political press coverage. Lanny Davis, a lawyer who worked for me in the White House Counsel's office and was appointed by President George W. Bush to the Privacy and Civil Liberties Oversight Board established by the 2005 Intelligence Reform Act, wrote a fiery short book, *The Unmaking of the President 2016: How FBI Director James Comey Cost Hillary Clinton the Presidency*. He cites all the major polling data and argues that no one can doubt that, had the election occurred on October 27, Hillary would have won. In about 150 pages he makes a case that has not been effectively refuted.

Throughout the campaign, there were some really perceptive journalists and commentators who tried to keep America's train on the tracks, warning the press early on not to make a mountain out of the email molehill and of the dangers of "false equivalency"—you have to say something bad about Hillary even if it's false, misleading, or just silly, if you say something bad about Trump, even if it's true. They bravely stood against the political press groupthink, but they didn't get television coverage.

From the very beginning, the political press knew they were peddling what Hillary's high school friends call "phony baloney." On March 10, 2015, right after the *New York Times*'s first big email article claiming that Hillary's use of her personal email and server was "possibly breaking the rules," Kurt Eichenwald, a *Newsweek* columnist and former *New York Times* reporter, wrote a rebuttal, "Why Hillary Clinton's 'Emailgate' Is a Fake Scandal." In his piece he proved that very regulation the *Times* cited as justification for its story contradicted the primary point of the piece by showing the paper had left out the words that explicitly allowed her to use her personal device, to store emails however she wanted, and even to declassify documents! The regulations also required anyone permitted to use their personal email to save work-related emails and turn them over when requested by the State Department record keepers.

The press quickly shifted its argument, saying that since they didn't know whether Hillary saved work-related emails, she "possibly" broke the rules by not saving them. That went out the window when the State Department asked all former secretaries of state to produce their emails and she promptly did so, just as the regulations then required. The State Department already had more than 90 percent of the covered emails and after reviewing them, they sent 1,000 back to her they'd deemed not work-related. The "possibly broke the rules" comment is like my saying if you're reading a hard copy of this book, you possibly stole it. It means nothing except I'm throwing shade on you.

When I was wrapping up this section of the book, I called Eichenwald to make sure I had read his article correctly—that the email story was not just overblown, it was false. He said, "That's right." Then he told me that the day after his story broke, he got a call from an executive at the *Times*, reading him the riot act for what he said. Eichenwald replied that he was agnostic about Hillary but he was for honest journalism, and he thought the *Times* piece failed the test. If the paper could demonstrate that he made a factual error, he would happily print a retraction. The executive hung up the phone.

On June 1, 2015, writer Anita Finlay, whose first job out of college was at *The New York Times*, wrote, "I never imagined that 30 years later, I'd be singling out the 'paper of record' for what appears to be a vendetta against Hillary Clinton. . . . [It] has taken on the role of Hillary Clinton's de facto opponent for the presidency . . . allowing debasing trash talk about a First Lady, two-term Senator and Secretary of State voted America's most admired woman for 19 years. . . . The once great 'Grey Lady' has fallen far indeed."

By contrast, most *New York Times* columnists from left to right were rational and objective. I already mentioned Tom Friedman's "WikiHillary for President" column. Paul Krugman, who set the standard for consistency, and wrote early on about the danger of "abnormalizing" all politicians, said in August of 2015 that the Republicans were great at creating cults of personality, while in the political press Hillary "is the subject of a sort of anti-cult of personality, whose most ordinary actions are portrayed as nefarious. (No, the email thing doesn't rise to the level of a 'scandal.')"

The editors and political reporters were too smart not to know Eichenwald, Finlay, Friedman, and Krugman were right, but they couldn't stop doing it. You know you're in trouble when the opinion pieces have more substantive and accurate information than the news in print, online, or on the air. *The New York Times* may have endorsed Hillary every time she ran for anything, but its real power lies in determining what gets covered and how, and sending a big signal to the rest of the political press, including television news, about what *not* to cover.

In 2012, the press jeered when Mitt Romney's campaign said his strategy wouldn't be "dictated by fact-checkers." By 2015, the political media had adopted the same practice. The major fact-checkers said Hillary was more factually accurate than Bernie in the primaries, and beat Trump by a country mile on that score. Yet by the last week of the election, polls showed voters thought she was less honest than Trump. Quite an achievement for the coverage.

When it was over, the press did take some hard hits. The Shorenstein Center on Media, Politics and Public Policy led by the nation's longtime expert on the presidency and the press, Thomas Patterson, captured every article in the major national and big regional newspapers and on the major social media sites, and every television segment on national network and cable channels. The center's report covered the pre-primary, primary, convention, and general election in four separate releases, the last titled "How the Press Failed the Voters."

Patterson's been calling the political press out for more than twenty years. Way back in 1995, Patterson, then at the Maxwell School of Citizenship and Public Affairs at Syracuse, wrote that a major factor in our 1994 loss of Congress was the relentlessly negative press coverage, creating perceptions that "are greatly at odds with the facts."

Marcie Bianco wrote a perceptive review for the Women's Media Center, "Harvard Study Documents Anti-Clinton Media Bias," noting its documentation of how the far-right media "garnered access to mainstream media outlets" and cited the success of "Breitbart Senior Editor" Peter Schweizer in getting mainstream media outlets to adopt its storyline and amplify it, "even though no actual evidence of wrongdoing was presented in the book [*Clinton Cash*] or in subsequent reporting."

The New York–based *Columbia Journalism Review* did its own review and piled on with its own analysis: "Don't blame the election on fake news. Blame it on the media," emphasizing the impact the print coverage had on television news. The three major broadcast networks devoted a grand total of thirty-two minutes to substantive issue coverage in the entire campaign, while about one third of Hillary's coverage focused on "fabricated and exaggerated scandals. . . . Attempts by the Clinton campaign to define her . . . on competence, experience and policy positions were drowned out while coverage of Trump associated with trade, immigration, and jobs was balanced with that on his personal scandals. . . . As long as extremist messaging and sensationalist disinformation continues to win elections while bringing in rich rewards to the networks that propagate them, the dynamic we observe here is likely to continue unabated."

Almost two years after the election, Kathleen Hall Jamieson, a highly regarded social scientist, said Russia's cyberattacks piled on top of Comey's interventions were effective enough to persuade voters in Michigan, Pennsylvania, and Wisconsin to vote for third parties or stay home. What the Russians did may have been enough to turn what would have been an Electoral College win into a close electoral vote loss. If so, Putin's enablers were Comey and the political press. The election wouldn't have been close enough without them. The coverage and Comey were the big factors.

So was there anything Hillary could have done *after* Comey's late intervention to change the outcome of the election? I'm not sure. Everyone was in a PTSD-like shock because nothing like it had ever happened before. I was on the campaign trail and no one at headquarters asked me what I thought. As I said, the campaign's focus groups and polls convinced them that after Comey, reachable voters were so down on Hillary that their only option was to argue that Trump was much worse.

It might have been better to run the issue-focused ads to revive the positive feelings of the convention and the debates, especially the last one. Of course, they'd need a different opening, something like: "There they go again [a great Reagan line]. They—the Russians, Comey, and the press—are trying to take the election away from you. Don't let them do it. Look at the real differences between Hillary and Trump on things that matter to you. Vote on that."

Her lead was about 6 points before Comey. Without the media's email coverage and their refusal to cover her positive issues, the lead would have been even bigger than that. Hillary's high points were the convention and the debates, because voters were free to hear her and think about what the election meant to them as Hillary and the people whose lives she had touched slowly turned the ugly cartoon the Republicans and the coverage had drawn into a three-dimensional human being, far more knowledgeable, presidential, and—God forbid—likable than she had been portrayed.

Would it have worked? We'll never know.

This whole thing is hard for me to write. I couldn't sleep for two years after the election. I was so angry, I wasn't fit to be around. I apologize to all those who endured my outbursts of rage which lasted for years and bothered or bored people who thought it pointless to rehash things that couldn't be changed. In this chapter, I've tried to calmly write about the darkest election possible in the United States, because it's important to understand what happened. Our country had, and still has, the best prospects for a bright twenty-first century. I still want that future, and we can't have it without a press that's on the level. I don't want 2016 to ever happen again.

Jim Fallows, a highly regarded author and journalist, always thought the email issue was way overblown, and said so during the election, citing Eichenwald's work. Afterward, when Hillary wrote *What Happened*, he responded to those in the political media when they unleashed their torrent of outrage. In his *Atlantic* piece, Fallows said:

> No sane person can believe that the consequences of last fall's election . . . should have depended more than about 1 percent on what Hillary Clinton did with her emails. But this . . . issue came across through even our best news organizations as if it were the main thing worth knowing about one of the candidates. . . .
>
> The press is among the groups that messed this up, badly . . . With this book, Hillary Clinton has gone a considerable distance toward facing her responsibility for the current state of the country. I'd like to see [the political press] be as honest about their own responsibility.

Don't hold your breath. On Trump's inauguration day, Liz Spayd, the *Times*'s public editor, wrote that the paper knew that the Comey-led FBI had opened its own investigation into Putin's connections to Trump but had decided not to run a story about it before the election. She also wrote, "At one point, the FBI was so serious about its investigation . . . that it asked the *Times* to delay publication." Comey presumably had his own reasons for holding back on any public acknowledgment of the investigation (not that he showed any such responsibility with Hillary's emails), but the *Times* had no reason to stay mum on what they knew. Yet their editor-in-chief still had the gall to say in response to criticism of the decision, "We wrote everything we knew—and we wrote a lot. Anybody that thinks we sat on stuff is outrageous. It's just false." Soon Spayd was fired and the public editor position was abolished.

Like I said, don't hold your breath.

But *The Washington Post*, which also caught the email virus early, did recover, and returned to professional journalism, including publishing a series of articles by David Fahrenthold on Trump's family foundation in New York for which he won a Pulitzer Prize. At some point during the general election, the *Post* had stopped practicing false equivalency and recognized Trump's—and Putin's—behavior for the threats they were, especially in tough, insightful articles by conservative columnists like Jennifer Rubin.

Although the press dropped it like a hot rock after the election was over, the email story didn't go away. In mid-October 2019, Congress received a nine-page report from the Trump State Department on Hillary's use of a personal email account to conduct work business, acknowledging that Colin Powell and Condi Rice's top aides had done the same thing. On the twenty-first, Ian Millhiser wrote a column in *Vox* saying, "And now we have an appropriate bookend for this media-made scandal: a State Department report that finds it was no big deal in the end, published on page A16 of the *New York Times*." In 2020, the same was true for the hyped investigations of the Clinton Foundation, run by the Trump Justice Department under Attorney General Jeff Sessions. *The Washington Post* reported they "found nothing worth pursuing." As the founder of CharityWatch later said, "If Hillary Clinton wasn't running for president, the Clinton Foundation would be seen as one of the great humanitarian charities of our generation."

I want to make one thing clear before I leave this painful subject. I don't "blame" the political media for Hillary's defeat. An election is a zero-sum game. To win you have to overcome whoever and whatever is arrayed against you. You win or you don't. Hillary and those of us who supported her failed to do that by a narrow margin in the Electoral College.

The blame is on us, but the evidence is overwhelming that the political media, Jim Comey, and Vladimir Putin deserve most of the credit for Trump's victory. At least Putin acknowledged his role in a press conference with Trump in Helsinki, admitting that he tried to barrage persuadable voters with false attacks on Hillary because he thought Trump would be better for Russia. In return, Trump pandered shamelessly to him, practically kneeling before the czar who possesses the kind of unbridled power he craves. When I saw them on TV, I was embarrassed for our country.

Comey and the political media should be at least as forthright as Putin and not hide behind "I thought she was going to win anyway." If I had a dollar for everybody who justified the damage they caused Hillary's campaign with "well, she's going to win anyway," I could take our whole family for a long dinner at a five-star restaurant.

For years, going back to my days in Arkansas, I kept handy a list of "Clinton's Rules of Politics" that I used to explain, enlighten, and lighten up political conversations:

1. Never tell anyone to go to hell unless you can make them go (Sam Rayburn told LBJ that).
2. Never drink in public—you might act like yourself.
3. Whenever you hear "it's nothing personal," brace yourself.
4. When someone can shift the heat from himself to you, prepare to be barbecued.
5. Everyone is for change in general but often against it in particular—it depends on whose ox is being gored.
6. When people say, "it's not a money problem," they're always talking about someone else's problem.
7. If you see a turtle on a fence post, it didn't get there by accident.
8. When you start to have a good time, you're supposed to be somewhere else.

9. You're always most vulnerable when you feel invulnerable, or when you're angry and exhausted.
10. Take criticism seriously but not personally (one I got from Hillary and well explained by Don Miguel Ruiz in *The Four Agreements*).
11. If you want to bring your feelings to work, get in another line of work.
12. Don't give up on people—if you dig long enough, there's almost always still a person down there somewhere.

The 2016 election forced me to go to a baker's dozen with a new rule: "If you're ever in the room with someone who says . . . 'but you're going to win anyway,' smile, thank them for their time, and get out of that room as fast as you can." They may want you to win, but they don't want to speak up for you for fear of criticism or punishment. "Anyway" is the tell word. When you hear it, get ready to move.

TWENTY-ONE

The Hazards of Rewriting History

In 2016, there was a slew of criticism from the left about the 1994 Crime Bill and the 1996 welfare reform bill. Both were characterized as reactionary cave-ins to the far right by Democrats who voted for the bills and me for signing them. This false revisionism is hurting Democrats today in their efforts to take a commonsense approach to empowering the poor and to crime, in spite of President Biden's firm refusal to go along with it.

Let's start with the Crime Bill. When I took office, violent crime had more than doubled over the previous thirty years, while the police forces in the U.S. had increased only 10 percent. People, especially in minority communities with a strong gang presence, wanted more police—not the kind of policing we saw in the Rodney King beating, the stranglings of George Floyd and Eric Garner, or the fatal shooting of Philando Castile, but policing by well-trained officers from racially diverse backgrounds, walking the streets and driving cars in pairs, relating to their communities, reducing tensions, and using force as a last resort. Community policing was already working in New York and a few other places and we needed more of it. Citizens also wanted alternatives to prison for first-time nonviolent offenders, and support for community nonviolence efforts to keep their kids out of trouble and safe from violent gang activity, which was spreading from big cities into suburbs and midsized cities in the heartland.

For a few years, Little Rock was one of them, with one of the highest murder rates in the country for cities its size. Across the country, young people, mostly Black and brown, fell victim to drive-by shootings, getting caught in the crossfire of gang wars, or sometimes becoming victims of gangs that required young men to kill someone before they could become fully accepted members.

The Crime Bill I put together, along with Senator Joe Biden and then-Congressman Chuck Schumer, provided money for 100,000 new police officers; funding for drug courts and other options to sentence nonviolent offenders to treatment, not jail; and $6 billion for prevention programs, including local block grants, recreation programs, community schools, and rape prevention and education. The bill also included the assault weapons ban and the ten-bullet ammunition clip limit, Senator Biden's Violence Against Women Act, and funds to implement the Brady background check bill, which I had already signed.

When several Democrats made it clear that they couldn't vote for the assault weapons ban and survive the next election (fifty-eight of them voted against bringing it to the floor), I had to negotiate with the Republicans or lose at least the assault weapons ban and the ten-bullet clip limit. The price of getting the votes to pass the Crime Bill with the provisions we thought essential was pretty steep, including $8 billion in prison grants to states that required serious violent offenders (murder, rape, manslaughter, aggravated assault, and armed robbery) to serve 85 percent of their sentences. It did not apply to minor drug offenses, burglary, larceny, or weapons possession. An Urban Institute study later reported that thirty states did nothing at all, and the Government Accountability Office said the grant programs, about 1 percent of previous spending, made an impact on the prison population in only four states. The Republicans also demanded that the death penalty be added to about fifty existing crimes. They knew they were unlikely to be used but would look tough and hopefully minimize the wrath of the NRA over the gun reforms.

The tougher sentences in federal law that had led to the dramatic increase in the prison population were enacted by Congress in the mid-1980s, *before* I took office. I tried to change one of them—the huge disparity in sentences for crack cocaine versus powder cocaine: 100 to 1. It took only 5 grams of crack to trigger a five-year mandatory sentence but 500 grams of the much more expensive powder to do so. Most of the crack offenders were people of color; most powder cocaine users were better-off white people. I asked Senator Orrin Hatch if he would support eliminating the disparity. He said he would but only if we raised the powder sentences to the crack level. He made it clear that his caucus wouldn't lower them.

In my second term I appointed a Commission on Race chaired by the eminent Black historian John Hope Franklin and asked them to look into the racial disparities in criminal justice (as well as the economy, healthcare, and education). The commission found there were still too many people in jail for too long. Their findings were the basis of my last message to Congress, asking that the effort to close the gaps continue. In 2010, President Obama signed a bill to lower the crack-to-powder disparity to 18 to 1. In 2018, a large bipartisan majority passed the First Step Act, allowing federal prisoners to earn time off their sentences for good behavior and President Trump signed it.

I think the Republicans came around on the sentencing because their evangelical supporters' views changed, in part because of the opioid epidemic, and because they learned that they couldn't keep building prisons and cutting taxes without starving their schools of essential revenue. Teacher and parent revolts in red states, including Oklahoma and Kansas, brought that home to them. President Biden has strongly supported First Step's vigorous implementation. It's the right thing to do.

The Crime Bill's sentencing provisions had little to do with the big drop in crime, other than helping get the votes to ward off a filibuster and pass it. But community policing with better-trained officers did. So did vigorous enforcement of the background check law, the assault weapons ban, the ten-bullet limit, the Violence Against Women Act, and the prevention efforts.

What happened to crime in the 1990s? The crime rate declined for eight straight years to a twenty-five-year low. Murder declined to a thirty-three-year low. Black deaths from homicide dropped 40 percent and all gun homicides were at a forty-six-year low. And mass shootings dropped for eight years. That's a lot fewer funerals. By the time I left office, the Brady background checks had denied more than two million felons, fugitives, stalkers, and domestic abusers the ability to buy guns, though it still needs to cover gun shows and all online sales. And the annual growth in the federal prison population dropped from more than 8 percent to 1 percent.

When it passed, the loudest criticism of the Crime Bill came from the right, as conservatives claimed we were spending too much on prevention and alternatives to prison for first-time nonviolent offenders. Gingrich Republican Jack Fields from Texas said it was "a touchy-feely piece of legislation that gives new meaning to the phrase hug-a-thug." Really? Sadly, more than a dozen Democratic House members lost their careers because they stood up to the NRA for safer streets and schools in passing the assault weapons ban and the ten-bullet limit.

On April 9, 2016, about a week after I was interrupted by protesters of the Crime Bill at a Philadelphia rally for Hillary, Dean David Yassky of the Pace University Law School wrote an op-ed in *The New York Times* responding to the event and my defense of the good done by the bill. In 1994, Yassky was counsel to the House Subcommittee on Crime, then led by Representative Chuck Schumer, now the Senate Majority Leader.

"I spent 18 months helping to draft and negotiate the Crime Bill," Yassky wrote. "Anyone who thinks the bill was just about locking people up is simply wrong." As Yassky pointed out, in addition to the 100,000 police, the Violence Against Women Act, and the assault weapons ban, the bill actually reduced sentences for federal drug crimes by *exempting first-time nonviolent offenders from the mandatory minimum penalties created before I took office*, "funded specialized drug courts, drug treatment programs, 'bootcamps,' and other efforts to rehabilitate offenders without incarceration, and allocated more than $3 billion to keep at-risk young people away from gangs and the drug trade, and growth in the federal prison population dropped from 8 percent to 1 percent per year.

"We didn't get everything we wanted. There are two parties in Congress; the Republicans won some concessions," including leaving many of the Reagan-era sentences in place and expanding the federal death penalty, but "it was indisputably a de-escalation of the so-called War on Drugs, a first step toward the more wholesale decriminalization underway today."

Then Yassky noted that between 1994 and 2016, violent crime rates were cut in half and "people who benefit most from decreased crime are residents of poor urban neighborhoods." He also called on us to fix the flaws in the current system because "far too many young African American and Latino men have been subjected to unconstitutional or inappropriate stops by police officers" and an "unacceptable number of Americans are in prison." More active policing produces more convictions and therefore more inmates. As I said, "We had the biggest drop in crime in history" but "we still had a lot of people who were minor actors who were locked up for way too long."

Yassky concludes by saying that we need to keep the active policing but move away from mass incarceration, with greater use of parole, halfway houses, and other forms of supervised release, and more mental health services. I would add education to that list. Colleges like Bard in New York pioneered programs to educate the imprisoned and the evidence indicates the recidivism rates for those who get degrees is almost zero. Universities in other states have been doing the same thing. We still need more schooling in prisons and the federal government should fund it through Pell Grants or otherwise.

In the end, if we are to keep our country safer from crime without police abuse and overreach by the courts, we need to keep pushing sentencing reforms that work, boost programs that prevent violence, and provide law enforcement agencies with what they need to provide top-flight training for officers.

———

On welfare reform, I ran for president on a platform to promote work over welfare and help welfare recipients get jobs, keep them, and be better off than they would have been on welfare. By then I had been interested in the welfare system since Arkansas received an experimental grant to help people move toward work in the late 1970s when Jimmy Carter was president. Next, we participated in the federal Workfare program started by the Reagan administration. Then for two years, representing the National Governors Association along with moderate GOP governor Mike Castle of Delaware, I worked with the White House and leaders of both houses of Congress on a reform bill that would promote work, strengthen families, and meet children's basic needs.

Castle and I testified before Congress and participated in the markup of the bill by the House Ways and Means subcommittee, chaired by Democratic representative Harold Ford of Tennessee. When President Reagan signed it, we were at the White House for a bipartisan celebration.

Unfortunately, a weak economy led to large increases in welfare numbers and increased spending on Aid to Families with Dependent Children (AFDC) by almost 50 percent. There was already a dramatic difference in support for the basic needs of poor people in the various states, from $923 per month in Alaska to $120 in Mississippi, and between 1970 and 1996, the real value of cash benefits after inflation declined by 40 percent or more in two thirds of the states.

When I became president, I decided we had to try again. Although most people moved onto and off welfare after a couple of months when they could find work, the number of recipients dependent on it for eight years was growing. So, in 1994, I sent Congress a bill that emphasized work and more child support. By the time the bill came up for a vote in 1996, Donna Shalala, the secretary of health and human services during both my terms, had worked with governors in thirty-seven states to fashion welfare reform "waivers" that would protect cash benefits and increase employment. It was working—welfare rolls were dropping and people were going to work. The number of states involved grew to forty-three by the time I signed the bill.

Then, in 1994, the Republicans won both houses of Congress. The new Speaker, Newt Gingrich, proceeded to push his Contract with America, including the GOP right wing's radical version of welfare reform. It was a people-destruction bill, with the biggest cuts in Medicare and Medicaid in history; slashing Social Security insurance benefits for disabled kids; block-granting Medicaid and food stamps so they were no longer federal guarantees; cutting the school lunch program; capping existing block grants for child welfare and foster care; making deep cuts in Head Start and in the Direct Student Loan program, which was actually saving students (and taxpayers) billions, and providing way too little support for childcare and for helping people move from welfare to work; and the cherry on top—the denial of food and medical benefits to fully documented immigrants, most of whom worked and paid taxes.

When they put all that and more in their first budget, I vetoed it and the Republicans shut the government down. When they sent me back a cosmetically changed version of the bill, I vetoed it again and they shut the government down again. Then I proposed an alternative balanced budget that had far more support.

Many Democrats urged me not to do that because it was already clear that the budget was going to be balanced anyway in a couple of years, thanks to my 1993 budget and economic plan which every Republican opposed, because it abolished their trickle-down theory and replaced it with a bottom-up, middle-out plan with tax hikes on the wealthiest Americans and big corporations, spending cuts in nonessential areas, and the critical investments needed to grow the middle class and help poor people work their way into it, while also bringing down the big deficit.

I disagreed with those who opposed our balanced budget legislation because I believed that America's future required us not just to abandon trickle-down economics but also to restore respect and support for the essential role of government in building a growing, fairer economy. That meant enacting a progressive balanced budget and humane welfare reform and getting some Republican votes for it. President Reagan had made a lot of hay talking about welfare queens in Cadillacs. We needed to show poor people empowered, far preferring a hand up to a handout, and the role government had to play. On welfare reform, that meant the chance to get a proper job that would pay more than the cash benefit and provide real childcare, transportation, and housing support, along with much stronger efforts to secure child support payments from noncustodial parents.

As I said, Donna Shalala had been working with governors, Democrats and Republicans alike, to develop waivers from the old rules to increase the movement from welfare to work. By the time Newt Gingrich launched his war on poor people, we had been working hard for two years. The welfare rolls peaked in early 1994 and had already fallen by more than a million before the bill passed.

I also vetoed the Republican budget for what it did to health and nutrition programs, and because it gutted the work of the Department of Education and the Environmental Protection Agency. As I said, in January of 1996, when Congress sent me a standalone welfare reform bill they had passed just before Christmas, I vetoed it, too. It had all the flaws of the first one, with too little support for the families of the working poor.

Then they sent a third bill that retained the federal guarantees of Medicaid and food aid; increased federal childcare assistance by 40 percent, adding $4 billion dedicated to childcare for families moving from welfare to work; gave states the ability to convert monthly cash benefits into wage subsidies as an incentive for employers to hire welfare recipients; included the provisions I wanted for stronger child support enforcement; and dropped the attempt to abolish our new college loan program that cost students less and saved taxpayers money because there were far fewer loan defaults.

But the bill left four big problems: a five-year lifetime limit without eliminating from the count the months we were in recession; denial of food stamps and Medicaid to legal (the word we used then) immigrants; a reduction in the overall budget for food aid; and the end of the federal guarantee of a monthly level of cash support. Gingrich was Trump before Trump.

Several of my advisors were deeply concerned about these problems. So was I. But in the end, I decided the good things we had put in the bill, including a generous tax credit for hiring people off welfare, plus forty-three states with their reforms already underway, made it worth the risk to replace a system originally designed to keep mothers out of the workforce with one designed to get them in. I felt sure I could use the budget process to reinstitute documented immigrants' eligibility for benefits, and we largely did that. I thought any future government facing a recession would include the lowest-income people in food and Medicaid assistance, and the Obama budget did that twice after the July 2008 crash. But to my surprise, the Democratic Congress didn't stop counting deep recession months against the five-year limit, or reinstate the federal requirement of some cash assistance and raise the benefit floor.

For the first decade or so, the bill worked as we had hoped, thanks in part to a provision that put a floor under total expenditures that was set in February 1994 when welfare enrollment and expenditures were at an all-time high, so that by 2000, when welfare rolls were down 58 percent, we were able to spend up to 58 percent more per family on childcare, transportation, and child support for those in training or already at work. With stronger enforcement, child support payments to single mothers and their children doubled. The coalition we put together to hire a million people off welfare, led by the late Eli Segal, the first leader of AmeriCorps, included 20,000 companies which hired more than 1.1 million people. And a nonpartisan study found that in the brief 2001 recession, employees who had been hired when on public assistance were actually less likely to be laid off than other workers.

When I went to speak at the Harvard Kennedy School in 2007, Dean David Ellwood, an expert on the economics of poverty who had thought I was wrong to sign the bill, said it looked like I was actually right, that the law was doing far more good than harm. In several states the reform spirit was still alive and the value of cash benefits was enhanced because people could keep them, for example, and own a car, something they couldn't do under the old law.

But in just a few years too many of the good things about the bill were allowed to die in too many states. The federal government began to permit the money to be spent on things that had no connection to helping poor people pay their bills, raise their kids, or find a job. And after the crash, several states—red and blue—slashed already meager cash benefits.

You can argue that I should have seen it all coming a decade out, powered by the hard move to the right in so many governorships and state legislatures. I didn't, and if I'd vetoed the bill we would have lost all the money that helped people support their kids and go to work, and later when the Koch brothers–funded long-term strategy to move state legislatures to the far right happened, they would have cut welfare spending anyway.

Still, you should work for the best but plan for the worst, and I should have urged the Democrats to restore the other half of my change formula when they won the House in 2006 and the White House in 2008, especially to restore a federal cash benefit to raise the minimum level of assistance to the poorest of the poor, because there will always be some families who can't make it out of dependency. After the Tea Party crowd won the House in 2010, the chance to do that evaporated. The Republicans at the national and state levels kept moving to the right, confident that they could always find a new hot-button culture clash to scare, divide, and conquer.

Thankfully, the Earned Income Tax Credit endured, and in all the states that kept at reform efforts, the results were good. And when things got really bad after the 2008 crash and with Covid in 2020, Congress stepped in with large relief packages to ease the misery and ensure that low-income people weren't left to fend for themselves. The economy needed their spending, too.

What should we do now? The same thing we should do with the Crime Bill. Thanks to the Affordable Care Act, low-income workers don't have to worry anymore about losing healthcare in states that have accepted Medicaid expansion. But we should double down on what works and fix what's wrong: restore a monthly cash benefit tied to cost of living but always make work pay more; don't count economic downturns as part of the five-year limit; push states that haven't expanded Medicaid to do so, with carrots and sticks (a lot of rural hospitals really need it); and don't permit states to use the funds on things unrelated to helping poor Americans. We need to fix those things, but we shouldn't abandon the focus on empowering parents to work and raise their kids.

On September 12, 2022, Jason DeParle published an article in *The New York Times* on the remarkable decline in child poverty from 1993 to 2019, falling from 28 percent to 11 percent. He cited a study showing that government aid played a critical role in the steady decline in every state, among children of all races, living with one parent or two, in native or immigrant households, and including "deep" poverty. While cash benefits shrank, other investment grew, starting with doubling the Earned Income Tax Credit in 1993 and, later, more increases in the child tax credit. So far Congress hasn't passed President Biden's proposal to maintain the most recent increases, which would cut child poverty in half again.

The study also found that increased labor force participation among single mothers, which spiked from 67 percent to 79 percent after the welfare reform bill passed, and state minimum wage hikes all helped. Over the twenty-six years, child poverty reduction measures shrank the number of children in poverty by 6.5 million, 2.2 million from that first doubling of the EITC in late 1993. Poverty fell most in the high-job-growth years of the late 1990s and 2010s, but in between, child poverty didn't increase very much, even during the Great Recession. Then it fell again before Covid hit in 2020.

The 23 percent increase in the minimum wage was all done at the state level. I raised the federal minimum wage once and proposed but couldn't pass a second one. The Republican Congress wouldn't vote for it. Neither will many GOP state legislatures. But culturally conservative, working-class Republican voters like minimum wage hikes. In Arkansas in 2014, a banner election year for right-wing candidates, a big minimum wage increase won 70 percent approval in a referendum, with all the major Republican candidates opposing it, knowing they'd win anyway.

The study says that the largest policy factors in child poverty reduction are, in order, the Earned Income Tax Credit, Social Security, SNAP (food stamps), housing assistance, free and discounted school meals, Supplemental Security Income, cash assistance, women/infant/children nutrition (WIC), unemployment insurance, and home energy assistance. Everyone who says that government is the problem, and can't be part of the solution, should read DeParle's piece!

They should also read the article by David Leonhardt, run in *The New York Times* two days later, with the chart showing the big drop in child poverty since 1996, and asserting the "conservative critiques of the old welfare state" were right that "poor single mothers were better able to find and hold jobs than many liberals expected." But the biggest cause of the drop in poverty was the continued expansion of the Earned Income Tax Credit and eligibility for food stamps, and of course the Medicaid expansion for those workers whose jobs didn't provide private health insurance. What welfare reform did was to shift our antipoverty efforts from people who weren't working to those who were. Leonhardt quotes Dolores Acevedo-Garcia of Brandeis University, who points out that "12 million additional children would be poor today" if the poverty rate were still as high as it was when I took office.

There are still 20 million poor people in this country and more just above the poverty line who have trouble making ends meet, and I'm sorry Congress hasn't passed President Biden's proposal increasing support for childcare and the Earned Income Tax Credit and making the child tax credit permanent (they seem to be the only tax cuts the Republicans oppose). With millions of jobs still unfilled in America, now is the time to do it. I hope the attention given to this report will help. Beneath all the noise and bad-mouthing of today's politics, real lives continue to unfold, and I still believe most poor people prefer being empowered to chart their own course over a lifetime of dependence.

Look at what we were able to do during my time in office when we worked together. Overall, family incomes rose by 15 percent, but by 32 percent for Black Americans, the largest of any racial group, followed by 23 percent for Latinos. Poverty, including child poverty, fell to record lows for Blacks, as did unemployment. Latinos also had the lowest unemployment rate on record, and the lowest poverty rate since 1979. All these policies should be judged by their consequences.

The $17.5 billion in Small Business Administration loans to minority-owned businesses in those eight years were more than twice the amount of minority business loans in the entire forty-year history of the SBA. The $34 billion in Development Block Grants to low-income communities was more than any other administration before or since. More than 90 percent of community reinvestment loans for home mortgages, small businesses, and community development in the twenty-four-year history of the Community Reinvestment Act came in those eight years, which led to a 58 percent increase in home mortgages to Blacks, and 125 percent for Latinos. Doubling the EITC lifted more than four million people out of poverty, more than half of whom were children. The Empowerment Zones brought needed investment in low-income communities. In Harlem, with large Black and Latino populations, unemployment fell by 60 percent.

To build a healthier environment, we cleaned up more than three times as many toxic brownfield sites as in the previous twelve years, almost all in minority communities; increased the number of Americans living in communities that met clean air standards by 43 million, which was predicted to reduce premature deaths by 15,000 and severe asthma cases by 350,000 per year; and thanks to Hillary's work and Senators Ted Kennedy and Orrin Hatch, we created the Children's Health Insurance Program in 1997, which had insured 2.5 million kids by 2000, with the number growing steadily to more than five million by the time it was included in the Affordable Care Act. It now insures seven million children.

In education, we almost tripled funding for Head Start and created Early Head Start for three-year-olds. With the public schools facing the first generation larger than the baby boomers, we provided more than a billion dollars to repair old schools with the most urgent needs for the first time since World War II; funding for 100,000 teachers to reduce class size; funding for summer and afterschool programs for 1.3 million students, which increased math and science learning and reduced violence. We also funded GEAR UP, an initiative designed for high-poverty middle schools to help more than two million kids by guaranteeing college admission to those who completed the program. Finally, we expanded internet access for our schools from 35 percent in 1994 to 98 percent in 2001, through the deeply discounted "e-rate" program covering schools, libraries, and health centers.

I'm especially proud of what we did in higher education, with the largest increases in college aid since the G.I. Bill, including a 90 percent increase in Pell Grants, a million more Work-Study slots, and tax credits to make community college free and lower the cost of other higher education and training by 20 percent. More than 10 million families had claimed the credits by the time I left office. We also offered college students the chance to borrow the money directly from the federal government with the option to pay it back as a small fixed percentage of their income, saving students about $1,200 for each $10,000 borrowed. This change saved students a total of $9 billion and saved the taxpayers $4 billion because the loan default rate dropped a lot. If we'd kept at it, student debt would be a much smaller problem today.

Finally, in the area of racial justice, the budget of the Department of Justice's Civil Rights Division increased 50 percent, and civil rights enforcement increased across all agencies. We cut the backlog of job discrimination claims before the Equal Employment Opportunity Commission by 60 percent, preserved affirmative action programs, and vigorously supported the preclearance provisions of the Voting Rights Act (which the Supreme Court would later gut); passed the Motor Voter law, which increased the number of voter registration sites and led to more than 28 million new voters in the 2002 election alone; defended majority-minority districts and fought Election Day discrimination, voter intimidation, and harassment by monitoring a record number of states and counties.

Beyond the criticism of welfare reform and the Crime Bill, the criticism I disagree with most strongly is that I aided and abetted the victory of the long Republican assault on government and somehow became a creature of corporate culture by saying in the 1996 State of the Union speech: "The era of big government is over." To get that, the political press had to omit the rest of the sentence, the argument for the necessity of government action, and the very issues I was speaking about. Here's the whole quote: "The era of big government is over. But we cannot go back to the time when our citizens were left to fend for themselves. Instead, we must go forward as one America, one nation working together to meet the challenges we face together."

Keep in mind the Gingrich Republicans had just shut the government down twice. In a heated meeting in the Oval Office during the shutdown with leaders of both parties, when Gingrich and his lieutenants threatened to destroy me if I didn't cave in to their demands, I told them I didn't care if my approval went to 5 percent, they'd have to get another president if they wanted to destroy the country. Al Gore dryly said it was a good line, but I should have said I didn't care if my approval rating dropped to 1 percent.

In the 1996 State of the Union address, I also introduced Richard Dean, a Vietnam veteran who worked in the Oklahoma City federal building for the Social Security Administration when it was bombed in 1995. He risked his life to reenter the ruins four times and saved three lives. Dean got a standing ovation from the entire Congress. Then came the zinger:

"But Richard Dean's story doesn't end there. This last November, he was forced out of his office when the government shut down. And the second time the government shut down he continued helping Social Security recipients, but he was working without pay. On behalf of Richard Dean and his family, and all the other people who are out there working every day doing a good job for the American people, I challenge all of you in this Chamber: Never, ever shut the federal government down again." This time only the Democrats were standing.

The reverse plastic surgery performed in 2016 on the "era of big government is over" speech ignores the pivotal role it played in one of the major projects of my first term—restoring the legitimacy of the federal government. The balanced budget and surpluses, Al Gore's Reinventing Government initiative, a more progressive tax code, the new student loan program, the Family and Medical Leave Act, and, most important, the broadly shared prosperity of those eight years dramatically increased confidence in the role of government, a case the Democrats can never stop pressing.

The big spending that occurred after the 2008 crash and during the Covid crisis was necessary because both caused multitrillion-dollar hits to the economy. For a long time, real interest rates were negative and government spending was necessary to keep the economy running and speed the recovery. That's why I wrote *Back to Work* in 2010, supported President Obama's recovery efforts after the crash, and back President Biden's initiatives today.

After the "big government is over" hit, the second big economic criticism is that I sided with big corporations and big banks, triggering the process that eventually led to massively overleveraged derivatives and the inevitable big crash of 2008.

In the 1990s, the big banks had three priorities: to make it harder for plaintiff law firms to bring lawsuits against investment banks when changes in the market resulted in losses to their clients; to repeal Glass-Steagall in order to allow commercial banks' holding companies to own insurance companies and allow banks to trade more securities for their own accounts; and to make sure neither the Securities and Exchange Commission nor the Commodity Futures Trading Commission (CFTC) could regulate large bets on highly leveraged housing and other derivatives.

I didn't like any of those bills and wanted to veto them all when they came before me. The bill raising the lawsuit bar passed Congress first. The bill went too far and would have resulted in meritorious suits being thrown out of court, so I vetoed the bill. Congress promptly overrode it.

Then, when Congress passed bills repealing the Glass-Steagall law and the bill limiting oversight by both the SEC and the CFTC on derivatives trading with veto-proof majorities even larger than the lawsuit bill got, I knew those vetoes would be overridden, too. So I got the Congress to put some good things in them, including an extension of the Community Reinvestment Act, which increased housing and small business loans in low- and moderate-income communities, in return for not vetoing bills they were going to pass anyway.

I thought the commodities bill was by far the most dangerous, and had an argument about it in the Oval Office with the Federal Reserve chairman, Alan Greenspan. Alan asked me why I cared about the high-risk trading, since it cost $100 million to participate in most big trades and those people could afford to lose the money. I responded that the high-risk derivatives market would grow, become increasingly overleveraged, and if future regulators weren't as vigilant as my appointees, SEC commissioner Arthur Levitt and Comptroller of the Currency Gene Ludwig, were in using the powers they still had, there could eventually be a crash that would reach way beyond the $100 million gamblers and hurt all Americans. Sure enough, once we had an OTS commissioner who posed for the photographers holding a chainsaw over a pile of federal regulations, it was only a matter of time.

One fight I should have taken on more personally was that of Brooksley Born, my chair of the Commodity Futures Trading Commission, when she was attacked by the financial interests for exposing Big Finance's bill to exempt large trades in derivatives from regulation by the CFTC or the SEC. I was unaware of the cold shoulder she was getting, not just from Federal Reserve Chair Alan Greenspan but also from some others in the executive branch. When she quit without talking to me, I was angry and didn't call and ask her to stay on the job and keep fighting. That's on me. In the end, we would have lost anyway, but I wish Brooksley would have stayed in the fight.

The anti-historical rewrite of the 1990s in 2016 has made it more difficult for the Democrats to be seen as both tough on crime and for civil rights and racial justice, both pro-work and for the support necessary to help poor people live and raise their kids in dignity, both pro-business and pro-labor. The treatment of trade as a con game makes it harder to reap the benefits of cross-border exchanges while getting funds on the front end to repair communities hurt by trade. We need an upbeat, forthright effort to combat climate change, inequality, and isolation by investing in physical and digital infrastructure and the education and training that will allow all Americans to access all kinds of work. Minimizing the importance of disciplined budgets to keep down interest rates and the percentage of our budgets that go to bondholders undermines our ability to win the race for the future with research and development and education and training for all. We have to beat the "brand and blame" crowd with a fair defense of our past and a fearless embrace of the future.

TWENTY-TWO

2017–2020: Back to the Foundation

Hillary decided she had to make good on her concession speech by attending Trump's inauguration. I agreed and off we went for root canals without painkillers. It was classic Trump. He gave a brief ungenerous nod to Obama, didn't acknowledge Hillary, and gave a dark inaugural address to a nice-sized crowd but nowhere near what he claimed or pushed the National Park Service to estimate, and smaller than the crowds in 1993 and 2009. Away from the cameras, the newly minted president thanked Hillary and me for coming.

Then we went home. As we turned into our short cul-de-sac, I thought of how our neighbors had decorated the entrance after the election with signs, notes, and flowers expressing love and support for Hillary. Some of them were still there. I was grateful to live in a county where Hillary had run ahead of the party registration, a place with good schools, libraries, parks, and nature preserves, filled with immigrants and native-born residents working and raising families side-by-side.

Despite the success of the demonize, divide, and dominate strategy, I went back to work trying to prove my neighbors were a better model for the future. I started 2017 by checking in with the foundation's major donors to make sure they were still with us, and urging President Bush to nail down GOP congressional support for PEPFAR before Trump could cut it, which sure enough he tried to do.

By the end of 2017, James Patterson and I had finished our book *The President Is Missing.* I had read hundreds of thrillers over the last forty-plus years and was excited to be working on one with the writer who'd penned the most best-sellers of them all. After our agent, Bob Barnett, got us together, we had to figure out how to do it. Jim asked me what I wanted to write about. I said I wanted to tell readers about the dangers of cyberattacks that go well beyond election meddling. Then he said, "I'm a storyteller. I want the president to go missing." I laughed and said it's harder for the president to go missing than the conspiracy spreaders think and so we'd need a believable plot line that required him to be alone to meet with the only person who could prevent a cyberattack. We started with those two ideas.

I learned a lot about thriller writing from Patterson, and really enjoyed working with him. We agreed on an outline, then he gave me about twenty questions that needed answering so we could make the White House meetings and the mechanics of the president going missing as realistic as possible. I worked on the questions and he sent me a draft of the first two chapters to review. Then we went back and forth with drafts until the end. The only thing he said I'd have to do by myself was the president's speech to the country near the end of the book.

Hillary and I like spending time with Jim and his wife, Sue. They are both ardent and good golfers. Between them they have more than a dozen holes-in-one. Sue's probably a better golfer but Jim has more aces. He's a competitive rascal. More important, they're serious philanthropists who promote universal reading with gifts to independent bookstores, including checks directly to their employees, support for effective school reading programs, and books given directly to kids and their parents. He's way ahead of me on that, but our foundation's partnership with Scholastic and others has allowed Too Small to Fail to put more than a million books into the hands of kids and their parents. We had a good time writing and promoting *The President Is Missing*, which became the bestselling novel of 2018.

Starting in February 2018, we did book signings, interviews with the press and with other mystery writers, and some TV interviews. The last one, on June 3, was NBC's *Today* show, with Craig Melvin, who had just transferred from MSNBC. He asked straightforward questions that Jim and I fielded for about 40 percent of the interview. We also discussed North Korea and the upcoming meeting between Trump and President Kim. Then Melvin asked, with the reckoning of the MeToo movement, if the same thing that triggered my impeachment had happened today, would I resign? I said no, because the impeachment process was not legitimate and had to be fought. Then he read from Monica Lewinsky's column about how the MeToo movement changed her view of sexual harassment and asked if I felt differently now.

I said, "No, I felt terrible then." "Did you ever apologize to her?" I said that I had apologized to her and everybody else I wronged. I was caught off guard by what came next. "But you didn't apologize to her, at least according to folks that we've talked to." I fought to contain my frustration as I replied that while I'd never talked to her directly, I did say publicly on more than one occasion that I was sorry.

The interview was not my finest hour. I was prepared to be asked why I hadn't apologized to Monica in person, but not to be accused of not apologizing at all. Melvin was barely in his teens when all this happened and probably hadn't been properly briefed. Regardless, it's always better to save your anger for what happens to other people, not yourself.

The network soon included a clip of me speaking to faith leaders at the White House in 1999, apologizing to my family, to Monica Lewinsky and her family, and to the American people. I meant it then and I mean it today. I live with it all the time. Monica's done a lot of good and important work over the last few years in her campaign against bullying, earning her well-deserved recognition in the United States and abroad. I wish her nothing but the best.

Meanwhile, the country was entering a post-truth era, and Trump was making the most of it. His cabinet was full of people with clear conflicts of interest, but he didn't care until they refused to obey his latest command because it was illegal or would destroy their reputations. Trump, his family, and many of his top aides also conducted official business on their personal cell phones, sometimes in public.

Thankfully, the people he assigned to renegotiate NAFTA took it seriously and basically updated the original agreement, which needed doing after almost twenty-five years. He didn't seem to care about the details. He just wanted to put a different title on the deal and proclaim it a vast improvement over the "worst trade deal in history." President López Obrador of Mexico and Canadian prime minister Justin Trudeau played along.

For Trump it was all about branding, erasing factual history with new myths. His tax bill was a big wet kiss to corporate America, with no requirement to share the benefits with their workers or use the money to make more investments in the United States. When I raised the corporate rate in 1993 to 35 percent, that was the average rate paid in advanced economies. By 2017, everybody else had lowered their rates. We needed to keep up with our competitors, but Trump's 21 percent rate was below the average in advanced economies and made no effort to close gaping loopholes which allowed many large corporations to shelter billions from paying any tax at all.

In 2022, the Democrats' Inflation Reduction Act turned the tide a bit, with a 15 percent minimum tax, but Congress wouldn't go along with the fix we need, and President Biden supports: a global 15 percent minimum. Nations would still be free to have different rates, but big corporations couldn't move operations to lower-tax countries or put money in tax havens and get off scot-free. According to news reports, big companies used most of Trump's tax cuts for stock buybacks and top management pay hikes, increasing inequality. Not exactly what he promised.

It didn't matter too much, politically. The years 2017–2019 were pretty good for the country economically, with economic growth that had begun ever so slowly in 2009, but picked up steam in President Obama's second term, helped by his policies and the significant minimum wage increases passed in several states. Trump was lucky again—even though job growth in his first two years was actually less than in President Obama's last two years, people finally began to feel it in rising incomes, with the benefits more widely shared, thanks in part to the state minimum wage hikes and a resurgent union movement.

In May 2017, Trump fired Jim Comey just four years into his ten-year term as FBI director. The deputy attorney general, Rod Rosenstein, whom President Obama had appointed U.S. attorney for Maryland, wrote a short bulletproof memo citing Comey's two violations of decades of FBI policy in 2016: his public statement on July 5 smearing three hundred State Department employees, including Hillary, for following long-standing State Department procedures; and his public announcement of reopening the email investigation right before the election.

Trump should have left it there. But he couldn't. He actually wanted Comey gone for two other reasons: his presence was a constant reminder of what really got him to the White House, and he wanted Comey to kill the investigation into whether Putin had worked to defeat Hillary, efforts already confirmed in 2016 by the Director of National Intelligence, Jim Clapper, and the Secretary of Homeland Security, Jeh Johnson. Comey's unleashing the dogs of war on Hillary and apparently dragging his feet on Putin's interference until after the election wasn't enough for Trump to keep him.

Trump set Comey up when he pressured him to let the investigation of General Michael Flynn go after hugging him at a White House meeting covered on national TV. Comey was clearly uncomfortable. But Trump wasn't. He soon fired him and later said he did it because the Russia investigation would interfere with his ability to work with Putin.

President Trump also kept his promise to move the Supreme Court to the right with the appointment of Federalist Society favorite Neil Gorsuch to the court fourteen months after the vacancy created by the death of Justice Scalia. President Obama had nominated Judge Merrick Garland, now attorney general, who earlier had been confirmed by a large bipartisan majority to the D.C. Court of Appeals. Majority Leader Mitch McConnell blocked a vote on Garland, saying the Scalia vacancy was too close to the election—eight months away—and should be decided by the voters. To confirm Gorsuch, McConnell had to abolish the filibuster for Supreme Court nominees, which he had recently agreed not to do when he accepted the bipartisan compromise ending it only for judges below the Supreme Court.

Hillary and I started 2018 with a trip to Hawaii. We stayed on the Big Island and got together with our old friend, former governor John Waihee, the first native Hawaiian elected to lead the state. After he finished two terms, John continued his efforts to promote Hawaii's history and culture, including teaching more young people to speak their native tongue. We visited a group of them who welcomed us with a Hawaiian song and showed us their project, a giant raft made like those that Pacific Islanders had first sailed to then-unsettled Hawaii about sixteen hundred years ago, navigating solely by the stars and ocean currents. The young people were also learning to navigate without instruments, a skill we could all use at times.

Not long after we returned home, I met another remarkable group of young people. I attended *Town & Country*'s Philanthropy Summit to introduce two survivors of the Parkland school shooting and two students from Chicago who had founded an anti-gun-violence group that also was lobbying for stronger gun safety laws. The Chicago group leaders represented inner-city Black kids who had long been at risk of gun violence. They lived in one of the five of Chicago's fifty wards where violent crime had increased over the last few years. The Parkland kids were leading a more racially, ethnically, and economically mixed group which had been activated by the deadly shooting at their own school.

I thought that these impressive young people's call to action had the potential to finally make it an issue for the voters who supported sensible gun safety laws but, so far, not with the same intensity as the opponents of any sensible regulations, like fully comprehensive background checks and a new assault weapons ban, or at least a reenactment of the ten-bullet ammunition clip limit.

These students and others like them had a chance to actually move voters, if we could keep them in the news. I was glad to help. The kids were great and made their case, although we'd have to suffer through more mass shootings, including the tragedy at Uvalde, when a teenager with an AR-15 killed nineteen children and two teachers when there were nearly four hundred armed lawmen nearby who did nothing. Uvalde finally prompted the Senate Republicans to support some modest improvements, but it was still not enough. In late 2023 in Lewiston, Maine, a mentally ill Army reservist killed eighteen people and wounded thirteen more after local law enforcement had been warned by his son, his ex-wife, and members of his Army Reserve unit that he was unstable and threatening to kill a lot of people. Authorities said state law required them to take him into custody, but they couldn't find him. The new GOP Speaker, Mike Johnson, said the killings were "a problem of the human heart." Since we have by far the highest mass-murder rate of any wealthy country in the world, does he mean that he thinks we have the darkest, hardest hearts on earth? Go figure.

On June 25, I went to Kennebunkport for what proved to be my last summer lunch with George H. W. Bush. He was frail but still had his sense of humor, wearing dark blue socks with a drawing of me on them. He was clearly still missing Barbara, who had passed away just a couple of months earlier. We had a good time, but I missed Barbara being there, too. She kept us all on our toes with her quick wit and no-nonsense wisdom. George didn't say much, but he didn't miss much, either. I could tell he knew his life was winding down and he wanted to finish it with family and friends, being gracious and grateful, with a smile on his face.

On July 10, I represented both of us at the renaming of two buildings on the campus of the U.S. Peace Institute in Washington for George and me. Both older buildings had been renovated to house a meeting space and peace tech lab. They're now respectable additions to the magnificent main building designed by the wonderful Israeli architect Moshe Safdie, whose work includes Yad Vashem, Israel's Holocaust museum, and Crystal

Bridges, the museum of American Art in northwest Arkansas. I was honored to support the project and liked the thought of being connected with George when we're both gone. I really miss him now, and whether the Republicans acknowledge it or not, they do, too. He was a tough campaigner, but when the elections were over, he governed in a way that left the door open for honorable compromise.

The rest of 2018 was dominated by two political stories. President Trump nominated Brett Kavanaugh, another Federalist Society choice, to the Supreme Court, and he was confirmed 50–48–1 after a contentious hearing, the tone of which was set by Kavanaugh's assertion in his opening statement that "what goes around comes around." Donald Trump and Mitch McConnell sure hoped so. In the nineties, Ken Starr and his henchmen implied that Hillary and I had something to do with our friend Vince Foster's death. After the previous special counsel, a respected Republican prosecutor, Robert Fiske, had already concluded that Vince's cause of death was suicide brought on by depression, Brett Kavanaugh aided Starr in reopening the issue, making Vince's death an "open question" and forcing the Foster family to relive their nightmare for three more long years. It was awful. I hope no one else ever has to go through anything like it when what goes around comes around.

The other big event turned out better for the Democrats. The efforts of the White House and the GOP Congress to repeal the Affordable Care Act without offering a remotely acceptable alternative made it clear that they were willing to take away coverage or explode the cost of healthcare for millions of people by ending the ban on charging people with preexisting conditions more for insurance, and by eliminating the Medicaid expansion that gave millions of poor people healthcare coverage and provided premium subsidies for millions more working families with limited incomes.

The voters noticed and gave Democrats the largest popular vote victory in the 2018 midterm elections in more than a century, 8.6 percent, leading to a net gain of forty-one seats in the House. The popular vote margin was larger than in the big Democratic losses in 1994 and 2010, but Democrats gained fewer seats because of reapportionment, gerrymandering, and efforts to make it harder for heavily Democratic areas to vote. The Republicans actually picked up two Senate seats, thanks to where the open seats were. Still, the victory was enough to save the Affordable Care Act, thanks to Senator John McCain's decisive vote, and give the Democrats hope for 2020. I was especially happy with Donna Shalala's victory in South Florida over a GOP incumbent, a tribute to her years of good work as president of the University of Miami and a smart campaign.

In January 2019, I stopped in Las Vegas to see former Senate Democratic leader Harry Reid, who was battling cancer but still focused on the future, determined to fight on as long as he had a breath left. After I got home, I did two long sessions with the film crew doing a documentary about Hillary. It was both exhilarating because I loved talking about her and painful because I had to relive the 2016 campaign and the problems as well as the joys of our long years together. *Hillary* was streamed on Hulu and did a compelling job covering her life and work. But it hurt when people who saw it said they wished America had seen *that* Hillary in 2015 and 2016. She was there all the time, but it's hard to see anybody when your view of them is blocked by mud.

I also did a long interview for a film on the late King Hussein of Jordan, who, when he was desperately ill with cancer, came to Camp David in 1998 to challenge the Palestinians to make peace with Israel as he had. He also weighed in, diplomatically, on the impeachment battle, saying in a press conference that while he had worked for peace with nine U.S. presidents and liked them all, no one had done as much for peace as I had, and he hoped I would be able to finish the job. With his life ebbing away, the trip took a lot out of him. Soon I would be marching in his funeral cortege in Amman. He was a brave, good man, and a loyal friend. He was succeeded by his son Abdullah, who along with his wife, Queen Rania, a Palestinian by birth, have continued to make Jordan a voice for peace and fairness in the Middle East. They often participate in CGI, and have been uncommonly thoughtful and kind to Hillary and me.

Throughout 2018 and 2019, the *Miami Herald* had been publishing stories about the financier Jeffrey Epstein, who in 2008 had been convicted and jailed in Florida for sex crimes. In part because of that rigorous journalism, Epstein was arrested again in 2019 for those and other crimes, this time by federal authorities in New York. The *Herald* stories and his rearrest raised questions about several well-known people's connection to him, including me. They deserved answers and I gave them. In 2002 and 2003, he invited me to fly on his airplane to support the work of the foundation, and in return for flying me, my staff, and my Secret Service detail who always accompanied me, Epstein asked only that I take an hour or two on each trip to discuss politics and economics. He had just donated $10 million to Harvard for brain research and he asked a lot of questions. That was the extent of our conversations. My only other interactions with Epstein were two brief meetings, one at my office in Harlem and another at his house in New York.

I had always thought Epstein was odd but had no inkling of the crimes he was committing. He hurt a lot of people, but I knew nothing about it and by the time he was first arrested in 2005, I had stopped contact with him. I've never visited his island. When it was suggested that I traveled there without my round-the-clock Secret Service detail, which would explain why there's never been a record of me being there, in 2016 the Service took the extraordinary step of saying I had never waived protection and they had never been there. Another person reportedly said she'd seen me on the island, but that I didn't do anything wrong. However, in early 2024, unsealed depositions showed that she'd only heard I was there but didn't actually see me. Then there was one of my former staffers who fed the story to *Vanity Fair.* He knew it wasn't true when he said it.

The bottom line is, even though it allowed me to visit the work of my foundation, traveling on Epstein's plane was not worth the years of questioning afterward. I wish I had never met him.

In May, I went to the University of Virginia, founded by Thomas Jefferson, to address a symposium on the presidency. I worked hard on the speech and its central argument: that all our presidents could best be understood by how they defined the two key ideas in the Preamble to the Constitution: who are "we the people" and what does a "more perfect union" mean? To support the case I went on a trip through American history, including the periods when we had strong movements to eliminate groups from "we the people" and shrink the definition of "a more perfect union," from the end of Reconstruction to the present day, and concluded that, so far, we had ultimately rejected division and chosen what I call "inclusive tribalism" to keep moving forward.

I had seen the ongoing argument on a recent trip back to Hope, Arkansas, to do a conversation at the Chamber of Commerce dinner with two of my kindergarten classmates, Mack McClarty, my first White House chief of staff, and Joe Purvis, a gifted lawyer in my state attorney general's office. By 2019, Trump fever had taken root in our hometown, but we had a good time saying what we thought and being well received, though it was hard to tell whether we were getting through or just being welcomed as respected relics of another time.

I also learned a lot going back to Arkansas for Alice Walton's seventieth birthday party, my fifty-fifth high school reunion, and the two-hundredth Anniversary Dinner for the *Arkansas Gazette*.

The *Gazette*, the oldest newspaper west of the Mississippi and a strong voice for civil rights during the integration of Little Rock Central High School, had been sold to *USA Today*, which couldn't make a go of it, then had merged with the state's conservative paper, the *Arkansas Democrat*, whose deeper pockets from other media properties had put the *Gazette* out of business to start with.

But the *Democrat-Gazette* was an old-fashioned paper in a good way. The publisher, Walter Hussman Jr., would beat me up on the editorial page but generally report the news as it unfolded. Hussman was also a good friend of Vince Foster's, and I appreciated his loyalty to our mutual friend and his unwillingness to sacrifice Vince's memory, and the plain facts, on the altar of power worship and personal vendettas.

TWENTY-THREE

The Virus That Affected Us All, and the Virus We Resisted

When the story first broke in January 2020 about cases of a coronavirus in China, I asked Chelsea about it. She said it was very serious, less deadly than Ebola but much more dangerous than the flu and far more likely to spread rapidly. And she said she thought the United States was especially vulnerable, unprepared, and our response would likely be slow, inadequate, and lead to a lot of deaths.

Besides being a wonderful daughter, wife, and mother, Chelsea's our in-house health authority. She's the vice chair of both the Clinton Foundation and CHAI, where she's served on the board for ten years. She also taught public health at Columbia University for a decade, and has three advanced degrees in global health. She's rigorous, blunt, and hyper-conscientious. She's one of those "experts" it's become fashionable in the U.S. to dismiss, until we need people who actually know something. I'm really proud of her, but this time, I was hoping she was wrong. She wasn't, of course.

Soon the director-general of the World Health Organization, Dr. Tedros Adhanom Ghebreyesus, asked Ira Magaziner to send some of our CHAI staff to the WHO headquarters in Switzerland to assist them in supporting countries that needed lots of help to fight the virus. The WHO, being a collection of humans, with a large variety of contributors and diverse constituents, is not perfect, but it does have a dedicated staff and an able and well-motivated leader in Tedros, whom I've known and respected for years from working together when he was health minister, then foreign minister, of Ethiopia. The WHO's response to this pandemic was more rapid and comprehensive than its initial Ebola actions, in spite of the limitations it faced in getting information and full cooperation from China.

I opposed the Trump administration's threat to cut off funding for and withdraw from the WHO, and was heartened when President Biden signaled his intention to continue U.S. membership and financial support. Whatever your politics, you should feel that way, too, because unless future health challenges are handled well in other countries, they will eventually spread to the United States and around the world. I strongly supported CHAI's efforts at the WHO, its work on the ground in twelve African countries, where our staff went all in to help governments and citizens deal with the virus, and in India, where CHAI had 215 people working at high risk, dealing with a severe oxygen shortage and other challenges. And, like Chelsea and Hillary, I wanted my country to lead the way in getting vaccines to as many people as possible, fairly dispersing any surplus we didn't need, and rapidly increasing the ability of reputable manufacturers around the world to make more.

In Washington, Congress passed and President Trump signed a bill backed by a large bipartisan majority to fund Operation Warp Speed to develop and deploy vaccines. There were daily briefings on the rising infections and deaths and what we could do to minimize them. And there was a big effort to build up essential medical supplies and equipment for healthcare workers and first responders, in part because the stockpiling of such things that I had begun in the late 1990s had not been maintained.

Dr. Anthony Fauci, who led the National Institutes of Health effort to develop a vaccine, and Dr. Deborah Birx, whose work on AIDS started in the Obama White House, conducted the briefings and did their best to keep us informed, urging social distancing and mask wearing until we could be vaccinated. For a while, President Trump attended briefings and often disrupted the flow of information with bizarre comments, from his assertion that Covid would soon disappear, to his reference to the healing powers of bleach, to his putdowns of his own experts. This was all the more ironic when Trump got a serious case of Covid and recovered with the help of lifesaving medicine and treatment. I felt especially bad about Fauci's treatment because he's given his entire professional life, fifty-four years, to the NIH. He oversaw the development of the first AIDS medicine when I was president and helped organize the PEPFAR program for President George W. Bush, who gave him the Medal of Freedom. He served into his eighties, leaving his last post as President Biden's chief medical advisor at the end of 2022.

On the home front, the Clinton Foundation did what we could to help. In Little Rock, the café at the Clinton Presidential Center worked with José Andrés's World Central Kitchen, the city, the county's two school districts, and others to feed children who were getting breakfast and lunch in the schools before they closed, the homeless, older people living alone, and others who needed food. The staff and more than five hundred volunteers, including fourteen AmeriCorps members, would prepare and package the meals, then leave them outside to be picked up and delivered to distribution centers. Everybody followed the health protocols, and the program, which ran from March through August of 2020 and again from December through February 2021, distributed a total of 718,480 meals. From June 2020 through the end of the year, the center also supported the distribution to families of more than 69,000 multi-meal food boxes provided by the U.S. Department of Agriculture's Farmers to Food Box Program. Those boxes pushed our distribution to more than a million meals.

I wish I could have done something to help the millions of small businesses who didn't get a dollar of the $680 billion congressional fund designed to save them, including the ninety-two-year-old McClard's Bar-B-Q in Hot Springs, Arkansas, a landmark run by the same family since it opened in 1928 and visited by people from all over America. They tried to get help from the payroll support program, to no avail. They had twenty-eight employees in a relatively small space that was often jam-packed, so reopening with social distancing would never cover costs. Happily, a local businessman bought the restaurant and got them over the hump. It's still managed by the McClard family and is even expanding.

I was also moved by the story of Burnell Cotlon, who ran a small market in New Orleans, catering to his neighbors in the Lower Ninth Ward. I called him when I learned he needed help, and sent him a little. His business has survived. There are stories like McClard's and Cotlon's in every state, red and blue. Many made it through Covid, but too many didn't.

In New York, our foundation's Too Small to Fail program, led by Patti Miller, added more than 50,000 children's books and home instruction materials for non-English-speaking parents to the feeding programs in city neighborhoods.

When Covid was raging in New York, Hillary and I were at home, with Chelsea, Marc, and our three grandkids next door in our guesthouse. Our Clinton Foundation staff all worked from home, keeping our projects going, including helping the faith leaders involved in our opioid alliance encourage their members to follow safe practices through worship and in daily life. The staff also moved our annual Clinton Global Initiative University, originally scheduled for the University of Edinburgh in Scotland in 2020, to an online format with panels and interviews on the pandemic in the United States and around the world. In 2021, we held another virtual conference with Howard University on how to build a more inclusive, more fairly shared economy during the recovery.

When the outbreak extended into the heartland, the spread was faster and the fatalities higher than they would have been had people not resisted wearing masks and getting vaccinated. In early February 2021, two of my high school classmates who lived on my block in Hot Springs embodied our national trauma. One, Carolyn Staley, my next-door neighbor and a Baptist minister, went to get her first vaccine shot at a local hospital, where she left a note for the other, Mike Karber, who was a patient there on a respirator. He died the next day—a man of great faith who rose before dawn to pray and help people in need before going to his day job, delivering the mail. COVID-19 proved we are all in this together, like it or not.

In spite of Covid's terrible toll, it was a blessing for Hillary and me in some ways. I loved having our family so close. It was such a kick to have then six-year-old Charlotte and four-year-old Aidan barge into the house and insist that Hillary and I stop whatever we were doing and play their favorite games, read books, or be characters in the plays they created. Seven-month-old Jasper happily observed the chaos.

I spent time exploring the internet—the magnificent music, the comedy routines, the humorous video clips, memes, and photos. (Did you see the guy singing "Don't Be Cruel" to two white cockatoos perched on a couch and rocking along to the music? Or the man out west who gives a ride in the backseat of his old convertible to a buffalo?) Hillary and I finally got into the streaming craze, spending Valentine's Day 2021 binge-watching *Bridgerton* all night long. We later binged *Ted Lasso* in smaller bites.

Just when the worst of the pandemic seemed behind us, and we were beginning to reopen the country, George Floyd was killed by a policeman who sat on his back with his knee pressing down on his neck for over nine minutes, although Floyd was lying on his belly on the ground handcuffed, no threat to anyone. The other three policemen there didn't try to stop it. Thank goodness the whole thing was caught on video, including the policeman, his hand in his pocket, adjusting his position to put even more pressure on Floyd. We would learn even more when the trial opened in March 2021, thanks to the eyewitness accounts of people who simply described what they saw and held up well under cross-examination. The officer who killed Floyd was convicted of second-degree murder and two lesser offenses. The prosecution did a masterful job of calmly presenting the evidence and arguing for the conclusion that flowed from it. And a lot of credit goes to Darnella Frazier, the young woman who bravely filmed the whole incident.

I was proud of the countless thousands of people who took

to the streets in peaceful protest all over America, and those who stood with them across the world. The crowds looked like America, as people of every race demanded justice for Floyd and other African Americans slain while being arrested, detained, or just stopped, and supported reforms to curb police abuses of minorities. Donald Trump, instead of condemning the indefensible and calling for national unity, tried to play politics with it, including having federal officials shove and gas protesters to clear a path between the White House and Lafayette Square so he could walk to St. John's Episcopal Church, hold up a Bible, say something forgettable, and walk back.

It was a shallow, unfeeling show. More than 780 retired high-ranking officers and national security leaders, including five former secretaries of defense, condemned the use of the military to stop American citizens from legally protesting. Still, Trump did finally finish a wall: reinforced fencing that protected the White House from Americans engaging in peaceful protest. I couldn't wait for it to be taken down.

In ways I still don't fully understand, the coronavirus and its stay-at-home imperative and the uprising changed me, and I suspect, you, too, especially in where and how we work and how much time we spend with family and friends. I laughed at the internet, then cried as I called friends who lost a spouse, a brother, parents. I worried with the people I work with and other friends, praying their infected family members would recover.

Yet I became more hopeful that—in our shared grief and worry, in our shared cheering for the bravery and devotion of those on the front lines who often don't look like us, in our shared laughter that makes the awful bearable, in our collective efforts to survive in a crippled economy, and in the outpouring of support for Floyd's family and for others whose loved ones were killed while being stopped, chased, or arrested, and for the idea that Black lives do matter—we might be recovering a sense of our common humanity, humility, and gratitude. The jury's still out on that. It could have the reverse effect, making too many of us even more determined to withdraw from each other and the rest of the world.

On June 22, 2020, my friend and longtime foundation supporter Steve Bing jumped to his death off a tall building in Los Angeles. His fifty-five years were turbulent, self-destructive, and isolated, yet full of kindness, generosity, and love. Less than a week earlier, I'd had a good talk with the Steve I usually saw. He was upbeat about a film he was doing on the life and work of Sam Phillips, the legendary founder of Sun Records and Sun Studios in Memphis, one of the only white promoters at the time to give Black musicians the chance to record their music in the heavily segregated city, and the producer of the first recordings of Elvis, Johnny Cash, Carl Perkins, and Jerry Lee Lewis. Steve wanted Mick Jagger and me to be coproducers. After Steve's death I had a good talk with Jerry Lee, who was heartbroken and said he'd do anything he could to finish the film. Sadly, we didn't even have a memorial. His father was adamantly against it and there were squabbles over what was left of his estate. Maybe we can still do the documentary. Lord knows there are enough of us who owe it to him to try.

Two thousand twenty was, of course, a big year in politics—the race for president, for the House and Senate, and another Supreme Court vacancy. In 2016, seventeen Republicans had run to succeed President Obama. This time, more than twenty Democrats sought the nomination to take on President Trump, the largest field ever. By November 24, 2019, there were twenty-nine of them, but by the Iowa caucuses, there were just eleven left. Pete Buttigieg won the most delegates in Iowa, lost to Bernie narrowly in New Hampshire, and Bernie came out on top in Nevada.

Then came South Carolina, where Congressman Jim Clyburn threw his support to Joe Biden. Clyburn liked Biden and was sending a signal that Biden was the most, perhaps the only, electable candidate. That did it. Biden won almost half the vote in South Carolina and it was all downhill after that. He was clearly the candidate most likely to beat Trump.

The virtual Democratic convention was good, showcasing the broad base of our party and Biden's significant and popular proposals, including a big infrastructure bill and allowing Medicare to bargain for lower drug prices, as the Veterans Administration already did.

The GOP followed its 2016 playbook: a critical smearing book by Peter Schweizer, a woman accusing Joe Biden of sexual assault, and accusations about Hunter Biden's business deals, in Ukraine and China. Unlike 2016, the political press, instead of signing partnerships with Steve Bannon and *Breitbart*, didn't take the bait. The coverage was light-years better and more on the level.

For the first time, Trump's Republican Party offered no platform. They just went after Biden and the Democrats as if the entire party was defined by its most liberal members. They closed the campaign saying Biden and the Democrats favored socialism and defunding the police. Neither was true, but they're better branders than we are.

The Covid-driven efforts to make it easier to vote prompted a record turnout for both parties. People who didn't want to vote for Trump heard Biden say he wasn't a socialist and didn't want to defund the police, but the House Democrats lost about half their majority margin through the GOP strategy of painting our mainstream candidates as something they weren't. They weren't socialists or for defunding law enforcement, but their more moderate voters were vulnerable to the divide-and-conquer strategy that doesn't work in the solidly liberal enclaves that elect the progressives. The loss I regretted most was Donna Shalala, who had done an excellent job representing a closely divided district in Florida.

The GOP strategy didn't work so well in the Senate races. After the victories of Senators Raphael Warnock and Jon Ossoff in hotly contested runoffs in Georgia, the Democrats picked up three seats to tie the Senate, which would give them a 51–50 majority when Senator Harris took her place as vice president and as president of the Senate, who can cast tie-breaking votes.

Before he lost the majority, Mitch McConnell gave President Trump, the Federalist Society, and the far right a big parting gift. When Justice Ruth Bader Ginsburg lost her long fight with cancer, less than two months before the election, McConnell rushed the nomination for her replacement through the Senate with a vote of 52–48, confirming Amy Coney Barrett just before the election. When Obama was president, McConnell said eight months was too close to the election to confirm a justice without giving voters a say. But this time, two months was fine. So much for giving the voters a say.

Not long before Justice Barrett joined the Supreme Court, when the political press was preoccupied with the presidential race, the Court, in *Rucho v. Common Cause*, ruled 5–4 that North Carolina had blatantly diluted the impact of Democratic voters (e.g., in 2012 the GOP got only 49 percent of the total vote for House candidates but won nine of the thirteen House seats) and in *Benisek v. Lamone* that Maryland had done the same on a smaller scale to help get an extra Democratic seat. But the Court said they couldn't do anything about it, because they couldn't decide how much gerrymandering was too much, and besides, the Constitution gave state legislatures the responsibility to draw district lines.

As Justice Kagan pointed out in her dissent, this was the first time in American history the Court had refused to remedy a constitutional violation "because it thinks the task beyond judicial capabilities." She noted that both the lower courts, which included Trump appointees, and other states, red and blue, had come up with fairer district maps based on easily developed computer models, and North Carolina refused them all to get its district splits to 10–3 in 2016, Republican over Democratic, regardless of how its citizens voted.

When the New York legislature tried to offset the GOP gerrymandering in other states by creating three districts more favorable to Democrats, its own Supreme Court overturned the plan based on the state constitution's equal protection mandate and a Republican judge substituted a plan even less favorable to Democrats than their existing map. The new map opened the door for several Republican pickups in 2022. Thankfully, state courts in North Carolina and Ohio moderated the extreme gerrymandering in those states, giving Democrats a chance to win two more districts, which they did.

The *Rucho* decision was the latest in a line of Supreme Court political decisions that helped Republicans, beginning with *Bush v. Gore* in 2000, which stopped the recount in Florida with Gore trailing by a few hundred votes, and was sufficiently embarrassing that the justices who voted for it said it could never be cited as a precedent in future cases. In the *Citizens United* case in 2012, the Court's conservative majority said the First Amendment's free speech provision prohibited limits on corporate contributions to "independent" political advertising. Corporations were no longer creations of the state, subject to state and federal restrictions. Now they were "just people" like you and me. *Citizens United* led to an increase in spending by such groups from $300 million to well over $1 billion by 2020. Then came *Shelby County v. Holder* in 2013, which gutted the preclearance requirement of the Voting Rights Act and led to a slew of restrictions on voting across the country.

Reading all the recent Supreme Court political decisions together, the Court seems to be saying that states can do as they please in making it harder for people to vote, in purging voter rolls, restricting eligibility to vote, and in gerrymandering to give more seats to a preferred party, but once the people vote and there's no credible evidence of fraud, don't expect us to overturn a legitimate election just because you don't like it. Otherwise, have at it.

While there's a lot of cynicism, and divisions remain in all corners of America today, we still need to believe we can move toward an economy with benefits and burdens, opportunities and responsibilities more fairly shared; a society committed to inclusive tribalism, rooted in the conviction that what we have in common is even more important than our interesting differences; and politics in which more people vote, the votes are honestly counted after every election, and on all the days in between, all people count and have their voices heard. That's what the American people voted to do in 2020, by a large popular vote margin, but another close vote in the Electoral College.

All those efforts toward a shared America are made harder when one party believes that the primary purpose of power is to hang on to it as long as you can, and when they're in charge will try to change the rules to make that happen. When I was dealing with Newt Gingrich and the Contract with America crowd in my second term, Gingrich told Erskine Bowles, my chief of staff who also led my budget negotiations, that I was a great politician but was at a disadvantage in dealing with the more militant Republicans because I wasted time and energy on efforts that didn't increase the Democrats' power, like restoring benefits for illegal immigrants (the term we used back then) who paid taxes but couldn't vote. He said to Erskine, "The president really believes we should all live under the same set of rules, doesn't he?" Erskine replied, "Yes. We think that's what a real democracy requires." Gingrich responded, "We don't believe that. We think everyone we elect or appoint should first do what's best for our party. Then we can talk about the rest." During the Trump presidency, Senator McConnell proved that by rushing through the Barrett confirmation after stonewalling a vote on President Obama's nomination of Merrick Garland for more than eight months.

The most extreme example of this single-minded determination to grab and hold on to power at all costs manifested itself on January 6, the day both houses of Congress met to certify Joe Biden's 2020 victory. Trump's claim to be the real winner of the race produced a large angry crowd that he whipped into a frenzy with his claims that the election was stolen from him, even though judges across the country, including some appointed by him, had quickly found the charges baseless. The judges were following the law—did all voters have an opportunity to vote and were the votes properly counted? But Trump and his supporters didn't keep score that way. The only question that mattered to them was: Did we win?

There was a method to Trump's madness. He'd lost Arizona by about 10,000 votes, Georgia by just under 12,000, and Wisconsin by just over 20,000. If he could have had those states' votes overturned, the electoral vote would have been tied, sending the election to the House of Representatives, where each state gets one vote, and Trump would have been reelected, despite losing by about seven million votes in the huge turnout. At least Putin's social media efforts to get people to vote for Jill Stein or stay home didn't go well this time. Perhaps our intelligence community had figured out how to plug at least one hole in our democracy's dike.

As I watched the crowd of thousands make its way toward

Capitol Hill on live television, I couldn't help but think of the mayhem that had broken out in Charlottesville at the Unite the Right rally a few years earlier, and its tragic result. The January 6 crowd included professionals, business owners, police officers, and retired and serving military, all fired up by Trump's lies and on the move to try to stop the democratic process in its tracks.

In 2017, I had written a review of Ron Chernow's compelling biography of President Grant for *The New York Times Book Review*. The Charlottesville events had given relevance to Grant's efforts during Reconstruction to establish the Justice Department and his strong support of its successful effort to dismantle the Ku Klux Klan. I wrote that, in the wake of Charlottesville, the events of Grant's presidency seemed in many ways "as much a mirror as a history lesson." Three and a half years later, the January 6 effort to overturn the vote count offered an even more chilling parallel.

Much has been written about the events that transpired when those thousands of people, egged on by Trump, reached their destination. The images are seared into our memory—for me, the photo of the Arkansan with his feet on what he thought was Speaker Nancy Pelosi's desk and a stun gun in his waistband was particularly piercing. Richard Barnett, a retired firefighter from the northwest Arkansas town of Gravette, was convinced that, in the words of the prosecutors, "the United States would be taken over by communists if President-Elect Biden became president and was prepared to do 'whatever it takes,' including occupying the Capitol, to prevent that from happening. He prepared for that violence by arming himself with a stun device and a ten-pound steel pole, both capable of inflicting serious bodily injury. And then he traveled to Washington, D.C., with those weapons."

Barnett is serving four and half years in prison for his actions, and as I write this 1,413 people have been charged with crimes related to the attack on the Capitol, with 881 people sentenced. The Justice Department has estimated that around 2,000 people committed crimes, and their investigations are ongoing. All of these ordinary people, from all walks of life and convinced they were patriots, were so moved by Trump's lies, promoted by right-wing media, that they attacked their own government.

Many of the Republican members of Congress who hid behind desks, stacked furniture against office doors to keep rioters out, or fled to safety, denounced the attacks right after they occurred. Sadly, after Trump denied what happened, even criticizing the law enforcement officers who risked their lives to protect members of both parties, most Republicans completely changed their tunes. Trump asked them the question we've all heard in bad jokes: "Who are you going to believe, me or your lying eyes?" Those who looked to Trump and said, "You, Master," lived to fight another day. Of the few who stuck with their lying eyes, most either left government service or were tossed out by the voters in their gerrymandered districts. It was almost comical to watch some of the GOP members who'd been photographed defending themselves whitewash the entire episode. The Republicans' alleged support for the police mysteriously evaporated when it came to the officers who were killed or injured defending the Capitol and members of both parties from Trump's foot soldiers.

Of course, Trump didn't invent this capacity to cast the law and facts aside to cling to power, but it was a parade he was glad to lead. Some people saw strength and conviction in Trump's denial—that's how democracy disappears from the inside out.

In 2021, Hillary and I were happy to attend the inauguration of President Biden, after we had voted for him in the Electoral College in Albany. He got off to a good start, appointing a diverse, impressive cabinet, many quite young, and an experienced White House staff, several of whom, including Ron Klain, Gene Sperling, Janet Yellen, Steve Ricchetti, and Bruce Reed, had served in my administration, and several others whose service began in the Obama administration.

In June, Jim Patterson and I launched a book tour for our second effort, *The President's Daughter*, about the kidnapping of a former president's college-age daughter in the U.S. by a terrorist group with a score to settle with her father for an attack on them when he was president. It explores the problems created when the adult daughter loses Secret Service protection after her father leaves the White House, the ex-president's smaller Secret Service detail and what they can and can't do, and the ambivalence of the current president who defeated him in mounting an all-out effort to rescue her former opponent's daughter. The book also describes an interesting aspect of postpresidential life in an age of terror: when a president leaves office, though you have much less security, and none for your adult children, you don't necessarily leave your enemies behind.

In July, I began taping the History Channel series on the presidency, which I edited and narrated with a lot of support from Sean Wilentz, a distinguished historian at Princeton, and the History Channel crew led by Jeff Cooperman. The first episode covered President Eisenhower's 1957 decision to federalize the Arkansas National Guard to enforce the Supreme Court's ruling to integrate Little Rock Central High School, and others touched on how some U.S. presidents have exerted executive power over the economy, the ways in which our presidents have tried to extinguish—and sometimes, to fan—the flames of extremism, and how presidents have wielded America's power in the world. Each episode gave me an opportunity to explain a piece of presidential history, why I found it fascinating, and hoped that those who watched it would, too.

On July 10, Hillary and I went to Plains, Georgia, to the celebration of Jimmy and Rosalyn Carter's seventy-fifth wedding anniversary. We had both worked in his presidential campaign forty-seven years ago, and though the long years had included both high and low moments in our relationship, we admired the Carters and were proud of our early support for them. I was glad to reunite with many old friends and to see the Carters still in good spirits and very much in love.

After our traditional family August vacation in Amagansett, near the eastern end of Long Island, I began to prepare for teaching my MasterClass. If you've never seen a MasterClass, via subscription through the internet, they're beautifully filmed sessions featuring different "teachers" explaining how they thought about and worked to succeed in their various fields.

I was looking forward to but a little nervous about my class on "How to Be an Effective Leader." It had been decades since

I'd taught law at the University of Arkansas, and I wanted to cover the ground in a way that would be both substantive and engaging.

Hillary had filmed her own MasterClass a few weeks earlier, and told me how impressed she was with the sets and the energetic, talented crew. On the first day of shooting, I saw why. The set included a desk modeled on the one I used as president, a comfortable chair off to the side so I could speak directly to viewers, and walls covered with photos and memorabilia borrowed from my home and office. The crew was friendly and professional, particularly the director, Davis Carter, who worked with me for three days, sitting directly behind the camera and asking questions that helped me give answers in a more concise, conversational way.

There were sessions on organization, conflict mediation and negotiation, public speaking, dealing with criticism, assembling and leading diverse teams, and—something we found essential at CGI—how to measure success. I wanted everyone who watched the class to believe that whatever their day job, they could play a role in making better tomorrows. Hillary and I also did a joint session, relating our memories of things we worked on together.

I enjoyed relating the lessons I'd learned in politics and life, including stories of my trip to North Korea to bring the journalists home, my work with President Bush 41 after the tsunami, my experience with the artists after the Haiti earthquake, and what I learned from my work and friendships with Mandela, Rabin, and others.

I especially enjoyed describing a lesson I learned from my eighth-grade science teacher, Vernon Dokey. He was a good teacher, intelligent and engaging, but not a conventionally handsome man. Arkansas teachers were poorly paid, and when he gained weight as he aged, his clothes got tighter and he didn't buy new ones. He wore big Coke-bottle-thick glasses in the days before contact lenses, and smoked cheap cigars in a plastic cigar holder clenched in his teeth in a way that gave his face a pinched look.

On the last day of class, Mr. Dokey said we might not remember much about what we learned in eighth-grade science, but "if you don't remember anything else, remember this. Every morning when I get up, I go to the bathroom, throw water on my face, put my shaving cream on, shave, wipe my face, then look in the mirror and say, 'Vernon, you're beautiful.' Remember that. Everyone wants to believe they're beautiful. If you just remember that one thing, it'll take you a long way." Sixty-four years later I remember that as if it were yesterday. Vernon Dokey was a beautiful man.

I tell the Vernon Dokey story often as an antidote to the current obsession to tell people we disagree with, in words, treatment, or tone of voice, how ugly, stupid, or inferior they are. Everyone wants to believe their lives have meaning, that they are special in some way, and can add their own particular piece to the puzzle of life. It may be out of fashion today, so full of identity-based grievances and attacks that leave no stones unthrown, no wounds un-salted. Yet after two thousand years, the Golden Rule still works.

In 2022, David McRaney wrote *How Minds Change*, a compelling account of successful efforts to bridge political and social divides. In essence he says persuasion is "changing a mind without coercion." People you're trying to persuade need to feel that you respect them and that you're trying to win them over but they have to make the decision. That's what makes change possible. It's hard work but better than name-calling.

Shortly after wrapping the MasterClass in October, I was on the way to Southern California for two Clinton Foundation fundraisers when I got a bad case of chills and shakes. I had been a bit tired for a few days but had consistently tested negative for Covid. When I got to my friend Nima Taghavi's house for a supporter dinner, I took some Advil and slept hard until just before it started. I felt better, but soon after the guests went home, the chills and shakes came back. So I went to the UC Irvine Medical Center, which thankfully was only a few miles away. By the time I got there, I was delirious, and the staff quickly determined that I had sepsis, caused by the spread of an infection in my bladder that had been treated a year earlier with a week's worth of antibiotics that didn't kill it. The wily bacteria had gone into hiding and had escaped detection in two previous tests. The excellent team at UCI Medical Center, led by Dr. Alpesh Amin, immediately put me in the ICU, determined the antibiotics that would defeat the infection, and started me on a thirty-day course. Hillary and Chelsea flew out from New York, and stayed by my side as my head cleared and I was allowed to walk around the hospital floor. After six days, with instructions for what to do until the treatment was complete, we flew home to New York where two fine, experienced nurses and my longtime medical team did the rest.

I had lost a good friend and a close cousin to sepsis, so I knew I had been very lucky. Nima's house was near the Cal Irvine hospital, and Dr. Amin was a specialist in my particular infection and the bacteria that caused it. The quick response kept the sepsis from spreading, and the emergency quickly passed. I'm eternally grateful to all the people who gave me such good care and yet another chance to go on.

Meanwhile, the country was reeling from Covid, running behind the vaccination schedule, and still burdened with significant underemployment. The Biden administration launched an aggressive effort to increase vaccinations and provided funding for the infrastructure to deliver them. The number of people vaccinated went up a lot, and communities began to reopen.

President Biden's $1.9 trillion American Rescue Plan provided direct payments of $1,400 to taxpayers (though, unlike Trump, he didn't sign the checks); loans to employers to keep workers on the payroll; a moratorium on evictions and foreclosures; an increased and refundable child tax credit; and funds for state and local governments to compensate for lost revenue (which could be used to hire and train more cops), money for schools from kindergarten on through eighth grade to safely reopen, and subsidies for Covid testing and vaccination programs. Every Republican voted against it, even though many would later show up at ribbon cuttings for new projects, or applaud the state tax cuts and surpluses the recovery act made possible. Still, Biden was on a roll.

Then things went haywire, as a small progressive bloc in the

House blocked a vote on the popular infrastructure bill, $1 trillion to rebuild crumbling roads and bridges, upgrade railroads, seaports, and airports, improve the electric grid, replace lead pipes that polluted drinking water in old systems, and provide funds for affordable high-speed internet access to every family in America. It would create a lot of high-paying jobs and support domestic manufacturing and supply chains, including a network of 500,000 recharging stations for electric vehicles. It also extended the Abandoned Mine Land reclamation fund, boosting employment in coal country, which had continued to lose jobs in coal mining under Trump, in spite of his promise to reverse the trend.

The most liberal House members thought that by holding up the infrastructure bill they could pressure two Senate Democrats, Joe Manchin of West Virginia and Kyrsten Sinema of Arizona, to vote for all of President Biden's Build Back Better program. They couldn't, as Nancy Pelosi and other leading Democratic House members tried to tell them. Trump had carried Manchin's West Virginia by 30 points, while Biden had won Sinema's deeply divided Arizona by just over 10,000 votes, the first Democrat to do so since I did in 1996, and only the second time since 1948 the state hadn't voted for a Republican.

Eventually, the bill passed in November 2021. Within six months there were 4,300 projects underway. Nineteen GOP senators, almost 40 percent of them, voted for the bill, but only thirteen of their House members did, about 6 percent of their caucus.

In that long gap between the proposal and the enactment of the infrastructure bill, three things happened that drove President Biden's approval rating down and made the 2021 off-year elections tougher for Democratic candidates: the messy withdrawal from Afghanistan; the constant coverage of the paralyzing split within the Democratic Party between the House "progressives" and Senators Manchin and Sinema; and a new round of culture war attacks.

I thought the Democrats should have passed the infrastructure bill first. Getting the projects up and going was the right thing to do for the American people, would have established a "can-do" image for the party and President Biden, and would have strengthened our candidates in Virginia and New Jersey going into the 2021 off-year elections. It was especially important to Virginia, which is plagued by traffic congestion, and where my friend, former governor Terry McAuliffe, was locked in a tight race with Glenn Youngkin, a wealthy conservative who had made his money in the Carlyle Group.

Youngkin was also boosted by the troubles of our Afghanistan withdrawal, because Virginia's electorate has the highest concentration of retired career military personnel in the nation. Many of them agreed that it was time to end our twenty-year involvement, but thought the withdrawal should be orderly and include all the Afghans who had supported us, not just our translators, drivers, and other staff, but also the women and girls whose rights, perhaps even their lives, would be at risk when the Taliban took over. We now know their worries were well founded as the Taliban government continues to restrict opportunities for women and girls in education and employment.

President Biden had said he would withdraw during the campaign and he was determined to keep his promise. Unfortunately, doing it in the best way possible was made much harder by the virtual surrender agreement that President Trump's secretary of state, Mike Pompeo, had signed with the Taliban in 2020, in which he pledged that the United States would leave even earlier than Biden eventually did and, unbelievably, would help the Taliban raise money! It shouldn't have surprised anyone when so many Afghan soldiers stopped fighting after the U.S., in effect, quit without even involving the Afghan government.

Biden had no intention of helping the Taliban as Pompeo had agreed to do, but the United States couldn't achieve an orderly withdrawal by the agreed deadline when there were no longer enough troops left to operate the U.S. airport at Bagram or secure the twenty-plus miles of roadway linking it to Kabul. Thankfully, a lot of other governments and concerned citizens, including Hillary, worked hard to get planes to take more people out and other countries to take more people in. Hillary worked her heart out on this, including persuading Albania to take a good number of Afghan women and their families. I was proud of her and all those who worked to get Afghans out, but it was still a big problem. The Biden administration probably did as much as they could, given their lack of control over Bagram and the road to it, eventually helping more than 120,000 Afghans to leave.

The third big problem was that the Republicans, especially Governor Ron DeSantis in Florida, Governor Greg Abbott in Texas, and candidate Glenn Youngkin in Virginia, had demonstrated a genius for discovering or creating hot-button issues that would move votes to them that otherwise would have gone to Democrats. As I said earlier, the GOP had already won the last two weeks of 2020 on "socialism" and "defund the police" when there were very few Democrats in Congress for either. The Republicans would tie the entire Democratic Party to a small minority of its most left-wing members to get the support of voters who disagreed with the vast majority of the GOP congressional members on economic, social, and political issues that affect far more people. In 2021 in Virginia, Youngkin managed to convince a fair number of voters that a single high school teacher's requirement that her students read Toni Morrison's *Beloved* represented a dangerous attempt to impose "critical race theory" on tender minds because the novel included a slave owner raping a slave.

How did they convince swing voters that they had more to lose from phantom Democrats than real Republicans? They're good at this and, consciously or not, the political press often helps them by giving a day's coverage to GOP leaders' radical and unpopular positions, hyping the stands of the social-media-savvy left-leaning Democrats, and saying the normal thing to do in midterms is to vote against the president's party, especially when there's inflation in food and fuel prices.

When President Biden finally signed the big infrastructure bill in late November of 2021, it was too late to help Terry McAuliffe in his Virginia gubernatorial bid (or Governor Phil Murphy of New Jersey, who barely survived) but not too late to help millions of Americans in red and blue states.

The new year that began with hope soon turned to heartbreak. On February 21, my chief of staff, Jon Davidson, called to tell me that Paul Farmer had just died in Rwanda. After more than a year of Covid confinement at home in South Florida—cherished time with his wife, Didi, and their three kids—he was eager to get back to work. Paul was in Butaro to deliver the inaugural address at the new medical school Partners in Health built, visit the students, and, as always, care for the patients. After seeing his last patient of the morning, a very ill Rwandan girl, he was feeling really tired and had his colleagues check him out. They said his vital signs were good and he should just go home and get some rest. So he went back to his room, lay down for a nap, and never woke up. He was only sixty-two.

The first person I called was Chelsea, who was devastated. After that I called Hillary, who had invited Paul to the White House when he needed help to gain access to Russian prisons where tuberculosis was rampant and he knew he could fix it. Then I went to my office in the hundred-year-old barn next to our house and cried for thirty minutes until I could get my bearings.

President Kagame sent a plane to carry Didi to Rwanda to bring Paul home. On February 26, his funeral was held at the beautiful St. Thomas Episcopal Church in Coral Gables. Didi, Paul's mother, Ginny, and his five siblings asked me to speak. By then I had twenty years of memories, starting in 2003, when CHAI's funding did what Paul had been demanding for years—bring high-quality, low-cost AIDS medicines to Haiti's poor—and also including our work together for the U.N. in Haiti before and after the earthquake; my asking him to go to Rwanda for a few months, which turned into an epic adventure so long that he and Didi had two more kids there; and his long, essential service on our CHAI board, where he worked to embed a culture of genuine openness, honesty, and cooperation.

I did my best, saying Paul surpassed Maya Angelou's observation that "People might forget what you said. They may even forget what you did. But they will never forget how you made them feel." For me and so many others, "I just thank God that he lived. I loved him for what he did. I loved him for what he said. And like all of you, I'll never forget how he made me feel."

If you want to know more about Paul, read Tracy Kidder's marvelous biography, *Mountains Beyond Mountains.* Or read one of the dozen books Paul wrote. Or watch the 2017 documentary *Bending the Arc.* Or Google the tributes of his daughter Catherine and those who worked with him. Before you know it, he'll be sitting on your shoulder, urging you to do good and have a good time doing it.

To support Democrats running in the midterms, in October 2022, I campaigned in New York, deep South Texas, and Nevada. It was toughest in New York. The Democrats were getting hammered on rising crime and cashless bail for people with minor, first-time offenses in a state where voters didn't think they could lose the right to choose, even after the repeal of *Roe v. Wade.* Too many Democratic candidates waited too long to respond to attacks on crime. I campaigned for Sean Patrick Maloney, Josh Riley, and Pat Ryan. Only Ryan survived, becoming the first graduate of West Point to represent the Military Academy in Congress. I was sorry for Riley, who ran a close race and will be back, and heartsick over Maloney's loss. He had a district with 70 percent new voters, a GOP opponent from Westchester County who presented himself as a moderate, and faced a ferocious negative campaign centered on a statement supporting cashless bail he'd made years ago, when running for attorney general, a position that he had long since recanted but was not effectively answered in the campaign. I pointed out that he opposed defunding the police and the Republicans were swooning over Governor DeSantis in Florida, where the crime and murder rates were still far higher than in New York. It didn't work.

In Laredo and Edinburg, Texas, I campaigned with Henry Cuellar and supported Vicente Gonzalez, two moderate-to-conservative Democrats who won their primaries and general elections handily, and with Michelle Vellejo, a progressive Democrat who won her primary by thirty-five votes, but lost to Monica De La Cruz in a redrawn district much more favorable to Republicans. She still carried the southernmost counties and ran a good campaign. I hope we'll see more of her.

Then I went to Nevada to campaign for Senator Catherine Cortez Masto, who had accomplished a lot in her first term but was trailing her opponent, former attorney general Adam Laxalt, until late in the campaign. She closed strong and won by about 8,000 votes. We did a hard charge through Las Vegas, where about half the votes are, and I watched her become more effective at every event. I carried Nevada twice and Hillary won there in 2016, but this was the first time any of us were trying to win without Harry Reid. I enjoyed doing the events and seeing the voters think hard about their choices.

The Supreme Court was a big factor in the election, though perhaps not in the way its very conservative majority wanted. By 2021, the Court had already established the most right-wing record since 1931, and in 2022, it doubled down with more decisions reversing established law. Of course, the most highly publicized was *Dobbs v. Jackson Women's Health Organization*, which overturned *Roe v. Wade* after forty-nine years. The Court said that *Roe* had robbed the states of their historic role in regulating abortion, including their ability to place "undue burdens" on a woman's right to have one. The opinion quoted Justice Scalia's previous argument from *Casey* that "undue burden" was "inherently standardless."

The reaction was swift. In deep-red Kansas and Oklahoma, referendums passed that protected the right to choose in the state constitution. In Michigan, where Governor Gretchen Whitmer was in a tight race for reelection, the Democrats put the right to choose on the ballot and their candidates ran on it. The Republicans opposed it. It was a clean sweep for the Democrats. Whitmer won by 10 points, and the Democrats won the other state offices and majorities in both houses of the state legislature for the first time in nearly forty years. I believe the GOP attempts to control women's lives will continue to benefit Democrats in most but not all states.

In *New York State Rifle & Pistol Association Inc. v. Bruen*, the Supreme Court ruled unconstitutional a 108-year-old New York State law requiring applicants for a concealed carry permit to show a special need for it. With gun-related deaths and mass shootings rising and nearly 80 percent of New Yorkers supporting the law, the Court threw it out anyway, saying it was too much of a burden. Apparently, states are permitted to ban all abortions but not to take reasonable steps to protect those already born. It seems this new Court has no problem finding "inherently standardless" "undue" burdens to uphold or strike down, depending on their political preferences. The same thing goes for their decision on who does or doesn't have standing to sue. Whether you have standing or just have to sit it out depends on what side you're on.

The 2022 election gave the Democrats their best performance in a president's first midterm election in forty years, in spite of inflation's negative impact on President Biden's poll ratings. Democrats gained one Senate seat and lost nine seats in the House, aided by the loss of several seats in New York thanks to court-ordered reapportionment and a belated and insufficient response to the spike in crime there over the previous two years. But all over the country, most Republican election deniers who ran for governor and secretary of state saying they wouldn't certify voting results they disagree with, lost.

So what did the results tell us? Election denying and disrespectful rhetoric were wearing out their welcome, though not enough to mortally wound the right-wing Republicans, as Democrats still struggled to define themselves as the party of common sense. The GOP won the House, though by fewer than 7,000 votes across the five closest contests, with the largest margin in those five being 0.8 of a percentage point. But Democrats won several close ones, too.

In effect, voters have given both parties another chance. They're thinking again. The mainstream press coverage is more on the level. A lot of people have figured out that inflation and the deficit will go down, and crime will, too, if we adopt the right policies. But losing our democracy, letting disturbed people buy weapons that can kill a lot of schoolkids in a hurry, failing to address climate change, and keeping America divided could be devastating for a very long time.

As I finish writing this book, President Biden has decided not to seek reelection, and Vice President Kamala Harris has been nominated to face off against Donald Trump. By the time you read *Citizen*, we'll know who won. I hope enough people will have chosen the benefits of inclusive economic and social policies, and of preserving democracy against abusive power, to turn the tide.

During this tumultuous period, we worked hard to save—and where possible, to expand—our charitable work. Since 2015, CGI had been fighting back against a blizzard of false charges. Donna Shalala was a great foundation president, steering us through 2017, when she returned to Florida to run for Congress. Kevin Thurm, her deputy when she was secretary of health and human services, stepped into the leadership role and has done a fine job keeping us going through Covid and being active in a very different environment. When Tina Flournoy left my office after eight active and productive years to become Vice President Harris's chief of staff, Jon Davidson took over the role. He, Angel Ureña, Rich Vickers, Corey Ganssley, and our staff in Arkansas made sure I did my part to support all our efforts.

We had downsized in 2016, when we stopped holding the annual CGI meetings, but didn't lay anyone off during Covid, thanks to loyal supporters and our endowment's investment income, and we kept getting top marks from the charity ratings agencies. Then, after the 2020 elections and the success of the vaccines, things changed. You could feel all the energy building for a return to a more normal life, in work, education, travel, and, yes, in grassroots do-gooding.

In mid-2021, when New York City restaurants finally began to open for outdoor dining, Hillary and I joined another couple for dinner one night in midtown Manhattan. Our outdoor table was open to the street, and two people I didn't know strolled by in quick succession and virtually shouted, "You need to bring back CGI. We all need something to work together on!" After two close, contentious presidential campaigns, and continuing divisiveness in Congress, at least these two people thought we should get back together to work on worthy projects.

I asked Bob Harrison to check it out. He had done a fine job leading CGI for years and was on the Clinton Foundation board. Bob talked to some of our biggest sponsors and reported back that about half would be supportive. Others thought the continuing economic and political uncertainty made CGI's successful return questionable, but the NGOs who made the commitment model work were more optimistic.

I really wanted CGI to come back, but in a format more relevant and attractive to younger social activists. Kevin Thurm and I asked Greg Milne, with the help of Luke Schiel, then leading our CGI Action Networks, to oversee the effort. We didn't have the staff to do the kind of massive commitment preparation of our halcyon years, but we had enough to do quite a bit. We shortened the program and recruited enough sponsors to cut the admission fee 75 percent and cover more expenses for mostly young NGO leaders from the U.S. and beyond.

We held our "new and improved" CGI at the Hilton in Manhattan on September 19 and 20. Our longtime partner the Sheraton was long booked, but the Hilton had good facilities for both the big plenaries and smaller meetings, and space for potential partners to meet and develop joint commitments. Thankfully, we also got lots of volunteers to help with the actual meeting, many of whom had done the same thing at the CGIs from 2005 to 2016. The Hilton was all in, going above and beyond to make things work. When the event was over, the Hilton staff was so excited about CGI that their employee fund contributed $5,000 to it.

More than 2,000 people came in 2022, with hundreds more on the waiting list. All told, 144 new Commitments to Action were made, addressing inclusive economic growth, health equity, climate change, and the refugee crisis, far more than the 96 commitments made in 2016. The largest was a $1 billion commitment by Water.org, led by Matt Damon and Gary White, to bring clean water to 100 million people across the world. We also had our first in-person CGI U meeting at Vanderbilt since 2018. Seven hundred eighty-seven students from ninety-two countries came.

The September 2023 CGI meeting drew 2,370 people from more than eighty countries to focus on the theme Keep Going. We opened with a Zoom conversation with the pope, with whom I'd had a meeting at the Vatican that summer. The Holy Father spoke about his children's hospital helping young people injured in Ukraine and invited CGI partners to help meet the rising need. We had already developed nine commitments for Ukraine, most of them to meet the health needs of children and families and other victims. Now we're working to help the pope with his hospital.

The 160 new commitments took us well beyond 500 million people helped over the life of CGI. Chelsea led a great panel with U.N. Under-Secretary-General Winnie Byanyima, the executive director of the Joint United Nations Programme on HIV/AIDS (UNAIDS), where she works to achieve universal access to HIV prevention, treatment, and care. After Hillary had a discussion about the post-Covid economy with Treasury Secretary Janet Yellen, she ended the meeting with a moving conversation with Michael J. Fox, who told us that genomic research into Parkinson's, which he has bravely and openly lived with for more than three decades, had brought us close to breakthrough treatment and perhaps even a cure. He was in strong voice and good humor, a fitting finale to the theme of perseverance.

In 2023, there were events both personal and political that highlighted the ongoing conflicts within and among nations between divisive and inclusive tribalism, between the drive for domination through division and the belief in the peaceful resolution of differences and shared responsibility for security and prosperity. On my trip to Northern Ireland in April to mark twenty-five years of peace, the ceremonies were hosted by Queen's University in Belfast, where Hillary had just succeeded George Mitchell as chancellor, who had urged her to take the post. Queen's did the honors because the long-dominant Democratic Unionist Party (DUP) had been defeated in the most recent election by Sinn Féin, which ran on an inclusive progressive program and offered new leadership through two young female leaders, Mary Lou McDonald and Michelle O'Neill. However, the Good Friday Agreement requires both the top two parties to cooperate in government as first minister and deputy first minister, and the pro-U.K. DUP refused to join, saying it had concerns about Brexit's impact on their rural economy. I'm convinced the holdouts just couldn't believe they lost and didn't want to sit second chair. George Mitchell, still a powerful presence at eighty-nine, gave a great speech, and Hillary did a fine job keeping the show on the road, well prepped by her long years of supporting the Irish peacemakers, especially through Vital Voices.

Thankfully, both Ireland and Northern Ireland are moving forward. In February of 2024, the DUP agreed to join a new government, with Sinn Féin's Michelle O'Neill as first minister and DUP's Emma Little-Pengelly as deputy first minister.

In July of 2023, I went back to Oxford for the fifty-fifth anniversary of my Rhodes Scholar class and the 120th anniversary of the scholarships. The first day I met with 250 current students, including Rhodes Scholars and others in affiliated programs, a group of young women and men from all over the world who are committed to an inclusive future and determined to meet challenges, not use them to divide people and destroy cooperation. The next day I was asked to speak for all the alums who had come to remember their years at Oxford. In my remarks, I urged them to use whatever time and talents we had left to give our children and grandchildren a future of democracy, freedom, and cooperation, and to deal with climate change while it is still an opportunity to build shared prosperity and security, and avoid a real-life sequel to the postapocalyptic Road Warrior movies.

Next I went to Albania, which in just thirty years had gone from the last Stalinist communist dictatorship to a growing, thriving democracy led by Prime Minister Edi Rama, an artist and former basketball star who governs with a cabinet and parliament full of young women and men who support their inclusive politics and programs. The prime minister presented me with one of Albania's high honors, the Great Star of Public Gratitude, in front of attendees that included young people who had been named for Hillary and me for what we did to help save Kosovo's overwhelmingly Albanian population from ethnic cleansing in 1999, and what Hillary did as senator and secretary of state to support them afterward.

The most awful thing to happen that fall, of course, was the terrorist attack on Israel committed by Hamas from Gaza, which killed more Israelis, including many children and frail elderly citizens, in a single day than Israel had lost in any day of its several wars. I was very proud of the initial response of the American people and of President Biden and his administration and members of both parties, affirming both our unbending commitment to Israel's security, the imperative of minimizing the loss of innocent Palestinian lives in the retaliation, and all sides' efforts to prevent the conflict from exploding into a regional war.

Arab states had largely abandoned the Palestinians after Arafat squandered the best chance for Mideast peace in a generation. That story bears retelling. With a little less than two months left in my term, Yasser Arafat came to the Oval Office for a private visit. I told him I was preparing a final peace proposal that was better for the Palestinians than anything that had been discussed the previous June in Camp David, and I thought Prime Minister Ehud Barak, his cabinet, and the people of Israel would accept it. It gave Palestinians a state on 96 percent of the West Bank and Gaza, including the Muslim and Christian quarters of the Old City of Jerusalem, their own capital in East Jerusalem, 4 percent of Israel to compensate for the settlers occupying land just over the U.N.-recognized 1967 borders, and the right of about 20,000 Palestinian refugees from camps in Lebanon to return to northern Israel, where their ancestors had been for more than 2,000 years.

However, as I mentioned when I related the story of the trip to rescue the American journalists, we also had a chance to resolve important security issues with North Korea that would open the possibility of dramatic positive changes in Northeast Asia. To do that, I would have to go to North Korea and to South Korea, China, Japan, and Russia. The trip would require almost two weeks at the very time I would need to be in Washington and the Middle East if we were going to sell a final peace deal.

Arafat blurted out, "You can't go to Asia." I asked if he needed me to stay so that I would be seen pressuring him to accept my proposal and then have time to make the plan as attractive as possible to his people and the region. When he said yes, I told him I understood, but said he had to tell me the truth. If he wasn't going to close the deal, I owed it to America and our friends in Asia to get the deal a trip there would produce. I said I wouldn't tell anyone, but I had worked very hard for a just and lasting peace in the Middle East and if he was going to back away, I had to know.

Arafat, with tears in his eyes, said, "If we don't do this now, it would be five, ten, fifteen years, maybe longer, before the chance comes again. We have to do it now." I didn't go to North Korea and gave both sides my two-state peace plan. Israel accepted it. But Arafat stalled until I was out of office and Prime Minister Barak was defeated. Then, four days before President Bush announced his own Road Map initiative, Arafat said he would accept my parameters. By then he had an Israeli government unwilling to agree to them, an Israeli public that no longer trusted him, and a U.S. government that wanted nothing to do with him. In the end, the press paid little attention to Arafat's statement.

In the years that followed that failed peace plan, Arab states now wanted to do business with Israel and to partner with it to block progress in the region by Iran and its proxies. That led to the Abraham Accords with the Emirates, Bahrain, Morocco, and Sudan recognizing Israeli legitimacy even though the Israeli government was dependent on a coalition that included right-wing parties committed to a hard line against Palestinian claims, and then under President Biden to an effort to forge an agreement to normalize diplomatic relations between Israel and Saudi Arabia and offer the Saudis additional security guarantees, access to advanced weaponry, and civil nuclear cooperation.

The future for those initiatives and any others is unclear, but I'm glad the United States is back to publicly advocating a two-state solution, which has been embraced by former prime minister Ehud Barak and should now have more resonance, even with

Likud and other less extreme elements of the Israeli right, but only if most Israelis believe they have a partner for peace.

Israel cannot be expected to make peace with Hamas after October 7. Hamas's goal is not to gain a Palestinian state but to make Israel unlivable, as its open partnership with Iran and its affiliates, the Houthis in Yemen and Hezbollah in southern Lebanon, demonstrates. On the other hand, the Palestinians cannot remain stateless, and if all Palestinians in still-occupied Gaza and the West Bank were to become Israeli citizens, Israel would no longer be a majority Jewish nation. Today Israel has about 7.3 million Jewish citizens, including 700,000 settlers in the West Bank, East Jerusalem, and the Golan Heights, and 2 million Palestinian citizens who live within the 1967 borders and are Israeli citizens eligible to vote. There are also 3 million more Palestinians in the West Bank and 2 million in Gaza. In other words, the Holy Land is about 50-50.

The Palestinian Authority implicitly accepted severe limits on the "right of return" when they supported the Oslo Accords in 1993, which was designed to produce a two-state solution. By contrast, Hamas never accepted Israel's right to exist, and rejoiced in seeing it run by increasingly fragile right-wing coalitions, including fringe parties that denied the legitimacy of Palestinian claims to statehood, even to control more land on the West Bank set aside for them when I was in office. What I proposed in 2000 is probably no longer practically possible, because of the massive expansion of settlements over the last twenty-plus years. But the Palestinian Authority in the West Bank has continued to oppose terror and embraced cooperation through it all. I hope the Hamas attacks will revitalize the Palestinian Authority with a resolute determination to reject terror and revive efforts to find a creative two-state solution. Soon, there will be more Palestinian Arabs than Jews in the Holy Land, making Israel's claim to be a democracy moot and its security more precarious.

Yitzhak Rabin saw this all coming, and gave his life to prevent it. Ehud Barak saw it coming, and sacrificed his political career and the viability of the Labor Party to prevent it. So eventually did Ariel Sharon, who set up a new peace party, Kadima, and unilaterally withdrew from Gaza. Now, someone will have to step into the breach, perhaps the revitalized Palestinian Authority committed, as the government of former Palestinian prime minister Salam Fayad was, to a peaceful path to statehood.

The Palestinians are an immensely gifted people. They have done well all over the world. When I was in office, it seemed there were no permanently poor Palestinians outside their homeland. They and their children deserve their chance, too, and America should help them find a way, and once more abandon our own ill-fated adventure into the fantasies of division and domination. Only then can our honest differences give us better tomorrows.

Meanwhile, in America, we have our own work to do. The House Republicans remain hostage to their most right-wing members and the Democrats have to flip the immigration issue by giving undocumented people who pass our longstanding legal test for acceptance into the country—that they are here because they're threatened by dangerous conditions in their home countries—the right to legally work so they can pay taxes and settle where they're needed and wanted. In the meantime we need to bolster our underfunded and understaffed facilities to house them safely and securely at the border until they can be properly processed.

We need to do this. Our current birth rate of about twelve per thousand people is below replacement level, and the lowest since the 1930s. Immigrants create six more jobs for U.S. citizens than they take, since so many become business owners. This is especially important in areas where there's already a labor shortage, including construction and the installation of green energy solutions. New immigrants are 80 percent more likely than native-born Americans to start new businesses. Most Americans are not anti-immigration. They're anti-chaos. We also need to take in more skilled immigrants if we expect to remain competitive across a wide range of high-tech fields, including A.I. and replacing outdated power lines with newer ones having twice the carrying capacity.

That's why it's tragic that the compromise President Biden and conservative Senate Republicans agreed to—a limit on immigrants accepted at the border in return for the necessary facilities and personnel to process them without breaking up families but with thorough vetting—was blocked by the House, then by the Senate GOP sponsors, when their Higher Power, Donald Trump, rejected it. They don't need solutions. Remember, solutions don't work for them. They need unresolved problems to complain about.

So where are we? There is no peaceful alternative to inclusive tribalism, with shared responsibilities that produce more security and more widely shared prosperity, through cooperation and compromise. Surely the current carnage in Israel and Gaza and chaos in the U.S. House of Representatives make that clear. If enough people on both sides want inclusive tribalism, they can find a way. We have to.

When I was a young man studying at Georgetown, Robert Kennedy, then running for president, famously quoted a line from Tennyson's "Ulysses" in his speeches and later in a book: " 'Tis not too late to seek a newer world." He made young people feel thrilled about the world's possibilities during an intensely troubled time. Looking back on those years from decades later, I'm struck by the fact that "Ulysses" wasn't written as a clarion call to the young. It was really about an old lion who gives his kingdom to his son but doesn't want to be idle for the rest of his life. So he brings what's left of his crew together for one last, great adventure, saying they are "Made weak by time and fate, but strong in will," still determined "To strive, to seek, to find, and not to yield," for "some noble work of note may yet be done . . . 'Tis not too late to seek a newer world."

There will always be conflicts between people, fueled by their politics, their faiths, or their other differences. Some will lead to violence and heartbreaking loss. Our oldest demons are patient ones, always eager to manifest themselves in new clothes, and, if we let them, to turn back our progress toward a more equal, sustainable, and peaceful planet. So many of our victories have to be refought and won again and again. The important thing is that, like Ulysses, we keep striving, keep seeking, and never yield. That's the only way to secure a peaceful, normal life for the Jewish and Arab children of the Holy Land, and for the children in a deeply divided America. It's the only path forward for us all.

EPILOGUE

In the ups and downs of the last twenty-plus busy years, I lost a lot of people I cared about, most but not all to old age or serious illness. Remarkably, only two young people doing foundation work were killed in the line of duty. Both were dedicated members of our CHAI family working in Africa.

On November 25, 2006, Ellen Verwey, a thirty-six-year-old nurse, was in Lesotho training doctors and nurses on how to care for HIV/AIDS patients. She and her husband and two other Clinton Foundation workers were spending the weekend at the home of Lesotho's trade and industry minister. She was killed by an AK-47 attack as they got out of the minister's car, apparently the unintended victims of an assassination attempt gone awry. Even after a healthy reward was offered for information, her case was never solved. Ellen came from a large farm family and had followed her dream to see the world and serve the poor. She deserved a much longer life, but she lived a very good one.

On September 21, 2013, four masked al-Shabaab terrorists opened fire in the Westgate Mall in Kenya, killing sixty-seven people, including Dr. Elif Yavuz, who was working out of CHAI's Tanzania office on malaria, vaccines, and diarrhea, and her partner, architect Ross Langdon. They were in Nairobi because she was eight months pregnant and it was the best nearby place to give birth.

I had met Elif just a few weeks earlier, with the rest of the CHAI staff in Tanzania. She was glowing in her coming motherhood. After her death, her coworkers helped her mother choose an orphanage for HIV-positive children in Nairobi to receive donations in honor of Elif, Ross, and baby Alicia. In 2017 in the Netherlands, I got to meet Elif's mother, Lia, and thank her for raising such a remarkable daughter. Elif and Ellen and thousands of others serving in CHAI in the last twenty years saved or improved millions of lives, as did those who built and grew CGI and brought it back in 2022, and all who've contributed to our other foundation efforts over the years.

What does it all mean in the grand scheme of things? I keep trying to figure it out. I got an inkling in early 2018, on our trip to Hawaii, when Hillary and I got a tour of the Mauna Kea summit, home to a number of the world's most powerful telescopes peering into the far reaches of outer space. We visited the largest ones there, the twin Keck telescopes, sponsored by American scientific groups and NASA. When our journey started at sea level, it was eighty-eight degrees. By the time we got to the mountaintop observatory, it had fallen to eighteen. After getting warm coats from our hosts, we looked through one of the Keck lenses at the universe well beyond the Milky Way galaxy, which contains our solar system and the stars that sparkle on clear nights.

Afterward we went back to the base for a talk with the staff over a hot cup of coffee. We had lots of questions, which they patiently answered. When I asked if they ever discussed the likelihood of life on other planets, the leader, a native of Germany, said, "Of course." Then I asked whether they had disagreements about it. He said, "Yes, big ones." So I asked "How big?" He said, "Some of us think it's 85 percent likely and others think it's 95 percent likely."

The conversation was mind-bending. When we left to drive back to sea level, I thought about our fleeting time on earth, a four-billion-year-old planet in a fourteen-billion-year-old universe with a billion galaxies. It's still expanding, and still full of surprises waiting to be discovered. Later we saw pictures of black holes, including one 55 million light-years away, bordered by a ring of fire. It was so large, with a gravitational pull so great that if our entire solar system passed by close enough it would be quickly sucked in and crushed into dust that would fit into a large thimble. Makes you think it doesn't matter so much who's on Mount Rushmore.

As I said early in this book, I'm fascinated by how the universe works, about the potential of human genome research to prolong and enrich life, and about the evident and likely future consequences of climate change. I've read books by Stephen Hawking, Lisa Randall, Brian Greene, Katie Mack, Steven Johnson, Steve Brusatte, E. O. Wilson, David Attenborough, and others. Though I don't fully understand everything I read, especially on physics, each effort has taught me something valuable, made me want to keep learning, and reminded me that they're far smarter than I am and how wise they are to argue for less certainty and more common humanity.

Recently, I discovered the lucid prose of the Italian theoretical physicist Carlo Rovelli. I've read three of his books, *Seven Brief Lessons on Physics*, *Helgoland*, about quantum physics, and *There Are Places in the World Where Rules Are Less Important Than Kindness*, a book of essays and articles that go beyond his scientific work. One of the essays is titled "Why I Am an Atheist."

Here's his argument: "I don't like people who behave well because they fear otherwise they might end up in Hell. I prefer those who behave well because they value good behavior. I don't trust those who are good for the sake of pleasing God. I prefer those who are good because they genuinely are good. . . . I don't like those whose belief in God gives them access to the Truth, because I believe in reality they are as ignorant as I am. I think the world is still a boundless mystery to us; I don't like those who have all the answers. I prefer those who are asking questions, and whose answer is 'I don't really know.' I don't like those who say they know what is good and what is evil because they belong to a church that has monopolized God . . . who tell others what they should be doing because they have God on their side. I prefer those who make humble suggestions, who live in impressive ways I can admire, who make choices that move me and make me think."

Like all Rovelli's writing, it's eloquent, moving, and made me think. I agree with much of what he wrote, but I don't think his argument disproves the existence of a creator God. The case for atheism can't be made based on the frailties and illusions of believers, especially those whose hunger for worldly political power seems to be the real goal of their religious zeal.

The believers Rovelli doesn't like, at least the Christians, ignore Saint Paul's most important lesson—that love of our fellow humans is a greater virtue than even faith, because in this life we all "see through a glass darkly" and only "know in part." The Christian New Testament says faith is "the substance of things *hoped for*, the evidence of things *unseen*," and that its two most important traits are, first, to love God with all you've got, and second, "like unto it," to love your neighbor as yourself. The Torah tells Jews that turning your back on a stranger is like turning away from the most high G-d. The Quran says Allah put all the different people on earth not to hate one another but to know and learn from each other. The Dhammapada of the Buddha says you're not fully human until you can feel an arrow piercing another's skin as if it were piercing your own. All these faiths are telling us to love our neighbors and to be open to people who are different from us. That's the God I felt when I looked into the universe through the Keck telescope.

My life after the White House, when they don't play a song when I walk in the room anymore, is filled with deep gratitude to the family, friends, foundation and personal staff, and partners who've made it possible to do things that save and improve lives, give children better futures, and try to keep bringing people together in the face of raging divisive populism.

Since that's the way I keep score, I'm happy. I still believe that despite our struggles with identity issues, most people are basically good, that we should live and work with hope, that the end of life is a homegoing, and that in the meantime, we should relish every chance to get caught trying. The song that matters most is the one you sing to yourself.

ACKNOWLEDGMENTS

A great many people contributed to bringing this book to life, with research, fact-checking, editing, and publication, and, of course, through the work covered in its pages. Often those who helped me get the facts and events right were the same people who had worked so hard on the initiatives, campaigns, missions, and other events I've included here. There were also people and events I cared about that I didn't cover because of the editorial constraints necessary to keep the story moving along. I am also profoundly grateful to those whose hard work was important and impactful, but whose contributions weren't included.

My lawyer, Bob Barnett, was, as always, in my corner, urging me to include or delete things based on his vast publishing knowledge of what has to be covered and what should be cut.

During the writing of the book, we lost my publisher and friend, Sonny Mehta, who, starting with *My Life*, always made sure Knopf was a welcoming home for me. Sonny was succeeded by Reagan Arthur and Jordan Pavlin, who kept that tradition alive. Thanks as well to the talented executives at Knopf Doubleday Group: president and publisher, Maya Mavjee, deputy publisher, Chris Dufault, and director of marketing, Kristin Fassler.

At Knopf I was guided by three gifted editors, starting with the legendary Bob Gottlieb, who never stopped asking me to not only talk about what happened, but how I felt about it. When Bob stepped down at age eighty-nine, just a few years before he passed in 2023, Andrew Miller stepped into some very big shoes. He was a steady voice and a marvel at discerning the core truths behind various passages and helping me come up with the final order of sections and chapters.

Finally, Jennifer Barth saw the whole project through to the finish line with good humor, finesse, and a fine eye for both the larger themes and the sentence-by-sentence focus a book like this requires, supported by Tiara Sharma, Claire Leonard, Nicole Pedersen, Casey Hampton, Felecia O'Connell, Anne Achenbaum, Arianna Abdul, and Meredith Dros. The great jacket was designed by John Gall, and Todd Doughty and Erinn Hartman headed up the brilliant publicity campaign. Thanks as well to Laura Keefe and Abigail Endler in Marketing, Suzanne Smith and Serena Lehman in Rights, Beth Meister in Operations and Sales, Kim Shannon and Annie Schatz in Sales, and Donna Passanante, Lance Fitzgerald, and Dan Zitt, who worked on the audiobook.

I had two chiefs of staff during the years I worked on *Citizen*. Tina Flournoy, who led my office for eight years with great skill and a big heart, was an early guiding hand in getting the ball rolling. After Tina left, Jon Davidson kept the project moving forward and kept me focused. Both of them reminded me to explain how my life and work fit into what I had done before I became a private citizen, and how my work evolved against the backdrop of larger forces at work in the U.S. and around the world. My deputy chief of staff and director of communications, Angel Ureña, helped center me throughout the process with his always insightful perspective and seemingly infinite patience, all while managing my other communications and press needs wisely and building his own busy and loving family life. Amanda Catanzano, Michael Fuchs, and Amitabh Desai made sure all the international and governmental affairs details passed muster. Oscar Flores was tireless, especially during Covid, in keeping my drafts, research, and queries organized while simultaneously running our Chappaqua home along with Mara Soto. They all worked hand in glove with Steve Rinehart, my chief in-house editor, who saw me through multiple drafts over several years, and somehow kept it all organized. All the while my director of scheduling, Corey Ganssley, protected the time I needed to write, edit, and research the book, and my director of engagement, Rich Vickers, kept all the pieces moving and worked with everyone above to make sure I had what I needed at any moment.

Many other people brought their own unique experience as readers and fact-finders. From the Clinton Foundation, Kevin Thurm, the Clinton Foundation's CEO during the period I wrote this book; Bruce Lindsey, my friend and trusted advisor for more than five decades; Craig Minassian, who's been giving me excellent advice since serving in my White House; Amy Sandgrund-Fisher, the Clinton Foundation's general counsel; Greg Milne, the Clinton Global Initiative's CEO; Luke Schiel, CGI's chief program and strategy officer; and Tom Galton, my longtime speechwriter, all lent invaluable help and guidance. For research into foundation initiatives, Julie Guariglia, Meghan Andrews, Chloe Sisselman, Liz Raftery, Eliza Oehmler, and Jesse Dozoretz were vital in tracking down briefings, correspondence, notes on trips, and other material I needed to flesh out the stories. Francesca Ernst Khan, Colin Bridgham, and Elise Barnes helped look through the thousands of photographs taken by dozens of gifted photographers over the years that included Joe Reilly, Barbara Kinney, Adam Schultz, and Sharon Farmer. In Little Rock, the Clinton Presidential Center, especially its director, Stephanie Streett, who has been with me since 1992, pitched in with research and guidance, with help from Ben Thielemier and colleagues Debbie Shock, Joy Secuban, Lena Hayes, and Tina Eoff. I'm grateful as well to the professionals at the National Archives and Records Administration, including Terri Garner, Dr. Jay Barth, Dana Simmons, and Shanna Weathersby, for their help in unearthing material from my administration throughout my postpresidency.

I'm particularly grateful to so many others who picked up the phone when I called and filled in facts, figures, dates, and events, many of them from the early years of my personal office and the foundation, including longtime aides Maggie Williams,

Eric Nonacs, Terry Krinvic, Bob Harrison, and Ed Hughes. Former members of my administration were also generous with their time and thoughts, including John Podesta, Paul Begala, Leon Panetta, Richard Clarke, Erskine Bowles, Gene Sperling, Bruce Reed, Marc Dunkelman, Kris Engskov, Minyon Moore, and Capricia Marshall. From Chelsea's team, we relied heavily on her chief of staff, Bari Lurie, and Sara Horowitz and Emily Young, and from Hillary's current and former colleagues we got help from Huma Abedin, Dennis Cheng, Nick Merrill, Dan Schwerin, Jake Sullivan, and Lona Valmoro, all of whom were generous with insights and anecdotes.

I'm also thankful for the many books, articles, and papers I've drawn on over the last twenty-three years to help jog my memory and organize my thoughts and make sense of the changing world. I'm especially indebted to Joe Conason's book *Man of the World* for his perspective on my postpresidential work. It brought our work to the attention of a lot of people who might otherwise have known only about my occasional involvement in politics and other high-profile events.

Finally, I'll be forever grateful to the scores of professionals who make my postpresidential work possible, beginning with my United States Secret Service detail, who keep me safe from Chappaqua to China and points in between. All of those travels are coordinated by skilled Advance teams who make sure all the movements go like clockwork, many of the members of which have been with me since the administration.

And of course, I'm grateful to Hillary and Chelsea, who read multiple drafts, fact-checking and offering valuable suggestions on what to add, delete, or rewrite, with their unique perspectives on the nearly quarter century the book covers, including their own full lives and their tireless work over the years with the Clinton Foundation. None of this would be possible without them. I love them very much.

A Special Thanks

All of the foundation efforts included in this book, and many dozens more, depend on the hard work and support of the Clinton

Foundation staff, CHAI staff, scientists, healthcare professionals, advisors, on-the-ground workers and volunteers, friends, and, every so often, on the kindness and generosity of strangers who start their days thinking there can always be better tomorrows than yesterdays. They number in the thousands, and very little of what you read in this book would have been possible without them. I could fill easily another 450 pages with stories of their dedication, focus, and enormous humanity. Space doesn't allow me to thank them all here, but I urge you to take a moment to visit PresidentClinton.com/CitizenThankYou and read through a more comprehensive account of the talented people who've made such a big difference in so many lives. They deserve a book of their own.

In the limited space I have in the meantime, I want to thank a few categories of people in particular. My personal office, with all of its myriad projects and responsibilities, was enriched and enlivened over the years by Laura Graham, Marc Gross, Jim Kennedy, Michael Kives, Matt McKenna, Hannah Richert, Helen Robinson, Ben Yarrow, and John Zimmerebner. On the foundation side, I'm particularly indebted to those who worked day to day to keep everything running smoothly, including Valerie Alexander, Elizabeth Bibi, Traci Carpenter, Brian Cookstra, Scott Curran, Lee Dugger, Omar Faroul, Erika Gudmundson, Linda Jean-Louis, Betsy McManus, Fred Poust, Trooper Sanders, and Zayneb Shaikley. And finally, the various foundation initiatives could not have been as successful as they were without the tireless leadership of Ragina Arrington, Mark Gunton, Sarah Hamilton, Jan Hartke, Rain Henderson, Kathy Higgins, Christy Louth, Terri McCullough, Patti Miller, Walker Morris, Scott Taitel, Christian Thrasher, Rachel Tulchin, Dymphna van der Lans, Howell Wechsler, and Bill Wetzel.

I would like to particularly thank the members of the CHAI and Clinton Foundation boards over the years. CHAI has benefited greatly from the experience and wisdom of its CEOs Ira Magaziner and Buddy Shah, and past and present board members Dr. Gro Harlem Brundtland, Ray Chambers, Awa Marie Coll-Seck, Aliko Dangote, Dame Sally Davies, Mark Dybul, Mala Gaonkar, Luis Alberto Moreno, Joy Phumaphi, Alan Schwartz,

Bob Selander, Ann Veneman, and two very special people we lost, Paul Farmer, and Dr. Tachi Yamada. Our Clinton Foundation board, past and present, has helped guide our larger work invaluably through the years, and for that I am grateful to Frank Giustra, Rolando Gonzalez-Bunster, Dr. Eric Goosby, Robert Harrison, Hadeel Ibrahim, Lisa Jackson, Ann Jordan, Bruce Lindsey, Terry McAuliffe, Cheryl Mills, Janet Murguía, Maura Pally, Cheryl Saban, Donna Shalala, Rodney Slater, and Nima Taghavi.

Finally, the hard work and guidance of our staff and board members hinges on the generous help of donors and supporters, from small donors, to annual givers of larger awards, to large individual business and foundation contributors, and to support from government agencies, conservation groups, and affiliated programs from all over the world. I am so grateful to everyone who supported our work in ways small and large, and in particular those individuals whose generosity kept our work going over the years, including Danny and Ewa Abraham, Bill and Tani Austin, Carlos Bremer, Beth and Mike Coulson, the Bill & Melinda Gates Foundation, Frank Giustra, Edythe and Eli Broad, Susie and Mark Buell, Susie Buffett, Fred Eychaner, Tom Golisano, Tom Hunter, Joe Kiani, Rolando Gonzalez-Bunster, Mack and Donna McLarty, Denis and Catherine O'Brien, Victor and Olena Pinchuk, J.B. and M.K. Pritzker, Haim and Cheryl Saban, Michael Schumacher, Carlos Slim, Nima Taghavi, Eddie Trump, Rumi Verjee, Ted and Michele Waitt, Alice Walton and the Walton Family Foundation, and Casey Wasserman and the Wasserman Foundation.

INDEX

A NOTE ABOUT THE AUTHOR

William Jefferson Clinton, the first Democratic president in six decades to be elected twice, led the U.S. to the longest economic expansion in American history, including the creation of more than 22 million jobs. After leaving the White House, President Clinton established the Clinton Foundation with the belief that everyone deserves a chance to succeed, everyone has a responsibility to act, and we all do better when we work together. For more than two decades, those values have driven the foundation's efforts to advance leadership and accelerate solutions across the United States and around the world. Flagship programs include the Clinton Global Initiative, which transformed philanthropy and has resulted in more than 4,000 projects and partnerships making a difference for more than 500 million people in 180 countries; the Clinton Health Access Initiative, which changed how the global community procured and delivered life-saving HIV/AIDS medication—reaching more than 21 million people worldwide; and the Clinton Presidential Center and Library, which provides year-round civic education and cultural programming to help inform future generations of leaders to apply lessons of President Clinton's lifetime in public service to the challenges of today. President Clinton and Secretary Hillary Rodham Clinton live in Chappaqua, New York.

A NOTE ON THE TYPE

This book was set in Janson, a typeface long thought to have been made by the Dutchman Anton Janson, who was a practicing typefounder in Leipzig during the years 1668–1687. However, it has been conclusively demonstrated that these types are actually the work of Nicholas Kis (1650–1702), a Hungarian, who most probably learned his trade from the master Dutch typefounder Dirk Voskens. The type is an excellent example of the influential and sturdy Dutch types that prevailed in England up to the time William Caslon (1692–1766) developed his own incomparable designs from them.

Composed by North Market Street Graphics,
Lancaster, Pennsylvania

Printed and bound by Berryville Graphics,
Berryville, Virginia

Designed by Casey Hampton